A History of Dolls' Houses

Stromer House, Germanisches National-Museum, Nuremberg

A History of Dolls' Houses

FLORA GILL JACOBS

BELL & HYMAN · London
in association with

Charles Scribner's Sons · *New York*

3 5 7 9 11 13 15 19 M/P 20 18 16 14 12 10 8 6 4 2
5 7 9 11 13 15 19 M/C 20 18 16 14 12 10 8 6 4

Printed in the United States of America
Library of Congress Catalog Card Number 65-24648

ISBN 0-684-14538-3 (paper)
ISBN 0-684-10276-5 (cloth)

For My Mother

Grateful acknowledgment is made for permission to quote from the following sources:

B. T. Batsford, Ltd., London, & Deutscher Kunstverlag, Berlin: Karl Gröber *Children's Toys of Bygone Days. The Connoisseur:* August 1917, December 1918, March 1919. *Cosmopolitan* Magazine: January 1904. *Country Life Ltd.:* March 6, 1942, October 19, 1951. E. P. Dutton & Co., Inc.: Lucy Crump *Nursery Life 300 Years Ago.* George G. Harrap & Co., Ltd.: Max Von Boehn *Dolls and Puppets.* Hodder & Stoughton, Ltd.: Esther Singleton *Dutch and Flemish Furniture.* Alfred A. Knopf, Inc. & The Society of Authors and J. Middleton Murry, Esq. O.B.E.: *The Short Stories of Katharine Mansfield. Ladies' Home Journal:* Frances Hodgson Burnett *My Toy Cupboard,* copyright 1915 by the Curtis Publishing Co. *The New York Times:* April 14, 1924; August 27, 30, 1924; February 3, 1925; May 29, 1932. James Nisbet & Co.: Sir Nevile Wilkinson *To All and Singular. The Spectator:* June 1907, December 1920, December 1928. *The Studio Ltd.:* Karl Gröber *A Royal Doll House,* November 1932. *Woman's Home Companion:* October 1913, December 1926, January 1938.

FOREWORD

*T*HIS BOOK WAS BEGUN MANY YEARS AGO, IN 1945, WHEN BOTH ITS author and the collecting of dolls' houses were very young indeed, and although its first edition did not appear till 1953, that version was sprinkled with many youthful errors of taste and style, including an encyclopaedic supply of exclamation points that it is merciful to have the privilege of correcting in 1965.

Exclamation points alone, needless to say, would not justify a re-examination of the subject, but the years between have brought to light not only much new information, but a whole new interest in and awareness of old dolls' houses on the part of collectors, museum curators, and antiquarians in general, and this edition has been extensively revised and augmented.

Although much of the original edition has been retained, a great deal of new material has been added, especially to Chapters 1, 4, 5, 6, 8, 9, 12, 15, and 20. Perhaps ninety per cent of Chapter 15 (The Contemporary Collector) consists of new material. Prior to 1953, when research for the previous edition was in process, one seized upon every dolls' house—every collector and collection—to appear on the horizon. Some of the information considered useful then has gone a bit flat, or has had to be excised for some other reason. On the other hand, the bulk of new information that has become available is so overwhelming that one can only hope, in recording much of it, to have done it justice to some degree.

There is no need to belabor here the value of dolls' houses as historical documents; their contribution, informative and charming, to domestic history is detailed elsewhere in this book. One might add only that the preoccupation with dolls' houses has grown; it has become considerably more than a preoccupation on the part of many, as we shall attempt to show.

In the Foreword to the first edition, the author saluted a number of museum people, librarians, and collectors who were helpful in its preparation. As many of these have since retired and a few are no longer living, there seems little point in re-listing them here, but they will be gratefully remembered always.

There is, however, one name which must be cited anew: that of Miss Siri Andrews of Concord, New Hampshire, who, as an editor, first discerned the merits of the subject of dolls' houses, and launched what had been a fragmentary idea.

Innumerable publications, listed elsewhere, have given us permission to reproduce illustrations and to quote, and we are grateful. I must acknowledge again a goodly debt to three pioneer toy historians from abroad who, unfortunately, even in 1953, were no longer present to notice my gratitude: Dr. Karl Gröber of Germany; and M. Henri-René D'Allemagne and M. Leo-Claretie, both of France. Their works, especially Dr. Gröber's, are a starting point for any toy researcher.

I would salute as well a corps of anonymous librarians both here and abroad for many courtesies to an author as anonymous as they, particularly in the Library of Congress, the New York Public Library, and the library of the Victoria and Albert Museum in London.

During the years since the original edition appeared, a number of persons have been helpful to one who is not only a dolls' house biographer but a dolls' house collector. Among these, I wish to give particular thanks to Dr. Elisabeth Wolffhardt of Munich who, out of kindness of heart, as well as interest in the subject, has checked numerous facts relating to dolls' houses, particularly to German ones and to dolls' kitchens, and has been helpful in innumerable ways. I also wish to thank Mrs. William Redd Mahony of Oak Park, Illinois, a collector whose knowledge and discernment have been reflected in many informative letters; Mrs. Henry Erath of F. A. O. Schwarz, New York, whose continued interest has been as helpful as the Schwarz catalogues she made available; and Mrs. Laura Treskow of London, who has been responsible for many choice additions to the author's collection, and, thereby, to her sum of dolls' house knowledge. Many museum officials have sent information and, through the years, many collectors have sent useful clippings. The names are too numerous to list, but I wish to express my gratitude to all of them.

Finally, I wish to thank my editor, Miss Elinor Parker, who bravely coped with the complexities of revising the present edition. And I wish to thank my husband, Ephraim Jacobs, who for years has endured with patience and stamina an unconscionable number of words about dolls' houses and dolls' house projects, both written and oral, as well as a most alarming number of the objects themselves on our mutual premises.

FLORA GILL JACOBS

16 West Kirke Street
Chevy Chase, Maryland
August, 1965

CONTENTS

CREDITS

Museums and Public Collections

Art Institute, Chicago: pp. 297, 300, 301, 302. Museum of Science and Industry, Chicago: pp. 268, 271, 272. Cleveland Museum of Art: p. 140. Denver Art Museum: pp. 156, 157. Mary Merritt Doll Museum, Douglassville, Pa.: p. 227. Rutherford B. Hayes Library, Fremont, Ohio: p. 115. Milwaukee Public Museum: p. 120. Guennol Collection, New York: p. 7. Metropolitan Museum of Art, New York: pp. 13 (Museum Excavations, 1919–20; Rogers Fund, supplemented by contribution of Edward S. Harkness), 164 (Sylmans Collection, gift of George Coe Graves, 1930). Museum of the City of New York: pp. 101, 102, 103, 175, 177, 317. Essex Institute, Salem, Mass.: p. 123. National Gallery of Art, Washington (Index of American Design): p. 175. Smithsonian National Museum, Washington: p. 236. Chester County (Pa.) Historical Society: p. 104. National Society of Colonial Dames: p. 100 (photo Alan Richardson). Wenham (Mass.) Historical Association & Museum: p. 118 (photo Robert E. Crosby). Rijksmuseum, Amsterdam: pp. 79, 169. Schlossmuseum, Arnstadt: p. 287. Historisches Museum, Basel: p. 146. Museum of Childhood, Edinburgh: p. 42. Historisches Museum, Frankfurt/Main: pp. 236, 327. London Museum: p. 50. Victoria & Albert Museum, London: pp. 31, 45, 49, 174 (Crown Copyright). Germanisches National-Museum, Nuremberg: frontispiece, pp. 16, 30, 34 (photo Peter-Jürgen Lüllemann, Verlag Henri Nannen, Hamburg). Rotunda Museum of Dolls' Houses, Oxford: p. 226. Musée des Arts Décoratifs, Paris: pp. 88, 89. Nordiska Museet, Stockholm: pp. 134, 135. Centraal Museum, Utrecht: p. 71. Museum Lydia Bayer, Würzburg: p. 225.

Private Collections, courtesy of the following:

Mrs. Eunice Althouse: pp. 59, 60. Mrs. E. J. Carter, p. 176. Mrs. Frank C. Doble: pp. 206, 235. Mrs. Estrid Faurholt: p. 232. Mrs. Frederick D. Hammons: p. 245. Mrs. Nicholas Longworth: p. 116 (photo *The Washington Post*). The Lord Chamberlain of England: pp. 55, 56 (Copyright Reserved). Mrs. William R. Mahoney: p. 234. Miss Elsa Mannheimer: p. 239. Mrs. Elizabeth Moskovszky & Mrs. Eva Horvath: pp. 151, 152. Mrs. Pat Monroe: p. 58 (photo Reni Photos). Mrs. Philip Ross-Ross: p. 213. Mme. Helena Rubinstein: pp. 306, 307. Lord St. Oswald: pp. 46, 47 (photo Photo Centre Ltd.). Miss Gertrude Sappington: p. 238. Mme. Madeleine Schlumberger: p. 234. Mr. & Mrs. E. H. Short: p. 154 (photo E. A. Phillips). Miss Ettie Stettheimer: pp. 312, 313. Mr. John Stover: p. 202. Mrs. Marg. Weber-Beck: pp. 147, 148, 186. author's collection: pp. 39, 54, 194; p. 111 (photo Elinore Blaisdell); pp. 107, 110, 112 (photos Glogau Studio); pp. 109, 129, 130, 184, 230, 231 (photos Harry Goodwin); pp. 4, 5, 8, 9, 10, 61, 62, 108, 124, 128, 138, 161, 163, 164, 167, 170, 171, 174, 190, 193, 207, 247 (photos Ray Harper); p. 190 (photo David Posner).

Books, Magazines, Miscellaneous Sources

Coleman, Evelyn, Elizabeth & Dorothy, *The Age of Dolls:* p. 196. *Amateur Work:* p. 212. *Aunt Judy's Christmas Volume for Young People,* Bell & Daldy, London, 1870: p. 323. Karl Gröber, *Childrens' Toys of Bygone Days,* B. T. Batsford Ltd.: pp. 76, 77, 148, 167, 172, 248, 250. *How to Make Dolls' Furniture and Furnish a Dolls' House,* Griffin & Farran, London: pp. 256, 257, 254. *The Nursery Play Book,* F. Warne & Co., London: p. 252. Wilkinson, Sir Nevile, *Yvette in Italy and Titania's Palace,* Oxford University Press: pp. 272, 278. d'Allemagne, Henri-René, *Histoires des Jouets:* pp. 19, 35, 94, 95, 96, 162. d'Allemagne, Henri-René, *Les Jouets à la World's Fair en 1904 à St. Louis:* pp. 37, 38. Lessing, Julius & Bruning, Adolf, *Der Pommersche Kunstachrank:* p. 21. Boesch, Hans, *Kinderleben der Deutschen Vergangenheit:* p. 28. Nachfolger, Karl Robert Langewiesche, *Die Puppenstadt:* pp. 290, 291, 292, 294. Muller, S. & Vogelsang, W., *Hollandisches Patrizierhäuser:* pp. 70, 75. *The Connoisseur:* pp. 321, 324. Country Life Ltd.: pp. 43, 52, 259, 260, 264, 265. *Homes and Gardens,* George Newnes Ltd. & Arthur Pierson Ltd.: p. 153. *Ladies' Home Journal,* coypright by The Curtis Publishing Co.: pp. 255, 329. *The Illustrated London News:* p. 166. *Playthings:* pp. 191, 197. *The Spinning Wheel:* p. 112. Catalogues from Althof, Bergmann & Co., 1874; p. 185; F. Cairo, 1892: p. 257; Montgomery Ward #67 & #71: p. 188; Schoenhut, 1913: p. 194; F. A. O. Schwarz, 1913: pp. 9, 178, 194, 195; Sears, Roebuck & Co.: p. 197. Radio Times Hulton Picture Library: pp. 279, 281. Washington Evening Star Photo: p. 142. U. S. Patent Office: pp. 204, 208, 209, 210.

INTRODUCTION

At the time this book was first published in 1953, there had been many a volume about dolls, but no previous history of dolls' houses. This was plainly an oversight, and to moderate it, there was only the well-known work about Queen Mary's Dolls' House, and an elaborate folio, by two Netherlands scholars, about five early Dutch dolls' houses.

There is still no other general survey of the subject but, since this one first appeared, there have been several additions to dolls' house literature, most notably, in 1955, *English Dolls' Houses of the 18th and 19th Centuries* by Vivien Greene, a sizable and delightful volume with many valuable illustrations. In 1956, *Tageslauf im Puppenhaus,* a slender, attractively illustrated book by Dr. Leonie von Wilckens of the staff of the Nuremberg Museum was printed in German about several of the museum's remarkable seventeenth century houses.*

Since dolls' houses may be of interest to such assorted members of society as architects, collectors, children, historians, housewives, and antiquarians of all varieties, it has seemed appropriate to direct this book towards as many of its likely supporters as possible. Of this miscellany, the collectors themselves are assorted; fanciers of antique dolls and toys being but a part of the gathering fraternity a book about dolls' houses is likely to engage. Because the dolls' house, during the four centuries in which its history has been recorded, has contained, in miniature, virtually every item that a full-scale establishment of its period would include, it perfectly reflects furniture of that period, china, glassware, silver, art, musical instruments; in short, and in little, anything that a full-size house might contain or a full-size antique collector collect.

---

* Victoria and Albert Museum in London has printed (1960), an attractive booklet, *Dolls' Houses,* picturing English examples, most of them to be found at the museum and its Bethnal Green branch.

The Rijksmuseum, Amsterdam, printed, in 1955, a booklet about its own *Poppenhuizen.*

There can be few more satisfying collections—to those of us who *must* collect—than antique dolls' house furnishings; such an assemblage cannot be surpassed in terms of either space-saving or diversity. The dolls' house specialist may store a quantity of furniture and china and lamps and clocks in one dolls' house, one cabinet, or one corner of a room, and yet have ventured into every field indicated by a moderately stocked museum.

This book hopes to tell all that it possibly can about dolls' houses of innumerable places and eras. And its theory is that in so doing, it will discover a great deal about arts, architecture, furnishings, customs, and, perhaps, the way of life, of many of the people who lived in those places during those eras.

The day after the galleys for the present edition had been returned to the publisher, we received, through the kindness of Dr. Rainer Rückert, Oberkonservator of the Bayerisches Nationalmuseum in Munich, information about a dolls' house mentioned in the inventory of the estate of a Bavarian duchess which may possibly pre-date the celebrated 1558 house, hitherto considered the first on record, of Duke Albrecht V of Bavaria. (Chapter 3.)

The Duchess was Duke Albrecht's mother, the Duchess Jakobäa, who was born in 1507. The inventory of her estate, made in 1581, the year after her death, states that "In the corridor between the panelled room and the large hall is a big case which contains the dolls' house, in which dolls are to be found in small rooms. The whole dolls' house is arranged in the manner of a court." A note in the inventory adds that this house and another case containing "many dolls in different costumes . . . have been given completely about half a year ago by the Duchess to the elder "Markgräfin."

The latter, Dr. Rückert tells us, may well have been Maria Salome, 1563–1600, granddaughter of the Duchess in the Grand-Duchy of Baden.

Although it is possible that this is the same dolls' house attributed to Duke Albrecht, there are many conflicting facts. As we indicate in Chapter 3, a thorough inventory of the Duke's dolls' house, and all of his possessions, was made by Johann Baptiste Fickler in 1598, and *his* house is believed to have perished in the great fire at the Munich palace in 1674. If Duchess Jakobäa's house was given "completely" to Maria Salome in 1580, it was likely to have been in the Rhine Valley in 1674 when the Duke's treasure was reportedly destroyed in Munich. In any case, it seems unlikely to have been in Munich in 1598 when Fickler catalogued the late Duke's possessions.

If the Duchess Jakobäa's dolls' house was made for her as a child, it would, of course, pre-date the 1558 house of Duke Albrecht by two generations, and it is tantalizing that an urgent deadline prevents further investigation. However, with thanks to Dr. Rückert, students of dolls' house history may pursue the matter further in Volume XVI, *Münchner Jahrbuch der Bildenden Kunst,* scheduled for publication in late 1965.

A History of Dolls' Houses

1

A MICROCOSMOS

PLATITUDES WILL NOT DO WHEN ONE ATTEMPTS TO EXPLAIN THE appeal of a sewing machine three inches long, with workable parts, or of a toy train. It is likely, in any case, that no suitable ones could be found. Platitudes are usually the result of irresistible definitions: phrases become hackneyed not if they are found wanting, but only if they are monumentally appealing. Perhaps platitudes begin as overly-successful epigrams, but whatever the case, there appears to have been no epigram, successful or unsuccessful, to define the elusive seductions of the diminutive.

Possibly Mr. A. C. Benson has come the closest to defining them at all, though a paragraph is hardly epigramatic:

"There is great beauty in *smallness*. One gets all the charm of design and colour and effect, because you can see so much more in combination and juxtaposition. And then, too, the blemishes and small deformities which are so inseparable from seeing things life-size all disappear; the result is a closeness and fineness of texture which please both eye and mind. One realizes in reading the travels of Gulliver how dainty and beautiful the folk and buildings of Lilliput were, and on the other hand, how coarse and hideous the magnifying effect of Brobdingnag was." *

* *The Book of the Queen's Dolls' House.* Methuen & Co. Ltd., 1924.

Mario Praz, who Edmund Wilson has said will "come to be known to posterity . . . as one of the best Italian writers of his time," touched upon a subtler and more metaphysical explanation. In a joint review of the first edition of this book and of Vivien Greene's about English dolls' houses* Signor Praz wrote,† "Let us not pretend even to skim the deepest portion of the subject, since quite probably we would have to move, in such a case, into the rarefied air of myth and investigate the mysteries of Creation in order to see, perhaps, in this penchant of ours for the little things the action of the Creator who amuses Himself with His creature, made, naturally, in His own image, only smaller."

The dolls' house, however, has more than mere smallness to recommend it. The ability to reflect, in a relatively limited amount of space, four centuries of architecture, household furnishings, and innumerable customs is practical as well as appealing.

Years ago, an antiquarian apologized in print‡ for having credited the origin of the rocking chair to colonial America in the mid-eighteenth century inasmuch as a toy rocker had been found which traced this beginning to England in the mid-seventeenth.

The authenticity of the dolls' house sized rocking chair, three and a half inches high, and clearly of Gothic styling, was not to be questioned. It was found in a plague pit near London in the company of other items proclaiming the reign of Charles I, and had to be treated chemically three times before it was deemed safe to handle, since germs as well as objects survived the frantic haste which cast such relics and their tragic owners underground three hundred years ago.

The antiquarian added that of the victims there is rarely a trace, but that such items when found are generally well preserved. "Even the little seat cushion of this toy rocker was intact," he pointed out, adding, "This tiny toy is a new starting point in rocking chair research."

It seems a logical starting point for a book about dolls' houses as well. And a talking point. It seems especially useful for talking to people to whom a dolls' house is no more than a piece of miniature real estate; a roof over a doll's head. Such people have encountered the dolls' house only as a plaything, though as a museum piece or an art treasure it has found roles of equal stature. They are unaware that for at least four centuries the dolls' house has so accurately reflected the life about it that a book about dolls' houses becomes a footnote, at least, to cultural history.

A social historian, with words, attempts to tell us a great deal about customs and tastes. A painter, with brush, lets us know even more, recording perhaps, and simply, the corner of a kitchen with the cook roasting a goose.

* Batsford, 1955. *English Dolls' Houses of the Eighteenth and Nineteenth Centuries.*

† This, it should be mentioned, is a translation from the Rome daily, *Il Tempo,* the original of which we had the privilege of receiving from Signor Praz himself, and we hope it does not blemish unduly the graces of his own style.

‡ Carl Drepperd, in *The Spinning Wheel.*

But the dolls' house reveals, at a glance, what has taken the writer many chapters and the artist much canvas to say.

An elaborate eighteenth century German or Dutch dolls' house furnished by the same craftsmen who "did" the great residence of its owner, often recalls more than paint or print or miscellaneous antiques about the arts and customs of its day. But even an awkward little Victorian cottage with spindles and scrolls possesses in miniature a charm it may never have had in full size, and lacking the artistic stature of these more stately toys, reveals a great deal about the tastes and times of the people who lived in its full-sized counterpart.

Such information, sought in libraries, is likely to require considerable digging. Some of it has not been discoverable outside the dolls' house, and the plague-pit rocking chair is not the only example. Other household objects, things which have not come down to us in full size, have survived in miniature form. The means of preservation is not usually so somber as a plague pit. There are commoner reasons for their survival. One may be that the lady of the dolls' house, living merely a part-time life, has had more time than a full-sized housekeeper to care for her possessions.

Styles in houses and furnishings change, and so do styles in dolls' houses and dolls' furnishings. But sometimes, with luck, a dolls' house is put away in an attic, or placed in storage. (Happily, the handsomest and most complete are more likely to be so stored.) Time stands still and a period is preserved as it never can be in a full-sized house. All sorts of things, however ephemeral, are left as they were in a dolls' house that would never remain in a human's. There can be no better example than a nearly modern dolls' house played with in the grim, dark London days of World War II by Miss Faith Eaton, a gifted English doll maker and collector. Her 1940 dolls' house has, she once wrote us, "an air-raid shelter and brown sticky paper X's on its windows and blackout-curtains because, when we did my own home I did my dolls' home as well and—mercifully—I put the house away in this condition when I grew up."

An isolated example? It must be more than a coincidence that a young English journalist, Miss Sonia Roberts, also wrote us (years ago) on this very subject. Only the details varied: ". . . I don't know whether you realise that although the war virtually halted toy production in Britain, a few dolls' house things were made and these were in keeping with the grim circumstances of the blitz. My own dolls' house was equipped wth miniature sandbags, a stirrup pump, and an additional supply of buckets and ladders for fire fighting."

Preserving history is all very well, and is perhaps the firmest purpose the dolls' house serves, but its other two roles must not be overlooked. Charm enough for a toy and magnificence enough for an art collection are qualities not common to every wooden jumping jack and jeweled snuff box, but since these characteristics bring together those two dolls' house fanciers, the child and the adult, the pages which follow will strongly suggest that both the young and the old always have enjoyed seeing their world reproduced in miniature. Whether or not, like Mr. Benson and Signor Praz, they will speculate about the reasons for their interest is immaterial.

Dolls' houses are just one expression of this interest. People forever have been making scale models of cities and ships and mules, and rationalizing thoroughly about their motives. The ancient Egyptians created miniature models of bake-shops and hair-dressing establishments—of much of their world—with the religious explanation that the dead, with whom they buried these things, would need them in the afterworld. They undoubtedly were sincere in this belief, but it seems possible, too, that they received pleasure in creating and regarding the miniature versions, *per se*.

Today what is known as a "working-model" is made of everything from a traffic light to a steamship, with the reasonable excuse that it is helpful to study a large project in small scale. We do not wish to doubt the worthy people who offer these businesslike reasons for commissioning such miniature models. It is true that building an automobile, say, in little before attempting it in full size is very likely to save time and expense. But it might be more graceful—and more truthful—if those involved with the miniature automobile (some of them anyway), happened to confess that they like what they have made, for itself alone, just because it is *small*.

Dolls' houses, it might be mentioned at the outset, have been from time to time, in their relatively recent (and English-speaking) history, known also as baby houses, toy houses, and play houses. As "baby houses," they are likely to be recorded in British publications of the eighteenth and early nineteenth centuries. Mr. G. Bernard Hughes, in an article in *Country Life* has pointed out that dictionaries of the period define a doll as "a child's baby, a girl's toy baby." The Westbrook Baby House of 1705 which he was describing was thus known to its first little owner. "Play houses," as applied to dolls' houses, as anyone who has either a play house or dolls' house knows, is altogether a misnomer. A play house refers to a small building large enough to contain doll owners as well as their dolls, but since this identification sometimes is mistaken for dolls' house and applied to accommodations suitable for dolls alone, it appears proper to expose the verbal culprits.

There are, of course, several spellings for dolls' house. The British invariably add the "s," plus an apostrophe fore or aft. They write either "doll's house" or "dolls' house," depending, apparently, upon the size of the family in residence. This attention to detail is in keeping, of course, with their national character, and it is perhaps a reflection on our traditional American haste that we practically always write "doll house." In the 1953 edition of this book, this national quirk was indulged and "doll house" was employed, a spelling which obliged Cassell, bringing out an edition in England in 1954, to insert an inordinate number of both "s"es and apostrophes.

For this edition, we have again checked Oxford and Webster for an opinion. While Webster continues to ignore the subject entirely, Oxford adds the "s'." Therefore, evidently, the British care and we do not. If some do not care, it seems logical to favor the spelling of those who do, and in this edition "dolls' house" will be our term.

Several diminutive matters not spelled in any of these ways have occasionally mingled in miniature with the dolls' house, and perhaps on the basis that they have assisted mutual interest, they deserve a paragraph or two.

One of these is the Christmas crèche. The German toy historian, Karl Gröber,* has linked it to the dolls' house in comparative terms, writing: "The dolls' house of the north, which had the life of the household as its model, has a parallel in the south, and especially in Italy, in the Christmas Crib which represents the life of the people in the open air." And he adds that both were meant principally to be looked at.

We describe in Chapter 3 a forty-foot specimen built for Charles III of Bourbon, King of Naples, in 1760 with 500 figures of people and 200 of animals "all made of finely carved wood, wax and costly fabrics," and some of those figures trooping from "shop, tavern and stall." A celebrated instrument maker wrought minute mandolins, lutes and harps; another artist modeled fruits and fishes. Such items as these demand a dolls' house, and it is possible that some of these very fruits and lutes have found their way into dolls' drawing-rooms.

The Noah's Ark is a simpler matter, and it is unlikely that its chickens and lions would turn up in a dolls' house (although "live" chickens were fattened in eighteenth century German dolls' house kitchens and the armorial lion had its own room in the princely Bavarian dolls' palace of

* *Children's Toys of Bygone Days,* Batsford, 1928.

A nineteenth century Noah's Ark

1558). But the Ark is built to dolls' house scale and it is possible that if a neatly carved Ham or Shem or Japheth knocked on the door of a dolls' house (which had an Old Testament on the parlor table) he would be warmly received.

The toy theater must also at least be associated in any account of the microcosmic world. Dolls' house residents were privileged to go to the theater some years ago, though they have had fewer opportunities in the current toy era. Miniature drama flourished principally in England, and also in the United States, in the second half of the nineteenth century. These theaters ranged from simple paper affairs to opulent stages with tin footlight troughs. Plays which were presented with live actors on full-scale stages had their scenery and cast reduced to scissor-size, and the show, after a tremendous painting and pasting, went on.

Dolls' shops, of course, are so closely associated with dolls' houses, that some museums, particularly ones abroad, list them together, along with kitchens, schoolrooms, and other related toys. They are discussed in their own chapter, and we wish there were another to contain the stables, swimming pools, fire houses, gardens, and other related members of the dolls' microcosmos. How does one classify (in the author's collection) a wooden gazebo, with faded roses climbing its turned posts, a blue-and-white striped fabric tent-like roof protecting, below, a table and four chairs in which a doll could take a spot of refreshment on a warm day? One knows only that it is a construction, nostalgic and beguiling, that mirrors a recreational appurtenance of the past.

Since a dolls' world has reflected so truly the actual one, it, too, in its small way, is vast, and two covers of one book are unlikely to contain it. We had hoped, for instance, to devote a chapter to the occupants of the small world—the dolls that inhabit it. Almost nothing has been written on the subject of dolls' house dolls, and rather little is known. There has been great interest in the subject, especially in those enchanting late Victorian bisque families in their accurate and evocative (though machine-made) late Victorian clothes. At least we are happy in our ability to offer a portrait of half a dozen of these small bisque personages, pristine in the late Victorian garments they were still wearing in a post-Edwardian 1913 Schwarz catalogue.

The late and beloved doll maker and collector, Martha Thompson, wrote the only article we have seen on the subject, in an issue of *The Toy Trader*,* and even this article is mostly concerned with instructions for copying the original clothes for similar dolls whose original ones have been lost. But her description is charming, of "an endless variety of well-proportioned bisque-faced little people who represented mothers and fathers and grandparents and household servants and even relatives in the 'service'."

"This would be Kaiser Wilhelm's service, of course," Mrs. Thompson adds, "as the little people were made in Germany and there is nothing so

"No. 2 Fire Station"
(Height: 17") and a wooden
gazebo (Height: 14½")

* An elusive issue for which we wish to thank doll-maker Mrs. E. J. Carter of Hyattsville, Md.

fascinating as those little resplendent Prussian soldiers that come our way from time to time." She shows a picture of a dolls' house father dressed for the opera (in his original box) and expresses regret that the firm which made these little dolls failed to inscribe its name somewhere, "for not even on the boxes in which they came is there a clue."

This series of dolls' house dolls which, as Mrs. Thompson wrote, began in the 'nineties and continued for about twenty-five years to the 'twenties, when small "flappers" were made, came, as the Schwarz catalogue indicates, in heights ranging from five to seven inches. Some had small wigs and glass eyes and others, like the Schwarz examples pictured, had molded wigs and painted eyes.

DOLLHOUSE DOLLS

For use in Doll's houses we have a large variety of small dressed dolls, such as Gentlemen and Ladies in different costumes, Maids, Nurses, Waiters, Butlers, Cooks, etc., etc. These dolls measure from 5 to 7 inches, and range in price from............50c. to $1.50

A dolls' house family as advertised by Schwarz in 1913

But, of course, delightful dolls' house dolls were made in all eras. There were the jointed "penny woodens" of the early nineteenth century representing such personages as Queen Victoria and her governess, dressed, and the small flat-heeled bisques of mid-century that small girls (and their mothers and their aunts) dressed themselves. And there are the dolls' house dolls that Kate Greenaway bought with her pocket money, also at mid-century, in London's famous Lowther Arcade.*

The Greenaway dolls' house dolls consisted of the Royal Family then in residence, including, needless to say, Her Majesty Queen Victoria, who had cost a halfpenny. Her garments are not described, but those of Prince Albert, who, quite properly, had also cost a halfpenny, are: His Royal Highness wore a white gauze shirt trimmed with three rows of cerise satin and, "for further distinction and identification, a red ribbon tied across his shoulder and under his left arm."

According to Miss Greenaway's biographers,† "These garments could only be removed by an actual disintegration"—which is also true of the clothes of their German descendants, the late Victorian dolls' house dolls. "The Royal circle was completed by the princes and princesses at a farthing apiece. Their dresses were made from the gauze bonnet linings just then going out of fashion, and such scraps of net and ribbon as had proved usable."

These dolls did not occupy a house, but a toy cupboard in Kate's bedroom which was well furnished, even though "furniture was hard to come by at a farthing a week." At this rate, it took twenty-four weeks to obtain a six-penny piano, but "once Aunt Aldridge came to town and presented the dolls with a work table." Unhappily, "so great a piece of good fortune never again befell."

Kate Greenaway's dolls' house dolls remind us that we, in this volume, longed to include a chapter relating to literary dolls' houses. Two, Katherine Mansfield's, and Frances Hodgson Burnett's, survive in Chapter 24, from the earlier edition, but there are many others, such as the one used as a model

* Lesley Gordon, in her delightful toy history, *Peepshow into Paradise*, George G. Harrap & Co. Ltd., London, 1953, (which should be reprinted under a less charming but perhaps more explicit title), has, with her usual kindness, referred us to her source for this enchanting information.
† M. H. Spielmann & G. S. Layard. Adam & Charles Black, 1905.

by Beatrix Potter for *The Tale of Two Bad Mice*. So many of the dolls' house articles the gifted artist reproduced exquisitely, in water colors, for the story—the plaster foods, the copper tea pot, the fireplace, and the stewing pans among them—are to be seen in every late Victorian English dolls' house worth its salt. Other literary dolls' houses include Sacheverell Sitwell's, and the late Denton Welch's (both the Sitwell house, dated 1835, and the lovely Georgian baby house the young English author restored shortly before his death having been attractively described by Mrs. Greene). There is Phyllis McGinley's considerably more modern "Connecticut country house" which she re-did for her daughters and then distilled—along with the essence of every dolls' house built by a father and furnished by a mother—in an exquisite poem.*

One cannot conclude these preliminary pages without reference to a species of miniature not made for dolls but one which unquestionably has found its way into dolls' houses of many vintages. This is the traveler's sample. Sir Nevile Wilkinson, whose miniature cannon, a traveler's sample, ca. 1590, is described in Chapter 19, wrote gracefully some years ago about how such miniature merchandise came into being. There was no postal service to carry catalogues, he said. "Petty rulers, robber barons or feudal chieftains to whom the goods appealed couldn't have read them anyway." There were so many brigands and outlaws upon the roads through the forests that it would have been tempting providence to send full-sized things without an efficient escort. And so traveler's samples, miniature replicas of the full-sized articles, were the ingenious solution. In later and more civilized times, Sir Nevile wrote, furniture miniatures were made for a similar purpose. And, for that matter, there are firms today which make such drummer's samples, although for rather different reasons.

There were also, of course, in the early days before the machine, apprentice pieces—articles fashioned to show the skill of the maker. Apprentice pieces, too, have unquestionably found their way into dolls' houses.

But that is another tale, and it is necessary to get on with the dolls' house story, a plump narrative populated with villains, heroes, and anecdotes as well as with tables and chairs. Dolls' houses have not only been furnished; they have been burglarized, by strictly full-sized burglars (see Utrecht, Chapter 6); they have been burned down, by entirely large-scale fires (see the Duke of Bavaria, Chapter 3). They have even been haunted! It is quite true that the latter state, as in life, is, so far as can be proved, fictitious, having been reported by M. R. James in a story entitled *The Haunted Dolls' House*. The Provost of Eton wrote this tale for the Queen's Dolls' House Library, but it has been reprinted in numerous anthologies, coming from its very limited (one copy) edition to a recent multiple printing in a pocketbook horror volume with the dolls' house's picture on the cover.

This book, though, will concern itself with dolls' houses more actual and less fictitious, but, perhaps, quite as informative.

* Printed first in *The New Yorker* and then in *The Love Letters of Phyllis McGinley*.

2

THE

ANCIENTS

EVIDENCE TO SHOW THAT EGYPTIAN CHILDREN, AND LATER, LITTLE
Greeks and Romans, had dolls' houses, is circumstantial. It is based largely
on the presence of a few scattered trinkets under glass in the antiquities
sections of the museums of the world. Several of the trinkets, for that matter,
are not conceded by all authorities to be toys. When one considers that
objects which are a mere few hundred years old cause controversy, it is not
surprising that some over a thousand have driven a few scholars to disagree.
Despite dissension, though, about possible survivals, there are few authorities unwilling to guess that ancient dolls had homes.

Although so many details about Egyptian life have come down to us,
few of them have been in relation to toys. It is unfortunate that the particular
sort of toys that furnish dolls' houses would, in almost any age, have been
made of wood and thus have only a mild chance of long-range survival. It is
therefore interesting that the most specific Egyptian dolls' furnishing in the
Metropolitan Museum of Art *is* of wood.

This is a folding traveling bed, approximately a foot long, and of
arresting detail. The six legs (the extra pair is at the folding joint) are fancy,
being delicately bulbous. There is a headboard and there are crisscross
"springs" of string. The latter have been restored, but this does not seem

surprising since this workable toy dates back to between 1500 and 1100 B.C.

One of the most curious Egyptian toys which has endured is also of wood, and is of a sufficiently domestic nature to qualify as a fitting occupant of an Egyptian dolls' house. Properly it is a mechanical toy, a figure kneading bread on a board when a string is pulled. Circa 2000 B.C., it is a crude figure with jointed arms and legs, but for our purpose it might be the doll that lived in the dolls' house. And the board may well be the earliest dolls' house breadboard. Certainly, if such subject matter was present in mechanical toys, it must have been duplicated in unmechanical ones, since mechanical and unmechanical toys have paralleled each other in every age.

Archeologists may accept responsibility for the most controversial element in this hazardous chapter, the small models they exhumed near the Nile. There is no doubt about the religious uses of the innumerable little houses and bakeshops and breweries placed in the sarcophagi of departed Egyptians to serve them in the other world, but several authorities have suspected that similar models have been used for toys.

A very young Egyptian, let us suppose, accidentally came upon a miniature house about to serve its usual burial purpose. If we are to believe only concrete evidence, he hadn't many toys of his own. Though risking parental wrath and even that of offended gods, was he likely to resist playing with this enchanting object?

The late Hendrik Van Loon, some years ago in a magazine article, described the religious purpose but toy-like appearance of these curiosities, observing, "Personally I feel rather inclined to believe that they were also used in the nursery." He added "other evidence" to bear him out:

"Many times during the history of the last three thousand years, the grown-ups have amused themselves by filling their houses with little objects which became toys the moment a child looked at them. In my grandfather's house there was a small glass case entirely filled with everyday scenes from Dutch life during the eighteenth century. Since all of these gadgets were made of silver, we children were never allowed to touch them. We could only look, but that was almost as good as playing with them."

Van Loon's idea carries the toy theory a step further. If the wayward child of our anecdote merely looked at the small house intended for a burial relic, it became a toy for him, and since such a mild claim hardly could have caused concern, such looks, and thus such toys, may have existed in many Egyptian households.

The Metropolitan Museum of Art has an illuminating group of models which were found in the tomb of Meket-Rē at Thebes in 1919. Meket-Rē, an important official of the Egyptian court about 2000 B.C., had them placed there to serve his needs in the afterworld. Among the models are his brewery, his bakery, granary, carpenter's shop, weaver shop, and garden, all animated by the neat miniature presences of a goodly population of slaves and other figures, including Meket-Rē himself. There is also a veritable fleet of boats of

Garden of Meket-rē.,
ca. 2000 B. C., at Metropolitan

various sorts, not surprising, since the people of the Nile were practically river folk, doing all of their traveling by water, and a good deal of relaxing in pleasure craft thereon. The vessels represented include a yacht, a fishing and fowling boat, a skiff, and a traveling boat with its kitchen tender. The traveling boat epitomizes the refinements of Nile travel: Meket-Rē sits in the bow smelling a lotus flower and listening to a singer.

Even though the Egyptians were at home, almost literally, on the water, a model of the garden of Meket-Rē comes closest perhaps to suiting a study of miniature housing. Not only is the garden represented, complete with a wall and seven identifiable sycamore trees surrounding a pond, but facing the garden is the house itself. Lotus and papyrus columns support the roof of the porch. We are indebted to the Metropolitan for the description, details of which are not all readily describable by a layman:

"Underneath, the roof is presented as consisting of logs resting upon cross-beams supported by the two rows of columns. The cross-beams are decorated with yellow stars on a blue ground—a ceiling pattern often employed in Egyptian temple architecture. At the back of the porch are shown a great state doorway with fanlight above, a side door, and a tall latticed window." The aspect of the model that no child would be able to resist, is the garden pond, made of copper, so that it would actually hold water.

Since one cannot speak for Meket-Rē, one does not offer this theory in respect to a dignitary who may have taken his religion very seriously. But there have been atheists and agnostics in every age; it is possible that an

13

occasional Egyptian, though he thought it all nonsense, philosophically permitted these after-life aids to be buried with him without protest, at least subconsciously preserving history. Thus, if these models for the deceased became toys when smiled upon by children, and museum pieces when tolerated by agnostics, they are, in two ways, suitable candidates for a book about dolls' houses.

A writer who has assigned a toy status to one of these models without question is Mrs. Emily Jackson, who, in her *Playthings of Other Days,* published in 1908, reproduces a picture of Egyptian kitchen utensils, a very complete outfit to judge by its variety. The implements are of bronze, the largest one and a half inches high, and Mrs. Jackson refers to them as "amongst the toys in the Egyptian Antiquities Section of the British Museum."

With respect to Greece and Rome, there is less need to be theoretical about dolls' houses. Speculation, for one thing, need not compete against the burial model identity which dogs Egyptian miniatures. No Greek or Roman dolls' houses remain, but as Gröber records, "They must have existed; for where else could use have been found for the little pieces of bronze furniture which have survived, if not in a doll's room? while the many little utensils belong of a certainty to the furnishing of a doll's kitchen."

In the same paragraph, Gröber, speculating about another matter, unconsciously offers a more direct clue to the dolls' house than the furnishings. "If Plato," he says, "can write that the future architect should from his earliest years busy himself with the building of houses, we can safely conclude that even in those days boxes of bricks, whatever they may have looked like, cannot have been wanting." Though boxes of bricks are all very well, we need not speculate upon the means here but the end. Gröber is dealing with a constructional toy; we dwell upon the toy after it is constructed and appropriated by little sister for her dolls' house. We hereby consider it constructed and appropriated.

Having thus, via Plato, and courtesy Gröber, built a Greek dolls' house, we turn to the Roman furniture which Gröber evidently had in mind to furnish his theoretical Roman dolls' house. A lead sofa and chair he pictures, less than three inches in height, are believed to be Roman of about 100 A.D.

These, in the British Museum, are undoubtedly the ones to which a writer in *The Spectator* was referring in June of 1907 when he wrote, ". . . nor is the tiny chair more clumsy which, belonging to the lead age, would have brought sudden happiness to the owner of a Roman dolls' house." The fact that the venerable *Spectator,* not given, after all, to making rash judgments, should thus concede the existence of Roman dolls' houses, is not to be taken lightly. *The Spectator's* theoretical Roman dolls' house is thereby placed alongside our theoretical Greek one.

French game historian Becq de Fouquières quotes Pausanias, Greek traveler and topographer, on the subject of a little ivory bed among the offerings in the temple of Hera at Olympia which, he had been told, had been a toy of Hippodameia, the wife of Pelops, and which she had offered to the goddess. Becq de Fouquières, writing in the 1870's, before toys were considered in historical terms, comments that "This bed ought certainly to be that of the doll of Hippodameia."

Although here, as in the case of the Egyptian models, speaking of this religious item as a toy may be taking license, it is not necessary to take as much as in the case of the models. Since the little ivory bed apparently was an art object rather than a religious symbol of any sort, it must have been a toy in the same sense that miniature furnishings in the old art cabinets were toys, and also in the nursery sense, since children would have adopted the little bed as promptly as the Egyptian child of our earlier illustration must have adopted the burial relic. Gröber, quoting the same extract from Pausanias sixty years later, is unhesitating about its toy origin. He used it to indicate that "such doll furniture could be very costly."

One exhibit of Greek and Roman toys in the British Museum, as set up in the autumn of 1948, included objects of bronze as well as clay, and two items of lead, a Roman tray and dish. Among the bronze miniatures were a tripod, Roman, from the first century A.D., and a carefully detailed water pot and a throne, both Greek, from the fifth century B.C. From the same period and place as the latter two articles, was a clay stool. The most interesting specimens in clay, though, as is often the case, were things which in full size probably would have been of the same material, a miniature clay lamp in the form of a grotesque head, wonderfully detailed, and a clay cup, similar to it. Both of these were Roman of the first century A.D. One small but striking fact about the group is that, despite the interval of centuries and civilizations, virtually everything in it is of the same scale often found in modern dolls' houses, one inch to one foot. A wispy clue, perhaps, for people who like to contend that things have not changed much.

But these are all the things there are . . . so far.

It seems regrettable if we are destined to find no doll noble's house of, say, the pyramid age, with painted ceiling (doves and butterflies), palm-trunk columns, and carved ivory couches, all exceedingly miniature. Or, turning to the Romans, a doll-size atrium with the kitchen in a corner and the bedding in another, and a hole in the roof for a chimney, would not seem much to ask. Perhaps one day some archeologist, digging just a little deeper, will turn up such treasures.

Even disputed dolls' house evidence cannot be traced to an earlier people than the ancient Egyptians. Gröber lists "little pots" among remains of prehistoric ages, but of little pots even this partisan book would not a dolls' house try to make. No one can say, though, that such did not exist, and we are content with the thought that a very small cave scooped out of the hillside was the dolls' house of the cave child; or, if you like, that the Garden of Eden once was produced in miniature, the handiwork, in their earlier and more peaceable days, of Cain and Abel. Since Adam and Eve did not have a daughter, we shall not venture too far on this last.

The kitchen of the Baeumler house and the nursery of the Kress house

16

3

1558 AND
THEREABOUTS

THE EARLIEST DOLLS' HOUSE ON RECORD IS A BAVARIAN ONE OF 1558. Since it was also one of the most elaborate which ever has been, and since it was the property of a well-publicized Duke, it is safe to assume that lesser dolls' houses, belonging perhaps to lesser personages, and therefore unrecorded, existed earlier.

In 1544, according to Hans Boesch,* the Abbess of the Cloister of Bernardenburg gave as a present to the children of a Nuremberg patrician, "a garden in a box so they should have some pastime and fun." It is likely if such externals of buildings were represented in miniature, that the buildings themselves had been thought of. If this is true, we are taken back fourteen years more in our quest, and every fourteen years counts. The Dark Ages seem to have been the relatively Toyless Ages. A few scattered playthings have survived, but since the amusing of children was unlikely to have been considered a prime objective by the preoccupied adults of the Middle Ages, the dearth of surviving toys is not surprising.

Gröber says that we know even less about the toys of the Middle Ages than those of antiquity, since "references to them are very scarce and few have survived." He also points out that with "the primitive manner of life,

* *Kinderleben in der deutschen Vergangenheit.*

17

the almost total absence of what we call comfort, we could perhaps hardly look for any work of art in this field. Again, the times were troublous, and in the many burnings and plunderings of castles and towns there were destroyed those little objects cherished by children though of no value to the destroyers."

Such toys as there were, then, would hardly include dolls' houses, which of all playthings would be most likely to fall into a category of "works of art." It seems possible, though, that some father, some true knight ahead of his time, whittled a few chairs, or even a whole dolls' habitation, with the edge of his sword, and one day it may turn up in a walled-up recess of some feudal castle, if it has not become dust. Clues have not been lacking. Medieval dolls' utensils of the fourteenth century, of German make, were found at Jena, and have been in the museum there.

Moreover, the Guildhall Museum in London, its archeological excavations at home spurred perhaps by the only benefit to come from the bombings during World War II, has been rapidly augmenting its collection of toys of ancient London. These include not only medieval treasures, but items dating to the days of the Roman conquest.

In *Antiques* in 1949, Mr. Oswald, Keeper of the Museum, wrote, "Below the City of London, to a depth of twenty or thirty feet, lie remains of the past 2,000 years." Pointing out that children liked to play house "as today," Mr. Oswald described a medieval "bronze cauldron with fluted feet and eared handle." He added that "Green glazed earthenware jugs much the same as the fragmentary bronze one were found in 1947 in deposits dated to the second half of the fourteenth century. Other small objects in pewter give an idea of the humbler dolls' house furniture of the past." The Guildhall curator also describes a first century wine jug, observing that the diminutive pottery vessels, being "faithful copies of the fashionable vessels of their times," are "perhaps most fascinating of all."

It would seem logical that Italy, knowing the Renaissance and its luxuries ahead of the rest of Europe, had the earliest dolls' houses. The one early Italian dolls' house which is well known (pictured in Chapter 9) dates no earlier than 1700, but a land which used forks before other countries thought of them, might also have thought first of dolls' houses.

We have suggested elsewhere that Gröber's comparison of the northern dolls' house with the southern crèche "especially in Italy" introduces another possibility—that these elaborate representations must have been related to dolls' house making. It is true that the link beween crèche scenes and dolls' houses would be more apparent in the northern countries, where the place of the Nativity became a snow-clad stable. In Italy the setting was more appropriately the open air. But even without a shelter, the crèche became so elaborate, and required so many minute accessories likely to amuse children, that they must have demanded duplicates for less religious uses.

Although it dates back only to 1760, the specimen which belonged to

Charles III of Bourbon, King of Naples (to which we have referred in Chapter 1,) is a spectacular example of how detailed these representations could be. Léo Claretie, the French toy historian, who called it the most beautiful in existence, wrote: "The scene represents the mountains surrounding the ruins of Paestum and the figures in the group represent shepherds, peasants, fishermen, the Samaritan women, the Magi and their suites, all wending their way, afoot or on horseback to pay their homage to the Pio Bambino lying on the lap of the Virgin who is seated on the ruins of a Temple to Apollo. With picturesque anachronism, all the persons represented in the procession, except the Magi and their Negro followers, wear the dress of Neapolitan fishermen and shepherds of the year 1760. Some carry on their shoulders gifts such as baskets of fruit, lambs, etc. while from roadside, doorstep, shop, tavern and stall troop up other worshipers."

The figures, delicately modeled from wax, were about nine inches tall. (Larger than an inch to the foot, this is the scale that is likely to be found in the big German and Dutch dolls' houses of the seventeenth and eighteenth centuries.) The most skilled artists of old Naples are known to have contributed. Miniature mandolins, lutes, and harps were the work of her celebrated instrument makers, fruits and fishes were modeled by her artists, and the dolls were dressed by the Queen of Naples herself. Our illustration of another elegant eighteenth century crèche, from the collection of the late Henri-René d'Allemagne, indicates similarly "picturesque anachronism."

Comparable splendor in these Nativity representations was to be found in northern examples. An amusing newspaper account of a specimen in a Munich museum is revealing: "One Tirolese took his fling when it came to

French crèche, eighteenth century, from d'Allemagne

the angels in heaven and dressed them in such a weight of gold and silver that even the strong wings he supplies hardly look equal to their task. Trappings of horses give another chance for jewels and color. The traders and workmen and farmers, however, are dressed to look like those of their time and place. Cattle, too, and poultry seem so accurate and complete, without a hair or a feather missing, that no doubt one who makes a special study of such things could trace breeds."

The same anonymous *N. Y. Times* author mentions that "the crèche led to models that made no pretense at having anything to do with Christmas decorations—models of the market place, of the hostel, a scene on the steps of the cathedral ... The market place has tiny loaves of bread, baskets filled with tiny cabbages, each leaf curled to perfection, mushrooms, fruit, strings of garlic, butter, eggs ... In the Italian models prettiest of all are the tiny ceramics—glass and majolica. The majolica is far more charming in miniature than that pompous glaze often is in life."

Probably a more likely inspiration for the making of dolls' houses in the north would have been the celebrated art cabinets on which people began to spend fortunes in the sixteenth century. The most famous of these, which were designed to contain curios and little works of art, probably was the one presented in 1637, when the practice was well under way, by the town of Augsburg to King Gustavus Adolphus of Sweden. It was built at a cost of 6,500 reichsthalers and has had two vast volumes written around it. This was from the studio of Philip Hainhofer, an art dealer, collector, and connoisseur, who designed many similar cabinets, as well as dolls' houses. It may be seen at the University of Upsala, and contains such toys as a little falconry, a peepshow, and a pair of dolls—a cavalier and his lady holding hands in readiness to dance by means of a mechanism which no longer works. According to Max von Boehn,* "the lady's head unfortunately is missing."

Von Boehn describes another Hainhofer cabinet of an even earlier vintage, one which was sold to Duke Philip II of Pomerania in 1617 and which was before World War II to be found in the Schloss-Museum at Berlin. "This represented a farmyard full of dolls, including soldiers, girls, farm servants, carriers, cavaliers, and peasants of both sexes. One woman was seated milking a cow, and even a 'closet', in which a girl is sitting doing 'the needful,' was included. There were many animals, and the various kinds of poultry were even covered with real birds' feathers." One might note here the resemblance of this bird-feathered poultry to the specimens "without a hair or a feather missing" described in the Tirolean crèche. Perhaps they were turned out, by the bin, for curio cabinets as well as crèches.

Since the model is about seven feet long, its corresponding dimensions may be judged. The animals were made by Johann Schwegler, an Augsburg

* *Dolls and Puppets.* Translated by Josephine Nicoll. London: G. G. Harrap & Co. 1932.

master noted for his exquisite contributions to a number of cabinets. According to von Boehn, the courtyards were popular toys among ladies of quality, and expensive ones, costing from 500 to 800 gulden. "Duke William of Bavaria gave several of them as presents; he sent various specimens to the Queens of France and Spain, some arch-duchesses, and other princesses, but these have all now disappeared."

Such wholesale distribution by an individual may account for the fact that the same Duke who proffered the courtyard that von Boehn describes, is credited, in the same year, with ordering a specimen considerably more elaborate, but no longer in existence, "the Meierhof," a house and courtyard, also from Hainhofer. So many details about it correspond to the courtyard in the Schloss-Museum that one might for a moment suppose that the two have been confused, and are one, but a brief study of the lovely water color drawing of the Meierhof (see illustration) will show that it is quite different from the courtyard of von Boehn's account. The water color of this tantalizing toy, done about 1640, and a sort of ground plan which details its curious

Hainhofer house and courtyard. ca. 1640

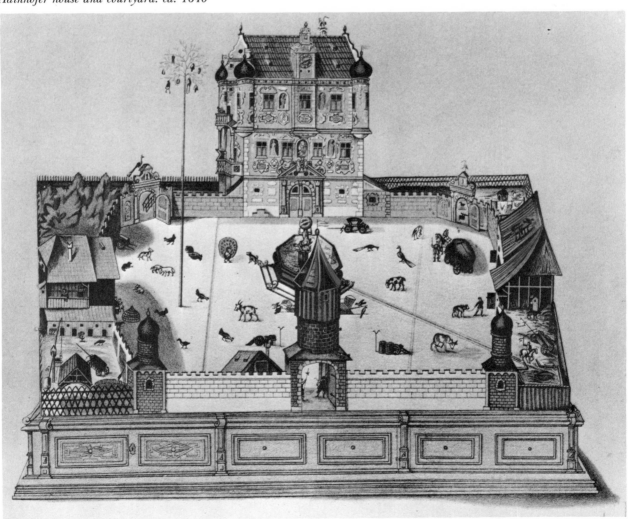

features are all, evidently, that is left of it, for it is said to have "vanished beyond trace."

Its picture shows it to be even more comprehensive than most dolls' houses as a likeness of its day. The courtyard is walled, like a castle, the main buildings forming part of this stone barrier. And the resemblance to such a fortress does not end there, for the place is full of turrets and towers. Very peaceful-looking beings are within the courtyard, despite its martial air. Goats and cows, peacocks and roosters, roam amid its cannon. The curious-looking tree-like pole in the left-center of the courtyard, we have been told by a Frenchwoman, is evidently the predecessor of a pastime still to be found at country fairs in France today where it is known as 'mât de cocagne.' Literally a "greasy pole," gifts are affixed to its top, and those agile enough to reach them are rewarded. The buildings of the Meierhof are said to have held exquisitely finished miniatures by Johann Schwegler, the same Augsburg master who did the cabinet presented to the King of Sweden.

Although most of the cabinets mentioned here seem to have concerned only the nobility, according to Gröber the formerly rare habit of forming collections was not confined to them, "for the middle-class merchant did not want to be behind in the fashion." He adds that "the new craze, as may be expected, stimulated the toy industry, since the loving purpose of giving joy to their little ones seemed to justify the parents in getting such toys made as also appeal, and have ever appealed to grown-ups . . ."

Earlier than any of the cabinets that have been described here, and obviously before Hainhofer's time, we hear of a toy as zoological as his farmyard, of a type often found in sixteenth century accounts—a "hunt." This early specimen, which was given to the twelve-year-old Prince of Saxony for Christmas in 1572 by his father, was a large one, "complete with huntsmen, and hounds, stags, roe-bucks, wild boars, foxes, wolves, and hares, to which horses, a mule, and a sledge were added. Probably the whole of this magnificent present was made of wood."

The Prince's two sisters, it might be noted, aged ten and five, got practically a dolls' house. There is a record of "A wonderful outfit for a doll kitchen which contained 71 dishes, 40 meat plates, 100 other plates, 36 spoons, and 28 egg cups, all of tin." Besides, they received such highly miscellaneous house furnishings in miniature as tables, chairs, cabinets, a wire cradle, sewing cushions, bathtubs (!), barber bowls, and inkstands. Moreover, according to Boesch, "The severity of life was shown by two rods such as those with which ducal children sometimes came in contact." The Princesses also received a little poultry yard, so Hainhofer was by no means the originator of these, nor was their distribution confined to great ladies. Of course, the figures in this yard, like the figures in the hunt, may have been made of wood, with such refinements as bird feathers lacking.

Christoph Weigel, writing a century or so later (in 1698), has left an interesting account of how the artists and craftsmen who made cabinet objects worked, which gives particular insight into the part taken by the omnipotent guilds.

"The materials of which these dolls and playthings are made are in part silver and are fashioned by gold and silversmiths, in part of wood, which the common carver of images and turner are wont to make, in part of alabaster . . . performed by the worker in alabaster. Others are moulded out of wax, and in particular many kinds of beasts and fowls are made of this almost exactly like nature, with their rough skins drawn over them or very prettily bedecked with feathers. Indeed there is scarce a trade in which that which usually is made big may not often be seen copied on a small scale as a toy for playing with."

Gröber tells us that toys were made in a large number of South German towns, and, of interest to us, that Augsburg and Ulm in particular were renowned for their wonderful dolls' houses and dolls' house furnishings. He adds, however, that the toy importance of these towns was slight compared to Nuremberg, "which was to become the center of the whole toy trade of the world." His description of toy manufacture in general by the guilds between the sixteenth and the eighteenth centuries is an interesting supplement to Weigel's:

"Childen's toys were made by all craftsmen as incidentals in their trade. The cabinet-maker made to order furniture for the doll's room, the tin and copper founder the little kitchen utensils, the potter small pieces of crockery.

"In the face of the stringent rules of the guilds, which limited the range within which a member might work, there was no such thing as a toy factory in the modern sense of the word. Each master could only practice within the circumscribed boundary of his own craft. The turner might not himself colour his productions, he must needs get this done by a recognized 'bismuth painter.' If, in the manufacture of a toy, any component part was needed which the master might not make himself he had to get it made by some member of the appropriate guild, however easy it had been for him to do the work himself.

"In the eighteenth century the city craftsman was really almost limited to the making of the finer sorts of toys, for he could not compete with the cheap and popular playthings which were being produced in ever greater quantities by the wood carvers of Thuringen, Berchtesgaden, and Oberammergau."

But we shall return to the sixteenth century, and an account of the first dolls' house on record. This dolls' house has the additional distinction of having had probably more misinformation printed about it than any that ever has been constructed.

Albrecht V, Duke of Bavaria, commissioned this much-misrepresented building for his little daughter in 1558, but placed it in his art collection.

Although, in some of the printed confusion above mentioned, it has been referred to in the present tense, it is believed to have perished in the great fire at the Munich palace in 1674.

Fortunately a detailed inventory had been made of the dolls' house and its contents in 1598, forty years after its completion. This document, recorded by a thorough inventorian named Johann Baptiste Fickler, who did a similar service for all the Duke's possessions, has been the innocent basis for most of the misinformation which has been printed about the Duke's dolls' house. Every toy historian has referred to the treasure, though always briefly, and even these brief references have managed to include the same error. The blunder, quite a vital one, since it alters the whole importance of the house, consists of the statement, made by almost every important toy historian since (and including) d'Allemagne in 1903, that this classic dolls' palace contained "three floors, four doors, and sixteen windows."

That a dolls' palace of such pretensions as these same historians also had described should have such a negligible number of floors, doors, and windows was disappointing, and somehow illogical. It proved to be inaccurate. We have not seen the original inventory, but a small book by Dr. J. Stockbauer, published in Vienna in 1874, contains a great deal of information based on it.

Here we learn that the dolls' house was four stories high with, on the bottom floor, five doors and fifteen windows; on the next, four doors and sixteen windows; on the third, three doors and sixteen windows; and on the top floor, five doors and sixteen windows; or, in short, the house contained a total of four floors, seventeen doors, and sixty-three windows, or one more floor, thirteen more doors, and forty-seven more windows than the number with which it often has been historically accredited. How the error came to be made is apparent: someone, looking quickly, jotted down the door and window total of only the second floor.

Discovering this additional floor, doors, and windows was, to a dolls' house researcher, a little like discovering America, and seemingly should be underlined in justice to the Duke's remarkable dolls' house.

But enough of the windows and doors! As for the whole, the bills for the work immortalize the names of the court box-maker, a painter, and two locksmiths: (respectively) one Wolf Greiss, one Hans Ostendorfer, one Hans Klein and one Casper Bauer. We even know how much each was paid, in florins, although the sums are fairly meaningless today. Many of the fittings came from Augsburg.

Stockbauer enumerates the rooms floor by floor, though in little detail, and it is not possible to know how accurately the old German has been rendered. We have found nowhere else so comprehensive a list; two other writers, Gröber and Boesch, have noted only a few of the rooms, and even these are in conflict, with Stockbauer and each other.

A picture does emerge from the confusion, though, and one which manages to show what an extraordinary dolls' house this must have been, and to cause antiquarians regret that it no longer *is*.

On the lower floor, according to Stockbauer, were a stable, which often appeared in early dolls' houses, a cow barn, the office, the larder, the wine cellar and the coach house. On the second floor were bathroom, kitchen, courtyard and orchard. The bath, of course, is the triumphant apartment here. In a day when the most fastidious nobles didn't wash much, this must have been an elegant establishment indeed.

The third floor included the ballroom which was fitted entirely with tapestry of gold material. Here were the Duke and the Duchess with six servants. In the middle was a table with a precious carpet on it—of the sort of thick fabric that was a table covering. (Floor carpets in that vulgar era were confined largely to ladies' chambers or boudoirs where they were less likely to be spat upon.) On this carpet there was a silver gold-plated lute and Indian bells, against the wall a buffet table with gold and silver dishes and, as Stockbauer regrettably adds, "etc." Next door was a chamber with richly embroidered tapestries on the walls and with curtains around the bed. Among the furnishings were silver chests, clothes, and the ladies' fire shade which, according to Dr. Stockbauer, the delicate ladies took along when standing in front of the fire "so that its heat wouldn't mar their delicate complexions."

On the top floor foremost was the chapel complete with priest and musicians. Adjoining the chapel was a church box in which the Duke and Duchess would sit and participate in the service—through a window. This chapel was next to a room containing chests, chairs, and three bedsteads. Then there was the working room of the court ladies full of weaving frames and spinning wheels. Next to this was another kitchen with silver fire dogs and silver dishes,* and finally there were the nurseries.

These are all the apartments that Stockbauer mentions, and omitted are several remarkable features reported by Gröber. The latter gives no account of the rooms in his toy history, but in a 1939 magazine article, he included this challenging sentence: "Everything was there, from the kitchens to the bathroom, from the armor room to the lion's house where the Bavarian armorial animal was kept." It is entirely possible that armor appeared in a room called by another name by Dr. Stockbauer, and that, perhaps, the lion's house was situated in the garden or courtyard. In any case, both additions are majestic and medieval touches which contribute a knightly air to the memory of these premises.

Hans Boesch mentions only that the house had "next to the stable a coach house, next to the summer house a zoological garden, also a ball room in which a ball takes place and even a richly furnished chapel." The zoologi-

* This second kitchen, known as the "best kitchen," is often to be found in Early German and Dutch houses. J. H. M. Leesberg-Terwindt writes that such a kitchen was a kind of sitting or dining-room. Many of the treasures from the housewife's dowry may be found there.

cal garden and the lion's house may very well be one—a recorder with the full inventory before him may have read "one lion" and jumped to conclusions. An anonymous account of the dolls' house in a trade magazine, possibly taken from a scholarly source, refers to a "menagerie," and this may have arisen from a similar misconception. These accounts, in which all sorts of beasts occur, make one wonder at Stockbauer's failure to imply the presence of any animal wilder than a cow, but he may have been limited by his preoccupation with the Duke's entire art collection.

It has been distressing not to have had access to the original inventory, but Stockbauer's account is, withal restricted, obviously firsthand, and perhaps enough has been set forth here to indicate the majesty of this first dolls' house on record which, if it *was* first in actuality, defies the rudimentary concept of things initial, and for all we know, may never have been surpassed.

We do know that its contemporaries regarded it with the most earnest admiration. This high regard overflowed in an ode composed by Augustin Maier in 1582. In lavish Latin it lauds the Duke's dolls' palace in a manner to cause Stockbauer to suggest that allowance should be made for hyperbole. We offer it here, untranslated, so that a reader or two who hasn't had a go at Horace or Ovid in a decade or so, may have a little fling:

> Lucent marmorie laqueata per atria campi,
> Calcantur vario per picta asorota nitore.
> Jurares Phrygio desectas monte columnas
> Et laeves Nomadum venis splendescere postes.
> Singula vix oculi capiunt. Hinc aere micantes
> Illinc e niyeo spirantes marmore vultus.
> Phidiacum hic laudatur opus: quodve arte Myronis
> Vel Polycletaeo meruit caelamine vitam:
> Illic Coa manus dubitantia lumina fallit.
> Quis florum species fuso referente metallo:
> Quis folia auricomo non miraretur in horto
> Crispari et levibus commota tremescere flabris?
> Hesperides cessent frondes jactare crepantes;
> Arbores Idaliae minus extollantur honores:
> Aurea virga latens silva Junonis Avernae,
> Exuat attonitis animis memorata stuporem.
> Ars haec cuncta recens felici imitamine vincit.
> Forte aliquis notas pertingens naribus herbas
> Captatoque diu tandem frustratus odore
> Vix possit regidae fraudes deprendere lamnae.
> Talia quae amplificis sparguntur plurima tectis
> Ut libet oblectant animos oculosque morentur.

4

DAS
PUPPENHAUS

*D*R. KARL GROBER WRITES THAT GERMANY MUST BE RECKONED AS the "peculiar home" of the dolls' house. A page or two later, though, he presents Holland's claim that the dolls' house originated there. And here his only defense, rather a vague one, is that "these toys go back certainly to the Middle Ages, and even into antiquity."

But the aforementioned dolls' palace of Duke Albrecht, so specifically 1558, and the earliest known to date seems an explicit defense for Germany's case. It will serve here to temper Holland's views, until an earlier Dutch dolls' house comes along. Moreover, in all the years since 1558, Germany has had an enormously illuminating dolls' house history. Her dolls' houses down to modern times have been famous; from the sixteenth century on, her craftsmen have been busy.

Her role, indeed, has been so conspicuous that it extends to several phases of the story. In an effort to bridge the hiatus between our speculations on the dolls' houses of antiquity and the more solid ground on which the 1558 house stands, we have considerably infringed on this German chapter. In particular, the manufacturing phase of the history, laden with the names of Augsburg and Nuremberg and Ulm, has been explored, and we shall be more concerned here with the consumer rather than the craftsman.

27

Having a dolls' house in the seventeenth century was a fashionable hobby; the well-to-do, the only citizens who could afford the mansions they were, became proud proprietors in numbers. Apparently even citizens who could not afford them could not resist them. A sad tale is recorded of an Augsburg lady, one Frau Negges, who so over-balanced her dolls' house budget that "she did hurt to her estate."

Not all ladies in pursuit of dolls' houses were so frivolous. A Duchess, Augusta Dorothea of Schwarzburg-Gotha, of whom we speak more fully elsewhere, saw to the construction, in the early eighteenth century, of almost a hundred dolls' "rooms," a remarkably full scenic representation of the life about her, complete with dolls. To her we are indebted for knowledge of her times, as much as to any historian.

Adults such as these invaded the diminutive portals of the dolls' house, but children led the way. It is made plain in contemporary accounts that dolls' houses were intended for the young, even though they captivated their elders in the bargain. There are several bits of history that plainly show this junior right of dolls' house ownership, though the first of these also involves an "elder."

In this one, Hans Boesch relates that, in 1631, a Nuremberg lady, named Anna Köferlin, an elderly spinster devoted to children, went to a lot of trouble to assemble a dolls' house which she exhibited in public. She even got up a descriptive pamphlet, a surviving document of great interest, with a picture of the house on the front page and the date blazoned in roman numerals on the front of the house. (See illustration.) The pamphlet explains how children will learn from her toy just how a proper household should look and how it should be managed—the first time, it may be, that this educational motif, later sounded over and over again as a justification of the dolls' house, appeared in print.

Anna Köferlin's dolls' house, dated 1631, from original pamphlet

Another notice, more than a century later, refers to the past. Paul von Stetten, in 1765, observed: "As to the education of girls, I must make mention of the toys with which many played until they became brides, namely the so-called dolls' houses. In these everything which belonged to a house and its management was reproduced in little, and many went to such lengths of sumptuousness that the cost of such a plaything would run to 1,000 gulden and more." Gröber tells us that, at the end of the century, Paul Stetten, the younger, brought this report up to date. While dolls' houses were "less made than formerly for children," he related, "they were not without their use for giving ocular instruction in the art of housekeeping, and other things."

To understand perfectly why this young home-maker theme so often appears, it is well to look in detail at a few seventeenth and eighteenth century houses, vividly laden with the means to housekeep, and the ways. Although museums throughout Germany contain dolls' houses, and there are excellent examples in such cities as Munich, Berlin, and Frankfurt, the foremost collections are unquestionably at Augsburg and Nuremberg. Some of the seventeenth century houses in the Germanisches Museum at Nuremberg were attractively described by Mrs. Emily Jackson, one of the first toy historians, as early as 1908, but they have been immortalized in a charming book of many photographs, by Dr. Leonie Von Wilckens, of the museum staff, in *Tageslauf im Puppenhaus*, published in 1956.*

Perhaps the most elaborate of the houses, which has its date, 1639, on a central dormer (the rope from the hoist dangles over the "3"), is the house which belonged to the Stromer family, and which is illustrated in the frontispiece.

A dominant decorative feature that gives distinction to so many South German dolls' houses of the period is the handsome balustrading across the front of the rooms which the writer had once thought possibly a practical dolls' house device to prevent the delicate furnishings from spilling out. Through Dr. Elisabeth Wolffhardt, a retired teacher of history in Munich, we learn that actually such galleried houses were built in full-size in Nuremberg during the Renaissance. Dr. Wolffhardt helpfully forwarded a booklet about the Fembohaus, the only such Nuremberg house not destroyed during the war. "I went to look at it," she wrote, "and from the courtyard I had the same optical impression of open galleries leading from the front part to the back part of the house, and these are the balustrades." Looking at the pictures of the galleried façade of the Fembohaus, one might well be looking at pictures of Nuremberg dolls' houses. Even the turned pillars between sections of balustrade are similar.†

The imposing house, which has three rooms on each of the two upper floors, has a curious ground-floor arrangement which is specific evidence

* Prestel Verlag, Munich.

† This type of architecture was not confined to Germany. Dr. Wolffhardt also sent a newspaper picture of the George Inn in south London which was described as "the last galleried inn left in the capital."

Bed-sitting room from the Stromer House, 1639. (see frontispiece)

that these houses were intended for instruction and play rather than as models of full-sized buildings. There are eight tiny rooms, in two tiers, almost like pigeon-holes in a desk, on each side of the spacious staircase hall with its arched double doors to the street. In one of these (lower left), a cow and a horse stand in their stalls, oblivious to the barrels and taps in the beer cellar on the other side of the wall. These rooms also include the store-room, office, and servants' bedrooms, and it is obvious that they are not arranged realistically, but were tucked in where they happened to fit.

There are many conventional and beautiful articles in this house, clocks and pictures and chandeliers, but they point out less about custom than some of the less elaborate pieces—the minor, homey accessories also to be found in these elaborately panelled rooms with their painted ceilings. It is plain that young dolls are in residence. An old wooden stand for teaching a baby to walk is, along with his cradle, to be seen in the nursery. In another room, there is a rocking horse two and a half inches high. There is also a bird-cage—there almost always is in these old German houses. The canary was brought to Europe early in the sixteenth century and became the especial pet of children. In Dr. Von Wilckens' book, one amusing picture shows a parrot in his cage.

The diversions of the senior members of the family are evident. On a table are checkers, a chessboard, and playing cards half an inch square, all representing recreations which have lost little favor in three hundred years. A passage-room upstairs includes a linen press with piles of sheets, napkins, and towels in bundles tied up with colored ribbons, all of which undoubtedly set a splendid example to learning maidens. The kitchen, crowded with rows of pewter plates, and multifarious utensils, as are all dolls' kitchens (which are fully considered in Chapter 11) is shown in all its glorious detail in Dr. Von Wilckens' book. Two varieties of plate racks—one in which the plates stand side by side, the other in which they are piled one upon another —are especially intriguing: the plates are trenchers and they are of wood. Most curious and informative are blackboards with articles of food and clothing most charmingly and explicitly painted on them. These are food and laundry lists, ones which could be readily interpreted, even by servants who could neither read nor write, and who could mark the amount in the space left alongside each turnip or shirt.

It is of interest to compare this patrician residence with a Nuremberg artisan's house of the same period, one which somehow found its way years ago into the Victoria and Albert Museum (then known as South Kensington). Of this house, which is pictured, Mrs. Jackson comments that "though the building, furniture, and fittings are all on a more modest scale, they are of the perfect workmanship which characterizes all the dolls' houses made in the Low Countries in the seventeenth century." Her description of the house, which has its 1673 date inscribed on the chimney, refers to a bedroom, kitchen, scullery, and sitting-room, but an article in an English periodical,* predating her account by about eight years, refers to a nursery, and, unquestionably illustrating how dolls can move about in eight years, notes that "There the little mother doll stands surrounded by her children . . . one little Dutch baby stands in a sort of circular cage to prevent it from falling." The photograph—views of this house frequently have been reproduced in both English and American periodicals—bears this out. As our later picture

* *Girl's Realm,* in a 1900 issue.

Nuremberg artisan's house, dated 1673, at Victoria & Albert   Height: 3' 6''

shows, the mother is alone in her bedroom; the father, in his workman's garb, who had also been above, has retreated below stairs; and the baby in the walker may be seen with a group of small objects displayed in front of the house. The other children, however many there may have been, have disappeared altogether.

Mrs. Jackson points out that the painted wardrobe in the bedroom is "a curious reminder of the painted furniture of old Austria and Bavaria," and that the "usual porcelain stove in the sitting-room" (which also contains a bed and is undoubtedly a bed-sitting-room), is "extremely plain, as befits the rank of the occupants of the house."

Her description of the exterior of the house offers a closer look at some of the detail: "The seven windows are latticed, thin sheets of talc being carefully divided with leaded squares. There are also three open attic windows; the centre one resembles the door of a warehouse—this curious survival of the combination of dwelling-house and warehouse having been left in the domestic architecture both of the Netherlands and Holland." (Did she mean, redundantly, to write "Netherlands and Holland"?)

She refers to flowerpots in some of the windows on the ledges which are visible in her rare view of the house with its front closed (it is considerably more photogenic open and generally has been so photographed). She comments on the "enormous bell," which can be seen above the front door on the inside, and "which must have roused the whole household when pulled." There is such a clutter of pewter and brass on the walls of the lower rooms that one can picture the lot tumbling down when the bell pealed, and augmenting the racket.

Mrs. Jackson shows the exterior of another handsome seventeenth century house at the Nuremberg museum, incorrectly identified as the Stromer house,* but her description is vivid and effective. The house itself measures a trifle over five feet "exclusive of the pitch of the roof," and is of unusual architectural interest. "There are strong iron gutters beneath the eaves, the gargoyles rival those of Notre Dame in grotesque elaboration, a dormer window above the door shows some beautifully carved oak, the bust of a man is at the top, above each attic window is a brass star, a weathercock is on each side wing." Then there is "a double flight of steps with elaborately carved balustrade which leads up to the panelled front door . . . pull the wrought-iron bell handle, near which the number of the house is painted, and remove the whole of the outside of the house, which divides into halves, leaving each room in the house displayed to view."

Dr. Von Wilckens shows a photograph of the hall of this house. Between the two pillars, there is a *vue d'optique* revealing a lovely garden between rows of trees and a fountain, plus what Mrs. Jackson refers to as

---

* Another photograph showing three of the houses, including the Stromer, in a row in the museum is identified as "five" in the caption. The blame for these errors of course may belong to Mrs. Jackson's editor rather than to Mrs. Jackson. In any case, the house described above is the Baeumler house.

"a summerhouse." The latter, however, is almost imposing enough to contain another patrician household. A large and handsome hanging lantern looks down upon the housekeeper, probably off to market with her basket. Perhaps she is going to buy fresh vegetables. She did not have to go far for most of her daily supplies. Two plants, two pigeons, and a garden bench are nearby.

The door on the right, Mrs. Jackson points out, "leads into the shop or store-room where it was customary in the seventeenth century when large houses were almost entirely self-contained, to buy, not only spices and every comestible, but also dress materials. A large blue cupboard with side compartment contains the stuffs carefully sorted in layers; in the drawers and on a narrow side table are pots, baskets, barrels, and hampers; sugar loaves are on a shelf, and loaves brown and crisp-looking; a bunch of sponges hangs on the wall. Weights and scales, a ball of twine, and a till are standing on a counter that runs down the middle of the room."

Intrigued by this description, we wrote to our friend, Dr. Wolffhardt in Munich, who found information about "the merchant's house in Nuremberg up to the seventeenth century" in a small book about full-sized houses.* "There used to be a spacious (court) yard with wide gateways leading to the street," Dr. Wolffhardt learned. "In the yard, the bales of goods were unloaded. Then they were taken to the vault (Gewölbe), a room beside the gateway. Here the goods were examined, entered into books, sold, or carried into store-rooms or lofts. In the vault retailing was also done, which was called Gewölbhandel (trade in the vault)." Dr. Wolffhardt concludes that the vault "was thus at the same time a shop and a countinghouse. Later on, a separate countinghouse was put beside the vault."

Although Mrs. Jackson refers to the room which has been described as "a hall," one suspects that it is a combination of courtyard and hall. Technically speaking, the ceiling is vaulted, as are the rooms on each side of it. Dr. Von Wilckens shows the shop in the Stromer house: there are rows of spices, coils of wax, and sugar loaves side by side with assorted weights for the scale. According to Dr. Wolffhardt, the goods in the Stromer house (she includes flax, which is not visible in the picture) "are quite typical of what the merchants of Nuremberg imported." In a separate picture Dr. Von Wilckens shows the account book and the "strong box," with coins spilling out of it. In the author's collection, an identical pewter, footed rectangular box, divided into four compartments, with a round pewter knob on its sliding lid, came in a Nuremberg kitchen, and had been thought a spice box. However, another identical one may be seen on the counter of an attractive store on the cover of *Altes Spielzeug*, which would seem to make this strong-box usage unmistakable.

Gröber shows photographs of two other South German houses at the museum in Nuremberg, both ca. 1600, and both 95½″ high. These houses resemble each other, as well as the other Nuremberg houses that have been

* Ludwig Veit, *Handel und Wandel mit aller Welt, Aus Nürnbergs grosser Zeit*, Munich, 1960.

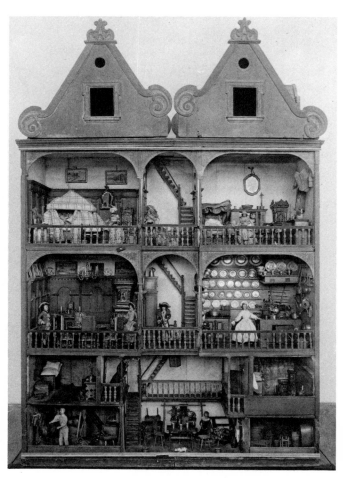

The seventeenth century
Kress house at Nuremberg
Height: 95½"

described, in many ways. One, which was partly refurnished in the eighteenth century, has on its ground floor a courtyard with galleried balcony around it, a little garden, and a pump. In both houses, kitchen and living-rooms are arranged on both sides of the elaborate stair well which, as in the other houses that have been described, extends to the attic. The one illustrated (The Kress house) has a galleried façade very similar to that of the Stromer house. There is a further resemblance to the latter: the sections at each side of the courtyard are divided into two rooms, up and down, though they are not further partitioned into four, as in the Stromer.

In her book, Dr. Von Wilckens shows the whole of this magnificent specimen with its handsome "M" roof, which is omitted in Gröber's photograph, giving it almost an additional dimension. With its dormer windows and rococo embellishment, the imposing roof, with these tall attic peaks, lends the house, along with its scalloped, solid wooden base, considerable grandeur.

The other Nuremberg house illustrated in Gröber has a similar balustrade in front of the staircase hall on the middle story, leading one to suppose that originally it may have been entirely galleried, like the other houses. This one, by the way, has enclosed basement and attic stories, in addition to the ground, first and second floors, which are open. In the attic story, a

34

semicircular shuttered window is centered, with two pairs of small leaded windows at each side. This nice balance, however, is lacking in the cellar in which a pair of panelled double doors are located considerably off center, and a couple of arched doors with wide hinges are set in a most random manner at each side.

Turning from Nuremberg, it is of interest to discover two early houses of somewhat different style made at Ulm. These houses are wider than tall, giving them a horizontal aspect quite different from the vertical look of the Nuremberg houses. One, ca. 1670, is pictured in Gröber who describes it ambiguously as a house "from Ulm; Dutch," and since it is in the Schloss-museum in Berlin, one can only suppose that it merely came from Ulm and was not made there. It is a handsome twelve-room house including a third story that looks, from its greater elaboration, as though it might have been added to the two lower floors at some point in the long history of the house.

There is no question about the history of the other house from Ulm (which is illustrated). This one came to Dr. Albert Figdor, a Vienna art collector, in the early twentieth century, having been in the possession of the same patrician family in Ulm for more than three hundred years where it had been handed down in the direct line as a cherished heirloom. According to Dr. Figdor (who described it in *Connoisseur* in 1913), it is possible that the house itself is not the original, but there can be no possible mistake about the furnishings, many of which have their age upon them—in apparent numerals. Most of this furniture is of earlier date than that of the Nuremberg houses, being from the sixteenth century.

There are four rooms, two upper and two lower. Those below are the kitchen and a sort of general room; the latter, we are told, of a type still common in the houses of the peasantry of thirty years ago, but which in the day of this dolls' house was a necessity of every patrician residence. (It has been succeeded by the scullery.) The two upper rooms are furnished as bed-sitting-rooms. It was then the custom to receive in the bedroom, which was the chief room in the house. Until quite recently this comfortable practice still could be found in some parts of Europe.

Among the most important furnishings in the Ulm house are impressive

Figdor house from Ulm, seventeenth century

old chests and cupboards. One cupboard, tall and proportioned somewhat like a tall-case clock, contains a built-in lavabo. A tank above stores water released by the faucet into a pewter basin below. This dates from a day that knew no knives and forks, when fingers frequently had to be washed. (Lucy Crump in *Nursery Life 300 Years Ago* quotes a Swiss student's account of a meal in his boarding house in the late sixteenth century: "We eat a soupe [sopped bread and broth] with turnips and carrots in it . . . Everyone ate the soupe with their fingers out of their bowls [supping the broth] . . . one of us . . . made a most unnecessary fuss by asking our hostess for a spoon of which there were none in the house. We had only one big knife, on the table, chained to it, which everyone used in turn. Our convenient [Teuton] custom of a separate spoon for everyone is unknown here.") A more conventionally shaped cupboard than the one for washing has an embroidered lining, one section on a door bearing, in needlework, the date of its origin—1568. There is also a curious table in this house, one with flaps, which has a hollow below instead of a drawer, and is said to be of about 1550.

Where English dolls' houses are supplied with fine old fireplaces, German ones are strewn with wonderful old stoves. Such stoves, one to a room, are still used on the Continent, and two in this house are particularly interesting. One, black glazed, trimmed in gold, is dated 1550, but it cheats a trifle as dolls' furnishings go, since it was made to serve as a sample for larger stoves, rather than as a toy. This traveler's sample, a genus we have noted in Chapter 1, is a very elaborate object. Its top is modeled like a house, with windows, gables, and pointed roof, and its lower part has two medallions, in relief, of Emperor Charles the Fifth, wearing the odd cap which was his crown in public.

The other, a true dolls' house stove, is green-tiled, and is said to be similar to many still found in peasant provinces. A very odd child's cot, which is more like a cage, being closed in at the top as well as at the sides, is another unusual piece. It is lattice-worked for air (but not much) and baby is put in and out through a door at the side. It is late sixteenth century.

There are splendid chairs in this house, upholstered in such divers materials as red velvet, stamped leather and Gobelin tapestry. There are two minute bird-cages. And there is a spinning wheel, seven inches high, with its flax still wound about its spindle and well enough made for real use. There is also a tiny loom in the general room, and a linen press is filled with its works, both linen and silk—gossamer looming indeed.

The Figdor house has also been described by d'Allemagne, and later, in almost the same words, by Claude Sézan. These accounts go into great detail about the kitchen and general room, the latter described as part kitchen, part dairy, and part servants' refectory. Says M. d'Allemagne, "Near the half-open door, one perceives a little personage who has come from the cellar where he was without doubt going to fetch several jugs full of old Rhine wine." The kitchen stove is full of pots, according to Monsieur, and one is reminded that the French idiom for "they live well in that house" is "*la*

marmite est bonne dans cette maison." Judging by the culinary clutter in this residence, its inhabitants lived very well indeed.

A picture of a dolls' house, circa 1820, in the Maximilians Museum in Augsburg,* indicates that more than two centuries later these toys were being made essentially the same way. This house with its four floors, the upper three cubby-holed into numerous rooms, with courtyard and garden below, is not as elaborately detailed as its seventeenth century predecessors, but this deficiency is not general, to judge by German toy catalogues of the period which illustrate elegantly fashioned toys indeed.

We are indebted to a volume by Henri d'Allemagne for specimen pages from the lavish toy catalogue of Georg Hieronymus Bestelmeier whose establishment was one of the most important toy houses in Nuremberg. This is the earliest known catalogue of its kind, according to Gröber, and it contains more than 1,200 different entries. (The German toy historian lists two Bestelmeier catalogues, those of 1803 and 1807, in his bibliography. After seeking vainly for such a catalogue in American libraries, the author had a disheartening experience in London in 1948. In the British Museum index, a Bestelmeier catalogue that pre-dated Gröber's, one of 1799, was listed. We sent for it eagerly, only to learn that it had been destroyed in the blitz.) "A pompously worded introduction asks the indulgence of the public for a [Bestelmeier's] 'pedagogical magazine' and in well-known advertising style boasts of the superlative excellence of his designers, the wealth of objects and the cheapness of his prices compared with those of similar articles previously produced," Gröber notes. He reports the presence in this expansive brochure of "all kinds of dolls' rooms, shops, hunts, farmyards, etc., often executed in the most elaborate and costly manner . . ."

There were many centers of this toy commerce, besides the greatest that was Nuremberg, and besides Augsburg and Ulm. A London publication in 1859, writing of Hesse Cassel, the center of toy soldier-making, related that the workmen of the principality were not entirely devoted to arms, and that little shops, parlors, and dolls' houses were made there. The account speaks, too, of an "exquisite" little interior of a cafe, with its fittings of marble tables, bottles, mirrors and plate, and reveals that it, and many similar enchantments, were made by felons in Prussian prisons.

In recent years, several charming books have been published, most of them with a relatively small amount of text, but with delightful illustrations, about toy collections in various sections in Germany. Of course, these include dolls' houses, shops, kitchens, and other rooms. One of these small books, *Altes Spielzeug,* by Juliane Roh and Claus Hansmann, published in Munich, in 1958,† shows in color two rooms in a dolls' house, ca. 1810, in Augsburg, and two delightful shops; a lovely Biedermeier milliner's shop

* The Augsburg dolls' houses were damaged in World War II but "have been reconstructed with great care," we learn through a German friend.

† Verlag F. Bruckmann, Munich.

Dolls' house chandeliers were available in variety in 1799, to judge by Bestelmeier's toy catalogue.

Merchandise from Bestelmeier's toy catalogue, 1799.

and a curiosity shop, ca. 1870. The latter is from the Stadtmuseum in Munich, and the milliner's shop, like so many of the houses described in this chapter, is from the Germanisches National Museum in Nuremberg.

Another small book, *Spielzeug,** entirely about the toys in the German toy museum in Sonneberg, shows mostly other types of toys, but includes a dolls' kitchen which contains furnishings of three generations of children who played with it. Most unusual is a Japanese porcelain shop, ca. 1880, from Tokyo.

Most delightful, of all, perhaps, is the small book showing old toys from Schleswig-Holstein—especially shops and rooms from the museum in Altona.† One kitchen, dated 1750, from an Altona family named Schmarje, has an unusual and handsome rococo frame with a huge pair of arched doors or gates which cover almost the entire front when closed. Similar arched doors with similar scrolled woodwork ornamenting the glass may be seen in a cupboard inside the kitchen. Another kitchen, ca. 1820, is in the form of a one-room house. There is a pitched roof with a chimney perched on the gable; eight windows in the same triangular shape are painted on the pediment beneath the gable. Larger windows and a door are painted on the sides. There are also a most decorative mercer's shop ca. 1830; a pair of rooms (salon and bedroom) ca. 1890 and full of the marvelous clutter of the period; and an absolutely irresistible confectioner's shop, also ca. 1890. The latter, in addition to the tall, ornate frame behind the marble-topped counters, above which mirrors glisten, has two galleried sections in front where a doll in need of a bit of refreshment can stop for an ice or—to judge from a huge bottle in a mammoth champagne bucket—something a bit more lively. There is even a menu in a stand on one of the two small marble-topped ice cream tables. A brief flight of three steps connects the galleried sections in what is, all in all, a most unusual and decorative toy.

The museum in Altona also has a remarkably attractive schoolroom, ca. 1880, in which a dozen pretty bisque schoolgirls, all of them in black china boots and hair wigs, sit on benches behind three long desks. Maps, and sheets of birds and animals hang on the two walls, and the hats and coats of the students, hang in a realistic cluster on pegs at the back of the room.

The celebrated Gontard house at Frankfurt is described in Chapter 24, and the formidable collection of Duchess Dorothea of Schwarzburg-Gotha has Chapter 20 to itself.

Having had such an early start in the dolls' house realm, Germany has appeared determined to keep her laurels green, and neatly trimmed. Her dolls' houses in the past hundred years, more than those of any other country, have kept to the glittering standards of her earlier works, and her craftsmen have helped to furnish more than their share of the dolls' houses of the world.

A late 19th century German house

---

* Otto Keil. Im Prisma-Verlag, Leipzig, 1963.

† *Altes Spielzeug aus Schleswig-Holstein,* Westholsteinische Verlagsanstalt Boyens & Co. by Hildamarie Schwindrazheim.

5

THE STATELY
(DOLLS') HOMES
OF ENGLAND

Notes & queries, that most British institution, in 1928 printed a letter from a Brigadier General which to those of us who are unfamiliar with the language of heraldry is a pretty piece of gibberish:

"I possess an ancient doll's house said to be in imitation of a house once belonging to the Norreys family of Fyfield, Bray, Berks. There are various shields of arms in the dining-room, in addition to that of the Norreys family, viz.:

"(1) Gu. a chevron between three fleurs de lys or.
"(2) Erm. three chevrons gu.
"(3) Vert a fess or.
"(4) Vert a pheon arg.
"(5) Arg. three hurts."

The general carried on, citing Papworth on the families these symbols indicated. "Can any reader identify any of the above as being families allied to the Norreys family—or suggest any possible explanation?" he concluded. *Notes & Queries* provided a suitably genealogical reply. Our only concern with the query here is that it seems to epitomize the character of the British dolls' house, a building which often has approximated, in miniature, the stately homes of England, and has been elegantly British, both architecturally and spiritually.

The late H. G. Wells, of all people, went on at great length in *Tono Bungay,* of all novels, about a dolls' house which he perhaps somewhat immoderately reported "contained eighty-five dolls." Even assuming that the house had twenty-five rooms, an inordinately large mansion as dolls' housing goes, that would mean three and two-fifths dolls per room, an arrangement which sounds, to say the least, cluttered.

It is true that the house Mr. Wells described was fearfully opulent. "We went to see," he said, "the great doll's house on the nursery landing to play discreetly with that, the great doll's house that the Prince Regent had given Sir Harry Drew's first born . . . that was a not ineffectual model of Bladesover itself [the fictional country house that held it], and contained eighty-five dolls and had cost hundreds of pounds."

The house which patterned Wells' fictional house was, of course, the dolls' house at Uppark (see page 43), where his mother was housekeeper.

Even the presence of the "Prince Regent" in this Wellsian fiction is not without foundation in fact. And this is another of those cases where fact is more extraordinary than fiction. We are indebted to a notation by G. Bernard Hughes (in *Country Life*) which introduced us to a letter written by Horace Walpole to his friend Mann in 1750. Walpole wrote, "The Prince is building baby-houses at Kew." Mr. Wells' Prince merely presented a dolls' house; Frederick, Prince of Wales, who died in 1751, *built* dolls' houses. Mr. Hughes points out that the Prince of Wales "had become attracted by the hobby of making dolls' houses during a visit to the Duke of Brunswick, where the dowager duchess, the Princess Augusta Dorothea, had occupied herself during a long widowhood . . . representing the entire Court of Brunswick in miniature." (See Chapter 20.)

Both the Brigadier General, fussing among his "chevrons gu" and "pheons arg," and Mr. Wells, trapped in a mob of eighty-five dolls, effectively if unconsciously suggest the atmosphere and scope of the early English dolls' house. As their miscellaneous words imply, traditionally such toys often were made as replicas of noble English town or country residences, taking the names as well as the diminished shapes of those lordly places.

The word "traditionally" is used advisedly. Often an English baby house traditionally believed to be a reasonably accurate reproduction proves to be otherwise.

A Georgian dolls' house designed, it was thought, after the front end of Cane End House, Reading, is a case in point. In the 1953 edition of this book, there is a brief description, based on an old newspaper account, of the six-room house with staircase hall containing, it was said, small models of mostly Chippendale furniture, and with dolls in their original eighteenth century dress (sitting about, presumably, on Chippendale's delicate chairs).

Mrs. Vivien Greene, having read a similar account, had the great good fortune, after diligent research, not only of locating the house, but of adding it to her extensive collection. Less fortunately, the original furnishings and dolls were already dispersed, and the legend about a replica house was about to disappear. When Mrs. Greene visited the original Cane End House it proved to be Queen Anne; the baby house façade, a story taller, is distinctly Georgian.

Even without its furniture, dolls, and replica tradition, the baby house, constructed in the Chippendale workshop, is, needless to say, a treasure. Most of the lovely eighteenth century wallpapers, printed from wood blocks, are intact, carefully salvaged by Mrs. Greene from beneath a later layer. A staircase of great beauty also survives, along with such delights as infinitesimal brass door handles (open-drop) and key escutcheons.

This house is described at length, and photographed, in Mrs. Greene's delightful and definitive work, *English Dolls' Houses of the Eighteenth and Nineteenth Centuries,** along with many other important English houses in her own museum,† among others. As we have said elsewhere, there would be little point in attempting to summarize even the highlights of a collection that has been so expertly described by its owner, but it may suffice to say that thirty examples, ranging in date from ca. 1700 to 1886 are displayed, many of them eighteenth century.

A very different sort of "replica house" from the one Cane End House was believed to be may now be seen at the Museum of Childhood in Edinburgh. An Elizabethan manor dolls' house which was "recently" built— just before the Boer War—it has qualifications from which its comparative youth cannot detract. In the first place, it bears the marvelous name of "Stanbrig Eorls," the ancient name in the old title deeds of the original house. This venerable structure, in the south of England, in Berkshire, was built in 1650 on foundations dating back to the time of Ethelwulf, and the dolls' house that is modelled on it is eight feet long and five feet tall.

This many-roomed mansion was the life-long pleasure of the late Miss Graham Montgomery, the last of an old Scots family, was begun in its owner's childhood, in approximately 1885. When she completed them, some seventy years later, the rooms were crammed with nearly 2,000 articles,

* Op. cit.
† "The Rotunda," at Oxford.

Miss Graham Montgomery's "Stanbrig Eorls," at the Museum of Childhood in Edinburgh

including many antiques. It has features which would have astonished Stanbrig Eorls' original residents—including electricity and hot and cold running water.

This small mansion has had a great deal of publicity, including a handsome color spread in the 1961 Christmas number of *The Illustrated London News* which referred to two catastrophes sustained by the house, a burst in the water supply, which stained the wallpaper in the vicinity of the imposing staircase (which is copied from the original), and the "Great Fire" of 1932, caused by a short circuit, which did further damage. In view of the extensive coverage the house has been given elsewhere, we shall dispense with further description here, except to mention that an enormous family of dolls, and an incredible overflow of furnishings, has been removed by Mr. Patrick Murray, the Honorary Curator and Founder of the Museum of Childhood, and displayed elsewhere.

Architects, persons bristling with blueprints and perfectly incapable of casting a family of dolls into a mere cabinet shell in the manner of the Dutch, did most of the earliest English dolls' house building. Thus they preserved for posterity the slant of a roof as well as what went on under it.

The prominent architects who "specially" designed these small structures, which were then made under their personal supervision, created them for the children of their clients, for these patrician edifices were not sold in shops. Moreover, this custom-made quality extended to the inside of the house as well as to its glittering exterior.

Stairways inside the houses as well as out were seen to in particular detail. In many of the German and Dutch houses, far more elaborate though they may have been, stairways were often halfhearted ornaments on one or two floors, leading to dead ends, or were missing altogether. In most English dolls' houses there were true stairways with genuine landings, and even dainty handrails which wayward dolls may have slid down from time to time.

"Among the treasures of that exquisite William and Mary house on the top of the Sussex Downs near Petersfield . . . ," said a writer in *Country Life* in 1942, "is the oldest and the most marvellously complete English doll's house." Writers about dolls' houses appear to have some sort of queer occupational failing which makes them incapable of supposing that the dolls' house they describe can be surpassed by any other. As this chapter will later show, a number of Queen Anne dolls' houses have preceded this Georgian baby house at Uppark which *Country Life* describes, but it is quite true that it is a wonderfully elegant building. (See illustration.) And most probably the Brigadier General of *Notes & Queries* would be interested to know that it has its arms in its pediment.

According to Christopher Hussey, who described this proud toy, "It was made about 1730 for Sarah, only daughter of Christopher Lethieullier, of Belmont, Middlesex, who, in 1747, married Sir Matthew Fetherstonhaugh. He had bought Uppark in the previous year, and the young couple immediately set about redecorating and furnishing their home, ordering the

Façade of the celebrated baby house at Uppark

best new things, buying pictures and other works of art on their honeymoon in Italy, and evidently bringing a good deal from the Lethieulliers' home. Sarah must have been very fond of her doll's house, for she brought that with her, too. At first it may have been put in the room intended for a nursery. But it now stands, and has stood for at least a hundred years, in the first-floor corridor near the head of the staircase. . . ."

A rather pastoral circumstance is revealed by Mr. Hussey in connection with its later history. Sarah's son, Harry (her only child), didn't marry till he was past sixty, and then he selected the dairymaid. How much of a flurry this event caused in Uppark circles, we are not told, but the marriage contributed to the preservation of the dolls' house. When his lady became his widow, she "and her young sister, Frances Bullock-Fetherstonhaugh, who succeeded to the place and lived till 1895, religiously kept everything about the house exactly (as Miss Frances used to say) 'as Sir 'Arry 'ad it.' " Combining this period of care with the neglect that Sir 'Arry, being a boy, naturally accorded it in an earlier era, Mr. Hussey very logically concluded that "When, by Miss Frances's will, Uppark eventually went to Admiral Sir Herbert Meade Fetherstonhaugh, his daughters were the first little girls to play with the doll's house—apart perhaps, from chance visitors—for 200 years. And as it stood in the passage, beside cupboards full of precious old china, they were very careful of it, when they were allowed to play with it as a special treat."

Mr. Hussey's description of the dolls' house tersely defines its architectural wonders: "The house itself has an accurately designed Palladian façade, of three storeys, seven bays wide, resting on a stand modelled on the arcade of Covent Garden piazza. The centre has two orders of Ionic and Corinthian pilasters supporting a pediment enriched with floral sculpture and a shield painted with the Fetherstonhaugh arms. Five gilt statues adorn the balustraded parapet. The front opens in nine sections, each revealing one room." Two glimpses into these may suggest that the furnishings and inhabitants are worthy of their surroundings. "Inside the front door," Mr. Hussey writes, "is the entrance hall with the porter taking a nap in his chair. He is not, however, provided with the alcoved and padded porter's chair still found in a few old houses, which was perhaps a later addition to his comfort. But he has a large pot of tea on the oak gate-legged table. . . ." And, "As we go upstairs, the quality of furniture and decoration goes up, too. Taking an unpardonable liberty, we discover that the ladies are wearing three petticoats." The illustrations accompanying this article suggest that a trip to Uppark, now owned by the National Trust, would be indeed worth while.

The same publication, incidentally, twelve years earlier had briefly commented on the same Uppark dolls' residence. This account, even more architecturally erudite than Mr. Hussey's, noted that the house "stands on an arched rusticated basement, and the detail of the Ionic and Corinthian pilasters on the advanced centre of the building, and the scroll-work on the tympanum of the pediment are finely executed. With doors, the furniture and fittings date from the first years of George II's reign; for instance, in the dining-room are a cabriole-legged table and chairs, a marble-topped side table, and a marbled alcove, for glass and china, in the centre of one wall, with its accompanying wine cooler and drinking glasses."

The scholarly writer, identified only by the initial "J," describes with the same special vocabulary two other highly architectural dolls' houses. The first, given by Mme. Georges Patry to the Victoria and Albert Museum, dates from about 1780, and there is no basement. "The cornice is surmounted by graceful urns, and the tympanum of the pediment carved with sprays of berried laurel. The pedimented front door opens into a small staircase hall, with kitchen to the left and dining-room to the right, each with its contemporary fittings. . . ."

But this small mansion is modest compared with the impressive and well-known Tate house at Bethnal Green. "J's" elaborate description supplements our illustration of this noble toy of 1760. "The brick of the walling, the stone for coigns and dressings, are carefully rendered; the pedimented entrance door at the *piano nobile,* with the Venetian window above it, forms an attractive centre, emphasized by the balustraded external staircase lead-

The Tate house, about 1760, at Bethnal Green Height: (with stand) 7' 2"

ing up to the first-floor level. The arched entrance in the basement leads to larders and kitchen, not so carefully lit as the upper floors, where the lantern of the top-lit staircase hall, seen above the balustraded roof, reproduces a device frequently found in Late Georgian houses. The windows of this façade open and shut, which gives an inhabited air to the house. The sides are carefully finished, the uppermost tier of windows being surmounted by tablets modelled with drapery swags and a garland of flowers. The chimney stacks at each side of the house are carefully detailed and provided with side ramps. . . ." The account by no means does justice to the double "balustraded external staircase" which mounts to two landings before the stairs converge at the entrance door.

Luke Vincent Lockwood in Volume I of his *Colonial Furniture in America* pictures an extremely prepossessing baby house, in this same highly detailed vein, and dating from the first quarter of the eighteenth century. Lord St. Oswald, of Nostell Priory, England, is the owner of this elegant toy. There are several strong similarities to the Uppark house—there are nine rooms, and there are statues mounted upon the balustraded parapet. Unlike the façade of the Uppark house, which opens in nine sections (one per room), this one curiously slides back, in two sections, from the center, a practical arrangement which we recall nowhere else. An impressive interior staircase, in the lower hall, is placed horizontally, a graceful digression from the vertical style usually found in dolls' houses.

Façade and interior of the elegant baby house at Nostell Priory   Height: (without stand) 5′ 6″

Mr. Lockwood's summary of the interior is of interest from the point of view of a furniture authority: "There are cabriole leg tables, double chairs and stools, a chest of drawers, a kneehole dressing-table with dressing-glass, a slant-front secretary with cabinet top, a basin-stand, a card-table, and a fire-screen. There are three bed-steads heavily draped in the fashion of the day; there is a rug on the parlor floor. In the kitchen is a turned chair in the form usually called Carver in this country. It is a significant fact that there are no highboys. In the American colonies at this time every house would contain several."*

The *Morning Post* (London) in October, 1926, under the heading "Queen Anne Curiosity Found in Country House" reported that "What may prove to be the earliest British dolls' house has just been discovered in an old country house near Chelmsford." We have remarked upon the tendency of antique dolls' house discoverers to consider their dolls' houses "unique" or "the oldest." Queen Anne dolls' house finders are decidedly the most persistent of this breed. No Queen Anne dolls' house finder or owner seems ever to concede the possible existence of another.

But this building does exhibit diverting aspects. And it is tantalizing not to know more about it, such as its present whereabouts: "It is a two-storied house," went on the *Post*, "about five feet high, built entirely of solid oak, and containing four large rooms, attics, and a balcony on top. 'The most curious feature of the discovery is that it is built of solid unpainted oak,'

---

* According to family tradition, the furniture in the baby house was made by Chippendale (who was born at Otley thirty miles away), and the house was built in 1740 by Robert Adam who was employed at the time on Nostell Priory itself. However, architectural historian Barbara Jones points out that Robert Adam was only twelve years old in 1740, and that "James Paines was the very youthful architect who, about 1740, began Nostell Priory to which Robert Adam made important later additions."

said Mr. Herbert Ellis, the Camden Road expert, who found it, 'and it is mounted on four cabriole legs—a remarkable curiosity. This and the panelling and the mirrors are of definite Queen Anne design and workmanship. As far as I know there is no other Queen Anne house in existence and those at the national museums are certainly later.' "

The Camden Road expert plainly had not heard about a dolls' house so Queen Anne that it had in fact been presented by that royal personage.

England's queens have taken practically as much of an interest in English dolls' houses as have her architects. One can hardly proceed three door-knobs in British dolls' house history without having to curtsy. The earliest majesty so involved seems to have been Anne. One would love to have discovered Bess in the act of dandling a dolls' cottage on her sturdy knee, but presumably she was too busy with state papers and sealing wax. However, good Queen Anne, a more domestic type, presented to her god-daughter Ann Sharp a splendid nine-room dolls' house which is a superb portrait of an English household in the closing days of the seventeenth century, and is considered at length in Chapter 24.

A Queen Anne dolls' house which sounds remarkably similar to the one found at Chelmsford, to a point where one would suspect that the same workshop produced it, has been described in *Country Life* by G. Bernard Hughes. This is the Westbrook baby house, a family heirloom handed down from mother to daughter for two and a half centuries. "In about 1705, a group of local tradesmen presented it to the daughter of a property owner who was leaving their district, evidently in the Isle of Dogs," Mr. Hughes records. "Nothing more is known of this little Miss E. Westbrook, but the subsequent history of her toy may be traced through the female line of the family down to the present owner, Mrs. Cyril Holland-Martin."

The resemblance of this baby house to the one found at Chelmsford is basic. There is the same two-storied cabinet-type arrangement mounted on legs; only the Westbrook legs are not cabriole but "plinth-mounted . . . of plain, tapering columns, and topped by a deeply arched frieze of extremely solid construction, a style tending to lose favour from about 1710." And the oak is the same, in this case (the stand like the house) "stained to a rich brown, brilliantly smooth with the patina of two and a half centuries." Mr. Hughes associates this exterior with the chest-on-stand popular at the turn of the century. This house, "a well-to-do home such as was being built in the main street of every town of the period," lacks the attics and balcony of the Chelmsford example, and has instead a shallow roof carved to simulate slates, and a tall chimney. Both of these Queen Anne baby houses are about five feet tall including their frames, and both are divided into four rooms.

Of the Chelmsford specimen, of course, we have no interior detail, as it appears to have been found unfurnished. Ann Sharp's house, which contains nine rooms, has the most detailed furnishings, and by comparison the Westbrook baby house is modest. But Mr. Hughes describes its walnut chairs, stools and tables with "sturdy" cabriole legs. Highlights include, in

Queen Anne "fragment" at Victoria & Albert   *Height: 2' 2½"*

the dining-room, a knife-box containing a complete set of cutlery with pistol-shaped handles of brass; in the living-room, a circular card table, "an indispensable piece of furniture at that time"; in the bedroom, a ceiling-high tester bed, every part of it fabric-covered "in the fashion of the period"; in the kitchen, the spit above the fireplace, "thrust through with a model goose." In a collection of silver toys associated with the dolls' house, Mr. Hughes describes a foot-stove used in wealthy families "to laye under their feet when they write, or studie, in cold weather, or in their coches to keep their feet warme."

This Westbrook baby house, like Ann Sharp's, and most of the other early English examples, is well populated with handsomely dressed dolls. The early Dutch and German houses were inhabited, too, but most of them, especially those of the Netherlands, with their bits of amber, ivory, gold, and silver, were toys for adults. The baby houses of England are another matter. They were made for children, even though, in most cases, the children were permitted only to look at them—and on state occasions at that. Almost all of them are occupied by large families of dolls whose long and beautiful names sometimes survive. The ones Ann Sharp named more than 250 years ago have the names she chose pinned to their garments or to the place in the room where they were to stand.

Despite some of the architectural marvels which have been described, the English dolls' house whose picture turns up oftenest in magazine articles is but a fragment of a dolls' house. This specimen—again Queen Anne— (in the Victoria and Albert Museum) actually is a room. Authorities nearly always engage in a little preliminary paragraph explaining why they think it a fragment of a whole and, if so, what fragment.

49

There *are* marks on the wood showing where hinges have been. Several observers point out that there undoubtedly was once a door, no longer in its place. In any case, it is a curious-looking affair, walled with Queen Anne windows. The effect is of many panes, with a goodly amount of hinged oak paneling (which folds into a room), and this leads one expert to guess that it "may have formed the hall or reception room in a dolls' house of considerable size." She inclines to the hall theory, since as a room there would have been so little wall space for furniture.

Detail of the hand-painted wallpaper, showing classical ruins, in the Blackett Baby House, 1740

(*Girl's Realm,* 1900, shows a photograph of what is undeniably this same fragment, but arranged this time as two rooms. In one, four dolls, one a country squire in a hunting cap, are taking tea. In the other, a lady nursing her baby receives a visit from three friends—all of these occupants the same ones who are differently assembled in the one-room version. Practically all the furnishings, with the exception of one table, appear the same; the discrepancy, while mysterious, may be based merely on the opinion of a curator.)

Whatever its original state, the room teems with all sorts of interesting plenishments, sandwiched amidst its singular congregation of dolls. The omnipresent warming-pan is there, and since almost every dolls' house which dates back more than fifty years seems to have one, it might be as well to mention them here and have done with them. The pierced copper specimen in this Queen Anne home was the usual sort, to be filled with live coals. There have been tales of a spark hopping out and igniting the heavy homespun sheets this type was required to warm, and, of course, there have been other, more precautionary versions of the warming-pan. A perfectly innocent-looking little vessel, in pierced work, throws an unexpected light on a curious drinking custom (and recipe) of quite another country. It is said to have been used for heating the "brandy wine" of the Dutch, which was poured upon hot raisins.

The patrician quality of the family who occupied this dolls' house is established by the presence of ten silver plates. The wooden trencher, from which several people ate together, was used by the middle class right through the eighteenth century. Apparently it occurred to hostesses only gradually to supply a plate apiece. Still, this custom was a good deal fancier than an earlier trencher procedure; in more distant times the plate from which the meat was served, though this at least must have been individual, was a good coarse slice of bread.

One historian notes that "Towards the end of the [eighteenth] century, the aged Duke and Duchess of Hamilton sat at the head of their table on a raised dais and ate from the same plate as a token of affection and a tribute to bygone customs." Since plates had rarely been used in England at meals till the sixteenth century, this custom wasn't really so bygone. (The trenchers of the well-to-do were of pewter rather than wood till Wedgwood's creamware and the porcelains of Bow, Chelsea, and Worcester replaced them.)

Tiny trencher salts, eight-sided, with depressions in the upper surface to hold the salt, are present in silver, a material of which there are many items in this room, hallmarked for only a magnifying glass to see. A large salt container occupied the center of the high table, but these small salts stood beside the trencher. An early sixteenth-century printer-and-Emily-Post, Wynkyn de Worde, said: "Sette your salt on the right side where sits your soverayne," and, "atte every end of ye table sette a salt-cellar." This is not so different from current etiquette which decrees one pair of salts and peppers for every two diners.

A three-legged contrivance in silver with four upstanding prongs contains ten silver plates. This article, complete with its load, was set before the fire to heat the plates. Often food had to come great distances, from below stairs, say, and any item which would help to keep it "piping" was not overlooked.

There is also in silver a two-handled porringer, bearing the date letter of 1713.* When tea first became a fashionable beverage, and it was not brought to England till 1664, the porringer was often used as a cup. A silver tankard is also present, intended no doubt for sturdier contents. This item (in full size) so easy to picture in the burly fist of some very early, very large warlike hero, drinking off, beside its hinged lid, great draughts of bitter beverage, wasn't known as a tankard till about 1575. Before that, we learn, the name was applied to wooden iron-bound three-gallon water tubs. And this borrowed name, for such is the way of words, may reflect upon the vast quaffing capacities of the earliest tankard-emptiers.

There are all sorts of elegances in this room, bits of Delft and Stafford-shire, besides the silver, and Dutch glass. But a few mundane kitchen matters, which escaped somehow into this surviving hall, are no less interesting than their "betters."

One of these is a mop, no ordinary mop indeed. Pure lamb's wool with a bone handle, it was described many years ago (by Mrs. Willoughby Hodgson to whose *Connoisseur* account we are indebted for much of the information about this "fragment") as a type still in use in the Midlands and the North of England. "It is an absolutely necessary article of domestic use in tiled kitchens, and the wonderful agility displayed in spinning it in the arms till all superfluous water is ejected is a feat only accomplished after years of practice." Mrs. Hodgson also gives a picturesque account of the walnut "dolly," "a long-handled article terminating in a clubbed end, still used in the Midlands, whose reverberant sound awakes the morning echoes in farm-house and cottage on washing-day, when the lusty housewife stands at her well-filled 'dolly-tub' and scatters the foaming soap suds far and wide as she belabours with the 'dolly' the soaking linen."

There are some interesting pieces of furniture among the miscellany

* There are three different kinds of hallmarks. One sort, the date letter, a letter of the alphabet for each year, is employed in a new style when the alphabet in one style is exhausted.

that is in this Queen Anne room, a Jacobean gate-leg table and a green lacquer toilet glass with three drawers. One of the most notable pieces, considered in terms of custom, is the typical walnut cabriole-legged chair with its high-backed seat, "shaped to suit the enormous periwigs of the men and voluminous head-dresses of the women of the day." There are tiny knives and forks in ivory with wooden handles and a delicate painted alabaster tea service. One could write a whole book, and an interesting one, about this fragment of a room.

For all we are able to learn, one of the most curious English dolls' houses may be in the United States. It was, at least, in October, 1942, when it was Number 643 in a Parke-Bernet catalogue. Unfortunately, it has not been possible to learn the present whereabouts of the house, but the very technical catalogue description is interesting in itself. This refers to the toy as a Sheraton inlaid mahogany dolls' house circa 1800, and further, "Mansion with a central clock and window recess above the door, flanked by three stories of windows in a façade with shallow returns; the whole surmounted by a demi-lune pediment faced with original mirror, and standing on a chamfered box base inlaid with marquetry dies and containing a small drawer." The height is thirty-five inches.

The description previously had identified the origin as "English (?)", and an appended note observed that since "doll houses seem to have been introduced into England from Holland, then the present example, if not Dutch, at least shows strong Dutch influence in the design, which is a pastiche of the architectural fashions of the period." The question mark would seem to be unnecessary, and the house unmistakably British, though, aware of the pitfalls in positive identifications, one must admire the discretion which prompted it. The house may suggest Dutch design but doesn't in the least resemble the unarchitectural form of most Dutch dolls' houses. Though the writer has seen no English dolls' house like it either.

Another unusual dolls' house which conforms in neither style nor manner to any other was believed to be, by its English owner, when the first edition of this book went to press, a "contemporary copy" of Sparrowe's House, Ipswich, a gabled relic which has been standing since 1567. Within recent years, however, identical copies began turning up here and there, and when the second copy appeared, the word "contemporary" had to be quickly discarded.

Through the courtesy of Mrs. William R. Mahoney of Oak Park, Illinois, and of Mrs. Margaret Whitton of Wilton, Connecticut, both of whom did considerable research on the subject, the small mystery was recently solved: "About twenty of the miniatures were made, around 1930, by F. Tibbenham, Ltd., of Ipswich, a furniture manufacturer who specialized in reproductions. They were mainly sold in London, to Americans, but one remains in The Ancient House itself."

Despite this disappointing recency (it seems astonishing that a back-

Mrs. Pumphrey's copy of Sparrowe House, Ipswich Height: 18½″, including chimneys

52

ground so modern could have been so promptly obscured), the dolls' house is a wonderfully ornamental affair with extraordinary pargeting upon almost every inch of space that is not occupied with windows. The whole front is lavishly decorated in this delicate plasterwork, with designs of animals, fruits, flowers, and other assorted devices. On the upper story are four oriel windows with, on the base of each, emblematical representations of Europe, Asia, Africa, and America. On the roof are four dormer windows, each ornamented with a different figure of Cupid engaged in some mythological business. The British Royal Arms with the familiar "Dieu et mon droit" occupies the center panel. A pair of magnificent Tudor chimneys crown the roof.

Like a dolls' house, and unlike a mere model, the front swings open in four hinged sections, one to each of the four main rooms. The latter contain panelled walls, beamed ceilings, and fireplaces. There are 42 assorted windows, leaded and engraved, a half stairway, and an air of ancient innocence which appears to have deceived at least one "knowing antiquarian."

Specimens may be seen in the collections of Mrs. Elizabeth Cheney of Oak Park, Illinois, Mrs. Homer Strong of Rochester, New York, and Fru Estrid Faurholt of Copenhagen.

When "Sparrowe House" was first written about in 1953, there was a question about its age which has since been answered. Therefore, when the writer later read of a single room which was said to date from the reign of James II* (a dating that would have made it the earliest English miniature room [or house] on record), it seemed imperative to check further.

Through the courtesy of the owner of the small room, Mrs. John F. Daniel of Lexington, Kentucky, who cooperated fully in trying to establish its age, we have learned that the room, which has a date, 1671 (and initials, "E. P.") carved above its recessed fireplace, is now believed to be "about 150 to 175 years old"—a ripe enough age to be of interest.

Of waved English oak with square paneling, the model, made completely without nails (it is put together with handmade dowels), is seventeen inches square and has an overall height of nine inches. According to Jane Hunt Clark, who described it,† the room is of typical English Renaissance style, and there are all the features one would expect of one of this vintage. "The walls have square flat bolection panels which project from the styles or vertical panels around the upper part of the walls." There are casement windows with minute diamond-shaped panes. The fireplace, with "its distinctive Gothic arch" is recessed into the back wall, and has a chimney made of fire bricks (a few of which were pulverized with age when the room arrived from England). There are recessed doors on each side of the fireplace.

The oak furniture, all of the Elizabethan and Jacobean periods, according to Miss Clark, includes refectory table, settle, press cupboard, dower

* Actually, the 1671 date above the fireplace would have been during the reign of Charles II.
† In a 1961 issue of *Antiques Journal*.

chest, four side chairs, two wainscot armchairs, two pew-end settles, and a small trestle refectory dining-table. The "large" (four by seven inch) refectory table has a stretcher base and deeply carved melon ball legs, the seat of the settle is hinged for storage inside and the hinged doors on the press "work perfectly and have inside latches." The hinges and other hardware, needless to say, are handmade.

It is of interest that the walls fit together with slots that slip into each other "making it perfectly secure and sturdy." At some point the top of the model was fitted with a thick piece of glass that has kept it in a remarkable state of preservation.

A "peg wooden" of the type Queen Victoria dressed, with a square pianoforte

Although we have seen only pictures of this unusual specimen, we have spoken by telephone to Mrs. Daniel, who told us that she bought it as an architect's model and not as a dolls' room. However, since that conversation, Mrs. Daniel's further inquiries about the piece, which she imported from England, have revealed not only a truer dating but also the fact that "it is believed to be a copy of an original house."

There is a goodly assortment of dolls' houses and related toys in Manchester. The property of the City Museum, these are now at a branch, The Queen's Park Art Gallery, where part are exhibited, and the rest stored.

Though some of this collection was also packed away in the autumn of 1948, we were able to see much of it, at Withenshawe Hall, an historic estate in the suburbs. A great part was given by Mrs. Mary Greg, one of the first collectors to perceive the importance of dolls' houses and their furnishings. (A few items from Mrs. Greg's vast collection, including her own dolls' house [ca. 1840] and an eighteenth century Nuremberg kitchen, are at Bethnal Green.)

Among a delightful array of houses, shops, and miscellaneous furnishings, there are a number of Georgian houses—early, mid, and late—including a late eighteenth century example with the rare addition of a garden.* The latter is formal with circular beds on each side of a walk leading to a curved stairway.

Because of the similarity of many of these to other early and elegant houses described in this chapter, we by-pass further reference to them to tell, perhaps waywardly, of a curiosity that was on view during our long-ago visit—a Victorian conceit which seems the ultimate in an era noted for such frivolities, and therefore worthy of note. This was a dolls' house that was in actuality a frogs' house, a two-room Victorian residence neatly labeled "The Home of the Frog Family," and very neatly furnished. Indeed, if the well-dressed wooden frogs were to move out, the premises would be very suitable for a family of dolls to move in.

* Just as this edition went to press, an arresting reference to the date of this house came to the writer's notice. Barbara Jones wrote in England's *Architectural Review*, "If the house and garden . . . is really late eighteenth century, its designer anticipated normal domestic architecture by some forty or fifty years."

Upstairs a dinner party is in progress. A roll nests in the napkin perched on each plate (in the fanciest Victorian fashion), so evidently the company has just assembled. It is quite a banquet, surely, for no less than four servers are laden with food. The diet is not frog-like. There is a soup tureen, and the second course appears to be a meat pie. The frog family, obviously very elegant, being served by butler and footman (frog), can survey with satisfaction their near-by treasures as they await the feast. No less than *two* clocks under glass bells are on the mantel. And the portrait plates hanging on the wall are of ladies and gentlemen—not of frogs.

A far less genteel scene is in the room below. A game of billiards is being shot by frogs with cues. One frog is racking the score with one (frog) leg while he holds his cue in the other. The chalk for chalking the cues is suspended (along with a gas chandelier) from the ceiling. A card game is in progress at the other side of the room. Several kibitzing, cigar-smoking frogs sit about on chairs and one reclining on a sofa has a large bottle next to him.

This exceedingly Victorian toy brings us to Queen Victoria in our procession (begun with Queen Anne) of royalty in British dolls' housing. A lady almost as noted for her large family of dolls as for her long reign, Her Majesty as a child had a modest two-room dolls' house (and some little shops) which still may be seen in the London Museum, Kensington Palace (where she played with it so long ago). It had merely a kitchen and a dining-room, so the dolls who lived in it must have been hard put to know what to do at bedtime, and even when they weren't sleepy, they may have felt cramped for sitting-room space. But with Her Majesty to tend them, they probably fared well enough under the larger roof of Kensington Palace.

However, practically everyone who has seen this dolls' house has sighed a bit about it. *St. Nicholas* in 1901 observed, "It has two stories and the furniture is not in the least royal. In fact, the kitchen is better equipped than the other rooms. A fine supply of pewter plates and cooking utensils is among its treasures. The present caretaker of Kensington Palace shows the visitor a small box where some scraps of time-worn yellowed muslin attest the industry of the child Victoria. There is a deal of laboriously neat stitching on the dolls' house linen and clothes, and there is an apron for the doll cook which is quite a triumph of dressmaking for the chubby fingers of a four-year-old."

Girl's Realm in 1899 referred to the dolls' house as "the most important of the Queen's toys" and went into detail: "It is two stories high, is painted to imitate red bricks, has a front door approached by a flight of steps, and there are nine windows in the front. . . . The kitchen is fitted with everything necessary to the most fastidious housekeeper. An ample dresser shows rows of shining pewter plates, and there are frying pans, saucepans and other culinary utensils placed neatly upon the walls or shelves. There is a capacious knife-box, filled with iron spoons and forks and wooden-handled knives. There are flat-irons, an iron-stand, a warming-pan, a coffee mill, and

The modest two-room house that Queen Victoria played with   Height: 3' 7"

a clock. The grate is one of the old-fashioned kind, and an iron kettle is on the hob. On each side of the fireplace stand doll servants. I grieve to state that they are neither clean nor trim. 'Biddy,' in a dirty, striped cotton bodice and a red petticoat looks a regular marchioness, while James, the cook, does not look as if he was a servant belonging to the 'quality.' There is a tea service of common wear, evidently intended only for kitchen use. As there is no staircase, you must reach the drawing-room by an imaginary flight. The furniture is not sumptuous. The square wooden table has some pretty little china cups and saucers on it. A kind of cabinet of plain wood stands in one corner, and a bird-cage, with a parrot in it, hangs from the ceiling. The chairs are all small, and do not apparently belong to the same suite."

When Frances H. Low wrote her charmingly illustrated book about Queen Victoria's dolls in 1894, she didn't bother to mention this dowdy but historic dolls' house at all. *Royal Magazine* summed up its "'racketty-packetty" aspect, somehow, a few years later. "The doll's house which now stands in the Osborne nurseries for the use of the children of Princess Beatrice," they sighed, "is a much grander affair than that which was the toy of the lonely little girl in Kensington Palace."

The late Queen Mary surpassed both Anne and Victoria in dolls' house activities. The phenomenal affair known as the Queen's Dolls' House, which was created for her by her subjects in the early 1920's, is considered in its own chapter. But the Queen, as a child, had her own dolls' house, which may be seen in the London Museum.

A section of the commercially-made house given to Princess May of Teck (later Queen Mary) Height: 3' 7"

This toy, a present from her mother, the Duchess of Teck, was arranged by Her Majesty a few years before her death, to show it as it was when she was a child. Besides the halls there are six rooms in the three-story house, the front of which opens in two hinged sections, and it is interesting to see what disposition the young queen-to-be made of them. On one side of the hall is the kitchen; on the other, the dining-room. Upstairs are the drawing and music rooms; on the top floor, a bedroom and nursery.

Queen Mary was given the house for her twelfth birthday in 1879 and it is filled with the charming commercially made furniture to be seen in many less royal Victorian dolls' houses. On the center table in the drawing room are tiny copies of the Bible and the History of England, just the literature one would expect in the dolls' house of an English queen.

Queen Mary's dolls' house interests did not end with the two examples she owned. English newspapers during her later years were filled with accounts of Her Majesty presenting a set of dolls' house furniture here, or buying a dolls' shop there. A 1928 London *Times* reported that as a result of a visit to the Bethnal Green Museum, which contains many dolls' houses, Her Majesty sent furniture for an empty dolls' house in the style of the second half of the eighteenth century, "having taken a careful note of the rooms to be furnished." The report added that the Queen "also lent a model white and gold room designed for one of the palaces, with a notable mantelpiece and handsome portraits. The furniture of this is modern, including a Chesterfield and easy chair and tiny occasional tables." The Queen included "a careful note," telling just where the furniture was to be placed.

This queenly interest in miniature interior decoration has been demonstrated in a somewhat different department. A magazine item notes that when Queen Mary was responsible for Buckingham Palace, she would have a model made of a room to be redecorated. Her Majesty, it seems, had her own royal ideas on the placing of furniture. Photographs would be made of the scale models and the housemaids would study these when doing their daily dusting, to be sure of getting things back where they belonged. (Evidently even royal domestics are not free of that dread dusting scourge—putting things awry.) After the pictures were made, the Queen often presented the models to the Bethnal Green Museum.

For many years, Bethnal Green, and its parent museum, the Victoria and Albert, have housed an outstanding collection of dolls' houses, and this collection has grown considerably. In addition to such well-known examples as the seventeenth century Nuremberg house (Chapter 4), the Tate, the Patry, and others that have been mentioned, there have been, in recent years, numerous additions. One is the lovely, late eighteenth century house bequeathed by the late Denton Welch, who in his *Journals* wrote so delightfully, before his untimely death, of his pleasure in restoring the small Georgian baby house given him by a friend. Another is the exquisitely furnished house (ca. 1830–40), teeming with an astonishing number and variety of peg wooden dolls—family and servants—superb both in quality and condition, given by J. S. Losh, Esq.

Other additions include a house, ca. 1903, designed with the simplicity one associates with Frank Lloyd Wright, and furnished to delight all partisans of the current revival of *Art Nouveau;* and a mammoth, 15-room, mid-Victorian mansion (approximately five feet tall and nine wide), with a clock in its pediment, and bronze griffins guarding the double flight of stairs to its front door.

It is a complete impossibility to do even moderate justice to the vast number of English dolls' houses which have come to light since the first edition of this book was published in 1953. Quite apart from the multitudinous examples, all of them important, in varying degrees, described in Mrs. Greene's definitive work on the subject which appeared in 1955,* the sheer quantity of material that has become known is staggering.

In *World of Toys,* a handbook of British toy collections, both public and private, compiled by the late Leslie Daiken and published in 1963 shortly before his death, there are listed some two dozen museums which contain dolls' houses; some of them with one or two, but many with sizable collections.

Several English houses of unusual interest have crossed the ocean,

---

* Many of which were described, of course, in *A History of Dolls' Houses,* 1953.

including the celebrated baby house of the late Mrs. Emmée Ricardo which was sold at Sotheby's in 1956.

This magnificent specimen, a huge affair six feet tall and four feet wide, is dated 1787, and is said to have come from the Adam workshop.

Mrs. Ricardo, a contemporary and friend of Queen Mary, with whom she used to exchange dolls' house furnishings, filled the four rooms to overflowing with rare and beautiful eighteenth and nineteenth century furnishings, including such uncommon pieces as eighteenth century Persian carpets and a writing desk of inlaid satinwood. Two of the rooms are panelled and one is lined with lovely Chinese wallpaper. The base, which contains a cupboard where the spare pieces may be stored, is concealed behind a handsome double flight of stairs when it is not in use (and accounts for much of the height). An unusual interior staircase is in the central hall.

The house, which was sold to an English antiques dealer (Mr. Leonard Knight) in the Sotheby sale, is now the property of Mrs. Christopher J. Devine of West Orange, New Jersey. Unfortunately, it has not been possible to communicate with Mrs. Devine, whose identity was not known to the writer till shortly before this edition went to press.

Mrs. Pat Munroe of Potomac, Maryland has, so far as the author knows, the only Queen Anne baby house to be found in the United States. The house, a lovely one, as its picture shows, was purchased by Mrs. Munroe from a long-established New York antiques firm (specializing in English pieces) which had advertised it as "ca. 1710."

The exterior, with its dentilated cornice, delicate fanlight, and balustraded roof top speaks for itself. It is the interior, with its charmingly detailed woodwork of the period, that warrants further description. Mrs. Munroe removed the excellent reproductions with which she has furnished the house so that some of this lovely detail can be seen in the photograph. Six-panel interior doors, some of which have their original butterfly hinges, connect the rooms, but the most unusual feature are the fireplaces: each mantel and over-mantel (or chimney-piece, as these would be called in the country of their origin) is of a different design, and, in each of the rooms (except, of course, the kitchen), is flanked by recessed alcoves containing butterfly shelves. In the kitchen, a dresser of unusual elaboration is placed so that its elegantly curving profile is done full justice.

Mrs. Pat Munroe's Queen Anne baby house
Height: 60″

The stand, without which an English baby house was almost never built, is of unusual simplicity.

One of the most thoroughly furnished of all possible dolls' houses, and one of the most attractive, is an English mid-nineteenth century one in the possession of Eunice Althouse of Oxford, Pennsylvania. This house, of fifteen rooms, plus stair halls and attic, was purchased by Mrs. Althouse, a collector and dealer, in 1962, and it is to her great credit that she will sell it completely furnished only, and has stood by this resolve for several years. It is a sad economic fact, which cannot be mentioned too often, that dealers have been buying furnished dolls' houses for some years now, and selling the contents piecemeal. In so doing, perhaps they cannot be blamed, but they are, of course, selling off history.

The house came from an estate near Burford, England, where it was built by the estate carpenter in 1856–58. His carpentry is relatively casual for that fancy era—the house itself is not the thing, but then its builder was beset with putting in all those walls, and with flights of stairs for three of the four floors (plus attic), he probably had little time for flights of fancy.

It was the decorator—a mother, a nanny, a sister?—who indulged in the latter and gave the house much of its character and charm. There are paper windows pasted on many of the richly-papered walls—with paper scenery showing through them. Much of this scenery is floral—potted plants and other assorted horticulture, as lush as the pages of a Victorian seed catalogue whence, perhaps, they originated. Ancient maps paper the walls of one room; a huge pair of colorful paper (Ming?) vases are glued to each side of the fireplace in another. The effect is colorful, ingenuous, and delightful.

Some of the furnishings are later than the house, but some, possibly dating from an earlier dolls' house owned by the family, are eighteenth century. In the dining-room, there is a marked Wedgwood oval tureen, ca. 1790. The square pianoforte in the music room is also about 1780–90, and two hand-painted "ancestors' portraits," over the sofa in the room where the little doll stands, are ca. 1800. The doll herself, a peg wooden who has lost her legs, is Madame St. Quintin. The house, Mrs. Althouse was told when she bought it, was always known as "Madame St. Quintin's House."

There is a fireplace in each room, and a tea set in each bedroom, both drawing-rooms, the music room, and the small sitting-room above the kitchen. It sounds like a house for a goodly family who entertain a great deal (and who drink a lot of tea). Why is Madame alone? Where are all the servants? Undoubtedly there is an explanation.

Madame St. Quintin herself, in her drawing-room

Surprising as it may be to find a dolls' house on exhibition at Wood-lawn Plantation in Virginia in a chapter about English dolls' houses, one has no choice. The house, ca. 1840, is as English as a Christmas cracker.

Purchased in England in 1959 for the Junior League of Washington, D. C., by Mr. George Payne of Woodward & Lothrop, the house was

restored by the League (and by Mrs. Alexander Foley, in particular), and is now on indefinite loan at Woodlawn, the estate given by George Washington to Nellie Custis (and his nephew, Lawrence Lewis) as a wedding present.

The house, a substantial three-story specimen with a typical English basement arrangement, has modest but pleasant architectural details, including a bell-tower on top, and was built in Truro, Cornwall, for Lady Octavia Catherine Onslow, wife of Baron William Roderick Onslow. In the family for three generations, it was purchased from a descendant who had put it in storage thirty years before.

The original furnishings, with a few additions added over the years, are largely Biedermeier in style. Most of Woodlawn's furnishings are contemporary with those of the dolls' house, and some are common to both. A striking example is a 19th century tin bathtub. Woodlawn's, referred to by the Crane Company, who lent it, as a "hat-tub," is identical except for paint color and size. Another example is a motif rather than an object. The lion's head knocker on the dolls' house door is matched by lion's head pulls on a Sheraton chest of drawers in Woodlawn's Lafayette bedroom, as well as on a sewing stand. There are also lion's head medallions on the pianoforte in the music room.

*A Victorian Gothic residence
Height: 46", with stand*

Included among half a dozen English houses in the writer's collection are a Victorian Gothic with turrets, buttresses, battlements, and chimney pots, and an early Victorian town house with a vast array of mirrors and pictures hanging in their original places against the perfectly scaled floral wallpapers. Sixteen looking glasses remain, in seven different styles, including an oval pair which boast pricket candle holders, and one with a cloak hanger at each side. A small, slender, mid-century town house came with only a few pieces of original furniture, but with something rare and interesting: an inventory of its original contents inscribed in a beautiful, shaded script. "Inventory of Lilliput House" is the heading, and the modest contents of kitchen, drawing-room, and bedroom (one to each of the three floors) are then listed.*

It is of interest to note what were considered the essentials in a well-run baby house at mid-century. We note bellows and toasting fork in the kitchen, and "jug and basin" and "towel rail" in the bedroom, but nothing is more engaging than the list of occupants themselves, dispersed at some unspecified date, but of unmistakable family to judge from their highly specific names. When the inventory was drawn up, most of them were assembled in the drawing-room, a cozy company consisting of "Mr. Woodhead, Miss F. Woodhead, Mr. Firbody, Harry Firbody, and Lucy Woodhead & Doll." Betty the Cook and Mary the Housemaid, their family tree unspecified, were properly below-stairs, while Mrs. Woodhead & Baby were in the bedroom.

* Because research established the fact that "TOWGOOD'S EXTRA SUPER," watermarked upon the aging page on which these words are inscribed, was that of Edward F. Towgood & Sons, an English stationer still in business, this house is usually referred to as "Towgood House".

61

LEFT: *"Madame St. Quintin's House," mid-nineteenth century, from an estate near Burford   Height: 5' 1¾"*

Lilliput House, mid-19th century, interior, exterior and an inventory of its original contents
Height: 28½"

The owner of the small house (28½" tall and with furniture approximately ⅔" to 1') will never see an unidentified "peg wooden" in future without wondering if she or he did not, perchance, once reside in this neat-fronted red-brick house with its lace-edged blinds and metal door knocker.

It is thought that dolls' houses were not sold in English shops until the reign of George III, although Nuremberg kitchens had been imported from the 1660's.* Nearly always the most elaborate surviving examples are the early ones designed by architects, built by cabinetmakers, and furnished by craftsmen, before the manufacturers invaded the dolls' housing field. Then, alas, the standard of the average dolls' house was lowered, though fine specimens did still appear. In the average house, three stories shrank to two; stairways vanished; furniture thickened and coarsened in dimensions and detail.

In *Jane Eyre,* Charlotte Brontë has her heroine refer to some dolls' house furniture scattered upon a window seat. She speaks of "tiny chairs and mirrors . . . fairy plates and cups," so apparently she found the dolls' furnishings of her time satisfactory. Dickens, though, in *The Cricket on the Hearth,* rambles on at some length about contemporary dolls' houses, and after what seems an enthusiastic beginning, registers an apparent complaint, placing the descriptive matter in the work room of Caleb the toy-maker, and the complaint in the mouth of the same gentleman:

"There were houses in it, finished and unfinished, for Dolls of all stations in life. Suburban tenements for Dolls of moderate means; kitchens and single apartments for Dolls of the lower classes; capital town residences for Dolls of high estate. Some of these establishments were already furnished according to estimate, with a view to the convenience of Dolls of limited income; others, could be fitted in the most expensive scale, at a moment's notice, from whole shelves of chairs and tables, sofas, bedsteads, and upholstery.

"In the midst of all these objects, Caleb and his daughter sat at work. The Blind Girl busy as a Doll's dress-maker; Caleb painting and glazing the four-pair front of a desirable family mansion."

Comes the complaint: " 'There we are,' said Caleb falling back a pace or two to form the better judgment of his work; 'as near the real thing as six penn'orth of halfpence is to sixpence. What a pity that the whole front of the house opens at once. If there was only a staircase in it, now, and regular doors to the rooms to go in at!' "

But Caleb worked for a manufacturer, and had no say in the matter. In the English press, from then on, and ending approximately now, one finds a whole series of regrets about contemporary dolls' housing, although certain elaborate specimens in British museums seem to belie such complaints.

* Mrs. Greene reproduces a 1762 toy-seller's trade card advertising "Fine Babies and Baby-Houses, with all Sorts of Furniture at the Lowest Price. Wholesale and Retail."

In 1875 the *London Daily Telegraph* reported that the Alexandra Palace was to have a Christmas exhibition of dolls and dolls' houses. "We shall see the dolls' houses of 1862, 1867 and 1873, ingenious in their arrangement, and superb in their appointments, which, however, have long since become as familiar to the educated eye as the automaton chess-player or Vaucanson's duck." (The latter was a creation of Jacques Vaucanson, the French eighteenth century maker of incredible mechanical toys. Says Larousse, "The duck on being placed in the water swam about, plumed its feathers, ate crumbs of food, which were swallowed, the muscles of the neck showing their course into the body of the machine.")

What the *Daily Telegraph* didn't figure on was posterity. Not only has posterity lost sight of that chess player and that duck, but it would be glad to have a look at those dolls' houses of '62, '67 and '73, which are not always available. This editorial writer of 1875 goes on bitterly about the dolls' houses of his time, but quite informatively, too.

"A clever carpenter and joiner," says he, "could put together a big dolls' house in a couple of days. It could be painted, glazed, and dried in another twenty-four hours. Toy warehouses are full of all the miniature goods and chattels which would be required for the most luxurious doll's house of the ordinary type. Admirably pretty upholstery, glass and china-ware, and drapery of this sort are made in England and France. The Germans excel in the construction of Lilliputian crockery, kitchen utensils, and imitation fruits and viands. A wagon-load of such articles could be obtained from Houndsditch in half an hour, and a doll's house as big as a cabinet piano could be swiftly furnished." Some editions of Gröber contain a picture of a fourteen-room, late nineteenth century residence that is furnished in such infinite and fussy detail that the contents could not have been obtained from Houndsditch or anywhere else in half an hour. Perhaps it postdated this critic and was the elaborate offspring of his protest. (Formerly at the Victoria and Albert, it was an unfortunate victim of the blitz, and the fine clutter of this residence is to be seen no longer.)

The *Daily Telegraph* would not have liked the latter residence. "This," it went on, "is by no means the kind of mansion which the friends of art-manufacture would care to see. Something like good taste, something verging upon real beauty in its sense of fitness and symmetry, and tending towards practical utility in teaching children the rudiments of household economy may be instilled into the arrangement of a dolls' house."

The critical gentleman then goes off into a lyrical account of the dolls' house at the Hague made for Peter the Great.* It is apparent that the "fit and symmetric" early examples of his own country are unknown to him. Though in justice to him, perhaps the wonderful houses of the Queen Anne and Georgian periods were still buried in the great dusty attics of the English mansions of which many of them were small replicas.

*Which the Rijksmuseum insists was not made for Peter the Great. See p. 74.

International Studio in 1916 pointed out what was indeed a curious state of affairs, and made what may be a justifiable complaint: "Perhaps the deepest pitfall some of the modern toy-makers have fallen into is to make their toys consciously picturesque or quaint, by simulating a look of age. The doll's house, let us say, appears to have a leaky thatched roof, its walls are painted with cracks and broken plaster."

The venerable *Spectator* in 1920 reports that "Of all toys, perhaps the doll's house remains the most delightful." A promising start, *The Spectator* thus makes, but then wistfully changes tune: "I wish that . . . some . . . of the many artist toy-designers would turn their attention to planning a really good architectural doll's house. I have searched fairly diligently, but have nowhere been able to find a satisfactory one. Copies of the jerry-builder's worst efforts, complete with sham bow windows and Ruabon bricks, are still with us, and even the best designs never seem to rise higher than the desperately picturesque suburban type found in the richer garden cities. The same low standard obtains in the furniture. It has not kept up with grown-up furniture at all. In the eighteenth century the most delightful 'Georgian' dolls' houses were made, dignified little structures with their orders and cornices, sash windows, and pediments." *The Spectator* was still fussing in 1928, reporting that "The dolls' houses were rather disappointing; some had no backs, others were like smug villas with ugly pink roofs."

It is only fair to say that not all English publications snarled about dolls' houses in these trying times. Some of the reports were quite lyrical. In 1907, *Royal Magazine* wrote of a dolls' house costing twenty-five pounds, which, since this was a goodly sum at the time, must have been elegant. This amount would purchase a "dolls' house that an auctioneer would describe as a very desirable town residence, containing whole reception-rooms, spacious bedrooms and possessing many other attractions suitable for a nobleman, Member of Parliament, or a gentleman of position.

"There is a balcony of graceful design around the outside of the house on the first floor, curtains and blinds to the windows, an imposing front door, even drains and waste-water pipes down the side of the house. The rooms are furnished in luxurious style. There are pictures and mirrors on the walls, a billiard-room, a motor garage, a lift to all floors, lock and key to the front door—in fact, there is nearly everything." Indeed, the billiard table had billiard balls made of sugar and there was a bathroom supplied from a cistern in the room, with water which could be heated by a little spirit lamp. Even this remarkable dolls' house was outdone in 1910. *Windsor* magazine told of reality in dolls' houses "being carried to such a degree that fires can be lighted and smoke go up the chimneys."

Thus, some dolls' houses did please some people. As a matter of fact, *The Spectator* much earlier, in 1892, had been satisfied with a good deal less. "There are beautiful dolls' houses at the toy show," they said, "with different sets of furniture in each room, and nice cool dining-rooms for meals. It is the wax dolls who will live in these; not the wooden dolls, who can make a shift anywhere."

The above reporter, probably very fat and fond of dinner, judging by his dining-room approach to the subject, has furnished our final testimonial on behalf of the dolls' house of his era. One other point this hungry man might have cited in its defense: those who have fussed as well as those who have praised when confronted with the manufactured English dolls' house must have had to admit that even if beauty dwindled when large production became the rule, there have been many more dolls' houses to go round than before. And lots more satisfied owners in pigtails and pinafores.

There *were* evidently small dolls' houses, though, unprepossessing little cottages, minus parapets and pediments, even in so tender a year as 1799. *The Children's Magazine or Monthly Repository of Instruction and Delight,* an entrancing publication of appropriately small dimensions, in February of that year ran a little story called "The Toys." This, if we may reproduce the typography of that oddly alphabeted era, was about George and his "fifter Charlotte" who were, in general, good children but "had one very filly trick, which was, that they always wanted the fame thing." Their mamma one morning went out and bought each of them a toy. "George had a very pretty cart and horfe in it, to draw about, and Charlotte had a nice little houfe with two windows in it, and one door." The rather harrowing complications which ensued, including a wheel off the cart and a broken window in the houfe, are rather beside the point here (save for the inevitable fact that these difficulties were resolved happily), but we are glad to suspect that dolls of modest fortune as well as their aristocratic contemporaries had, in 1799 (though it seems not to have survived) some sort of houfing.

Individual houses, made by craftsmen for their own pleasure, are to be found in England as elsewhere, and we turn from manufactured houses to note two remarkable ones, both made in relatively recent years, but representing two very different eras and genres.

To those who consider comparisons odious: we do not mention the Batty dolls' house at Brighton with reference to the Queen's at Windsor, nor Titania's Palace near Dublin, except to remark upon one of those curious coincidences in which two people—in this case three—hit upon a similar idea at the same time.

This coincidence is also remarked upon in Chapter 19 in relation to the elaborate mansion made by her subjects for Queen Mary, and the similarly imposing "palace" created by Sir Nevile Wilkinson. We did not learn till recently of the Batty dolls' house, and though it is, in terms of extent at least, a considerably more modest exhibit, there are several irresistibly analogous aspects, particularly with reference to Titania's Palace.

Where Sir Nevile began building in miniature in 1906, a Yorkshire-man named Mr. Tom Batty (of Drighlington, near Bradford) set to work upon his model house in 1908. Where Sir Nevile was an artist as well as a craftsman, Mr. Batty, as the Brighton booklet says of him, was "a man of 100 trades and crafts." Instead of a palace of many rooms, he built a residence of four rooms with an elaborately marbled staircase hall. For twenty-two years—a time span almost identical to that of Sir Nevile's work for Titania, he was "its cabinet-maker and carpet designer, its glazier and its bookbinder, its electrician and its decorator."

In aspect, the result is already a period piece; both the architecture of the house and its interior decoration have a distinctly Edwardian flavor that is one of the appealing features of Mr. Batty's creation.

The crafts he employed included the making of needlepoint carpets, hand-painted windows, gold-leaf furniture, and parquetry floors. Each of the carpets contain approximately 2,400,000 threads, and two years, averaging eight hours a day, were required to complete four of them. For an eight-octave grand piano (three and three-quarter inches high), Mr. Batty cut each of the sixty-four white keys separately from billiard balls (and the black ones from ebony stick). All are wired and can be pressed down.

Mr. Batty was also something of an inventor, and some of the ingenious conveniences he incorporated into his house are beguiling indeed. In one of the bedrooms, a handsomely carved bed has an imposing headboard which reaches to the ceiling with good reason: inside this headboard are a radiator, a medicine chest, and what the Batty house brochure describes as "a really secret safe."

Another extraordinary notion has to do with chimney-sweeping. This device, "whereby the chimneys can be swept without entering the respective rooms," involves a removable portion of exterior wall which permits the sweep to work on the outside. This device may be impractical for houses of full size, but it is a lovely thought.

What is perhaps Mr. Batty's chef d'oeuvre, though, when it comes to inventions, is disclosed when a penny is inserted in the letter box: the door-bell rings, the door opens, and the lights in the house go on. Originally this was made to operate with a shilling.

The house was first opened by the then Duchess of Devonshire with a golden sovereign which had belonged to her son, who was killed in the First World War.

With the exquisite and careful craftsmanship of the eighteenth century, Mr. Jervis Roscoe, of St. Albans, Hertfordshire, has made a model of an existing Georgian house at Reigate, Surrey. Like the gifted estate carpenters of old, Mr. Roscoe (who teaches mathematics), has also made the furniture. Indeed, he has made everything, including the glass chandelier in the hall, the curtains, the cushions, and even the patchwork quilts. Asked about the chandelier, Mr. Roscoe wrote, "Yes [it] is blown from glass, and a finger-burning job, too!"

Three flat-topped dormers look out from a pitched roof flanked by two chimneys. The two floors below have a simple façade with beautifully proportioned twelve-light sash windows, five across the second story, and two on each side of the front door. As though to atone for his restraint elsewhere, the architect (assuming Mr. Roscoe followed him precisely), lavished all his embellishments on the doorway. Topped by a lovely arched fanlight, and flanked by columns with Ionic capitals, the panelled door is crowned with a dentilated pediment of great beauty, all of which is effectively, and cannily, set off by the surrounding simplicity.

We regret the lack of space to show Mr. Roscoe's pictures of this beautiful house.

In writing of England's dolls' houses in 1956, an English authority on architecture, Barbara Jones, complained about the lack of variety and imagination to be found in them.* "The strange thing . . ." she wrote, "is that these ideal clients requiring neither plumbing, pampering, nor, indeed, material consideration of any kind, should inspire so little fantasy and surprise. One would expect the second half of the eighteenth century to show us a long series of Gothic, Chinese, rococo, singerie, and rustic dolls' houses; conceits that either rivalled the follies and pavilions already in the park, or allowed people who could not afford such embellishments an opportunity at least to have them in little.

"Instead most of the dolls' houses are extremely severe, echoing only the starkest mansions and the simplest cottages . . . Curious, for the eighteenth century that delighted in, for instance, dressing tables that opened and extruded a dozen trays, drawers, boxes and mirrors at the touch of a hand; and still more curious of the nineteenth when patent furniture of all kinds was so fashionable, elaboration and ingenuity were the breath of life to so many people, and both furniture and houses were designed in an infinite number of styles."

Although Miss Jones is one of our favorite writers (her *The Unsophisticated Arts* is a most sophisticated and beguiling book) we cannot agree with her evaluation of England's dolls' houses any more than we can resist quoting it.

Perhaps the dolls' house specialist has an inordinate prejudice in favor of what he studies and collects. As for us, with but six English examples in a largely American collection, all of which, from a battlemented Victorian Gothic to a simple Georgian, seem most marvelously diversified, and all of which contain furnishings of a most astonishing variety, the wonder to us, rather, is that so many of the "conceits" and "embellishments" and "surprises" are reflected—that the choice, reduced by fire and accident and, particularly, by childhood caprice, is so very wide.

* *Architectural Forum.* October, 1956.

6

THE
DUTCH
CABINETS

PIETER BRUEGHEL . . . PETER THE GREAT . . . A SEVENTEENTH-CENTURY admiral . . . a burglary . . . all of these improbable but tantalizing elements mingle in the history of the "poppenhuizen"—the dolls' houses of the Netherlands. Since the venerable specimens which survive in the custody of Dutch museums and favored families are among the most magnificent which ever have been built, such associations as great artists and brave admirals are not astonishing.

All Dutch dolls' houses are so splendid, so thoroughly supplied with precious ores, gems, and works of art, that most historians consider them the least likely to have been entrusted to children. The same theorists suggest that the superb condition of most of the survivors indicates that adults had them made for their own amusement. "After all," says Karl Gröber, "the grave, worthy Dutch burghers who spent their good money on these costly creations were themselves but big children."

The question isn't too disturbing one way or the other. Dr. Gröber might note the honest delight of today's adult dolls' house fancier and miniature collector and conclude that big children are not extinct. However, the excellent condition of Dutch antique dolls' houses need not point to an exclusively adult ownership: the little girls who were to grow up into the most noted housekeepers in the world, most likely to succeed at soap and mop, were likely to care lovingly for their toys. It is probable that, as today, dolls' houses were made for "big children" and little ones.

As noted for their cabinet architecture as for their splendor, the dolls' houses of the Netherlands are generally contained in handsome pieces of furniture which give no hint, till their doors are swung open, that anything more extraordinary than a decanter and some glasses are inside. These are deceptive exteriors, often long-legged and resembling nothing so much as elaborate radios, circa 1928, but they are likely to be constructed of rare woods, painted by noted artists, and inlaid with such choice embellishments as ivory and amber.

They are thus generally shy of windows and miniature doors, or any inkling, for us, of the architecture of their period. This is particularly true of the earlier ones. Several of the eighteenth century examples preserve the cabinet casing over an architectural façade. One might, as in the case of the Blaauw dolls' house, open the scenically-painted cabinet doors and find two additional doors with many-paned windows set realistically into them. Another house preserves only the legs of the cabinet form and is almost as structurally informative as the highly masonic British specimens.

The disconcerting thing about Dutch dolls' houses, a matter equally disquieting about all perfectly made dolls' houses is the difficulty in remembering that what is represented on a photograph is in miniature. In the beautiful folio volume, *Holländische Patrizierhäuser*, (by Professors S. Muller and W. Vogelsang), published in 1909, there are forty splendid plates, and except for the dolls, who are handsome but have dreadful posture, the full-size illusion is complete.

Although five dolls' houses are covered in the professors' book no less than twenty-eight of the plates are devoted to the famous example at Utrecht. Of all Dutch dolls' houses, it is best known, and since it is one of the oldest, going back approximately to 1680, it seems to deserve, in all its splendor, every fragment of its fame. A great deal of its history is available; all, that is, save what we would most wish to know—whose idea it was in the first place, and why.

Of the latter, there are legends. Since an old lady is inevitably the center of these traditions, once on behalf of an only grandchild, once on behalf of herself, the probability of this elderly person's participation is better than a guess. If the first century of its ownership is obscure, thereafter there is enough recorded ancestry for a forest of family trees. In 1738 it belonged to a rich tobacco merchant who gave it to his daughter who married a gentleman of a more dainty ancestry than his surname of Slob would convey. His mother was a member of a noble French family, of interest to us because it appears to account for several French contributions to the house, including miniatures of a Louis or two, and several contemporary Cardinals.

As this would imply, there have been changes in the dolls' house, additions and subtractions, as there are in any house over a period of years.

The celebrated Utrecht house, ca. 1680

The most notable subtraction was owing to an unfortunate felony in 1831, a (dolls') house-breaking in which the drawing-room chandelier, the silver fire-irons, a tortoise-shell inlaid cabinet, an amber chest inlaid with gold and ivory, and a plate chest full of baby spoons and forks were ruthlessly stolen. Several of these items, including the flat silver, were replaced by the contemporary owner, but one wonders what sort of obscurity may have claimed the originals since they were snatched from their noted nest.

One writer has suggested that of some of its most valuable treasures the house could not be despoiled—chiefly the scenic drawing-room ceiling and walls painted by a master who also did full-scale murals, F. de Moucheron. A number of noted painters and sculptors are represented among the art works and it is a mercy that their more portable productions were ignored.

There are fifteen rooms, including a garden. (See illustration.) The latter is French in character with espaliered fruit trees and fruit trees in pots, statues, a summer house, and even a game of ninepins. Utilitarian apartments are represented along with luxurious, but despite the fidelity to form and usage of their furnishings, we can't always count on one aspect of their reality. Opulence seemed obliged to triumph over detail, and the most mundane kitchen implements are to be found in silver. This exaggerated

ABOVE: *Drawing-room from the Utrecht house*   Height: 15¼″

CENTRAL MUSEUM, UTRECHT   BELOW: *Art chamber from the Utrecht house*

state of affairs persists in a number of elegant Dutch dolls' residences. Even the pump in the Van Teinhoven dolls' house has silver handle and taps.

The way of Dutch living is reflected in diversified departments. In the Utrecht house there is testimony to music matters—in the salon are a harpsichord and two flutes. A less intellectual pastime is suggested in the office where a wicker basket profusely piled with long earthen pipes is on the floor. To fuel these the smoker cut with a knife a proper swatch from his available rolls of tobacco. In the storeroom are ice skates and sleigh, suggesting in this instance Dutch geography rather than history. Mingled with these tributes to her wintry situation are items to fortify the household against it— bottled beer, tubs of meat and bacon, and other rugged provender. In all of the rooms of most of the houses are fashion notes, wherever a doll is present. The professors tell us that "the simple black is almost entirely gone; varied shades, mignonette, salmon pink, vivid yellow, are very becoming to the ladies." As this miscellany implies, no category of living is neglected.

Professors Muller and Vogelsang make an interesting comparison between the Utrecht house and the Van Teinhoven,* or Haarlem specimen, which they believe may have originated in the same atelier, probably in Amsterdam. The cabinets are treated in the same way, the inhabitants appear to be related, and the pictures and collections are similarly "rich and valuable."

In both houses these treasures are placed in the art chamber against whose plain white-washed walls the paintings attain additional luster. The collections are of particular interest in this book because they reflect the same taste for curios and miniature art that caused the dolls' houses that contain them to be built. The professors tell us that many of these small wonders seem to have been chosen for rarity rather than intrinsic value. Among them are shells, gold coins, and Chinese porcelains.

If the Utrecht house is the most publicized and the most lavish of all the Dutch houses (and there are several specimens to challenge its position), the one with the most interesting history is the Amsterdam beauty forever linked with the formidable name of Peter the Great. We say "forever linked" with trepidation. There are various theories about which, if any, of the surviving houses was the one commissioned by this most impressive Russian Czar. There are also numerous stories about why it was commissioned.

Of the latter, the commonest relates that when Peter, as a young man, was visiting Holland, he became so delighted with the dolls' cabinets he saw that he was bound to have one for himself. Accordingly, he commissioned an elaborate one, returning to Russia, and leaving his Resident, one Christoffel van Brants, to look after his interest. When the house was completed, after a period of five years, its cost exceeded the 20,000 florin esti-

* Now at the Rijksmuseum in Amsterdam and believed to be their oldest (fourth quarter, seventeenth century).

72

mate, and he refused it. Thus it remained in Holland, which presumably was glad to keep so splendid a treasure in the family.

The variations are infinite. There is even a deviation in regard to its raison d'être. Professors Muller and Vogelsang, telling the "traditional" story, say that Peter ordered it for his daughter, which seems reasonable, and doesn't particularly alter his own attraction to the cabinets.

A far more attractive tale than any we've seen elsewhere is worthy of record here, if only as a delicious example of how folklore comes into being. This story appeared in an English magazine (*Mentor*) in 1923, and where its author obtained his information we cannot imagine. Since all of the versions seem to have someone standing near ready to contradict them, perhaps this one is no further from the truth than any, though some of its facets glitter like paste.

In any event, in this rendition, Brandt (the spelling also varies) is mysteriously metamorphosed from Peter's Resident into a retired merchant who had made his fortune and then turned to creating "diminutive items" for his own amusement. This worthy man gave his productions to friends and museums, and never accepted pay. When Peter admired his work, he graciously offered to make him "a little palace excelling all others."

Mentor goes on: "For twenty-five years Brandt labored. At last he sent word to the Czar that the task was completed. Townsmen protested that such a masterpiece should be lost to the country, but the promise had been given. When Peter received the message he had just concluded advance peace with Sweden and was turning his attention to conquest in the East. But he had not forgotten. He directed that a reply be sent asking what he'd have to pay for possession of the masterpiece. Deeply offended at Peter's gross tactlessness and disposition to bargain, Brandt replied that even a Czar had not money enough to pay for twenty-five years of a man's life. He presented the dolls' house to the nation."

This tale, it is plain to see, has everything. Emotion, pathos, but especially, that advance peace with Sweden. That and Peter turning his attention to conquest in the East lend to the dolls' house story a kind of international significance that even *it* never expected to have. Before abandoning it to the history books, however, we feel bound to examine the twenty-five year production time which has multiplied by five the figure more commonly mentioned. Brandt, the writer makes plain, had already retired when he undertook the project for Peter, and it would seem that either he had retired at a quite early age or he lived to an exceedingly ripe and active old one. Meanwhile, Peter, who lived only to fifty-three, was nearly ready to die himself, according to *Mentor's* statistics, when the house was completed, and seems to have acted very decently about the whole thing under the circumstances.

Nevertheless *Mentor's* man has got his information from somewhere. He has all sorts of interesting detail about the house itself. "He made the molds, which afterwards he destroyed, for the articles of plate and for silver and copper utensils. Regardless of expense he had suitable carpets manufactured and ordered chests of table and household linen woven in Flanders. The books that filled the miniature shelves came from Mayence, each volume had golden clasps . . ."

The house believed to be the one made for Peter is one of the three included in the professors' 1680 group. Although extremely handsome, it is not from the pictures quite as impressive or interesting as either the Utrecht house or the one at the Hague, a fact which, since it was said to be so extraordinary, is ammunition for remaining disbelievers. (Gröber, writing in 1928, and therefore one of the most recent commentators, tersely dismissed the topic by saying that we do not know if the house is still in existence, or if so, which cabinet it could be. Since he had access to the Muller-Vogelsang material [cited in his bibliography] it is hard to know what caused his divergent point of view.) The *London Daily Telegraph* in 1875 referred, without speculation, to the Peter the Great house as the one at the Hague, but despite the fact that 1875 is ninety years or so nearer to the truth than today, and the Hague house would seem a more logical candidate in point of location as well as splendor, the statement seems to be the innocent blunder of a hasty journalist.

If the Amsterdam house is not as striking as several, it bears a distinction which so far as we know is unique. Its portrait was painted (see illustration), and the result, imbedded in a heavy gold frame, is nearly as informative as the model. Since this portrait was contemporary, it is interesting to compare it with the original, and discover what changes the furnishings have undergone. This is the only Dutch house we have seen that does not contain dolls, and whether they have disappeared, or whether Peter the Great (if it is his house) considered them beneath his dignity, it is hard to say. However, the house of the painting has a much warmer look about it, being fully populated.* The artist seems to have contributed little people rather than dolls; the attitudes are realistic and graceful. There is a vast number of children. We've a theory that the painting may be an indirect bit of evidence in support of Peter the Great ownership. Perhaps other dolls' houses have been additionally immortalized on canvas, but this is the only example we've seen. Plausibly, the maker of Peter's house, regretting its anticipated departure for another country, would have wished to keep some token of his masterpiece, in the form of an equally artistic facsimile.

It must be added here that in its official booklet, printed in 1955, the museum discredits all associations with Peter the Great, saying "We must free ourselves from this legend." Instead, ownership is attributed to Petronella Oortman, wife of Johannes Brandt, who married in 1686. This, however, leads one to wonder why such a legend, if it was only a legend, found in numerous versions for at least a century past, would have been

* The Rijksmuseum believes that these were dolls that have been lost.

initiated. What reason would anyone have had for concocting such an improbable tale? And why would it be perpetuated in so many versions?

The professors describe and picture two eighteenth century dolls' houses, both of which, while preserving their cabinet aspect, are far more architectural than the earlier representatives. Of these, the more interesting is the Blaauw family dolls' house, whose two "fronts," cabinet and façade, we referred to earlier. The second has preserved only the legs of the cabinet form. Windows, many-paned as in the Blaauw house (an average window has forty-five panes), do not appear as in that house only on the front façade; they also march, two abreast, up the sides, a pair to a floor. Instead of an elaborate cabinet top there is a pitched roof with four chimneys. There are two front entrances, a sort of service type on the ground floor, and above it a majestic pair of double doors surmounted by a noble variation on the fanlight. These doors are led to by dual flights of fourteen steps which meet in a landing, all of which projects from the main building.

But the Blaauw house is the more interesting internally. There seems to be a certain amount of printed confusion about most of the important Dutch dolls' houses, and this one is no exception. It is not quite clear why the most remarkable apartment in this house, the study of the wonder-doctor Ludeman, is included when the artistically interlaced initials above the front door, on the outside, "P. V. A.," represent the name of the original owner, the family Ploos van Amstel. Muller and Vogelsang suggest that possibly it was "just the fascination" to build something as complicated as a cabinet including "pharmacy in miniature instead of the well-known art chamber. And so the famous name of Dr. Ludeman came later on, all by itself."

Portrait of the
controversial house
at the Rijksmuseum,
Amsterdam

Whatever the reason, the results must be an informative glimpse into medical history. There are jars of powders and insects, as well as medical books. The most curious item present, which sets the tone for the whole apartment, hangs from the ceiling where ordinarily the chandelier would be. This, a medical symbol, is a death skull of crystal. Dangling from the crossbones is a touch of prettiness which only can be described as macabre, a little pearl-adorned pendant. The inventory for the physician's study lists among many strange articles a monkey. Since we cannot locate it in the photograph, we don't know whether this was meant to be alive or stuffed, but in either state it appears, in this scientific realm, to be a plausible presence.

This house is built with such a consciously artistic balance in the parallel arrangement of its rooms, that one must be a bit suspicious of its realism. An interesting example of this is to be found in the salon which has a superb built-in silver cabinet with sliding doors. The silver is displayed on brackets, against a formal pattern of painted swags and scrolls. It parallels in dimensions, manner, and position the pharmaceutical cabinet in Dr. Ludeman's study, across the hall from it, reaching almost theatrically to the ceiling. It is hard to know whether the installation duplicates similar "buffets" of the time, or whether the small treasures are exhibited in this manner in the dolls' house as an effective balance to the room opposite, and an attractive means of display.

There is much for the specialist in the book of the five Dutch dolls' houses. It is difficult to imagine anyone attempting to write about any sort

The magnificent house at The Hague, ca. 1743   Height: 72"

Salon from the house at the Hague   Height: 15″

of Dutch furnishing within the eighty-year scope of the book without recourse to this work. For our limited purpose here, it is of less interest to condense its technical progression of furniture styles than to note the random minutiae that give such history its quaintness and charm.

A tall cane is resting against a tall canopied bed. It hasn't been left there by mistake; such canes were standard bedroom accessories for scaling the dizzy heights to the mattress. We are told that practically every piece of furniture in the Utrecht house has astragals twisting along its pedestals, its arms or legs, and we glance with amusement at a set of brooms, their handles similarly screwlike. In the Utrecht house, the fireplace opening is hidden by an ivory image of Mercury, a summer-time ruse still to be found in numerous variations. There are bundles of dried fish in the granary. A linen press is in the omnipresent drying-and-ironing room. In the Amsterdam house is the spoon case which was employed by a diner-out to pack along his own spoon and knife.

It is surprising that Muller and Vogelsang didn't include the dolls' house from the Hague (circa 1743) in their book. Possibly, since their work was written over fifty years ago, this exquisite example (see illustration) had not yet been placed in the Gemeente Museum, and was lurking obscurely in some alcove or attic. The cabinet is more patently a piece of furniture than most. Where the usual cabinet appears to have been made especially for the dolls' house, this one seems to have been a furnishing first, one which its owners later had the happy thought of converting to dolls' quarters. There are three drawers below, present rather arbitrarily, and it is plain that the nine rooms were built to fit the interior, three on each shelf, quite casually.

This is most apparent on the top floor where the swirls of the cabinet top cause parallel dips in the ceilings of the rooms, which must eternally astonish the inhabitants. Surrounding each of these three cubicles there is considerable air space, something of a never-never land, surely, for even the most adventurous doll.

But these occupants have all sorts of compensations. Their salon, a most extraordinary apartment, is practically a museum in miniature. The walls are positively cluttered with bric-a-brac on shelves or brackets. A central alcove has twenty shelves with incredible bits of pitchers and vases and jugs, mostly Oriental porcelain—in an idle moment a dolls' house historian counted to a hundred before desisting.

The curious custom of putting dolls' houses into cabinets intended for quite different purposes was still more evident in an odd piece auctioned by the Red Cross during World War II (and pictured in *The Illustrated London News* in 1944). This was British from point of residence, since it had been sent in 1715 from Holland (for "a very spoilt little girl"), but its ancestry appears to have triumphed decisively over its environment. The cabinet is tall carved oak and is considerably simpler than others we have been discussing, containing but three rooms—bedroom, drawing-room and kitchen. What is curious and interesting about it is that it seems originally to have been a desk. There is a panel, with lock, that opens out between upper and lower regions, and the kitchen has the curious relationship to the upstairs of being divided therefrom by little drawers and pigeon holes. One can picture cook clambering over four quill pens and scaling five billet-doux to tell madam that there are no pickled eggs left for dinner.

Several early Dutch poppenhuizen have found their way into private collections.* An attractive eighteenth century example may be seen in Mrs. Homer Strong's private museum in Rochester. Another, a very early eighteenth century Dutch house, is in the possession of a Chicago importer. This typically magnificent example, which we learned of through the courtesy of Mrs. William Redd Mahoney, is in the two-inch-to-one-foot scale that is usually to be found in the big Dutch baby houses of the period. (This one is seven feet tall.)

There are, according to Mrs. Mahoney, "beautiful fireplaces" in each of the four rooms (there are also upper and lower halls with a stairway which continues to the unfinished attic) with "oil paintings set in the panelled chimneybreasts, and handsome chandeliers." There are the usual exquisite bits of Delft, silver, and brass in settings which include floors covered with parquet or needlepoint, and walls lined with carved panelling or tooled leather. Furniture is painted, inlaid, or carved. Mrs. Mahoney noticed, in a bedroom, a fire screen dated 1703.

* Formerly in the collection of Dr. Fritz Rosenberg of Colorado, and now in the Denver Art Museum, are two Dutch dolls' houses, one eighteenth and one nineteenth century. See Chapter 9.

She was told that for more than 200 years, the house was "one of the show-pieces of a famous old hotel in Amsterdam," and before the latter was torn down, was a major item in "a widely publicized auction attended by antique dealers from all over Europe."

At an exhibition of dolls' houses in the Baltimore Museum of Art in the late 1950's, we saw a tiny eighteenth century Dutch room which is in interesting contrast to the huge houses described in this chapter.

The property of Mrs. Campbell Lloyd Stirling of Baltimore, it was brought over from Holland by her great, great, great grandparents, Libertus Van Bokkelen, M.D., and his wife, née Dederika Van Gzendoorn, who were married in Holland in 1772 and came to New York after that date. Dederika, who, Mrs. Stirling believes, had possibly inherited this from some of her ancestors, was the granddaughter of Adrian Wor, admiral in the Dutch navy. (All of these facts, with additional dates, are taken from the family Bible.)

The curious little room, all of eight inches square, is made of wood with a glass front. In this space, there is a surprising amount to describe. In addition to a nun seated at a table on which are her supper dishes, there are other furnishings which, in Mrs. Stirling's words, "include two chairs, a wardrobe, a chest or altar holding a candlestick and books, with a crucifix on the wall behind, and a canopied bed beneath which is the usual little

Dolls from the house at the Rijksmuseum

receptacle. Several tiny pictures are on the wall, and a casement window with side draperies is indicated at the rear.

"Rather luxurious furnishings for a nun!" Mrs. Stirling concludes.

There is too much information available about some Dutch dolls' houses, and not enough about others. A trade magazine writer who had just been abroad in 1925 mentioned a house in an Antwerp museum that was claimed by its curator to be the third finest in Europe. Unfortunately, all he told of it was that it stood about eight feet high by almost five feet wide and "it was considered of sufficient value and importance to issue a special descriptive brochure describing it, the cost of which is one guilder [about fifty cents]." We have sought vainly for a copy of this booklet.

Esther Singleton in her *Dutch and Flemish Furniture* (1907) included some tantalizing information about Dutch dolls' houses, which it also has been impossible to substantiate. The most challenging paragraph declared: "At the exhibition of Amsterdam in 1858, among a number of these curiosities, was a notable one veneered with tortoiseshell and with painted glass doors—a present from the King of Denmark to Maarten Harpertz Tromp. Another was a typical Dutch house of walnut-root wood, furnished with silver furniture and wax dolls; there were also two of Italian make with tortoiseshell, ebony and brass ornaments, the doors of which were painted with Italian sea-towns; and one of ebony, the door-panels of which were painted by Peter Brueghel."

To a dolls' house researcher, several items in that paragraph are breathtaking. Unfortunately Miss Singleton included no bibliography, and even letters to the Netherlands have elicited no record of the wondrous 1858 exhibition.

In his journal, that noted Dutch admiral, Tromp, is rightfully more concerned with sea battles than dolls' houses, and no mention of the unique trophy appears. Since Tromp's dates were 1597–1653, his dolls' house would necessarily have been of earlier vintage than any of the other Dutch cabinets (since the King of Denmark presented it, was it of Danish make?) and it seems a pity not to know more about it.* In any case, the item is a luscious morsel, pointing more than any other we've found to the esteem in which these toys were held. What a strange little flurry a monarch of today would cause were he to present a dolls' house, however elegant, to a Chief of Staff!

Since Brueghel's dates are 1520?–1569, he would necessarily have been painting the door-panels of one of the earliest dolls' houses on record,

---

* It is a most curious coincidence that another celebrated Dutch admiral, an associate of Tromp's, is related, by the official Rijksmuseum booklet, to the oldest dolls' house in the museum. Admiral Michael Adrianzoon de Ruyter, who seconded Admiral Tromp in a great battle against the English in 1652, was the father of Margareta de Ruyter, whose "nut-tree" dolls' house is mentioned in an inventory of her possessions made after her death in 1689. One wonders if Tromp, presumably presented the dolls' house by the King of Denmark, might not in turn have presented it to de Ruyter for his daughter? De Ruyter was later ennobled by the Danish King, a further small coincidence.

if not the earliest. Of course there is the possibility that he painted the doors of a cabinet which was not made into a dolls' house till a century or two later. The biographical material available in English about the Flemish master doesn't appear to mention any cabinet-painting activities, dolls' house or otherwise, and we report with great reluctance the reaction of the Netherlands Information Bureau. Queried on the subject, the Bureau flatly replied, "That Peter Brueghel would have painted a door panel is impossible."(!)

Miss Singleton, discussing Dutch dolls' houses generally, mentions that the death chamber often was included. "The latter was draped in black with a canvas or silver coffin containing a tiny wax corpse." Here again, we are completely indebted to Miss Singleton. None of the famous dolls' houses we have mentioned appears to have contained such an apartment. And of all save the Antwerp house, we have studied many photographs. It would seem more likely that the Italian dolls' houses contained this somber feature; it would appear a more probable accessory to the residences of such a highly religious people.

We feel on surer ground with Miss Singleton when she mentions that the Dutch dolls' houses often included a miniature garden "embellished with a quantity of coral-work. . . ." She tells us that one Margaretha Godewyck had a dolls' house with a garden and arbour, about which she wrote verses. One of these appears to make a poetic companionpiece to Augustin Maier's Latin eulogy of the Duke of Bavaria's dolls' house (Chapter 3), and since Miss Singleton was thoughtful enough to provide both, we include translation as well as original.

OP MYN CORAAL WERCK

Hier siet ghy van coraal in 't cabinet besloten,
Een baeckermat, een wiegh, een korf, een stoof, een mandt,
Een kleerben opgepronckt, een bedsté, ledikant
Gevloghten van coraal en na de kunst gegoten,
Gemaeckt van suyver glas, en van verscheyden kleuren,
Aen d' Aemstelstroom gevormt van blaeuw, van groen en peers,
Want sulck corale werck verdient oock wel een vers,
En Pallas sou het self voor wat bysonder keuren.

ON MY CORAL WORK

Placed in my cabinet here, you see made of coral
A baby's basket, a cradle, a child's foot-warmer and a
    warming-basket,
An ornamental clothes cupboard, a bed and bedstead of
    twisted and cast coral
And of pure glass, of different colours,
Shaped at Amstel's stream of blue and green and purple.
For such coral-work deserves indeed a verse,
And even Pallas would judge it more than ordinary.

7

LES MAISONS DE POUPÉES

*I*N A CURIOUSLY NATIONALISTIC FASHION, MOST TOY HISTORIANS
appear to stress the toys of their own countries and give the once-over-lightly,
or no mention at all, to those originating beyond their geographical borders.
To some extent this is understandable; this book, originating in the United
States where its author is necessarily more in touch with American toy
collections, probably has more space devoted to American dolls' houses than
it would have had if an ocean hadn't abbreviated research abroad. Still it is
odd that in Europe, where countries are as close together as states are here,
toy researchers often have been so internationally myopic.

France has suffered most from this limitation. Anyone reading only
English or German toy histories would suppose that French children had
been deprived of dolls' houses until practically the nineteenth century.
Almost all English and German authorities content themselves merely with
mentioning the very historical French dolls' rooms (considered later in this
chapter) which, after all, scarcely can be ignored. Fortunately for France,
she produced two competent toy historians of her own about five decades
ago, Henri d'Allemagne and Léo Claretie, who returned a compliment by
noticing the toys of other countries secondarily.

If toy historians have slighted France, however, doll historians (they are
two distinct species) have attributed dolls' houses to her which she cannot

claim. The trap has been an innocent phrase, "petit ménage," which because of its household implications in full scale almost invariably has been translated into English as "dolls' house." The times this error has caused the heart of the dolls' house researcher to beat faster have been numerous.

It may not be strictly fair to refer to the translation as an error. A sixty-year-old French-English dictionary does indeed give "baby house" as a meaning, and perhaps those who have fallen into the trap were relying on this pocket definition. A recent Kettridge, however, offers "miniature (or dolls') home set," a more reasonable interpretation of a phrase which had a wider meaning three hundred years ago.

Lucy Crump discusses this term in detail in her delightful book (*Nursery Life 300 Years Ago*) based on Héroard's Journal, the amazing record by his physician of a little dauphin's (Louis XIII's) first years: " 'Un petit ménage' was a frequent present, tiny toys packed in a box which the children would have the delight of unpacking and peeping in to see what sort of a ménage it was. Héroard uses the term for all sorts of small objects; a chalice and a censer, a cock and a woman all made of pewter and packed up together in a box; two little glass dogs made in the glass works of Nevers; a dinner-set; pots and pans to cook with, and once 'two tall candlesticks with white tapers such as are used in church.' " (As for a ménage of pots and pans "to cook with"—this could be literal: Héroard in 1607 records that the dauphin "went to the chamber of the queen where he made a fire, and put there his little stew pot in which he put lamb, pork, beef, and cabbages.")

Incorrect translation of this word "ménage" has been responsible for innumerable reports of "little silver doll houses," which sound like such quaint and fascinating affairs, but which, except in a translator's mind, never have existed at all. For example, Esther Singleton, a social historian of wide experience, in her doll history pertinently mentions the fairy tales of the Countess d'Aulnoy whose stories picture the life around her at the close of the seventeenth and beginning of the eighteenth centuries: "In the version of the Cinderella story called 'Finette Cendron,' when Finette's two cruel sisters begged her to take them out of the woods with her they promised as a reward that 'they would give her their lovely dolls and their little silver doll's house and their other toys and sugar-plums.' " Checking on the Countess, we discover that Finette's cruel sisters have promised her their little silver toys, a much less interesting inducement. Collections of silver toys at the time were as popular as dolls' houses. Many of these silver miniatures could be used as dolls' house fittings, but that is as far as the resemblance goes.

A similar error appears in the same book in reference to the order which Claude de France, Duchesse de Lorraine, in 1571 gave in writing to "the celebrated goldsmith of Paris, Pierre Hotmann, bidding him send four or six dolls not too big, the best dressed that are possible to find, for the child of the Duchess of Bavaria and also a little doll's house all complete, including a buffet, plates, dishes, pots, pans, and everything, such as are made in Paris." Here, too, a "ménage" and not a dolls' house was plainly the intention.

Esther Singleton also attributes the ownership of a dolls' house to Louis XIV. (Little boys were not ashamed in those days to play with such toys.) She undoubtedly is referring to a "petit ménage" given him which included, according to Alfred Franklin in *La Vie Privée d'Autrefois*:

"a little brazier with eight pieces
a little basket with eight pieces, fashioned of wicker
four little candlesticks, two inches high
a spinning-wheel
five chairs and an armchair
an octagonal table
four little snails
two egg cups
ten little wicker baskets of several types."

These items, however, seem to have been a good start towards furnishing a dolls' house.

Probably the tallest story resulting from the ménage confusion was told in print about thirty years ago. This read: "Perhaps the most famous dolls' house of all Europe in olden times was the property of Louis XVI. It was made entirely of silver and its completion required the services of many artists for years. In later years during reverses in France the royal dolls' house went into the melting pot and the silver was used to pay some of the ruler's debts." What first cast suspicion upon this inviting tale was its strong resemblance to the famous incident of Louis XIV's silver toy soldiers made by Merlin which were later melted down for the same pecuniary reason. Since silver miniatures, of a ménage type, were dissolved along with the soldiers, this probably explains the silver dolls' house legend.

There have been other references to dolls' houses in the Bourbon family about which it seems impossible to locate more detailed information. An isolated sentence in an article which cannot be traced to its source reads: "Louis XVI made locks for the Royal children's dolls' houses, Marie Antoinette dressing the inmates of these miniature palaces." Attempts to check bits of the vast library written about this pair have failed to substantiate this pretty story, but there must be some glimmer of truth to it.

Marie Antoinette herself had a dolls' house about which there appears to be no doubt, although about it there is very little information available. Claretie told, in English, in a magazine article about sixty years ago of "a delicate little bust of crystal [which] was a part of a gorgeous dolls' house made for the little Archduchess Marie Antoinette." In his book, published almost twenty years later, he mentions "a pretty little crystal chandelier [belonging to] Mme. Pellerin. It came from a dolls' house which Marie Antoinette had made for her children; and judging by their richness so, necessarily, were the furnishings, tapestries, costumes and stuffs of this royal boudoir."

A French doll historian, Claude Sézan (in *Les Poupées Anciennes*), has a wistful paragraph about the son of Marie Antoinette: ". . . the little Dauphin Louis, before going to sleep in his Temple prison under the guard of the shoemaker Simon, must have dreamed of the beautiful dolls' house which had been given him by his beautiful and gracious mother, Madame the Queen, in other times. . . ." It is difficult to judge here whether M. Sézan has been carried away by the beauty and sadness of his thought, or whether he is referring to a specific dolls' house, possibly the one for which the Dauphin's mother made the linens and his father the locks.

However, there are French dolls' houses about which a great deal of information survives, because the houses themselves have come down to us to tell their own stories. The earliest of which we know is a remarkable Alsatian example of 1680.* The property of a Strasbourg family living in Paris, it was the subject of two full accounts recorded four years apart, in 1920 and 1924. These descriptions, however, are in some respects so divergent that one might more easily suppose that a generation of furniture-moving doll housekeepers had intervened. But between the two, it is possible to give a composite view of the dolls' house and Alsatian bourgeois family life in the late seventeenth century that is generously informative. We shall permit the machinery to show here, dependent as it is upon our limited French, and let M. Claretie (in *Les Jouets de France*) and M. Forrer (in an article in *Vie en Alsace*, 1924) battle things out for themselves.

To let M. Claretie begin: the dolls' house "is contained in a large chest six and a half feet long and over three feet high. It consists of four parts, two to the ground floor and two to the story." One of its chief fascinations is its goodly amount of exterior detail, for: "Below, to the right, the great door, with copious ironwork alongside it and heavy lock, faces the courtyard, paved with pebbles. A shutter window permits sight of arrivals before opening to them. In the wall, above, a sundial is embedded. The bell hangs from a gibbet. On the ground, a barrier isolates the poultry-yard from the wood-house which is supplied with faggots. An apiary is set back against the wall; the stone well occupies the center. . . ." All that M. Claretie appears to have omitted there, to judge from the account of M. Forrer, is the watchdog.

M. Claretie: "We pass through an archway, through buckets, shovels and ladders; we greet the two servants and the little girl who watches us while holding her doll in her arms. The women are wearing pointed hats of black felt, tight bodices with padded sleeves, broad smooth skirts. Here we are, at the side, in the lower room, of which the door is carved, sculptured, with columns; some *vitraux en grisaille* ornaments the windows." (Larousse defines *grisaille* as a type of painting which imitates sculpture and in which only gray tones are employed. The great windows in this room, therefore, had panes so processed.) "From the ceiling hangs a chandelier with six

* Dr. Elisabeth Wolffhardt has pointed out that inasmuch as Strasbourg belonged to the German Empire till 1681 when it was occupied by Louis XIV, there are "both French and German elements" in this house.

tapers; the floor is of flagging. A vast clothes-press, a washstand, a cupboard full of stuffs, a dresser with shelves and posts loaded with jugs and pewter mugs, a clock in a case, some green chairs, and some framed pictures of saints complete the furnishing."

But not according to M. Forrer. He calls this apartment "le salon d'aujourd'hui" and pictures there (he also pictures her upstairs, so perhaps *he* is to blame for the confusion) "the mistress of the house . . . receiving a very distinguished man to judge him at least by the rich lace work ornamenting his attire." For the rest, M. Forrer gets the same results (from looking) as M. Claretie, but says of the pewter washstand that it is a furnishing the lack of which was not noticed in any *bonne chambre* at the time of the Renaissance.

M. Claretie: "From the ground floor, the wood staircase mounts to the room above which is a kitchen, its window decorated with oiled paper. Some tubs are in the sink, which is surmounted by a roller-towel. The kitchen range is large and well-stocked. Casserole covers adorn the large mantel. Kitchen utensils fill the shelves. Little copper chamber candlesticks stand near some andirons; a copper warming-pan hangs on the pot hook. On a block is a mortar and pestle and a still. Jugs, pewter and earthenware dishes stock the dresser. In the open drawer one perceives an assortment of tableware. Some hour glasses are ranged on a cabinet. A winch is attached to the chimney where it is necessary to turn the spit. The oven door pierces the wall on one side; a keg is placed on a gantry; some implements of all sorts, rat-trap, clock, cat-o'-nine-tails, scales, battledore, feather duster, encumber the chairs, tables, chimney-piece, at the service of the cook in black silk corselet and white apron, who watches a chimney-sweep armed with his tools, near whom the little dog of the house is yelping. A maid is sweeping."

Weavers of dolls' house whimsy, coyly describing dolls' house occupants perpetually preparing for events which never take place, may be brought up short here. In 1920 when M. Claretie described the cook in the Alsatian dolls' house she had her eye on the chimney-sweep. In 1924, when M. Forrer immortalized her, she had turned her attention to the maid. The only other addition M. Forrer offers in the kitchen is a goffering iron, a highly indispensable instrument in the be-ruffled seventeenth century.

M. Claretie: "A door communicates with the neighboring room above the courtyard. It is a rich chamber, of which the walls have columns, the panels are sculptured, with pediments; near a pewter washstand and a large, beautiful clothes-press, the spinning wheel awaits the skeins of prepared hemp; glass pots of preserves are ranged on shelves; some tankards, goblets and pewter mugs adorn the buffet. The bed and the cradle are columned and curtained with green serge. The cradle is on pivots and balances itself. We make no noise for a baby sleeps there, as does a bird in a cage. There are chairs, arm-chairs, stools; at the round table, madame sews; monsieur, dressed in black . . . examines his account books, near an old and curious inkstand of which the two copper cups are set in a small boat of the same metal. The bell is there, within reach of hand, to call the servant."

M. Forrer doesn't bother with the inkstand at all, but we learn all sorts of things from him which M. Claretie seems to have ignored. For one thing, he is specific about what room this is. He calls it a bedroom, but adds that "it is at the same time dining room and sleeping chamber as this was the custom in middle class families of Strasbourg, as it is still in many peasant houses of Alsace." M. Forrer found the master and mistress engaged in the same account books and sewing as did M. Claretie, but instead of discovering the baby asleep, he located this young person holding "by the nursemaid to the leading-strings and [attempting] thus its first steps."

M. Forrer supplies such important details as the 1680 date above the entrance door of this room, and also on the wall, "One of the concave mirrors much in use in the middle ages, and a very large hunt trophy. . . ." He also spots an odd stove used to dry the baby's linen. He sees *two* cages suspended at the back with *two* birds *singing*. He also locates the chessboard "ready to serve monsieur and madame," if, presumably, they give over their old sewing and account books. They are plainly more static creatures than the birds and the baby.

Eighty years earlier, even nobles' houses in France were likely to be scantily furnished by our standards, and part of these limited furnishings were absent some of the time since even a queen took bed and table appointments along with her when she traveled. Therefore this Alsatian dolls' house appears to point to remarkable progress in fourscore years.

One curious little dolls' house, dated 1791 and called Trianon, has only two rooms, a bedroom and a salon, but it has the distinction of a glass roof, through which the Louis XVI decor may be inspected. For those who prefer vertical views, there are also four "great windows."

The approximate date of this brief apartment has been established in an interesting way: on the console, in the salon, along with two vases of flowers, are two books of music manuscript dated the 1st of October, 1791. A French writer commenting on this elaborate toy cried, in print, "Here is what amused Paris during the torment!" This would imply that he considered this particular dolls' house more a plaything of adults than of their children. Since the furnishings are exceedingly elegant, this seems not improbable.

Both rooms have fireplaces, of course, and in front of the one in the salon, small chairs and armchairs are arranged around the table. A statuette is on the mantel. The sofa is of striped material and is furnished with cushions. Small oval pastels are hung on the walls. Blue silk curtains are at the windows. Moreover the room is occupied: two women, dressed impressively in silk, are seated "chatting about topics of the day."

The carpeted bedroom, connected by a door to the salon, has an elaborate bed crowned by a yellow silk canopy ornamented with four plumes.

Salon and exterior of a
dolls' house, ca. 1840,
at the Musée des Arts Décoratifs
Height: 24½″

M. Claretie writes: "The commode contains provisions of household linen, delicate and perfumed; the fireplace and the consoles hold vases of flowers and statuettes in Nevers glass. All is intimate, calm, silent; one would believe himself in some provincial house, that of the wife of the bailiff or another of the elect. Madame seems to be preparing herself for rest after a journey without bustle, and monsieur is in dressing-gown and cotton nightcap, like a man who is not at all troubled by the latest news from Paris."

The lovely French house illustrated may be seen at the Musée des Arts Décoratifs (the Louvre.) With its double panelled doors, arched windows, and metal grillwork, it is the very model of the French town house, ca. 1840, that it should be. Of the rooms, we picture the salon, but all are as exquisitely furnished, and the whole is infused with the sense of style which one expects in French décor as well as in French couture.

Two interesting dolls' houses of the time of Napoleon III survive. French dolls' houses of that period appear to have been even more elaborately detailed than Victorian examples in England and America, their exteriors outdoing even the interesting clutter going on inside.

Again we shall translate M. Claretie, and with a hope that we do not too often tread upon the niceties of his style, or too readily misinterpret the technicalities of the household vocabulary. The first house he describes is "a four-story building, with porte-cochère, staircases, landings, garret-windows, bedrooms and drawing-rooms, furnished and inhabited by accessories and dolls which date from 1860. . . . The interiors, very full of objects, give well enough the idea of middle-class apartments of our time greatly encumbered with cheap furniture and knickknacks. It is the progress of industry that facilitated this diffusion and inclined modest middle-class homes towards imitation furnishings, and the gewgaws and ornaments in bronzed zinc with which the Saint-Antoine quarter flooded the market.

The kitchen of the ca. 1840 house

"The other house is prettier, more tidy, more finished, less cluttered. It represents the homes of our fathers the middle of the last century, that is to say the nineteenth. It is in the form of a little cabinet of polished oak with pointed roof. . . ." And, if you please, balustraded windows.

There is a ground floor and three stories. A salon and bedroom are on the ground floor, but of most interest there is a bathroom, "with a little bathtub of gilded copper." Finding a bathtub in an American dolls' house of this period is extremely unlikely.

"On the first floor is a green room furnished with red armchairs. On the mantelpiece is the bust of a child, large as a pea, flanked by two candelabra. Wall glass, pictures, sconces, vases, all the comfort of a middle-class home. The dining room is in oak; initials are entwined on the front of the buffet which is stocked with plates and dishes and crystal to scale. Two ladies take tea, and the little dog watches them. A bedroom is on the other side, of the same style. . . .

"On the third floor, the dressing-room is comfortable enough; the wash-stand is of white marble. Two well-furnished bedrooms complete the lay-out. The kitchens are in the basement; a beautiful dormer window lights the garret. . . ."

M. Claretie concludes by noting that the accessories "preserve all the insipid enough flavour of the domestic elegance of the reign of Napoleon III."

A writer reporting the Paris Exposition of 1900 described a dolls' house shown by a manufacturer from the provinces which surpassed even these for detail and clutter. "Its architecture was important, with turrets, a bell-tower, banisters, flights of steps, balconies and encorbelments; dolls were at the windows watching a croquet match briskly played by their little sisters in the courtyard fenced with beautiful iron grill-work."

None of these individual buildings, no matter how ornate, can be quite as revealing of life in France as a contemporary toy apartment house described in a 1911 trade publication: "Six floors of varying decoration, furniture and social status, each flat strangely complete from parlor to kitchen, all inhabited, with a doll janitor in his lodge by the great front door; two stairways and two elevators, like the most expensive modern houses, the second elevator being a coal and provision lift for servants . . . there was electric lighting in each room of each apartment and complete electric heating."

There indeed was a microcosmos, displaying at a glance, as could few buildings, miniature or full-scale, of any era, different levels of society. This curious French living arrangement, in which the wealthiest families dwelt luxuriously on the first floor, and families above were successively poorer until the miserable occupants of the top story might be approximately in rags, becomes strange social comment in a dolls' house, and one would wish this doll building, beyond all relatively recent ones, preserved in some attic somewhere.

It is not surprising to find French dolls' houses more than ordinarily lavish in detail and arrangement. France has never been a mass market for cheap toys, but almost always has had a world-wide counter for elegant ones, particularly dolls.

In 1917, *International Studio* reported that French artists had turned to toy-making, and featured illustrations of a dolls' drawing-room, dining-room and bedroom made by one Marguerite de Félice. These have a quaint, pre-war, continental flavor.

In 1924 Pierre Calmettes was writing, in a book called *Les Joujoux,* "Doll houses are no longer in fashion; one encounters only rare specimens in the luxury stores, and sometimes a specimen in foreign catalogues. One must regret the actual rarity of these toys, for they were made to give little girls a taste for housework. . . ." A few paragraphs later, M. Calmettes, who has been talking of the necessarily cumbersome dimensions of dolls' houses and "the continual reduction of habitable space in modern apartments," tells us that "The stroke of the broom and the feather duster are the most implacable enemies of dolls' houses." Thus dolls' houses, which Monsieur was recommending to housekeepers of the future paradoxically were being outlawed by housekeepers of the present.

Of course dolls' houses, like many things, are popular in cycles, and writers of successive generations can be seen discovering them for the first time, or regretting their passing—it depends very much upon the experience of the writer. Dolls' house history is full of such statements as "there never have been such doll mansions as we see this year" and "one no longer finds dolls' houses such as existed a generation ago." Both writers may be writing at the same moment.

Most countries which built dolls' houses constructed dolls' rooms, but the French gave them historical and intellectual dimensions apart from the average dolls' chamber. For this reason, and because the rooms we discuss are, to a large degree, French,* we consider dolls' rooms in this chapter, rather than in one of their own.

* Since this was written, the author has acquired from different sources two pairs of rooms. These folding cardboard rooms, attractively lithographed, appear to date from the end of the nineteenth century, and both came, at different times, from Vienna.

The dolls' room, since at first glance it is but a rudimentary version of the dolls' house, would seem to be an economy measure, designed to save space and purse. Such a lowly status is true of it today, where practically the only examples made are approximately paper, but in the seventeenth century a dolls' room often was costlier than an elaborate dolls' house, and the things that went on in it were fabulous.

Fabulous is a word used deliberately here, and in its most literal sense, since dolls' rooms often contained enactments of little stories or contemporary goings-on. Some of the early dolls' rooms conservatively consisted of no more excitement than dolls and furniture, but a number, especially in France, practically anticipated the toy theater.

Héroard tells of several which belonged to the Dauphin's little sisters and date back to the first years of the seventeenth century. In one of these the main piece of furniture was a bed. On it lay Holofernes, general of Nebuchadrezzar, with Judith in the act of slaying him. Since the incident is from the Old Testament (the Apocrypha), the macabre subject matter may be partially accounted for, but the toy would seem a reasonably positive source of nightmares even for the elderly children of those candid times.

Another room that little Mademoiselle, the Dauphin's sister, possessed, was of a less alarming nature, but it is interesting to consider the questions a parent of today might be obliged to answer about such a toy. This, however, was a type which was traditional for two centuries—a lying-in room: "a bed with mamma and the baby in it while the midwife stood by in attendance."

The most celebrated of these lying-in rooms may attribute part of its fame to the personage who bestowed it. Cardinal Richelieu in 1630 presented this little room, complete with six dolls, to the Duchesse d'Enghien. This, according to the contemporary account of Tallemant des Reaux, included, besides the mother lying in bed, "a nurse almost lifelike, a child, a servant, a midwife, and the grandmother. Mlle. de Bouteville and others played with it. The dolls were undressed and put to bed every evening; they were dressed again the next day; they were made to eat; they were made to take their medicine. One day she wished to make them bathe, and had the great sorrow of being forbidden."

Another lying-in-toy, also seventeenth century, and also of noble ownership, is described by d'Allemagne. (The monopoly of great names, by the way, as owners of these toys, need not imply, as so many historians suggest, that only the great could afford them. Probably many a daughter of the wealthier bourgeoisie had comparable treasures, but no writer near by to immortalize theirs.) This is a group of furnishings for a lying-in room rather than the room itself, and d'Allemagne has an interesting reconstruction of it sketched in color in his book. These things he had seen, in a private collection, were believed to have been made for the Princesse de Nassau.

"The principal personage is lying in a sumptuous bed munificent with four columns and surmounted with eagles of gilded bronze. The curtains and the canopy are of green serge decorated with lace forming rich arabesques. Not far away, near the fireplace, is a nurse looking after her baby whom she is rocking by means of a large thong of cloth." This comfortable means of baby-rocking is practical—the cord is attached through two loops across the cradle, and the nurse, with the long end in her lap, can, by gently tugging it, soothe the most indignant infant without stirring from her seat. "Finally, there are two personages, come probably to felicitate the new mother."

In reference to this scene d'Allemagne has aptly pointed out a possible religious origin, which might apply to lying-in rooms generally. His theory is that at first the different objects may have been meant to represent a Nativity, though none of them has a religious character. We have seen that most crèche scenes anachronistically reflected the times and settings of the countries in which they were made rather than accurately picturing the holy time and land they were meant to represent, and d'Allemagne undoubtedly is relating his surmise to this fact.

Lying-in rooms, though, cannot help but express also a point of view diametrically opposed to these holy motivations. They visibly suggest the early age at which children hardly more than infants were exposed to the facts of life, inevitable accompaniment of the lack of privacy in living arrangements of that candid era.

Lucy Crump's account of such apartments in full-size tells us that "In most rooms where a birth was to take place, it was the custom . . . for a dresser to be set up on which a display of silver vessels and other valuables was made; if a household had not enough to satisfy its vanity relatives would lend what they could spare for a few weeks. Sweet-scented flowers were strewn on the ground and flagons of wine and dishes of sweet-meats were placed among the silver ready for the constant stream of neighbours and friends who made merry in the house, cheered up the mother and admired the baby. Citizens' wives copied the noble-born ladies, making the best display they could while the poorer women had at least a dish of spiced comfits and some pungent scented herbs to welcome their gossips."

One would like to have seen the miniature silver vessels upon the miniature dresser, with flagons of wine (2 fld. drops) and dishes of sweet-meats (sugar crystal size) placed among them. One can picture the same little girl who wanted to bathe the dolls in the room Cardinal Richelieu gave her picking minute sprigs of germander and hyssop, which were, according to John Parkinson, "good to strew floors with," and strewing hers.

The most famous of all dolls' rooms returns us to a realm where actual personages are represented, though unlike the Holofernes example, any action to this scene is cerebral rather than physical. In 1675, according to the *Ménagiana*, Mme. de Thianges gave as a gift to M. le duc du Maine, a room all gilded, big as a table, below the door of which there was in large letters: *Chambre du Sublime.*

Inside was a bed and a balustrade with a great armchair in which was seated M. le duc du Maine, made in wax, a decided likeness. Near him was M. de La Rochefoucauld, to whom he was giving some verse to examine.

About the armchair were M. de Marcillac and M. Bossuet, then bishop of Condom. At the other side of the recess, Mme. de Thianges and Mme. de La Fayette were reading verse together. Outside the balustrade were Boileau, and a little farther off La Fontaine, to whom he was making a sign to advance. All these figures were of wax, in little, and each person represented contributed his own likeness.

This intellectual gathering, unless it has been preserved in some unknowing garret at a temperature kindly to wax, evidently has not survived, but it has left all manner of speculation behind it. Mr. Edmund Gosse, as his brief contribution to Queen Mary's dolls' house library, wrote a lament at not being able to see it. But some of its admirers have dealt with it more controversially. M. Claretie wrote almost a little essay about it, one quite relevant to our dolls'-house-as-a-document theme.

"And see," he begins, "to what extent toys could at times be useful to learning. Note this little detail: Boileau is making the sign to advance to La Fontaine. Now then, one knows that in his review of poetry types, in the fourth verse of l'Art poétique (1672) Boileau did not name the Fable, and did not speak of La Fontaine for reasons purely literary, which are too long to relate here. But people had inferred from it a misunderstanding between the two poets, and a violent enough blame fell upon Boileau because La Fontaine was not very much in favor with the king.

"The 'legislator of Parnassus' thus bore the accusation of having sacrificed equity to flattery. The little toy of which I have spoken establishes by the amiable air with which Boileau welcomes La Fontaine that they were by no means at loggerheads or enemies.

"You are conscious of all the importance. Boileau passed for a bald courtier. His good reputation is re-established and redressed by a children's toy."

Having considered that bit of irony, note Gröber's interpretation of the same plaything, and know why researchers take almost everything with grains of salt: Herr Gröber refers to the little Duke of Maine's room as "a serious affair representing a tourney of poets, made of wax, in which the good poets sought to keep the bad ones from approaching the duke."

So much for the room's intellectual pretensions.

No one who has translated the episode into English seems to have accounted for the balustrade amid the furnishings, or even mentioned it. Quite an interesting explanation is possible: Lucy Crump in her description of the castle at St. Germain tells us that "Every room opens from another; nowhere is there any privacy; a screen, a curtained bed, a portion of a room reserved for special use by a balustrade or dais, an ingle nook, these were all that the age could give and indeed all that it desired." Later she goes more into detail about balustrades, particularly in respect to the Dauphin. "This balustrade divided the room into two portions; a quite usual arrangement in the houses of people of high rank. The portion near the hearth was kept strictly for the use of the Dauphin and those whose immediate attendance on him gave them the right of entry; here stood his cradle, later on his own little chair, a table for his meals, chairs for the king and queen, a stool for his nurse and such things as were wanted for his own use. The other portion of the room was more or less public. Now and then Héroard specially records that a visitor was allowed within the balustrade and sometimes we can infer that such was the case."

Since such notables as Boileau and La Fontaine are on the "public" side of the balustrade in the Duke's room, one might gather that this furnishing was included out of custom and not as a symbol, though if Gröber's impression of a tourney of poets is accurate, one can see what symbolic value such a barrier might have.

Mrs. Jackson describes another specimen (see illustration) with "portrait models" in the house of Madame de Sévigné in Paris. "Voltaire, represented by a figure nine inches high, is seated at a table on which are all the implements for writing; the face is well modelled in wax, the hands and feet are of the same material, his cloth clothes fit with great nicety; the meagre stand, table and chair, however, do not attain to the dignity of a furnished room."

Dolls' rooms could be expensive without being symbolic. Cardinal de La Valette paid two thousand écus (a silver coin) for a doll, the room, the bed, all the furnishings, the déshabille, toilette accessories and changes of dress. All this bounty he presented to young Mlle. de Bourbon.

Voltaire (in miniature) works on his tragedy, Irene

94

Mme. de Maintenon's prayer room in cardboard and gilt paper

Probably the strangest of all dolls' rooms is one which belonged to Mme. de Maintenon, consort of Louis XIV, according to Gröber, "in the days of her brilliancy." He refers to it as "a very sumptuous dolls' room which was later turned by this repentant sinner into a penitent's closet, furnished with a bed of bast and a kneeling chair as a sign of her change of life." Gröber provides a photograph of this strangely tattered cubicle, which belonged to d'Allemagne's collection. D'Allemagne, on the other hand, in his book shows a "toy in cardboard and in gilt paper representing the prayer room of Mme. de Maintenon at Saint-Cyr." It is difficult to account for the startling metamorphosis—practically miraculous—of the mutilated chamber. D'Allemagne's drawing is evidently of an entirely separate toy, perhaps a religious plaything made for a later generation. The grotesque chamber of Gröber's photograph was obviously not of such flimsy materials as cardboard and gilt paper. The elegant satin drapery of the bed curtains is still intact.

D'Allemagne shows delightful drawings in color of three dolls' rooms exhibited by contemporaries of his at past expositions. One of these is a Louis XVI bedroom. Dolls in this room must have been great ones for knowing the correct time; in addition to a clock on the marquetry commode, there is a pair, hung, on either side of the bed. A warming pan is suspended from the wall, courtesy a lavish blue bow. There are two dolls, one standing rigidly by herself, the other sitting on the floor, an indignity to which the latter is subjected, no doubt, because she can't stand alone and looks too large for the one small chair.

An Empire bedroom (see illustration) has mahogany furniture trimmed in gilded bronze and is, says d'Allemagne, "of incomparable richness. What is most delicious . . . is that little sofa covered in red silk of which the arms are ornamented with cornucopias from which escapes a sort of palm leaf; the bed, the commode and the console are in harmony. Each of these pieces is supplied with its tiny decoration, so fine, so well-proportioned, that one might say that the bronzes had been carved in the country of Lilliput . . .

"The principal clock [here again, time is of the essence] placed for convenience on the commode, is in light copper, stamped and surmounted by a crown of artificial flowers of a taste perhaps a little doubtful, but it is necessary to take into account that we are confronted with a doll ménage and must not be too exacting.

"On the wall one perceives two little pictures, in which the subject is presented by means of fine cut-out work: they represent some landscapes of several poetic countries glimpsed in the dreams of the mistress of the house, who is gravely seated on the sofa. In the rear of the room are two other clocks, one in the form of a lyre surmounted by a bronze bouquet, the other in a rather Gothic style that seems to recall the Restoration.

"Near the front, a brave soldier, in brilliant uniform, gets ready in all probability to dance a minuet with a beautiful person whose severe dress is in conformity with the style of the room's furnishings.

"This little interior," sums up one who should know, "of a remarkable harmony and proportion, is assuredly one of the most curious relics of the past which we ever have encountered."

The furnishings of the Directoire Room are less elegantly made, but it has fascinations of its own. Monsieur tells us that this room would appear to be a salon rather than a bedchamber but adds, "however, we cannot attribute to it another purpose when we perceive the doll lying in a bed enriched with gold who holds in her arms a delicate creature come without doubt to kiss her mamma good morning . . .

Empire bedroom "of incomparable richness"

"In order to give the scene a great aspect of verity, one has not forgot to place there the Argand lamp, vulgarly known under the name of Quinquet: it is ornamented as always with its lampshade of green paper." (Webster defines this as "a lamp with a tubular wick which admits a current of air inside as well as outside of the flame.")

It was apparent to d'Allemagne that although the furnishings of this room are "rich and intricate," they were not models but had been especially created in order to amuse children. "Most of the dolls which one perceives in the front of this charming little interior, have been dressed by the children themselves, for the cut as well as the needlework of these garments denotes a touching naïveté.

"From the point of view of the cabinet-maker, the construction is of the most simple: it is of white wood simply fastened and adjusted in a manner a trifle summary." These furnishings are painted a soft green, and where in the Empire Room minute metal is used to represent ormolu trim, here a dash of gilding is made to do.

Interesting advertisements may be found of dolls' rooms in both the eighteenth and nineteenth centuries. In *Mercure* for 1745, one Raux "junior," a merchant in the rue du Petit-Lion announced that he had for sale, "little cardboard cabinets [Singleton thinks these were probably lacquer] in the style of the Chinese cabinets containing little figures of enamel, men, women, actors, musicians, little buildings of the same material with some very pretty apartments where veritable history takes place." The Goncourt brothers tell us that "no woman considers her house complete without a Chinese cabinet." In Bestelmeier's catalogue of the period (see Chapter 4) there are several dolls' rooms on view, and Georg Hieronymus Bestelmeier carried "all kinds."

A very curious sort of dolls' room appeared in the earliest years of the nineteenth century. These were rooms made by pastry cooks of a substance called gum tragacanth. The results were "for the most part edible," being composed of sugar, meal, and the tragacanth (an aromatic gum). This was molded into appropriate shapes which after hardening were painted. According to Gröber, the work was so delicately accomplished that it became "almost an imitation of porcelain," but he adds that today the art is lost.*

He shows a lying-in room of this material, which has survived both time and hunger, noting elsewhere that such toys were popular "particularly in Alsace." Forrer, in *Vie en Alsace,* shows an eighteenth century room executed in paper and colored paste by a Strasbourg pastry cook and to which Forrer refers as "the interior of a middle class bedroom where preparations to celebrate a baptism are being made. The mother with the child is still in bed; around the table one sees the sponsors, there to assist the father—not

---

* A toy stall, ca. 1810, with many small wares of this substance, is shown on p. 170.

to forget the mid-wife—ready to make the great traditional Gugelhopf disappear. At the back one sees the crockery frying-pan painted in blue Delft, a commode, a clock in a case, and also Alsatian chairs in sculptured wood."

Before taking leave of the French *chambre,* we multiply it again into a *maison* to tell of a weird affair Grimm has described. As translated from the French of Léo Claretie: "The good Duke de Penthièvre brought a dolls' house one day to the convent of Abbaye-au-Bois for his granddaughter, who was to become the unfortunate Princesse de Lamballe. Little personages could be seen through all the windows of the luxurious rooms. But an innocent bystander accidentally pressed a hidden spring, and the dolls disappeared and were replaced by the most daring figurines of Aretin. The good Duke had been duped by an unscrupulous merchant who had not warned him that this plaything was not for children. The Superior was very much amused that Providence had chosen the wisest man on earth to be the butt of this practical joke."

Which is as Gallic a tale about a French dolls' house as one is likely to find.

8

AMERICA'S
DOLL
HOUSING

*T*HE EARLIEST AMERICAN DOLLS' HOUSE OF WHICH WE KNOW IS A MOST beguiling specimen in the nursery of the Van Cortlandt Mansion at the edge of New York City. It is dated 1744.

It is also dated 1774. The numerals of these two divergent years are prominently painted one at each side of the second story. No one affiliated with the Van Cortlandt Museum seems to know to what event in the existence of the dolls' house the 1774 refers. The obvious speculation is that at that point it came into the possession of a different young mistress. There are names, as well as numbers, for amateur genealogists. According to the society that sponsors the museum, "The House was made in 1744 for a member of the Homans family of Boston. It then descended to the Greenough family of Long Island—and was given Van Cortlandt by the late Mrs. Edward Townsend, née Alice Greenough."

The house itself is far more interesting than these few unadorned branches of family trees. As its photograph plainly shows, it is a distinctly Early American dolls' house. In its straight simple lines, it bears no resemblance to English dolls' houses of the same period which might very well have been imported by well-to-do colonial families. It stands on the floor in the center of the delightful collection of toys in the top-story Van Cortlandt

The baby house dated 1744
at the Van Cortlandt
Museum   Height: 50″

nursery. Visitors looking through the metal grill that guards the room, however, are likely to know (unless they are omniscient) of only half its attractions. They see two stories, one room apiece, above a drawer which provides storage space for more toys, and under a gambrel roof with a chimney in the middle.

But this is not a two-room house. The front and back of this very practical doll residence are identical. Just as there are two open rooms on the front, there are two open rooms on the back. By an additionally thoughtful device, palings, admitting extra light, instead of solid walls, separate the rooms thus back to back, in areas where wall is not used. The only windows are painted onto the sides of the house which also have drop handles for moving it about.

Unfortunately the original furnishings do not survive. But there are extremely attractive built-in fireplaces with accompanying shelves, and the general aspect of this nursery treasure with its dull red roof and dull green trim would be sufficiently impressive without so much as a chair.

It is a much simpler matter to locate American dolls' house furniture for these early years than the dolls' houses themselves. Always, of course, there is the problem, when either is found, of determining whether the toys were actually made in this country, or imported.

The Parke-Bernet Galleries in New York auctioned in 1939 the only other American dolls' house of early vintage of which we know, though additional specimens may be lurking obscurely in historical societies and museums. The Parke-Bernet house, of which a picture may be found in the gallery's October, 1939, catalogue, was of the early Federal period. This the catalogue described as "Constructed of painted wood, the hinged front opening to reveal a six-chambered interior with hall, each room furnished with an assortment of miniature furniture, various utensils, decorative objects and china and glassware." The kitchen was on the second floor while the third story topped by a slanting roof formed attic bedrooms similar to Mt. Vernon's.

The catalogue noted that the house had "descended to the present owner from her great-grandmother," but it has not been possible to learn from Parke-Bernet anything more about its history or whereabouts. A printed report stated that it had gone to a New York private collector for $100, an absurdly low figure which seemed scarcely credible. The gallery later said the sale had not gone through, which is hardly surprising, so perhaps the house is still in the anonymous hands of the great-granddaughter.

Probably the most important American dolls' house to come to public notice in recent years—and certainly one of the most appealing from every point of view—is the Brett house at the Museum of the City of New York.

The Rev. Dr. Philip Milledoler Brett spent two years, from 1838 to 1840, in the building of this engaging toy residence. The fact that he built it in the Sail Room of the family shipping firm on South Street is a picturesque detail that heightens in our imaginations a dolls' house that could hold its pitched roof high (if an anthropomorphic reference may be forgiven), even if its distinguished and picturesque pedigree were missing.

The builder, whose framed portrait hangs in the drawing-room, scorned the usual box-like arrangement of rooms to be found in most dolls' houses— and, indeed, in most houses. In this one, as its picture reveals, three rooms connect on the ground floor; attractive pairs of fan-lighted French doors lead into the drawing-room from the library on one side, and from the dining-room on the other.

*The Brett House
at the Museum
of the City
of New York
Height: 36″*

Garden of the Brett house, with the grandparents having tea

In splendid isolation, a bedroom, directly above the drawing-room, is crowned by a pitched roof with a shuttered twelve-light attic window. Inasmuch as the lovely façade of the house has been removed for viewing purposes, this bit of attic, plus gabled roof sections on the wings, are all of it that may now be seen. Mr. John Noble, Assistant Curator of the Toy Section, has sent us a charming sketch of this façade with diagrams showing how the four panels that comprise it are held in place with pins and sockets. There are multi-lighted windows with workable shutters similar to the one visible on the attic section, and the entrance doors are French ones, with fanlight above, that match the others in the drawing-room. Mr. Noble tells us that on this attractive façade, painted a rich brown that he has always known in England as "Indian red," a pattern of sizable bricks is outlined in yellow ochre. This façade eventually will be displayed with the house.

Even without the façade, it may be seen that the architect has been generous with exterior detail. Although he chose to omit a kitchen, he supplied a lovely garden, surrounded by a garden wall, with entrance gate; and there is even a latticed side porch and—a detail seldom noticed by doll architects—a three-holed outhouse.

Most of the furnishings are contemporary with the house, but there are some pieces, especially among the rare collections of miniature books and silver, which pre-date it. Among the books, most of which, somehow, are in the drawing-room rather than the library, there are a 1786 edition of Robert Burns' *Poems* (1¼″ × ¾″), and, in similar postage-stamp scale, a *Lilliputian Folio Edition of a Description of England,* and an English Dictionary. A Bible printed in 1780 may be found on the slant top of a rare (perhaps unique) four-shelf book stand in the drawing-room.

Also in the drawing-room, on the music stand, with its handsomely turned pedestal base, is a song book, a volume of British songs with distinguishable printed notes. This stands alongside a lovely harp and an inlaid mandolin.

The hallmarked silver includes a caudle cup, from London, 1775, and a French wine cooler, ca. 1800, both in the dining-room.

Much of the furniture is Biedermeier, of the early, classical genre, to be found in many dolls' houses of the period, both here and abroad, but with numerous rare additions such as a late eighteenth century French wood-box and a chess table. Important in a house with which four generations of the Brett family played, are two objects hanging on its walls. One, to be found in the dining-room, is the framed Brett coat of arms. The other, a tinted engraving hanging over the mantelpiece in the library, is an early nineteenth century view of Rutgers College, of which the Rev. Philip Milledoler Brett, grandfather of the builder of the dolls' house, was president in the long ago years from 1825 to 1840.

Another notable house, virtually of the same period as the Brett house, but unlike it, is a glass-fronted cabinet with little exterior detail. This huge (7' 10") house, built about 1836, and complete with its original period furnishings, is displayed by the Chester County Historical Society in West Chester, Pennsylvania.

Even in an unarchitectural dolls' house such as this one, there is a broad hint—a period reflection—of era. As Edward F. LaFond, Jr., the Society's Curator, has pointed out, "The roof line resembles the Greek Revival Temples in vogue at that time." Three classical columns which embellish the front also reflect this motif.

Early books and silver are among the treasures in the Brett house. A 1786 edition of Robert Burns' Poems *no larger than a postage stamp, and a Monteith bowl from London, 1775–6 (John Lautier), are among them.*

Although the Society does not know for whom the house was made, they do know that it was the work of a Philadelphia cabinetmaker and upholsterer named Voegler. It is not surprising, in view of his calling, that most of his work is inside the four large rooms where the lovely furnishings, in a remarkable state of preservation, are what one would expect of a master craftsman of similar pieces in full size. Most of the late Empire furniture is mahogany (veneered on pine and poplar). There are carpets of needlepoint and chair seats of petit point. There is a tall-case clock, in the drawing-room, and there is a magnificently carved poster bed. There are lovely taffeta draperies beneath gilt cornices, and, in the dining-room, hand-painted scenic wallpaper (classical ruins).

The painted kitchen furniture is simple. There is a drop-leaf table with nicely turned legs and, as in the other rooms, an iron fireplace stove. Throughout the house there are such embellishments as oil paintings and silver napkin rings. Lest anyone get the notion, however, that this house is a model and not a dolls' house, it should be mentioned that there are dolls. There are three—two with china heads (hair-dos ca. 1835–50, says Mr. LaFond), and one a jointed wooden. The latter reposes, appropriately and comfortably, on an Empire sofa in the drawing-room of this magnificent house which, to judge by its condition, has never been played with even, alas, for a moment.

The bedroom of the 1836 house at the Chester County Historical Society

A handsome, early 19th century cupboard house was acquired some years ago by Mrs. Milton K. Brandt of Lewistown, Pennsylvania, from an antique dealer who carefully documented its colorful history: "This doll house was purchased by us from the last remaining member of an old Pennsylvania family . . . whose great-grandfather bought it second-hand in 1845, from a very wealthy man in Warren County (Penna.). In 1870, the doll house was brought down the Allegheny River on a raft, to Rochester, Penna., where it remained until recently, when purchased by us. Most of the furniture and furnishings are the original ones, but a few Victorian replacements had to be made after the voyage down the river, as a few things were lost overboard."

The writer saw this house not long after Mrs. Brandt acquired it, and no picture does it justice. Housed in a lovely crotch-mahogany Empire style cabinet (39 inches high) are four rooms with, curiously enough, beautifully curtained windows in the two rooms above, but no windows whatever in the two below. Handsome brass cornices crown the curtains which, in the parlor, are supplemented by tasselled crimson valances. All curtains and floor coverings are original, and these and the lovely furnishings are of the early dark-wood pieces in Empire style.

Among these, a pier mirror (there is also a built-in example between the parlor windows) and a sleigh bed are notable. Sleigh beds, according to the Bogers,* were "popular in America for a few years after 1820," and allowing for the lag of a few years in which a toy copy might be made, this

* *The Dictionary of Antiques and the Decorative Arts* by Louise Ade Boger and H. Batterson Boger, Scribners, 1957.

bed may help to date a house "secondhand in 1845," and dating perhaps fifteen years earlier. The date of the bed's origin may be forever shrouded, but not by the bed linens: these are delicately and specifically embroidered: "Coral, 1852."

One of the most remarkable of American dolls' houses belongs to Mrs. William Redd Mahoney of Oak Park, Illinois, whose excellent collection is mentioned in Chapter 15.

A majestic mansion, seven feet tall, with four stories, an attic, and innumerable balconied windows, this came from a Plymouth, Massachusetts, antiques dealer accompanied by a booklet with these words on its cover: "Book of the Baby House built by Wm. S. Watkins, about 1845, for his Grandchildren." In mid-nineteenth century couplets, as complete and careful as the fine cabinetmaking in the house itself, the architect and poet has described the rooms, with a substantial stanza for each and every one, kitchen, pantry, dining-room, parlor, nursery, bedroom, withdrawing room, and—of all things—the Hall of Science, which turns out to be the library.

It is obvious that the builder, who, except for his name, is a mystery man, one whose identity Mrs. Mahoney longs to discover, was also one of considerable learning. The verses are filled with classical allusions and lofty sentiments. Mr. Watkins' couplets are nearly as well constructed as his house, and we long, with Mrs. Mahoney, to discover where he built it. (She knows for whom—his granddaughter, Camilla Brown.)*

Curiously, the writer was making plans to go and examine this house (with a view to its purchase) when it was sold in 1960. A bit later, she received a letter from Mrs. Mahoney telling of a choice dolls' house she had purchased—this one, of course. Mrs. Mahoney's description in that letter does Mr. Watkins' baby house full justice:

"The house is in five sections, which fit together with shallow drawers between the floors. Four windows on each floor in front, and one at each side—a total of 24 windows and 12 drawers. An attic room at each side has windows in its double doors, and there is a secret compartment which can only be reached from a trapdoor in the back . . . very difficult indeed, as it stands against the wall and weighs about 350 pounds! . . . The finish is grained walnut over walnut—a very fine job indeed and I have trouble convincing people that it *is* grained! I found, of course, that that was the thing to do at that period—several historic houses have doors so finished. It is all the original paint, inside and out, and I am sure it is all the original glass."

The finish is a lovely color, dark and rich. There were about 75 pieces of furniture with the house when Mrs. Mahoney bought it, though most of it was later in period than Mr. Watkins' marvelous mansion.

---

* Handwritten on the printed booklet are also the following names which we include in the hope that someone with the key to the mystery will come across them: ". . . (for his grandchildren) Ann Amelia Yard (Hill) & Camilla Brown (di Pollone). The existing house belongs to Katherine Brown di Pollone (Pease). Mrs. Hill's house was given away also one made for . . ." (other names not clear). Obviously, the gifted and energetic architect made three such houses!

Another American house of unusual interest in Mrs. Mahoney's collection came with its original furnishings and again enough of its history to tantalize. A two-story house, with four rooms, two up and two down, on either side of a stair-hall, this one, reportedly from the Hanna family of Fort Wayne, Indiana, is believed to date from the 1860's. Although the house has an open front, and little architectural detail (there is a dormer in the roof, and amusing scroll-cut brackets on the beams fronting the walls), the attractive furnishings, in excellent condition, and the colors, carefully chosen, give the house an appeal that is best seen to be appreciated.*

Many other fine Victorian dolls' houses whose histories are known, or are partially known, are to be found in private collections.

A magnificent specimen in the possession of Miss Lenore Thomas of Mesa, Arizona, came to her with its original dolls and furnishings in virtually mint condition—and with every detail of its history.

The house, which was begun in 1870, and completed in 1880, was built for Mrs. Bernadine Zumbusch Terry of Hackensack, New Jersey, by her father. The furniture was made by her step-grandfather, and upholstery, curtains, draperies, carpets, doll clothes, and bed and table linens were the work of her aunt.

It was even possible for Miss Thomas to know where the purchased pieces had come from—"Schwarz' Toy House" (to no one's surprise)—and which they were: mostly accessories—such things as books, dishes, cutlery, lamps, jardinières, pictures, dolls, and a Christmas tree.

The large six-foot house is of a handsome glass-fronted cabinet style with a pitched roof (covered by 1,200 shingles) and side windows, including well-designed bays. The roof and windows are its only concessions to architecture. The wood of the cabinet is rich and beautiful and there is an impression of solidity that is echoed by the handsomely made furniture in the rooms. Inside, there is also solidity—and authenticity. One has the feeling that if Hunca Munca had somehow got in, she'd have gazed in awe for a moment or two, and then made a rather mousey exit.

* A curious footnote to the history of this house was revealed a few years ago which demonstrates how small the dolls' house world literally is (however full of houses it may be). Again it involves a personal note (Mrs. Mahoney and the author seem always to be related to the same houses—indeed Mrs. Mahoney's purchase of this one resulted from the purchase of another to which we referred her).

When Mrs. Mahoney first sent a snapshot of the Hanna house, there was nothing in it that jogged a memory or rang a bell. Later on, however, we were looking through some old clippings and came across one about a Victorian dolls' house, a feature story written years ago when the author was a cub reporter on a Washington paper and knew nothing of dolls' houses. We had not even remembered writing such a thing. There was one picture with the story—of one room in the dolls' house. Somehow it looked familiar, and, as things turned out, it was. Examination showed it to be one room in Mrs. Mahoney's Hanna house. Many years before, the dolls' house had been on view in a Washington department store in some sort of joint promotion with a concurrent film showing of "The Magnificent Ambersons." A print of the very photograph in the story was in Mrs. Mahoney's possession, one of a set she was given when she bought the house. Unfortunately, this episode cast no light on the earlier history of the house, but it does seem a surprising and amusing coincidence.

Author's mid-nineteenth century
South Jersey house   Height: 44"

The average American Victorian dolls' house is not always of architectural interest. Often it is a big box-like arrangement, usually run up by the neighborhood carpenter in time for Christmas, and without the superb cabinetwork of the Dutch cupboards. Sometimes, like the Dutch specimens, it is literally a cabinet without so much as a window; more often it is a rectangular building with windows and doors, but a big box nevertheless. Occasionally, however, one encounters a Victorian dolls' house whose exterior tells as much about its fancy era as the gingerbread clutter inside.

In a New Jersey barn, part of a rural antique shop, the author was fortunate enough to locate a most elaborate specimen (see illustration). This surprising edifice had been in the barn eight years, the last support of rickety chairs and several layers of other miscellaneous unsold antiques, a great credit to its strength. It was cobwebbed and dirty, with a discouraging number of broken windows, and was known to its new owners only as "the haunted house" till its restoration.

It is believed to be the model of a South Jersey house of about 1850.* That is all that it has been possible to learn of its past. The rest of its story could only be surmised by small clues, gathered like footprints, from its deserted premises. Although scaled an inch to the foot, it is of impressive proportions, with a base approximately thirty by forty inches, and a height of four feet. Its photograph speaks best for its Victorian personality, but specifically:

The exterior is of a sandpaper texture probably intended to represent stone, its dull, mellow red trimmed with dull, mellow green. It has an

* This house is featured in *The Doll House Mystery* by Flora Gill Jacobs, Coward-McCann, Inc., 1958.

imposing number of glass windows, of all descriptions: bay windows on the ground floor, stained-glass windows at the doors, casement windows which swing out on little hinges in the bedrooms, dormer windows in the attic. Almost all the windows have pediments.

The convex mansard roof (a rare mansard—the average full-size example seems to be either concave or straight) is painted in a subtle checkerboard of gray and black and dull rose with blue and crimson medallions at the corners, and might have amused François Mansart, the seventeenth century French architect who invented it. (A law was passed in Paris establishing all cornice lines at a certain height, which Mansart got around by adding a story in the roof above the cornice line.) An elaborate frieze runs beneath the dolls' house roof, under the cornice, in a motif reiterated at windows and doors.

The interior has ten little hand-carved doors (there are so many doors and windows that there is scarcely wall space for furniture) similar in style to the double pair at the front. The walls are painted in plain colors rather than elaborately papered, possibly to avoid detracting from the designs daintily painted on the ceilings. The ceilings and walls offer the most clues to the past life of the house. Small girls for whom the ceiling designs were perhaps not quite fancy enough must have pasted the valentine stickers (now difficult to remove) at what they deemed appropriate spots. They must also be held responsible for flame smudges on ceilings and walls, indicating, along with empty hooks, where candle-burning chandeliers must have hung.

The house has eight rooms, four large and four small, exclusive of the garret formed by the mansard. The large rooms, fifteen by twenty-four inches, give by their inch-to-foot dimensions the feeling of the large, high-

*Rear view, interior,
of the South Jersey house
Height (of the two stories
under the mansard): 27″*

Drawing room of the South Jersey house, with ormolu trim on the furniture Height: 14¾″

ceilinged chambers of their day. Two of the small rooms, which bisect the big ones, form the upper and lower hall, containing staircase with landing. Access to these rooms is through the back which opens in three windowed sections. The restoration of the house by the late R. K. Helphenstine, Jr., of Chevy Chase, Maryland, was a large-scale project, beautifully accomplished. A three-inch "stone" foundation, of which only one side remained, had to be replaced, and an outside staircase to bridge this foundation to the entrance was missing altogether, and had to be provided, or the dolls would have been obliged to jump three inches (three feet to them, after all) to enter or exit. This staircase, Mr. Helphenstine's chef d'oeuvre, is surmounted by a pair of French toy street lamps, pewter bases supporting ruby isinglass lanterns with a wick to be really lit (if the owner would be given permission by her family), and a little wheel on each by which the flame may be raised or lowered. These are French (embossed on the pewter is "Déposé JS. Paris") and are believed to date from the mid-nineteenth century.

But New Jersey hasn't the only mid-century town-house architecture to have been immortalized by the dolls' house. The Museum of the City of New York has a splendid brownstone, a modified reproduction of Peter Goelet's house at 890 Broadway, built in 1845 for the three little nieces who came to live with him and his sister. It lacks the flowering hawthorn trees, the cow grazing on the lawn, the pheasants and peacocks near by, and the tall iron fence that guarded these, but it has many other features of the original house. It has the high stoop and the areaway, and, always welcome in a dolls' house, an address—890 is upon the stained glass above the door.* However, these details are minor compared to the brass rails adorning the front steps and the areaway, agleam from what must be a brisk daily polishing.

The interior is of less interest since none of the original furniture has survived the activities of the vast number of little girls who played with it, but the daughter of one of them has undertaken to refurnish the house as she remembers 890 to have been. The winding staircase, which in the original house was circular, has a decidedly period balustrade—of bonnet pins. The pier glass between the parlor windows, a mid-century decorating notion, reflects an alabaster Venus, an equally inevitable accessory. Since the double parlors of 890 "were hung with great crystal chandeliers of prisms and wax candles," a similar specimen is in the dolls' house, this one a copy of one in the Trianon.

On the sitting-room walls are two pictures of an order that all dolls' houses should have, one, a photograph (from a daguerreotype) of the original owners, Almy,† Jean, and Elbridge Gerry, and one of the original house, nostalgically, "taken from a woodcut given to the family by Miss Dean of the famous establishment very near to 890 Broadway which supplied ice cream, jellies, and cakes for all the family parties and weddings."

Another mid-nineteenth century New York town house came to the author's collection with some of its original Biedermeier furniture, and the tradition that it had been made for a member of New York's Tiffany family. Although it has not been possible to verify this history, its architecture, clearly, is everything one would expect. Its "vaguely Italian detail" is a by-product of what Mr. John Maass‡ calls the "Italianate interlude." It has the typical low-ceilinged English basement on the lowest of its three floors, contrasting with the high ceilings of the "company rooms" above. A bracketed cornice is all it should be, and so are the eight tall windows that light the façade. Double windows on the sides make the window total impressive and the curtain problem formidable!

(An imposing town house, also in the author's collection, which has an almost astonishing resemblance to "Tiffany House," is, curiously enough, from Somerville, Massachusetts, a copy of an existing house. In addition to an identical arrangement of rooms, both houses have double chimneys, a bracketed cornice under the eaves, and a similar arrangement of windows. It is almost as though a cousin in Massachusetts had sent a sketch to a cousin in New York! Even the buff paint with brown trim is nearly the same.)

Mrs. Sumner Parker has a typical Baltimore (doll) town house complete with little white steps. Mrs. Parker, who, with her husband, the late architect, made of their estate, "The Cloisters" in Green Spring Valley,

The big mid-19th century house from Somerville, Mass., bears a surprising resemblance to the Tiffany house from New York   Height: 5'

* A smallish, slender three-story house from Beverly, Massachusetts, in the author's collection, has an address, "46 Hunt," painted on its door.
† Mrs. Frederic Gallatin, whose descendants gave the house to the museum.
‡ *The Gingerbread Age.* Rinehart & Co., New York, 1957.

110

Maryland, one of the most diverting private museums in the country, has an attractive collection of dolls' houses.

Among them are a cupboard dolls' house (played with by five generations of Mrs. Parker's family), an American farmhouse of about 1850, a German eighteenth century cottage of a Gothic turn, a mid-Victorian country house with turrets and spires, a Charleston mansion, circa 1860, with porticoed columns, and the Baltimore town house, somehow the most interesting of all.

There are iron balconies under the windows. The latter, being four-paned, have the long, piercing look of most Victorian windows. There is a dark, handsomely turned balustrade on the inside staircase. There is even the checkerboard marble pavement in front of the house which the family servant was obliged to scrub along with the white marble steps.

A celebrated Civil War dolls' house was built for a Fair held in 1864 to raise funds for the relief of sick and wounded soldiers who fought in the war. There is no question about which side the builders and exhibitors were on: a silver name plate on the front door reads: "U. S. Grant." A patriotic suggestion of a more general nature is emblazoned on the glass light above the double doors: "1776."

Although they were made by Philadelphia craftsmen, and exhibited at the Great Central Fair for the U. S. Sanitary Commission held in Philadelphia, the house and its elaborate furnishings are now in a neighboring state,

The Tiffany House,
a mid-nineteenth century
New York brownstone
said to have been made for
a member of the Tiffany
family   Height: 4½′

111

The double drawing-room from the Somerville (Mass.) house with iron furniture patented in 1867   Height: 14¾"

the property of the Delaware Historical Society in Wilmington. The substantial building, five and a half feet tall, contains three stories, and nine rooms, one on each side of a center hall, in front, plus—what is more unusual—an additional room on each floor at the back.

Certainly the most extraordinary room in the house is the art gallery. A copy of a list of the paintings it contains, taken from *Our Daily Fare,* Philadelphia, June 13, 1864, has been sent us by Mr. Dale Fields, Executive Director of the Society, and it is an intriguing document. A number of Philadephia artists are represented, but there is also a treasure, "Ruins of a Temple of the Sun," by the Neapolitan seventeenth century master, Salvator Rosa, among the twenty-five paintings listed. Landscapes dominate the list, but one finds also such contrasting subjects as "Rubens, after the original by himself in the Uffizi Gallery, Florence" (by one Mardelli) and—

The Civil War house at the Delaware Historical Society, Wilmington

112

"Puss in Boots." For the dolls' greater comfort in viewing (and the house is fully inhabited), there is, in the center of the room, one of those large circular ottomans (sometimes called a *causeuse**) that seems the ultimate in Victoriana. This is the only one we have come across in a dolls' house.

At the time of its exhibition at the Fair, the house, given by a Miss Biddle (whose name lends further Philadelphia flavor to the Delaware treasure), was valued at $1,000. Reportedly, each of the three marble fireplaces gave an expert marble cutter three days of employment and, as one would expect in such an imposing residence, there were magnificent curtains, draperies, and carpets. Much of this glory has become tattered, however, and the house, in the process of restoration, has been (in 1965) temporarily withdrawn from display.

Contrary to prior reports, it is a house that has been played with. At the close of the Fair, there was evidently an auction or lottery, and Colonel Henry S. McComb of Wilmington became the owner. The Colonel had a seven-year-old daughter, Nellie, and it is not known whether it was Nellie or some of her descendants who are responsible for the present need for refurbishing. Since the draperies appear excellently preserved in what must be a relatively recent photograph, perhaps we must look not to Nellie, but to time, that arch-enemy of the fragile, for the blame.

Mr. and Mrs. Walter Kueffner of St. Paul, Minnesota, are the owners of a more modest Civil War dolls' house, built about 1860 for the two daughters of Mr. Kueffner's uncle, a general in that war. The General also practiced law in Belleville, Illinois, and the house, built by a client, is believed to be a replica of the General's house in Belleville.

In 1894, when the General died, the dolls' house was shipped up the Mississippi River to St. Paul, where a younger brother's five daughters played with it. The daughters of a nephew, Mr. William Kueffner, then had a turn, and they turned it over to the children of its present owners. With those children grown, it is now reserved for the Kueffner grandchildren—to look at only.

Pictures show it to be a clapboard cottage of nostalgic appeal. There is a side porch "elaborately decorated with tiny spindles and scalloped scrolls," as Mrs. Kueffner has described it, with "each little shingle of the roof . . . carved by hand." There are no bedrooms: "The interior of the house consists of a parlor and sitting room in the front, and a kitchen at the rear. Upstairs is an attic with unfinished rafters. Originally (the house) had a spindle stairway and curved bay windows with shingled roof off the kitchen."

---

* In *Decorative Arts of Victoria's Era* (Scribners, 1950), Frances Lichten calls this "an ottoman or 'causeuse'." In *The Dictionary of Antiques and the Decorative Arts,* (Scribners, 1957), neither of the definitions given of these two words applies to such a piece. *The White House* (White House Historical Association, 1962), refers to the White House example as "a large circular ottoman," which phrase we borrow.

After so many small girls had finished with the house, it needed restoration, and Mrs. Kueffner said the inspiration for refurnishing was supplied "by a touching poem which the General's wife wrote when he went away to war."

"We decided to put the General and his family back in the doll house to illustrate the poem . . . Only furnishings of the period were to be used, making it necessary to do some research work. We made several trips to the library and had many consultations with a friend, Miss Elsa Mannheimer,* who is a genius at miniature furnishings . . ."

That traditional fixture, the American front porch, was given as much thought as any room with ". . . the baby asleep in her elegant carriage with parasol above it," an American flag, a basket of vegetables on the steps, with a hand trowel beside it, a Boston rocker, "the General, field hat in hand, in blue uniform of the North . . . bidding his young wife goodbye." But that isn't quite all of the General: the attic "has discarded furniture and china, spinning wheel and yarn, mouse browsing along mop board behind old cat's back, and a painted bride's trunk of very early days. The General's civilian clothes hang suspended from pegs on the wall. Toys and tools are scattered about." It doesn't seem in the least surprising that this thoughtfully refurnished doll cottage won a Minnesota State Fair first prize one year for early American antiques.

It is unusual to find a Victorian dolls' house architect immortalizing in miniature any era other than his own. But Leonidas Vergil Badger in 1858 had a substantial reason for wanting to reproduce a Portsmouth, New Hampshire, house built in 1690. The 1690 house was the home of his ancestors. He built it in 1858 for his children "to preserve in miniature the original family homestead." He made the furniture and even the braided rugs. According to Elaine W. Rogers, who wrote about the house: "A teak-wood chair in the lower parlor is a reproduction of one brought to the Badgers in 1700 by a seafaring captain. Another is a careful copy of a plain slatbacked chair once used by John Alden; still another is a replica of a chair that belonged to Governor Carver."

However, there are inevitable Victorian touches. There is a Steinway upright in the parlor with a painted design on the front board above the keys, and according to Miss Rogers, the tables are set in the middle of the rooms in Victorian fashion. There is also an orange tree in a wooden tub which sounds like a frivolous touch for a pioneer New England family, even if imported by a seafaring relative.

One of the most satisfying dolls' houses to be rescued from obscurity in recent years is the one presented to ten-year-old Fanny Hayes while her father, Rutherford B., was president of the United States. Any White House dolls' house would, of course, be of interest, but the handsome Hayes dolls'

---

* Miss Mannheimer, who turns up, seemingly, whenever a Minnesota dolls' house appears, may also be discovered in Chapters 8 and 15.

house, the ultimate in Victorian splendor, would be outstanding even if its important and fully-documented history had been lost (as, alas, so many dolls' house histories are).

It was in February 1878, when President and Mrs. Hayes attended the Methodist Fair in Baltimore, Maryland, that the dolls' house, which had been especially made by a Baltimore carpenter, was presented to Mrs. Hayes for their daughter.

Happily, this marvelous three-story mansion, with its mansard roof, window balconies, and towering center turret, has been brought back to its former splendor by Mrs. Webb C. Hayes of Chevy Chase, Maryland, whose husband is a great-grandson of the nineteenth president. The furniture had been lost, but Mrs. Hayes spent two years collecting, with fidelity to period and scale, antique dolls' house furnishings.

When the dolls' house was restored in 1959–60, the maker's name and address was found inscribed inside the steeple: "Made by George C. Brown, Baltimore, Md.," and the date was added, "February 13, 1878." According to Mr. Watt Marchman, Director of the Rutherford B. Hayes Library in Fremont, Ohio, where the dolls' house, which was shown for a while at the Smithsonian, is on permanent display, a Baltimore directory for 1878 shows that George C. Brown was a carpenter and builder, living at 186 Saratoga Street.

The house, which is open at the back, has bays at three sides, and four chimneys. Its center stair halls are almost spacious enough to qualify as rooms, and they, like the rest of the house, are thoroughly furnished.

It is also through the courtesy of Mr. Marchman that we are able to quote from the account of Miss Grundy (Austine Snead), a lady correspond-

The dolls' house played with, in the White House, by the children of Rutherford B. Hayes. It was presented to Fanny Hayes while her father was president Height: 75" (including steeple)

The dolls' house played with by Mrs. Alice Roosevelt Longworth when she was a small girl Height: 35"

ent in Washington during the Hayes Administration, who was permitted by President and Mrs. Hayes to tour the living quarters in the White House in March, 1878. She wrote an article entitled "How Presidents Live— Description of the White House at Washington." In her article, she said: "Most agreeable reminders of the presence of children are the two large 'baby houses' standing in the hall, in which the President's only daughter, little Fannie, between 10 and 11 years of age, and the youngest child, Scott, some three or four years younger, take great delight . . ."

According to Mr. Marchman, the second dolls' house was not preserved. It was made for the Hayes children in Washington for $16, and is remembered by one of President Hayes' grandsons, Walter S. Hayes, of Perrysburg, Ohio, as more of a frame house for rooms of doll furniture.

The only other White House dolls' house that appears to be known seems to have vanished without a trace. The loss is great because the house, made for the Cleveland children during their father's administration, was a miniature copy of the White House itself!* Grover Cleveland's daughter, Mrs. Marion Cleveland Amen of New York, remembers the house and thinks it may have been given to a cousin. Perhaps one day it will reappear.

Recently, an observant friend of the writer's, who happened to notice a Victorian dolls' house in the Washington sitting-room of Mrs. Alice Roosevelt Longworth, thereby discovered another dolls' house that was played with by a White House daughter—but before she and her father lived in the White House.

When President Theodore Roosevelt and his family moved into the Executive Mansion in 1901, his daughter Alice was a girl of seventeen who had left her dolls' house behind in the family residence at Oyster Bay and, of course, had not played with it for years before that. Mrs. Longworth believes that she may have been given the house in 1890 or '91, when she was six or

* From *They Lived in the White House*, by Frances Cavanah. Macrae Smith, 1962.

116

seven; she has no recollection of its arrival. If her interest in it as a child was moderate, however, she has made up for her lack of enthusiasm within the past few years.

Her daughter Paulina, who had been given colonial-type houses with plumbing and electricity, had little to do with Mrs. Longworth's dolls' house, but other children in her family had done quite a thorough job of destroying the furniture. Some years ago Mrs. Longworth's sister-in-law and friend, the late Mrs. Theodore Roosevelt, Jr., meticulously restored the house, using Chinese tea papers among others and, as Mrs. Longworth fondly remembers, "exquisite taste."

"And then, about two years ago," said Mrs. Longworth, a lady who defies all laws of age (and gravity—she gaily relates a tale of falling down a flight of stairs not long ago, at age eighty, with not even a bruise to show for her adventure), "I just went wild . . ." She obviously had a marvelous time, refurnishing the house with the finest of reproductions, mostly of eighteenth century pieces, from the New York studio of Eric Pearson.

Mr. Pearson's handsome furniture has been fitted into a graceful commercially made house of foreign origin. As its picture shows, it is a mansard-roofed structure with French windows and considerable charm. Its front swings open in two sections to reveal the two lower floors, and the top of the mansard lifts off to give access to the attic. The children who did away with the furnishings were kind to the house itself—its pale peach façade trimmed with soft green is mellow and lovely. Metal knockers glint intact at the double doors, and even the original scalloped white curtains show above their tie-backs through the windows—all twelve pairs.

It is interesting that a variation of this house may be seen in F.A.O. Schwarz' 1913 Christmas catalogue. The pretty French windows of two decades earlier have been transposed into late Victorian ones with drooping lintels, and the turned balusters on the window balcony have been replaced by a simpler fret-worked rail, but the fine mansard roof has been kept intact, and even in toto!

It is not surprising that Miss Elsa Mannheimer of St. Paul, Minnesota, whose attractive collection of houses and rooms is discussed in Chapter 15, and who combines her own meticulous craftsmanship with antiques, has been asked by the Minnesota Historical Society to restore a historic Minnesota dolls' house.

The house was ordered by Governor Alexander Ramsey (Minnesota's first territorial governor) in 1887 as a Christmas present for his younger granddaughter, Miss Laura Furness. "It is an approximate replica," says Miss Mannheimer, "of the Governor Ramsey Mansion," and that is not surprising inasmuch as it was built by Mathew Taylor, the master carpenter of the mansion itself. The original bill—for $25—is shown with the house.

Although the writer had seen pictures of the dolls' house unrestored in the *Gopher Historian* (Fall, 1958), thoughtfully sent by a friend, Miss Mannheimer's own comparison of the full-sized mansion with the small one is worth quoting: "The mansion," she writes, "is of gray limestone and has several porches, but the doll house is innocent of both. However, the carpenter undoubtedly meant to suggest his larger effort, as the doll house is painted stone gray (though, of course, made of wood), and has the roof, dormer windows and general look of the house façade. No effort is made to reproduce the interior, which consists of four rooms, and two halls connected by a rather elaborate stairway."

The house was restored once before, in 1949, for a territorial centennial celebration which took place that year. It was evidently at that time that it was re-papered and therefore, says Miss Mannheimer, "It wouldn't hurt to do it again." However, she adds, "The outside (not as shabby as you might imagine) remains untouched, and only such furnishings have been added as were necessary to replace what had been lost or otherwise destroyed."

If one were obliged to confer an award for the dolls' house that seemed to represent the ultimate in Victoriana, one unquestionably would be found, pacing back and forth, somewhere between Milwaukee, Wisconsin, and Wenham, Massachusetts. The two houses shown nearby clearly illustrate the dilemma: for fanciful elaboration and meticulous gingerbread, neither the vertical doll residence at the Milwaukee Museum nor the horizontal example at the Wenham Historical Association can prevail over the other.

To consider them in order of date, the glorious specimen at Wenham was built in 1884 by Benjamin H. Chamberlain, a Salem, Massachusetts, silversmith, as a Christmas present for his two daughters, Mamie and Millie. Their names are inscribed on the front door on, appropriately enough, a silver name plate. There is no point to having a silversmith father if he is not going to make a silver tea service for one's dolls' house, and this one did.

The house at Wenham, made by a Salem, Massachusetts, silversmith for his daughters in 1884 Height: 38″, including cupola

(Since other silversmiths have undoubtedly had daughters, we wonder how many of the lovely silver miniatures collected by adults were actually initiated for children?) Mr. Chamberlain also made a silver water pitcher for the dolls' house, fashioning it from a silver thimble and a letter seal which he used for the base.

However, as even the most cursory glance at his dolls' house will show, his talents ranged well beyond silversmithing. He not only made the eight-room house, which is shown without most of its removable façades (for front, front porch, kitchen porch, and cupola), but he also made and decorated most of the furniture.

The house is inhabited by a family of dolls who wear their original dresses, all in the styles of the 'eighties.

A date—in this case, 1893—in stained glass over the front door—is a peculiarly specific and satisfying clue to the history of a dolls' house, even when it comes as well documented as the one at the Milwaukee Museum.

When Mrs. Joseph E. Uihlein, Sr., was seven years old, she found the house "under her Christmas tree" says a *Milwaukee Journal* reporter in a burst of enthusiasm. The house was a present from her parents, Mr. and Mrs. Fred Vogel. "It is especially delightful," a Milwaukee collector wrote the author at the time the house was first displayed, "as it represents several generations—even to a set of twins (at various ages) being added when they joined the family tree."

Unlike the house at Wenham, this one has no windowed façade to gild an already delectable piece of gingerbread; a set of stairs which hooked into the front were missing, we are told, when the house was given to the museum. All of the embellishments are heightened by the colors with which the fanciful frame is painted—a warm coral against the palest possible olive*— and perhaps the most diverting of these are the heads that surmount the exterior corners of the four principal rooms. Suspecting a Muse, we inquired, and received an interesting reply from Mr. John W. Luedtke, Curator of Fine Arts at the museum: "The woman's head generally represented a Muse and was very common in the decoration of Milwaukee architecture at the time the house was built. One of the houses in which this rested for many years had a large pottery head of the same type built into a side wall."

Mr. Luedtke also informed us that the majority of the furnishings and dolls are original, though a few of the furnishings are replacements from "the same time, period, and sets" (of furniture). It is of particular interest in this connection that although "the dolls' house remained in fairly continual use up to the 1930's" and "there are additional sets of furnishings that reflect the changes in taste . . . oddly enough the newer pieces are generally more spotty than the original ones."

This bit of intelligence tends to support what one might suspect: that

* The colors may be seen in the handsome photograph of the house in the December, 1963, issue of *Country Beautiful*.

The Uihlein dolls' house at the Milwaukee Museum, with its 1893 date in stained glass over the door   Height: 5' 2"
MILWAUKEE PUBLIC MUSEUM

later generations of children often may have by-passed and set aside furnishings that were out of date and with which they didn't identify in favor of later ones contemporary with themselves. Mercifully for dolls' house history, the children who played with the marvelous Milwaukee house were gentle with what they rejected.

Since we never have seen another dolls' house in this astonishing and delightful style, we were especially pleased to learn from Mr. Luedtke that at least one other exists. Made obviously by the same unknown cabinet-maker, this one may be seen at the Milwaukee County Historical Museum.

It is curious and interesting to find a dolls' house built about 1890, at the height of the gingerbread era, in purest Greek Revival style—or, to put it in the term more customarily used, to find a "Georgian Colonial."*

The Western Reserve Historical Society in Cleveland is the owner of this sedate dolls' house. Known as "The Bingham Doll House," it was built for two sisters, who are now Mrs. Dudley S. Blossom and the Honorable Frances P. Bolton, Congresswoman from Ohio.

Four classical pillars support the pure Greek pediment. There is a

---

* But here again, architectural history is reflected: "A Colonial revival, which McKim, Mead and White introduced," writes Russell Lynes, in *The Tastemakers,* "was beginning to spot the country-side as early as the eighties with columned houses with Palladian details in the windows and cornices." (The author lives in just such a house—by Mr. McKim.)

120

double-doored entrance, shuttered windows, and a carriage entrance (but no porte-cochère* as an 1890 reminder).

After the house was found, some years ago, in the dark corner of a cellar, the sisters decided it should be restored. It was taken in hand by an interior designer who has decorated the interior with the perfection of model rooms, in the manner of Mrs. Thorne and Mrs. Hammons, in the style of the architecture rather than in the period in which it was made. There are fine reproductions of Chippendale chairs, Gilbert Stuart paintings, and Louis XVI love seats. It is all very elegant, and one wonders a bit wistfully how it was furnished originally.

Since other American dolls' houses fall mostly within the mid or late Victorian radius, it appears more suitable to consider them museum by museum rather than in any chronological order. The delightful Museum of the City of New York, with one of the most attractive toy collections in the United States, is something of a shrine for dolls' house researchers. We have mentioned the Museum's Brett and brownstone, and its Stettheimer dolls' house is considered in its own chapter, but the collection also includes several other large dolls' houses, a few attractive dolls' rooms, and shelves of miscellaneous dolls' house furniture.

Among the Victorian dolls' houses, a fetching example is in what one is tempted to describe as mint condition, so perfectly kept are its lavish appointments. "Altadena," the name of the little girl to whom the dolls' house belonged, and "1895," the year in which it was presented to her, are emblazoned in paint, and in a manner decidedly of the period, upon the house-front. These emblems are at a discreet distance from the splendid double doors which have white porcelain knobs and a lock and key that work. The form of the house itself is unusual. A two-room wing appears to have been added later to the main portion, the latter consisting of four conventionally shaped apartments surmounted, under a fancy roof with gables and a tall chimney, by two attic rooms.

Despite these architectural attractions, the furnishings are the most arresting part of Altadena's dolls' house. Some of them, it is true, are of another vintage. The daughter of the little owner, Mrs. Gardner Whitman, who presented the house to the Museum, furnished several rooms very handsomely in eighteenth century reproductions and with a miniature silver service, pearl-handled flatware and other embellishments of great elegance. But other rooms are richly supplied with the original furniture and bric-a-brac, all of it looking as though it had just come from the shop. Actually, F.A.O. Schwarz labels are still affixed to many of the pieces.

Among such refinements as brass crisscross frames and cloth folding screen (stretched on metal frame) in the bedroom, an especially delectable item is in the richly-furnished parlor—a glass epergne on the parlor table,

---

* Webster says this term is used erroneously in the U. S. to define "a carriage porch". We so mis-use it here.

fitted with delicate white flowers above and highly realistic fruit below. A look of yesterday-just-a-moment-ago is lent by a straw hat pegged to a wooden hat tree in the bedroom; impeccable knitting (knit imperceptible one —purl invisible two) on ivory knitting needles the size of the straight pins which usually must serve the same miniature purpose nowadays.

This and most of the Museum's dolls' houses are the customary inch to the foot. But one of its houses is a mammoth building with its furnishings scaled to correspondingly jumbo dimensions. Child play theorists who complain that dolls' houses and their contents are too small to accommodate a girl's favorite dolls could have no quarrel with this one. The three floors and eight rooms are crowded with pieces that the most over-grown doll could use. There are some discrepancies, it is true; the square piano in the parlor could swallow up the nearby fireplace three times without noticing it, and the four-poster bed with its patchwork quilt could practically serve as a moving van for some of the other pieces, but such disparities express true dolls' house personality. This house, circa 1860, has flowered Brussels carpets and gilded candelabra, but gives very little thought to windows and doors.

Another house, comparably enormous, but with furniture more diminutively scaled, is considerably more architectural. This is not surprising, since a Mr. James Van Orden (of Islip, Long Island), a builder and contractor, was responsible for it. Mrs. Bayard James, whose mother's full-size house was built by the same contractor, presented the dolls' house to the Museum. It has a little balcony supported by two columns at the front entrance, and a neat widow's walk on the pitched roof. The Museum at one point had the house placed against windows, and the rays of sun which slanted through the smaller windows of this realistically conceived house lent such a living air to its 1880 dimness that someone five inches high appeared likely to walk across the parlor floor at any moment.*

A chapter alone might be written about the miscellaneous furnishings in the museum's collection. There is, for example, a set of furniture made from an officer's bureau which was on the battleship *Minnesota* when it was shelled by the *Merrimac* in the Civil War. This, made by Captain John Watters for his daughter Annie, consists of bureau, sofa and chair—the seat of the seafaring, battle-going chair daintily upholstered with a bit of Mrs. Watters' bonnet ribbon.

The Essex Institute in Salem has several notable dolls' houses. One of these, dating from the turn of the century, has gables and turrets and bays, and a very American front porch. It was built to scale, by a local carpenter, from the plans of a Salem house believed to have burned in the Salem fire of 1914. Mrs. Lawrence S. Philbrick, to whom the house was given when she was a little girl, furnished some amusing details regarding its early history. It was, in the first place, occupied by a family named Sterling, "for the very simple reason," said Mrs. Philbrick, "that that was one of the first

* The remarkable Brett House, recently given to the museum, is discussed elsewhere.

122

words I learned to spell (from the back of spoons), and thought 'Mr.' Sterling a very remarkable man to have made so many pretty things."

But the Sterlings were not the only residents. Mrs. Philbrick wrote that her family customarily closed their Salem house in the summer and went to the country. "One year when we returned in the fall the dolls' house had obviously been occupied by mice. They had pulled the stuffing out of the chairs and made nests, lugged the 'Sterlings' into different rooms from where I had left them and had stored bits of food all over the house, exactly as it happened in Beatrix Potter's *The Tale of Two Bad Mice*." Mrs. Philbrick said that after this procedure was repeated for three years, her mother, weary of having to re-cover the chairs each year, drove a wedge into every door and window so the mice couldn't open them.

The most imposing dolls' house in the Institute is notable not for its architecture but for its elaborate furnishings, which reflected an aristocratic Boston residence. This house was planned by Mrs. J. Mason Warren (born Annie Crowninshield) for her four daughters about 1852. Made in Salem by a cabinet-maker who had done a great deal of work for Mrs. Warren, it is a tall cabinetlike affair of three stories, six feet high, five feet wide and twenty inches deep. (See illustration.) There is a tall glass window for each of its eight rooms and the front door is graced by side lights and top light. This door did have a brass plate with "Warren" on it, which seems to have disappeared, and a doorbell. Such name plates seem to have been fairly traditional on dolls' houses of that period and region; in the Harrison Gray

The 1852 Warren house at Essex Institute, Salem, Mass.   Height: 6′

Otis House collection in Boston, one little door acknowledges its small owner's name more informally, on a little silver plate marked "Estelle."*

The affection the Warrens felt for this dolls' house, as well as the years of attentive interest they must have lavished upon it, is apparent to the most hasty inspection. There are monograms, exquisitely worked, on approximately everything entitled to a monogram—tablecloth and napkins in the pantry, sheets and pillowcases in the bedroom—all are marked with "W." Mrs. Warren worked the drawing-room carpet to represent Aubusson, roses and leaves on a white ground. But this and a handsome firescreen, near by, are only a fraction of her contributions, which undoubtedly included such gossamer needlework as bedspreads and matching curtains, blue satin in the "Mother's room," and cherry satin in the "Eldest daughter's"—with satin slippers to match!

Mrs. C. H. Gibson, one of Mrs. Warren's daughters, who presented the dolls' house to the Institute in 1925, took the trouble to submit with it a detailed history, a thoughtful procedure which regrettably has occurred to few other dolls' house donors. We have seen a number of museum dolls' houses, standing in dim corners without the barest identification, and for which even the office information was meager and garbled. But from Mrs. Gibson's account, it is possible to know all sorts of things. Inside a tall desk in the dining-room, for instance, is "a walnut shell with white gloves enclosed which was handed to Mrs. Warren at her engagement dinner." (A bit of intelligence which would seem to imply that Mrs. Warren was interested in miniatures before she ever had her four daughters, and planned a dolls' house for them.)

The most historically interesting piece is also in the dining-room. The mahogany drop-leaf dinner table "is said to have been captured from a British ship in the War of 1812 by the Crowninshield privateer ship *America*. The former was all fitted with furniture, brocades, and even toys for a family going to India, and this little table was going to India."

The library is copied from the one in the Warren house at 2 Park Street, Boston, which was torn down, about 1876, "for business purposes," with only this dolls' house replica to commemorate it. Mrs. Gibson's description is comprehensive: "Tall oak bookcases on either side of the fireplace reaching nearly to the ceiling, with marble busts on top. Red silk curtains cover the front, as there were not enough books to fill them. A red velvet valance with gold fringe hung from the mantel, over which was a mirror with beautiful carved gold frame. A quaint English grate with coal in it, and clock and figures on the mantelpiece. On left of room a little real square piano. and sofa on opposite side, the furniture being the same color as the bookcases and covered with rich velvet. A round table in middle of room with a tiny pack of cards on it, and equally small books bound in red

"Gertrude's House, 1904"
Height: 34″

* In the author's collection, another Massachusetts house has two little silver door plates, one bearing the owner's name, "Gertrude," and the other a date, "1904."

124

leather printed in French and (I think) dated 1825. In front of the fireplace stood a small chess table carved in black and white ivory with legs like a stag's antlers, and on it a little green box containing the chessmen no larger than a grain of rice." The house is populated by dolls, including black Dinah in the kitchen, who has her own settee there, as well as such general fixtures of her labor as a scrubbing brush, a clotheshorse and a pump.

The third house in the Essex Institute is also worthy, though furnished and built in less detail than the two which have been described. For us, one of its most delightful features was revealed in a note from Miss Edith S. Price, who presented it to the Institute some years ago, and was able to reply quickly to our 1947 inquiry though, as she wrote, "My father had it made for me about 1868." Miss Price did not say how old she was when her father had the house made, but it is splendid to be able to comment briskly, "It always seemed to me a very perfect period piece and, of course, it is a much better bit of cabinet work than most houses of the kind" of a toy one's father had made for one eighty years before.

Also at Essex are the Bessie Lincoln house, built by a Salem cabinet-maker in 1876, and the so-called Vaughan "doll house." The latter, once described as one of the few "outdoor doll houses," is in actuality a play-house, capable of accommodating doll owners as well as their dolls.

The Harrison Gray Otis House in Boston has an attractive collection of Victorian houses. One of them, made about 1860 by a Cambridge carpenter, originally had "Cambridge Cottage" painted across its front. The alteration was just one of a number. Although the past has not always recorded such repairs, a dolls' house is often no more safe from ravages of era than a full-size residence—unless it is fortunately tucked away in garret or closet for a generation or so where era (and small hands) can't get at it. In 1880, stairs, mantelpiece and curtains were added to the Cambridge cottage, and borders put on at the top of the rooms. But that wasn't all.

The latter were, after all, additions rather than subtractions. Miss Mabel H. Cummings, who presented the cottage to the collection, has written us of more shattering changes, and why they were made. The house itself was built for two of Miss Cummings' older sisters. "I remember," she writes, "when I was eight and my sister Lillian eleven, the doll house was made over for us, and all new furniture was put into it; that was 1880. That year my three sisters, Emma, Alma and Elizabeth, went to Europe for six months and when they returned, they brought back the furniture for the doll house."

These remarks demonstrate a few of the hazards of dolls' house dating. When a date, unlike this one, is not even approximately known, and when generations of children have conspired, by additions and alterations, to confuse—they confuse.

One of the most impressive houses in the Harrison Gray Otis collection, given by Mrs. Albert Gardner Mason, was made for her by the family car-penter about 1895 and given to her for Christmas a few years later. "The ell," Mrs. Mason once wrote in answer to an inquiry, "was added as I felt I must have a laundry and 'clothes yard.' " This house is furnished in great detail. There is delightful gilt furniture in one room, and a piano marked "Julius Bleithner." Who enjoys dolls' houses most, children or parents? Says Mrs. Mason: "It was as much of a hobby for my mother as it was a joy to me to play with and keep in order; for my mother was always buying and adding new things to it."

The Harrison Gray Otis collection has several other interesting dolls' houses, and some rare rooms of dolls' house furniture. The oldest is a quaint bedroom set with Chinese decoration used by the children of Mrs. Lucia (Pickering) Dodge of Salem. Since Mrs. Dodge was married in 1776, the antiquity of the furniture may be surmised. There are also Empire bedroom and drawing-room suites used by the children of Mrs. Eliza (Dodge) Devereux, presumably a daughter, in 1809.

Determining the ancestry of old, anonymous American dolls' houses can be difficult but is no problem whatsoever in connection with a large dolls' residence in the Newark Museum. "The house is a Newark product. It was built by a Newark carpenter in 1882 for a Newark girl's Christmas. It was decorated with papers and carpets made in Newark and the furniture was bought in shops here and in New York." (Much of the furniture, of course, was probably imported.)

So said *Playthings,* the toy trade magazine, in 1927. The house is not always on view. Except for photographs and an inventory, we were unable to see it, but it has been possible to gather from the trade magazine account, the inventory and the photographs, that realism has been more than usually seen to. This is most evident in the floor plans. There is an alcove off the upstairs sitting-room, for example (with a bird cage in the window), and there is a dressing-room behind one of the bedrooms, where the washstand reigns. For that matter, there is a hall just off the kitchen with an icebox in it, containing a piece of imitation ice.

There are daisies on the blue parlor carpet; a family album and a portrait of Schiller on the center parlor table. But our favorite items in the inventory are the total number of curtains: "19 pr. white net, 3 dotted swiss," and the total number of curtain pins: "13 quatrefoil, 7 bouquet-shaped." The numbers don't seem to come out quite matched, but the spirit of the thing is there.

The Newark Museum has a considerably less impressive dolls' house, of an earlier vintage, but which is amusing and which it was possible to see. This was made for Hattie Maslin, a little Brooklyn girl, about 1861 by a member of her family. It has just two rooms, but they have carpet and wallpaper, windows with ledges, and the spirit of their times. One can't ask more of any dolls' house.

The Newport Historical Society has a paper dolls' house of the same era which sounds unusual, particularly because it appears to be a factory product. This house, which we have not seen, cannot be of paper in its usual thin sense, since it has windows of glass, six panes to a window, and, what sounds most dazzling, a glass cupola on top. According to the librarian of the Rhode Island society, the house is octagonal in shape, has two floors, is papered inside, and has a very elaborate crystal chandelier hanging upstairs. The evident clue to its having been factory-made is that Miss Mary Cotton of Newport has a similar specimen, different only in its smaller size. The remarkable fact that two similar houses should both appear in Newport might imply that the manufacturer was there, or near by. The Society also has a Victorian house, of wood, one of the Civil War period made like a bookcase with glass doors that open out, and a relatively modern house, made in 1919. The latter, which is very complete, was made and exhibited to help the French war orphans after World War I.

It is to our great regret that some years ago, during a visit to the Shelburne Museum in Shelburne, Vermont, we examined the delightful collection of dolls' houses with pleasure, but without a notebook. Since it was not possible to pay a return visit before this edition went to press, we wrote to Shelburne in the hope of obtaining a summary, at least, of what the collection contains.

"During Mrs. Webb's* lifetime, it was impossible to catalogue properly much of the material here because of the extremely rapid growth of the Museum," a member of Shelburne's Research Department replied. "The collection of doll houses is one of those as yet-to-be done projects." The only information available was that there are fifteen houses "of various types," including an imposing eighteenth century English house formerly in the Victoria and Albert Museum which we had remembered and specifically inquired about.

However, like everything at Shelburne, the dolls' houses are marvelous, and a visit to the collection is earnestly recommended.

One of the interesting things about dolls' houses is the ingenuity their architects have employed to make them accommodate small hands and moving day every day. Usually, of course, front or back opens (on hinges), or, occasionally, sides. Sometimes the hinged area will comprise a whole façade of the house, and sometimes it will consist of a number of sections, one to a room. An elaborate house, in the Western Reserve Historical Society, built in the 1870's, has an entirely different system. The second story and the attic lift off the ground floor.

Mrs. Ernest Wilmer Marlow, Jr., of Chevy Chase, Maryland, has a good old dolls' house which carries this type of accessibility a few steps further. Her house, of which there is no way of knowing the exact antiquity, and which she found in an antique shop in Washington, D. C., comes apart in five sections. Here, as in the Western Reserve house, the second floor and

* Mrs. J. Watson Webb, founder of the museum.

attic lift off, but first two turret sides with towers are removed. The house is "stone" and the pieces are set on individually. The very thorough builder also provided twenty-four sash windows which open and close.

Another unusual arrangement is to be found in a dolls' house belonging to Miss Betty Whale of Muskegon, Michigan. This house, which bears a surprising resemblance to one in the extensive collection at the Queen's Park Art Gallery in Manchester (England), contains four rooms, back to back, on each of the two floors, with each of the long sides swinging open in two sections.

The Manchester house, its approximate twin, may be seen in Vivien Greene's book,* in which she refers to it as the "Noah's Ark House." The same pitched roof and similar proportions, even the same arrangement of windows are to be seen, along with a comparable method of access. The only essential difference is that Miss Whale's house has an attic story with three additional rooms and is necessarily taller (40 inches high rather than 26). Both houses contain a staircase.

Mrs. Greene estimates the date of the Manchester house as 1830–45, and says that it may even be Regency.

Miss Whale's house is of considerably later date, if the furnishings which came with it may be considered a guide. Many of the pieces were marked "Catharine S. Chapin, Xmas, 1895 from Papa & Mama," but, of course, the house may very well have been built earlier—for Mama, per-haps—or even Grandmama—and refurnished in 1895 by "Mama" for Catharine. It came, incidentally, from Rhode Island (where Chapin is a well-known name).

Another privately owned antique dolls' house, which belongs to Mrs.

* Op. cit.

Interior of author's cupboard-type house from Pennsylvania Height: 50"

John Harrell, of Potomac, Maryland, architecturally demonstrates a part of the country the author, being far from the West Coast, has not seen in other dolls' houses. This domicile, which Mrs. Harrell discovered almost completely furnished in a San Francisco antique shop, is an excellent replica of Golden Gate architecture of its period. The family who sold the house was very "hush-hush" about it, for some reason not wanting their name known, but Mrs. Harrell was told that it was built in 1886.

One curious feature is that it was probably a copy of a row house. This Mrs. Harrell deduces from the fact that there are no windows or any embellishments of any kind on the sides. The front is well supplied with bays, a bell with a pull rope, and a nice selection of gingerbread. The rear has a proper flight of back steps, which many dolls' houses ignore. Mrs. Harrell has thoughtfully installed a nest of storks in the roomy eaves. She is continuing to furnish the house in The Ugly Period, an excellent thought, because even though the house came well cluttered to begin with, she can use The Ugly Period as an excuse to go on and on and on. Her house, which has one of the earliest bathrooms we've seen in the doll world, is delightful.

In the author's possession is one of the frequently found cupboard-type dolls' houses, of no architectural pretensions, but of the type usually run up (in the United States) a few generations ago by the family carpenter. This one from Pennsylvania was furnished mostly in the late eighties, and is divided into four square rooms, each disclosed by an individual door, and fastened with an old-fashioned revolving catch. The only architectural features are rear windows and a pitched roof.

Chandelier with workable wicks; author's collection Height: 6½″

Clock, candelabrum, seal and inkstand; author's collection Height of candelabrum: 3½″

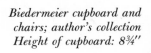

Biedermeier cupboard and chairs; author's collection Height of cupboard: 8¾″

But, the original wallpapers and draperies are intact and, as our photograph shows, the furnishings are remarkably complete. In the dining-room, in addition to a wall telephone, there are such treasures as half a dozen fringed damask napkins in pewter napkin rings and half a dozen wooden breakfast eggs in papier-mâché egg cups. There is also a complete dinner service, including a tureen, in this ware. Pewter sugar tongs are of the same pattern as the flat "silver." In the drawing-room, desk furnishings appear in two varieties and two scales. (Two scales, inch-to-the-foot, and another, somewhat larger, are to be found in this house.) In the smaller scale there is a brass set consisting of ornate inkstand with double glass wells, roller blotter with handle, and infinitesimal chamber stick; in larger scale there is a considerably older piece, perhaps eighteenth century—a china inkstand with two removable china receptacles—one for ink and one for sand. This is pictured in the company of two pieces not of this house but which may be of the same era—a pearl-handled, silver-trimmed letter seal incised with thistle design—and a silver candelabrum with blue and white Oriental figures on its Chinese porcelain base. Its six branches are of the style which pierced the candle rather than cupped it. This silver portion is possibly Dutch. Both seal and candelabrum were purchased in England. In the same photograph, there's another piece from this cupboard house; an ornate brass clock under a glass bell.

A cupboard and pair of chairs (shown) are of a type of dolls' house furniture made in Germany in various sizes, styles, and qualities during most of the nineteenth century. There were obviously several manufacturers

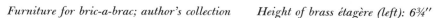

Furniture for bric-a-brac; author's collection   *Height of brass étagère (left): 6¾"*

130

involved, and Mrs. Greene may be justified in calling the best of these the Dolls' Duncan Phyfe, but this seems a somewhat cumbersome term, and Biedermeier appears to cover all varieties aptly. An 1880 catalogue described it as "imitation ebony and gold." The cupboard, larger than an inch to a foot, has the fine detail of the earlier and better pieces, and it has withstood well the ravages of time. The gilt pattern looks as new, the two narrow drawers beneath the glass doors glide perfectly after a century, and the bone embellishments are intact. Also in this room is an étagère (illustrated) laden with choice bric-a-brac. It holds a white-and-gold Staffordshire vase of traditional shape, an inch high, and a pair of perfectly done figurines in colonial dress: the gentleman in tricorne hat and knee breeches, the lady in tiered skirt which conceals a surprise when she and said skirt are parted— a place for (doll) trinkets!

We refer elsewhere to the japanned black-and-gold tin furniture in the bedroom of this house—bureau with swivel mirror and workable drawers, canopied bed, and lift-top table containing linens. (The latter with its china chamber set is shown in Chapter 12.) The bureau contains feminine under-garments as perfectly made and of the period as anything in the house. Cheval mirror, fireplace with fringed lambrequin, Franklin stove, hinged coal box with coal, are other high-lights of this select boudoir which is rather over-populated by dolls, including minute twins in a filigree cradle and a child whose sheets and blankets are stamped with her name, "Bethel." Particularly attractive is the illumination provided for these young ladies. A lead filigree chandelier with wicks which can actually be lighted—given a little fuel—contains bristol glass globes (as our illustration shows).*

Having lingered over-long in the other rooms, we can only touch upon the kitchen where a delicate china tea service features dainty rose-and-green floral sprig decor and octagonal cups. A blue ceramic pudding mold, made to accommodate half a dozen doll desserts, may be considered by kitchen-ware collectors (of full-scale utensils) the most remarkable object in this room. But gentlemen tool collectors would not agree. They'd probably choose the perfectly made miter saw, rip saw, hammer, and plane, all thoroughly capable of miniature carpentry.

And what of the children who played with these dolls' houses now taken over by museums or adults with antiquarian fancies? We submit random clues to the personalities of two of them:

One of these appeared in *Harper's Young People* for May 8, 1888. It offers not only a key to the role the 1888 child accorded her dolls' house, but it also touches on dolls' house play of a generation earlier, and we set it forth in full: ". . . a young person of tender years escorted me to her nursery where her play-house was exhibited with great pride. The doll house was very like what I remember in my own childhood—a three-story dwelling, with a very convenient front, for, by turning the knob of the front door, three stories of windows, entrance, and all, opened on hinges, and disclosed

* In England this delicate ware is known as bristol; in France, as opaline.

the interior of dolly's family residence. But how different was it from the doll house I cherished nearly twenty years ago! We felt ourselves luxurious then with furniture selected from a large tray at our toy-shop for a penny each. But in my little friend's doll house I saw a drawing room which was an amusing imitation of the one in which I had just been having afternoon tea. The furniture was decorated with odd bits of drapery, and the floors were painted and carpeted with a capital imitation of rugs. The mistress of this artistic dwelling was seated in the drawing-room near a low tea table, and dressed in a most becoming tea gown. My little companion and I, sitting comfortably on the floor before the doll house, regarded her with proper respect, and talked about the kettledrum she was going to give in about five minutes to the row of paper and china dolls waiting in another corner of the room. My companion informed me that the occasion of the tea was Mrs. Cleveland's visit to Philadelphia, and after a little search we found the Lady of the White House at a proper distance from the rest of the company. My little friend said the invitations were for five o'clock and as soon as the company had assembled Mrs. Cleveland would appear . . ."

A more modest dolls' house was described by the owner herself in a quaint little magazine (whose circulation survived only two years) called *The Doll's Dressmaker*. A Letter to the Editor (one Jenny Wren) from Eulalia O'N., Brooklyn, N. Y., printed in the September, 1891, issue informed her fellow, and undoubtedly envious readers that, "Last Christmas I got . . . a new doll house, with real glass windows, a mantelpiece and doors that will open and shut. It has shades and curtains to the windows, a clock on the mantel, and furniture. Afterwards my sister gave me a pug dog, a grey cat and a stove and coal scuttle, and a darkey doll named 'Dina' to take care of the house. They are all the right size for the house and make it look real."

Note that pug dog, a sign of the times. But mostly note that "look real." Those modern toymakers who scorn realism might pause and consider the words of Eulalia O'N. of Brooklyn . . .

9

AN
INTERNATIONAL
PROCESSION

ERE WE HAVE A MISCELLANY, A CHAPTERFUL OF COUNTRIES whose dolls' houses have been either elusive or few. It is rather an arbitrary assortment; the intention of the present volume has been pioneer rather than definitive, and it is possible that a number of countries whose dolls' houses should be represented, or represented more elaborately, are slighted. This report, dependent to some extent upon which foreign museums answer their mail, and which do not, attempts to be only a cross-section.

An occasional country confesses its indebtedness to neighbors. Sweden, for one. The Nordiska Museet in Stockholm lists thirty dolls' houses in its possession, representing three centuries. This number strongly rivals the assemblage of the Victoria and Albert Museum in London which, with its branch at Bethnal Green, has one of the largest dolls' house collections in the world. A Stockholm museum official once wrote that Sweden's dolls' houses are of two types: "the one is like the German doll houses made as real houses; the other is like the Dutch doll houses made as cupboards with glass doors."

However, this highly geographical circumstance has not triumphed completely over the personality of Swedish dolls' houses. Museum pictures of both types show marked national individuality. This is particularly true of

Swedish cupboard-type house, ca. 1740, Nordiska Museet

Late seventeenth century Swedish manorhouse, Nordiska Museet

the oldest house, which dates from the late seventeenth century and is of an architectural aspect. (See illustration.) This house, which resembles no other we have seen, even *looks* Swedish. This quite unscientific observation, based probably on simplicity of line, does have support from fact, supplied by a former curator:

"The shape of the roof is typical for the Swedish manorhouse (sätesgård) from the baroque. The first floor is a sort of store-room, in the centre floor is the kitchen with lining of imitated glazed tile, and the top floor contains a big hall with painted friezes around the walls both above and down in the lower part but the tapestries between the friezes are lost. Only one or two of the pieces could possibly have belonged to the original furniture." The roof is peaked with windows in an indented crown at the top. In the front, there are four large windows on each of the two upper stories, and two paned ones at either side of the curious, grooved door on the ground floor. Each story opens individually from the center of the front. But this is drab information indeed compared to the romantic place-name of the house's origin. It hails (a most dream-like hail) from Norra Lindved Castle in Scania.

A cupboard house, circa 1740, also has decided personality, though this stems principally from its furnishings which are largely original. There are four floors (shelves to the literal), only one of which is partitioned into three rooms. The other apartments are spacious affairs occupying entire floors, including a kitchen and what appears to be a ballroom. (See illustrations.)

In the kitchen a china-cupboard holds a faience set signed Rorstrand, Stockholm, 1746. A pewter service, twenty-seven plates of which line the walls in rows of racks, and which is additionally present in tall stacked piles, dominates this room in which the cook is incautiously sitting on the stove.

The ballroom, if such it is, is a beautiful and unusual room. There is an elegant marble checkerboard floor, and a continuous woodland wallpaper is above the dado. The furniture is very formal in arrangement. An odd and handsome stove in the center of the wall goes to the ceiling and a row of quaint little chairs (in an exaggerated Queen Anne style), which appear to be gilded or silvered, stands on each side. A corresponding row of mirrored sconces, scalloped and identical, hangs above the chairs, interrupting the scenic wallpaper at intervals.

Of the other houses in the museum, many are in cupboard form. Of the others, one is a cardboard house from the eighteenth century, certainly one of the oldest surviving dolls' houses of any country made of that ephemeral material. Another specimen which sounds unusual is a summer-house from the early part of the nineteenth century with original furniture.

Of two relatively modern dolls' houses that sound interesting, one is described as a "house in two storeys with a lower part," and was made in 1900–1905 by the chemist and druggist C. D. L. Carlsson, Skinskatteberg, the first chemist we've come across in a dolls' house world dominated by architects. The other building, made in the 'twenties, is a copy of Hersbyholm Manor at Lidingo, near Stockholm, and must therefore be quite a mansion, and possibly a rival to Titania's Palace or the Queen's Dolls' House of the same period.

Through the kindness of Mrs. Flora MacDonald Judd of England, and her son-in-law, Lektor Hartveit of Norway, we received from the Vestlandske Kunstindustri Museum in Bergen in 1960 a list of dolls' houses which had been shown there at a special exhibit in 1953. The list was accompanied by small pictures.

Some years later, while studying these, we were especially struck by the pictures of a four-room house which was accompanied by a date: 1893. The house was obviously eighteenth century—there were even chairs and ottomans upholstered in flame-stitch*—the only ones in miniature we have ever encountered, and we wrote to the museum to inquire. A prompt reply from Mrs. Thale Riisöen, the Curator, assured us that the house does indeed date from the eighteenth century, and that 1893 was the year it was *acquired*.

* Known also as bargello, Florentine or Hungarian work, and used largely in the late 17th and early 18th centuries.

Ballroom of Swedish cupboard-type house, ca. 1740

This was interesting information from several points of view: it seems remarkable that in 1893, when the collecting of old toys must have appeared as remote to most museums as the year itself now seems to us, any museum should have had the foresight to accept such a bequest. Although, a decade or so later, the two Dutch professors, Muller and Vogelsang (see Chapter 6), were writing about the valuable poppenhuizen in Netherlands museums (houses made for adults, and filled with rare bits of silver, porcelain, and other items which were *per se* valuable), this house is modest by comparison, and more patently a toy.*

The rooms, which are curiously arranged with bedroom and kitchen on the lower floor, and with two sitting-rooms upstairs, are contained in what Mrs. Riisöen describes as "A cupboard of green-painted deal with glazed doors . . . The cupboard has a distinct Queen Anne style from the first decades of the eighteenth century." Mrs. Riisöen also gives us the size of the rooms: each is 16¼″ high and 23¼″ wide, and therefore the furniture is evidently somewhat larger than inch-to-the-foot (one-twelfth) scale.

Unfortunately the pictures are not as clear as might be wished (having been photographed through the glass), but among the features of special interest that may be discerned, there is a scenic wallpaper, or mural, in the drawing-room revealing birds, trees, and a turreted castle; a bed with a circular half-tester and, also in the bedroom, the flame-stitched pieces that have been mentioned.

Pictures show the other houses in the 1953 exhibition at the Vestlandske Kunstindustri Museum to be an attractive and varied assortment, mostly of the second half of the nineteenth century. One, the property of Gamle Bergen (the town museum), is a four-room, two-story house of unusual character, owing in great measure to a clever and attractive arrangement of hinged glazed-and-panelled doors which form, four sections to each room, the entire façade, and give it a distinct personality. One room in this house contains a homemade set of furniture which obviously stems from the great fret-saw revival so avidly pursued in the United States in the 1880's, and obviously elsewhere, too. The wooden lace that someone with a gifted saw fashioned for this dolls' house is of unusual intricacy.

More than twenty dolls' houses—which include shops and kitchens—are to be found in the collection of the Dansk Folkemuseum in Copenhagen. A museum official lists which among them the museum considers its best and, of these, two are complete dolls' houses; one of them a two-story house from the end of the eighteenth century with the mansard roof which one tends (despite its seventeenth century origin) to associate with the nine-

---

* It is possible that we belabor this point, inasmuch as this dolls' house was at least a century-and-a-half old in 1893, and obviously there have been antiquarians in all eras, to whose perceptions we owe the 17th and 18th century houses that have survived in Germany, England, and elsewhere. However, in saluting the 1893 donor of the Bergen dolls' house for giving it, and the Bergen museum for accepting it, we hereby presume, on behalf of all dolls' house partisans, to salute all collectors and museum curators of bygone days who have shown similar perspicacity!

teenth. The other, most intriguingly named "Villa Olga," is dated 1884, contains three floors, a cellar and *two* garrets, and obviously reflects the solid comfort to be found (in all countries) in the substantial upper-middle-class houses of that substantial upper-middle-class period.

Two pairs of dolls' rooms, both dating approximately from the end of the nineteenth century—the popular combination of sitting-room and bed-room—are also on the museum's preferred list, along with an early 19th century milliner's shop, and three kitchens from the eighteenth, nineteenth, and twentieth centuries. Even the twentieth century example may now be considered a period piece, being dated 1907.

A delightful booklet, *Dolls and Toy Soldiers,* published in 1961 by Finland's National Museum, has pictures of several attractive dolls' houses and rooms in the museum's collection, all of them complete with their histories.

The oldest of the houses was made for a merchant's daughter in Raahe who was born in 1856, and most of its furniture "was produced locally." The house is a rather uncomplicated three story building (three feet tall) which appears to be considerably less interesting than one two sisters played with at Linnainen, Lohja, two generations later: "Both inherited antiques and contemporary pieces are often used to furnish dolls' houses;" Riitta Pylkkanen points out in the museum's booklet, "The dolls' house assembled by Mrs. Marie Luther for her children in the 1890's is an example."

We learn that the grandmother of the doll family, Marie, dates from the 1860s, "But was given a new wig and fashionable dress in the 1890's. The grandmother used to sit next to the stove, and the children were not allowed to disturb her. General Otto and Madame Thea sit in their drawing-room, which was fitted with furniture inherited from the early 19th century." Madame Thea is playing the mandolin for the General who, with an impos-ing array of military decorations on his jacket exceeded in grandeur only by his fierce moustache, appears unbending.

The writer notes that the manufacturing of dolls' furniture didn't begin in Finland till the latter half of the 19th century, and that much of the furni-ture to be found in Finnish dolls' houses was imported, "primarily from Germany." It is evident, though, that Finnish manufacturers also were busy. Examples pictured include "a drawing-room fitted with furniture in the Neo-Renaissance style made by M. Nordensvan's toy factory in Kuipio" and a bedroom set for which M. F. Tamlander's toy shop in Pori won a prize at the Helsinki General Exhibition of 1876.

One wishes the toy makers of other countries were as well documented.

Turning, for a change of pace, to the Orient, it is possible to become almost hopelessly involved with the Girls' Festival of Japan. Almost every-one knows something about Japan's annual doll festival, but the centuries of symbolism which have come to surround it can be adequately interpreted only through study of a correspondingly vast maze of ritual, both religious and social. Such folklore is better explained in an entire volume, but since the paraphernalia of this Hinamatsuri is in part the dolls' houses of Japan, it seems appropriate to give a smattering of the background.

A Japanese can most suitably explain the Festival, and one Tekiho Nishizawa has given a terse definition of its religious meaning in a beautiful booklet put out by the Society for International Cultural Relations.

"On March third of each year," wrote Nishizawa, "it is traditional for Japanese parents to pray to the gods for the protection of their babies and the happiness of their little daughters by celebrating the Doll Festival." This Festival is epitomized by a court scene in which the dolls and their equipment are arranged on shelves (five or seven tiers draped with red cotton cloth) with occasional buildings supplementary. The arrangements are highly ritualistic and traditional, though there are infinite variations in the details, depending on the budget of the family providing them.

Nishizawa's description, like his definition, is stripped to the essentials, and makes a sufficient frame for the additions of other commentators: "At the center of the top shelf sit a Court noble and his lady (Dairihina) behind whom are placed small standing screens. On the shelf immediately below are three Court ladies (Kanjo). On the third shelf are a singer and four musicians, holding a flute, drum, and two tambourines respectively. The fourth shelf has two seated dolls, a military and a civil dignitary, between whom are lacquer boxes containing offerings. On the fifth shelf are three male servants kneeling between miniature cherry and orange trees in bloom. The lower shelves contain furnishings and other articles in black lacquer decorated with gold, intended for the use of the royal couple. These consist of miniature chests of drawers, a palanquin, a carriage, braziers, swords,

Late nineteenth century Japanese Doll Festival display for the Hina Matsuri; author's collection Height: 18"

mirrors, etc. There are also various offerings, principally of cakes made of cooked rice or beans.

"The dolls are dressed in the ancient richly embroidered costumes of the Court which are prescribed by custom. The collections possessed by some Japanese families have been increased with the addition of some new ones in the course of successive generations, and they are treasures of high artistic value."

In a very beautiful book (*Dolls on Display*—C. Caiger) about Japanese dolls, to be obtained in the rare book room of the Library of Congress, there is a clue to the antiquity of this precise panorama. About 900 years ago, one self-immortalized Lady Murasaki noted in her diary that "The diminutive stands, dishes, chopsticks, rests, etc., are likely to be requisites of hina-playing," which developed, according to Caiger, into the ritualistic festival. Probably basing his opinion on this notation, he observes that "The inclusion of diminutive household furniture seems to have been a part of the ceremony in ancient times."

One U. A. Casal, who evidently had no access to Lady Murasaki's diary, in a "brief paper read at the Kobe woman's club" said that "the furniture was a comparatively late introduction. During the seventeenth century there were already in use certain objects in lacquer and utensils . . ." However, his list of the reproductions likely to be found on the tiers in imitation of the Japanese household is of interest.

In addition to the food trays on which offerings are made to the prince and princess, he notes chest of drawers, traveling trunk, writing table and box, toilet stand on rack for hanging up dresses, musical instruments. "There may be an out-fit for the tea ceremony or for the game of matching incense." All of these objects, perfectly made, are, he tells us, on a scale of less than the usual inch to the foot. (Like the scale of the people to us?)

"On the lowest shelf," Casal adds, "or more correctly on the mats in front of it, there will even be miniature kitchen utensils, and in these the little hostess should herself prepare a fancy meal to treat her guests. Tiny dishes loaded with small fish, little piles of vegetables and minute cakes will be served on tables but hardly larger than those on the shelves."

This matter of the miniature food is of particular interest, for at least two reasons. For one, it emphasizes the play and education phases of her toys rather than the usual religious ones for the Japanese child. Esther Singleton quotes a Japanese woman in this regard who tells us that "The doll family remains for three days, and the proud and happy little mistress is busy all the time. The daily food for the tiny dishes is planned and purchased, if not really cooked by her, and she serves it not only to the visiting dolls, but to all who call to see the beautiful room."

But the enchanting aspect of this miniature gastronomy is something for which the artificially filled bins in the dolls' houses of other countries might yearn in vain: literally miniature, and altogether edible viands. Miss

Singleton's Japanese informant writes that during the Festival "every fish-market is stocked with tiny fish; every bake-shop has a wonderful display of wee cakes of every kind; vegetable sellers bring, with their usual stock, the smallest vegetables that can be grown by gardeners who are specialists in this line." While dolls of other nations subsist a few generations on painted sawdust, there seems to be a nutritional reason why Japanese dolls survive centuries.

The modern (1934) Japanese Doll Palace at the Cleveland Museum of Art

Caiger discusses the use of "A Palace," a miniature building which may be used separately as a setting for the Imperial Dolls and their attendants. He offers a photograph, and his criticism of the palace it pictures is almost as informative as a description. "Conservative Japanese," he writes, "prefer a replica of the Enthronement Hall of the Imperial Palace in pure Shinto style, much simpler than this, and of unpainted wood. The illustration shows a confused style of building—too ornate. The pair of dolphins on the roof are commonly seen on castles, and the attendants should be seated at the foot of the staircase, not in the Hall itself.

"The illustration shows how commercialism is affecting the Doll Festival in the loss of accurate representation and the growing desire for display." Caiger adds that the palaces are not in wide favor even among the well-to-do because "they need a big room for display and also take up much space in the box room during the other eleven months."

The Cleveland Museum of Art owns one of these palaces, made about 1934, which contains fourteen dolls, eight pieces of furniture and seventeen dishes. This one also, we are sorry to say, has dolphins on the roof, but most of the attendants, we are glad to report, are suitably situated at the foot of the staircase. However, there is a vast amount of lacquer and floral ornamentation, and all manner of gewgaws—tassels and pediments and chains—and it is probable that a Shintoist wouldn't let it in his house.

The only furnishings manifest amid this somehow ordered confusion are the pair of floor lanterns, gilt lacquered and of rice paper, which, according to Caiger, are sometimes to be found on the top shelf of a tiered representation, often in the company of a ceremonial tray and two dogs who symbolize faithfulness and loyalty. Folding screens of golden colored silk, he further writes, frequently form a background. His own illustration shows some of another type "that once were used to partition large rooms and to gain privacy in the houses of the aristocracy." His book is a small trove of such smatterings of Japanese household history.

Because of the frequent inclusion of palaces and other buildings on the tiers, it is difficult to know where the Doll Festival leaves off and dolls' houses begin. Mrs. Jackson has a picture in her toy history of what she calls a Japanese dolls' house. This, a one-room affair, looks more like a kitchen than a house, and despite its fascinating and cryptic appearance, is nowhere described. Mrs. Jackson has also an exceedingly tantalizing sentence: "Of the Japanese dolls' house and the lovely miniature fittings we

140

speak elsewhere," she says; "suffice it to say here that Madame Chrysanthemum has the most charmingly furnished house in all doll-land, and her equipment is complete, even to a two-inch lacquer box with dollie's writing-brush, Indian ink tablet, palette, and water-bottle, lest she should wish to write a letter." This is all tantalizing because if Mrs. Jackson has spoken elsewhere of Japanese dolls' houses, she must have spoken in another book.

The late Stewart Culin, former ethnology curator of the Brooklyn Institute, had an article on Japanese toys in *Asia* in 1920 which is illuminating. He wrote that "notable among the wares" of toy stores in Japan "are carefully made models of shops with every kind of merchandise, of interiors of temples with all their appurtenances, and of living rooms and kitchens showing details of the daily life of the people." He added that "Cheap as things are in Japan—and toys are exceptionally cheap—these models are by no means low in price, frequently commanding as much as 100 yen."

Ruth Field Ruggles of the Cleveland Museum of Art once wrote that she had seen several models of Japanese houses "made of a wood like bamboo, complete as to their four walls and roof, doors, gateways, etc. They are very carefully made, but unfortunately inclined to warp in our climate." She referred us to such a house given to the American Museum of Natural History by Mrs. Henry M. Lucas, of Cleveland. We saw it there and recommend its delicate detail to anyone who visits the New York museum.

One might rather wistfully report upon "The Story of a Goodwill Project between the Children of America and Japan" which was published in 1929 by an optimistic group called "The Committee on World Friendship among Children." In a hopeful pre-war gesture, the children of both countries exchanged dolls and the American specimens went to the Tokyo Education Museum to take up residence in a two-story Japanese dolls' house.

In this, the unofficial enrollment of royalty in dolls' house circles took on a new member. Her Imperial Majesty, the Empress of Japan, presented the dolls' palace in which the American dolls were to dwell. This building, it was said, possessed "several rooms," and a Mrs. Bowles wrote from Tokyo that "it is a perfect Japanese house, surrounded with an exquisite Japanese garden, the whole enclosed in a huge glass case. . . . All over the garden are articles used for kindergarten games. Some dolls are sliding down the slide; others are on the see-saw; some are picking flowers. There are just enough Japanese dolls to act as caretakers and hostesses."

Gardens evidently have been customary accompaniments of Japanese dolls' houses, which, since gardens are nearly as much a part of Japanese lives as are their houses, is not surprising. In a little book called *A Diplomatist's Wife in Japan,* a series of letters written by an Englishwoman, Mrs. Hugh Fraser, at the end of the last century, the enchantments of such dolls' house gardens are vividly set forth.

Mrs. Fraser, in an 1890 letter describing the Doll Festival, wrote of the doll collection of "the little daughter of one of the great nobles. . . . It was hard to find words to express proper admiration of the dolls' country house, with gardens, farms, lakes, and pine trees all complete, which she showed me in another room. Real flowers had been planted around it in light earth brought up for the purpose; and her mother, when I returned to the drawing-room, told me that 'Nobu cho' arranged this part of the show entirely."

The prominent role these diminutive goings-on have been allotted in Japan was indicated some years ago by an observation that Mitsukoshi, "the Wanamaker of Toyko," had a "wonderful display" of miniature furniture and household utensils and that one entire wing of the immense stage was devoted to the dolls and their possessions. The latter included everything, even, as one writer put it, "The infinitesimal toilet utensils for painting the face and blackening the teeth and making oneself generally attractive . . ."

A rare and beautiful dolls' palace, the only one of such elaboration we have encountered, belongs to Mr. and Mrs. Walter Nichols. Mr. Nichols, a Foreign Service officer with the United States Information Service, was stationed in Japan when the palace, a diminutive version of the one in the old capital of Kyoto, was acquired.

With its carefully thatched roof, two staircases, central balcony, and Ceremonial Hall, the Nichols' imperial palace belies its substantial appearance by packing intricately—150 or so sections—into a box. Thirty-four other boxes, of Paulownia wood, lovely themselves with their sliding lids and decorative labels, contain the dolls and paraphernalia.

The Nichols' magnificent Japanese doll palace, with dolls and furnishings for the Hina Matsuri

Although in the traditional display, as we have suggested, the court ladies, musicians, dignitaries, and servants are arranged on rigidly prescribed shelves below the Emperor and Empress, the Nichols' well-sheltered royal family is situated in and about the palace itself. (The magnificently dressed Empress wears twelve layers of undergarments!)

Shelves below the palace hold the handsome lacquered furnishings; their gold leaf decorations are individual works of art in themselves. The crest of the family to whom this exquisite set belonged is emblazoned upon every piece. Small drawers contain infinitesimal accessories—bronze mirrors, ivory combs, bamboo brushes, and an abundance of wigs and garments. The palanquin of the Empress and the carriage of the Emperor, complete with ox (the latter's horns and fur as specific as the rest), await their royal passengers on the lowest tier.

Turning from these beauty secrets to a different department of the Orient, we find Chinese dolls' house information as spare as Japan's was lavish. The Counselor of the Chinese Embassy in Washington wrote, "Although we do have doll houses in China, I know of no source of information concerning them. . . ." But Mrs. Jackson throws some light on a related matter. "Some of the toy shrines of the Chinese are beautifully made," she writes, "and in a superb wall painting of the Ming dynasty we see a toy shrine where the children are worshipping and where even the baby squats on the floor at the back in conventional attitude." Such a plaything Mrs. Jackson refers to as "an ecclesiastical toy . . . largely made and used, without levity or offense, for what we 'grown-ups' have come to look upon as play" but which "is the serious business of child life."

A dolls' house of worship we might call this little Ming object which may have been related to more secular miniature interiors. If this toy shrine may be considered a dolls' house, and if Mrs. Jackson's "wall painting" is *early* Ming, Duke Albrecht's dolls' palace may be only a pretender, and this toy the earliest dolls' house on record!

Russia is another reluctant dolls' house country. A notation in the rear of a small volume by Miss Elizabeth Hooper of Baltimore, a writer of informal books about her dolls, that Gatchina Palace (now called Palace of the Young Pioneers) near Leningrad is "full of doll houses," seemed fraught with promise. Some years ago, when research for this book was begun, the author corresponded at great length with the American Russian Institute in New York in respect to this challenging sentence about Russian dolls' houses. The Institute, in turn, corresponded with VOKS, All-Union Society for Cultural Relations with Foreign Countries, also at great length. Finally VOKS sent two research papers on the Palace of the Pioneers to the Institute, containing no reference to dolls' houses. But a paper on the Zagorsk Museum briefly described toys of the seventeenth to nineteenth centuries, including ". . . engraved and filigreed metal miniatures . . . tiny cups, chairs, sofas, vases and all kinds of dolls . . . and a great assortment of furniture—a mahogany parlor set, an entire three-wall room set up with shelves, chests and so forth . . ."

In 1915, *International Studio* discussed "Toys by a Russian Artist," and mentioned, as one group, "architectural models of various kinds which include a farm, a harbour and a monastery." The last, it added, "enjoys a great fame in Russia." The article also discussed the toy industry which had flourished in a Moscow province since the end of the eighteenth century.

The *New York Times Magazine* in 1932 referred to the toys from this same "region of the Volga known as Sergeievsy Passad where generations of craftsmen have copied the playthings their fathers made." The writer, though, was engaged in describing "toys cast in the Bolshevik mold" and mentioned that "dishes and furniture instill an attachment for personal property and lead small girls to play at bourgeois domesticity."

He described something less likely to corrupt them, a toy factory kitchen, a collective plaything to be used in grade schools and kindergartens, in which individual pots and pans had been "replaced by the cooperative soup kettle." Such an item would be a startling note in our toy kitchen chapter, and we have resisted the temptation to put it there. The same writer described a toy collective farm which sounds adequate only to the impersonal precincts of an orphanage or school.

Much pleasanter sounding was a plaything of an earlier regime reported by the same author, who noted its presence in Leontovsky Lane in Moscow "where a whole museum is devoted to the toys of yesterday . . . A galleon in full sail is heaped with a cargo of tiny bowls and jugs, chairs and tables, all in red, black and gold lacquer." This was one of the toys made by the Sergeievsky peasants whose cargo might, with only slight adjustments, have been installed in a dolls' house rather than a galleon.

The opening of what was probably this same Moscow toy museum was in 1926 commented upon by *Playthings*, the toy trade magazine. "One can see there," said the writer, "the toys of aristocratic children of the last century. There are complete doll houses all furnished with costly furniture in which charming dolls are reposing in beautiful armchairs dressed in crinoline dresses." Though this seems to be rather a flighty account, it may be a reasonable bit of Russian dolls' house evidence.

Children in Russia at the beginning of the present century had homemade dolls' houses if no other kind. An autobiography, published in 1935, of a Russian woman now in the United States (Tatiana W. Boldyreff's *Russian Born*) has several references to her dolls' quarters. One item displays the importance which dolls if not houses had before the Revolution. The author tells of a doll magazine supplement she read as a child. This was appropriately doll-size—being about three by four inches—and contained not only doll stories and serials but jokes which the author's father enjoyed reading. The year's issues were bound, and the little volume that resulted was a treasured item in the dolls' house which the author's grandmother made for her, vying with a "tiny real oil painting" her mother copied from a seascape by the Russian artist Aivazovski.

This dolls' house must have been in very large scale to accommodate a bound volume of such dimensions. This outsize is implied in another place where the autobiographer refers to a kaleidoscope given her by an aunt and which "later became a telescope in my doll house for my learned dolls who studied astronomy and watched the comet of 1911." We do not mean to infer from this that all Russian dolls' buildings were scaled large, though a contemporary (and rather plain) Russian dolls' house on a photograph belonging to Sovfoto, the Russian picture agency in New York, is also relatively jumbo to judge by the children playing with it.

In *Alt Wiener Spielzeugschachtel* (Old Vienna Toy Box), a charmingly illustrated book by Herbert Kaut, many attractive Austrian toys are shown. Among these are the salon and nursery of a lovely 1880 dolls' house made for the Vienna artist, Ella Rothe (now in the Historisches Museum der Stadt Wien), a "mixed goods shop," ca. 1840, at the Österreichisches Museum für Volkskunde, and a Vienna kitchen, ca. 1900, from the collection of Gabriele Folk-Stoi.

Two pairs of folding rooms in the author's collection are late Victorian toys from Vienna. One pair is the customary combination of drawing-room and bedroom, the latter, as one might expect, a considerably smaller room. The handsomer pair is divided into rooms of equal size, identically provided with two glass windows apiece, all of them splendidly hung with crimson silk draperies and crowned by gilt-fringed cornices. A checker-board floor is also common to both rooms. The only difference, and a very pretty one, may be found on the walls, which, in one room, are besprinkled with lilies of the valley, and in the other, with parrots and pansies.

Considerably more sedate than its setting, unpainted fret-work furniture of considerable delicacy came with these rooms. The pieces are meticulously dovetailed and far more delicately wrought than most of the fret-work revival pieces made in such multitudes in the United States in the 'eighties, but they seem a trifle primitive in a setting of crimson draperies and lavishly lithographed walls. (We have wondered whether they were originally with the rooms, or were a later addition. Very similar fret-worked pieces are to be seen in a Norwegian dolls' house described on p. 136.)

Several important collections of dolls' houses and related toys are to be found in Basel, Switzerland. Foremost, at the Historisches Museum, is the magnificent cabinet house, of nut-wood, ca. 1700, that is pictured. Dr. H. Lanz, Curator of the Museum, has pointed out that some furniture, such as a cooking stove, which had been added in the nineteenth century, has been replaced by eighteenth century pieces. However, most of the furnishings—of wood, faience, tin, brass, and iron-plate—are original, including a covered

dish of silver made by the Basel goldsmith Peter Biermann and dated 1709. The house came from the Basel family of A. Wengen.

Among five other dolls' houses in the museum's collection—all from Basel and all of the nineteenth century—of astonishing detail is a five-story house of many rooms, made about 1850 by Ludwig Adam Kelterborn, a Basel artist, for his three daughters. This house has a true staircase from the ground floor to the attic, with a separate flight leading from the ground floor hall to the arcaded cellar. In addition to the rooms in full view, realistic glimpses of others are disclosed through half-open doors, and one looks forward to a trip to Basel and something more than a camera's eye view.

The museum also has a collection of eighteenth and nineteenth century related toys—a kitchen and some shops. The latter include a confectionery, a spicery, and a milliner's shop, all from Basel, and a spicery and cloth shop of Trogen (Canton Appenzell). The museum's collection is delightfully housed in the "Kirschgarten," an eighteenth century mansion which is a branch of the museum proper.

An even more sizable collection of dolls' houses may be seen in the Schweizerisches Museum für Volkskunde in Basel: there are more than twenty houses as well as shops, kitchens, and related toys in this museum of Swiss folk art. Through the kindness of Dr. Robert Wildhaber, Director of the Museum, we have received the catalogue of a comprehensive toy exhibition at the museum which ran from December, 1964 to June 1965. A nineteenth century kitchen, a pair of late nineteenth century rooms, and an early nineteenth century doll's parlor, all from Basel, are shown, along with many other rare toys.

An important part of this collection was given to the museum by the Basel collector, Mr. Hans-Peter His, who has since formed a second collection. In a delightful letter, Mr. His writes of this second collection which includes a dolls' house made in Basel in 1873, with its original wallpapers, furnishings, accessories, and dolls intact—"never touched by children," (alas for them, poor things, but merciful for domestic history)—nor restored in any way. All furnishings in the four-story cabinet are of the Biedermeier genre made in Germany, but all were purchased at a celebrated toy shop in Basel and still bear its labels.

Mr. His has also constructed dolls' houses and shops himself, using old furnishings and wallpapers, among them "The Room of Madame Bovary," (a chamber of a literary aspect not often found in miniature), "Confiserie, France, about 1860," a toy shop, an antiques shop and (another highly original notion) a Paris Hotel, all carefully true to their respective styles and periods, one is certain.

It seems of unusual interest that the firm of Franz Carl Weber in Zurich, probably the largest toy shop in the world (with twenty-three branches in Swiss cities), now has a museum of antique toys, begun on the occasion of the firm's 75th anniversary in 1956.

A charming parlor, ca. 1840, in the museum of antique toys of the toy firm, Franz Carl Weber in Zurich

Detail of a charming milliner's shop in the collection of Mrs. Marg. Weber-Beck

At this writing, there are only two dolls' houses and one shop in the toy collection, but these, to judge by the beautiful room shown, and by pictures of the milliner's shop Mrs. Marg. Weber-Beck has also forwarded, are of unusual quality and charm.

The delightful furniture in the ca. 1840 parlor is half wood and half cardboard, covered with white paper, and trimmed with the gold paper embellishments to be found, with infinite variations, on furniture in houses and rooms of both the middle and late nineteenth centuries. Furniture with this gilt paper trim is nearly always French. The set shown here, including the sewing stand with mirrored top at left (note the key case hanging above), and the marvelously fancy piano, has an unusual degree of elaboration (an attribute usually associated with earlier pieces in a sequence of dolls' house furniture made over a period of decades).

Two unusual and early shops from Zurich (author's collection) are described in Chapter 11.

Italy is represented in this procession by one dolls' house (to which we have alluded in Chapter 3), but it is such a worthy specimen that there is scarcely need for another. This is a representative of the mid-eighteenth century, and is to be found in the Museum of Industrial Art at Bologna.

To judge it from photographs, this dolls' house is an unusual, curiously nationalistic plaything. This one, as we said (in kind) of the Swedish dolls' house, *looks* Italian. It is marbleized, one story and low, decidedly unlike the tall, thin, cupboard-like dolls' houses to be found in most of Europe.

An Italian writer, describing it shortly after its acquisition in the twenties, remarked that the Ministry of Instruction labeled it "a *model* of a settecento palazzino." The Italian writer, however, earns our gratitude by declaring that, "The fact that it is open on all sides with large glass doors which open and fold back, and the absence of any constructional characteristics, remove any doubt: the object is a superb, aristocratic *toy*." The checkerboard marble floors and Palladian arches of the interior are accompanied by all manner of detailed scroll-work and other elaborate ornamentation, gilded, it would seem, wherever possible. Equally characteristic of the time and place are the furnishings. In the entrance hall, our informant refers to the "indispensable oval paintings of the Petronian palaces of the time." A

Italian dolls' house, ca. 1700, at Bologna
Height: 28¼"

less stately item, hanging from the ceiling rather than upon the wall, is a blackbird in a cage.

The dining-room is even more a symbol of the sunny land it epitomizes. Its countryman notes "Two elegant winestands (and the bottles of Cyprus wine standing in a circle make a brave display)." These are among a miscellany of interesting items on the dining-room walls, which also hold Venetian-style mirrors and, fastidiously enough, a wash basin. A pair of gilded and decorated sideboards contain the collection of plate.

The bedroom is so "of the place and period" that only our historian can do it justice: "The double bed . . . attracts attention behind the rich curtains of the recess. Standing on a square base painted white and gold and festooned with flowers, with a rich canopy and carved and gilded volutes above, it is provided with all the comforts of the settecento. . . . There is a 'comò' or 'bombé' chest of drawers in the Louis XIV style lacquered in gold on black with numerous drawers. On this stands a gilded clock between two statuettes of cupids in *biscuit*. There are two mirrors with gilded frames in an obviously Bolognese style. Inside an oval pointed frame is a Madonna painted in the manner of the Gandolfi. . . . On the ceiling are frescoes of playful little angels, and pleasant landscapes inside baroque frames."

There are frescoes, incidentally, on all the ceilings, perhaps the most specific identification of all. There is also a most specific clue to the original ownership of the house. On the sitting room table is a work-basket, of pearls, bearing the name "Giuseppe Sorm," believed to be Sormani, a rich and noble Emilian family with one branch living in Parma and another at Reggio with their own palaces. This, perhaps, was one of the palaces.

Sitting-room and entrance hall in the dolls' house at Bologna   Height: 28¼"

We have seen only one picture of a Spanish dolls' house, and that obscurely placed (by a photograph which is unsuitable for reproduction here) in a far corner of the room, but it is, from its appearance, a most impressive edifice. This picture, reproduced in a book published by the Hispanic Society of America,* is of a parlor on the estate of San Roque in Vigo (Pontevedra). A letter to the Count, who in 1939, when the book was printed, still lived on the estate, brought no response, but several notable things about the house are apparent from the picture.

It is a towering structure like the northern dolls' houses, though its façades, unlike those of the average German dolls' house, are complete. It stands on the floor on a platform which has a balustrade around it. There are four stories, crowned by a pitched roof, and the three upper floors have in front three elaborate windows apiece, with one each on the one visible side. The most striking feature, however, is the lowest level, an arcade with wide arches. The only other dolls' house we have seen with an arcade is the classic English specimen at Uppark. There, however, the bays are of an entirely different style; they are smaller and lighter and there are considerably more of them. It doesn't seem possible to fathom the vintage of this structure.

Despite the two lone antique specimens, one of Italy and one of Spain, we are inclined to hold to our theory (more fully developed elsewhere) that these two countries, by right of Renaissance, are likely to have preceded northern nations as makers of dolls' houses.

We owe to Mrs. Estrid Faurholt of Copenhagen the knowledge of a "marvelous" collection in Budapest.

Some time ago, in a letter, Mrs. Faurholt mentioned that friends had seen this collection of dolls' house furniture, that of Mrs. Eva Moskovszky Horvath, on a visit to Budapest. It is possible to see from pictures of pieces in Mrs. Horvath's collection the truth of a remark made by the visitors from Denmark: whereas most private collections of dolls' houses and furnishings are "bürgerlich," Mrs. Horvath's things are "from castles." There is an impression of beautiful woods with intricate inlay and a lovely patina on pieces of exquisite design.

A long letter from Mrs. Horvath herself tells us not only about her own small but select collection, but about others in Budapest, pointing out that though she is the only collector there whom she knows of at present, a Baroness Grodl, now deceased, was the most famous. Most of the Baroness' collection perished during the war, and some was sold, it seems. Mrs. Horvath is happy in the possession of some of it.

There are, in the National Museum, "a dolls' house, a toy shop— middle of the nineteenth century—some furniture, and a nice Empire doll or two," Mrs. Horvath tells us, but these, of no great distinction, one gathers, are about to be impressively augmented—regrettably too late for

* *Gallegan Provinces of Spain: Pontevedra and La Coruna,* by Ruth M. Anderson.

this edition: ". . . two old ladies have donated a collection their ancestors have collected, and the family heirlooms. Among these there is a little village, a church, some houses, workshops, everything furnished. It is partly in boxes as yet."

According to Mrs. Horvath, although there is "some fine 18th century doll furniture" in the Sopron Municipal Museum, "toys were rather neglected by museums, and many private collections or family possessions perished during the war." She adds that dolls' houses were "never so *en vogue* in Hungary as in Holland or England. "If there were complete dolls' houses from the seventeenth and eighteenth centuries, they must have been destroyed." Mrs. Horvath says that she and her mother have seen beautiful old doll furniture. They personally possess "some very fine specimens."

"My mother, Mrs. Elizabeth Moskovszky, is the mother of our collection," Mrs. Horvath writes. "The interest for toys is in her family." When she was married, Mrs. Moskovszky began collecting miniature crockery, pewter, and silver, and later she turned to furniture.

The collection consists mostly of "beautifully elaborated sample pieces, made by cabinetmakers' apprentices as their 'master work.' Of course they were used for toys afterwards." Mrs. Horvath and her mother have arranged them in two rooms, ". . . the one being quite small—the chairs about three inches—the other one rather big, but neither of them very old—about 1840–50."

Mrs. Horvath lists many of the items, and the list reads like a catalogue from one of Sotheby's more impressive sales. Oldest is "a little wardrobe, Hungarian, about 1700, the wood painted black, imitating ebony . . . both of the sides are beautifully inlaid in various woods . . . A buffet, 18th century, Hungarian, quite charming, inlaid with checkerboard marquetry work . . . Of Hungarian peasant doll furniture, [a table] is the most interesting, because it has the date of 1860 inlaid in boxwood in the carved oak, besides the name of the little owners is inlaid, too, as well as a religious inscription. The [style] is Louis XVI—it is interesting that it lasted eighty to ninety years till the [style] reached the people . . ."

It has been difficult to choose which of the distinguished pieces to include in this limited summary.

World's Work in 1903 had an article on Irish toys for Christmas with two charming illustrations. One of these was "Toy Model of an Antrim Cottage" and the other was the interior view. This enchanting toy, made at Ballycastle, was, to judge from both photographs and description, an excellent representation of Irish peasant architecture:

"The cottage itself has the thatched roof and the half door, a fire on the hearth with crook and griddle and gravelled yard. Inside, the settle bed, which serves the dual purpose of 'a seat by day, a bed by night'; the kitchen dresser or open cabinet—on which the usual wooden food utensils are dis-

Stove, white faience, 18th century, Upper Hungary. The vase in the niche is blue and white Chinese (obviously made to order since the name of a girl, Gisela, is incised in its back under glaze)   Height: 13″

A wardrobe, ca. 1700, inlaid with trompe l'oeil stars Height: 14½″

Peasant wardrobe, dated 1875, painted. These toy wardrobes were sold in markets.   Height: 7″

played—the homely chairs and stools and wooden platters of an Irish cottage will all be observed in their places, while a colleen bawn (fair girl) is spinning at the wheel and a colleen dhu (dark girl) carries home a creel of turf, the native fuel, upon her shoulders. The churn and staff are there, and the utensils for making butter and rolling bread and washing potatoes, with the milk-pail (piggin), and the three-legged pot that hangs over the hearth, and the pig at the trough."

The cottage appears to have two rooms, and is in its simplicity as socially informative as many a dolls' mansion. "Toy-making," the 1903 author commented, "is in Ireland at present in its juvenile stage." Four years later *Playthings* noted in a squib about Irish novelties the availability of "little cabins with thatched roofs, wee pigs and other farm animals." But from that day to this we have read no more about the Ballycastle toy industry.

Stove, bronze, partly blackened, partly gilt, end of the eighteenth century. Urvolgy, former Upper Hungary, now belonging to Slovakia Height: 5¾"

Scotland enters the procession at this point geographically, though properly her dolls' houses, of undoubted similarity, would be considered with England's. An item from the *Glasgow Herald* of March 1907 describes a house to be featured at a local exhibition. This, it seems, had six rooms and was "fitted with every appointment." The house dated from 1844, and the *Herald* thought it "probably the best-appointed dolls' house in Scotland."

The *Herald*, it would seem, was not fully informed. A house of a similar six rooms, but a century older, was lurking in Scotland all the time. And well before the *Herald's* report, this rival residence was on its way to becoming a thirteen-room mansion.

This, the "Farie" house, originally at Baronald in Lanarkshire, belonged till recently to Mrs. Clayton-Mitchell (née Farie), and was described fully by John Ramsay-Fairfax in the June 1953 issue of *Homes and Gardens*. It is now in Mrs. Vivien Greene's museum, The Rotunda.

Roughly two hundred years old, this elderly toy "came into the possession of the then Mrs. Farie . . . in the late-Victorian era." The past seventy years have seen it grow from its original six rooms to thirteen. Seven feet high, and with a frontage of five feet, it has, according to Mr. Ramsey-Fairfax, a "lived-in appearance . . . [and] has maintained that slightly over-crowded late-Victorian atmosphere one still associates with childhood memories of visits to aged relatives."

Buffet, "Marie Theresa," chessboard pattern, with "a charmingly provincial look" according to its owner. Height: 17"

Modern improvements during the seventy years have included such practical additions as a staircase in both ground and first floors, doors between the rooms, and three bow windows. Electric lighting has been installed (with fuse-box and switchboard in the attic), and so has a "somewhat 'Edwardian' bathroom on the top floor. One of the smaller bedrooms has been sacrificed for the much-needed improvement, for which the necessary sanitary fittings (there is a very impressive geyser) were bought in Switzerland. They include a toilet roll with perforated paper."

Some of the most beguiling furnishings in the house are to be found in the "Empire Room." The Empress Eugénie herself presented the Empire-style love seat and armchairs to Mrs. Farie (then a little girl who played in the grounds of Chislehurst where the Imperial family were in exile). As Major Ramsey-Fairfax suggests, there can be no dolls' house furnishings in existence more decidedly "Empire."

The drawing-room includes such *objets d'art* as Japanese statuettes, a violin, and a daguerreotype photograph of Queen Victoria. There is a solid-silver tea set said to be "superb," and a peacock firescreen which is "a complete miniature bird with tail erect." The pictures include "five beautiful French coloured prints in gilt frames," and there is a Regency work-table. "The newspaper lying on the settee is Swiss, but the newspaper-stand holds a miniature copy of the *Illustrated London News* of 1887."

Featured in the dining-room are such oddments as pottery bowls and cups from India, a stone ginger beer bottle and a "heart-shaped menu card." No details of this bill of fare are given, and one would like to know what miniature courses are to be served at the meticulously set table.

This is a patrician household, for "the bed-linen and coverlets in the best bedroom are hand-embroidered and edged with real lace. The tiny

A group of dolls from the 'Farie' house in the robes they wore to the coronation of Edward VII

The Empire Room of the 'Farie' house with furniture presented by Empress Eugénie

ewer and basin are made of Venetian glass, and on the dressing-table are scent bottles, brushes, combs and a silver-backed mirror." The enumerator of these wonders lists the contents of the writing-table—"notepaper, envelopes, silver-nibbed quill pen, paper clips, bunch of keys and a pair of spectacles," but, gentleman that he is, dismisses in one sentence the wardrobe as "full of female attire, including hats, coats, shoes and hand-bags." Really, Major Ramsay-Fairfax—there *are* ladies present.

The nursery, "peaceful and untidy," is best inspected with a magnifying glass. Dolls' dolls are no surprise in a dolls' house nursery, but this one also has rattles, a picture book and a cuckoo clock. The latter folds its hands demurely (and permanently) at 7:30.

What was once a schoolroom for the nursery children has been converted into a basement smoking-room, and a very elegant one, it would seem. It contains some "very fine antique furniture, including Queen Anne chairs and an inlaid Empire table."

The most considerable clue to the personality of the residents is to be found in the hall where luggage, golf-clubs and big-game rifles suggest an imminent safari to links and jungle. A trophy from a previous expedition is on the floor—a monster of a mouse skin, fully two inches long. Its ferocity is not lessened when we learn that this treasure was presented to Mrs. Clayton-Mitchell by the gardener's boy years ago.

One of the really nice things about a dolls' house, very often, is the family in residence, for in a really well-established dolls' house, the ancestors needn't be displayed merely in portraits on the walls. Dolls and doll ancestors are immortal and a few centuries of relatives may mingle in the ancestral doll mansion. So it is with the Farie house.

There are many generations though "they have no family tree, and the identity of many of them is obscure." A prominent member, it seems, is "General Brown, an imposing gentleman and the present master of the house. His age is uncertain, but it must be considerable, for one of his daughters is [to be seen] in . . . the robes she wore at Edward VII's Coronation." Three other members of the family are similarly bedecked in velvet and ermine for that event long past, another Royal link—with a Scottish accent—to Britain's historic dolls' houses.

The New Zealand residence of "Miss Queenie Watson" Height: 6'

In 1955, we received with pleasure a letter about a Victorian dolls' house in New Zealand—the only one from that faraway part of the world known to us (except for Katherine Mansfield's literary one, p. 331).

The letter was accompanied by pictures of an attractive, late Victorian house, six feet tall and three stories high; with a twin-gabled roof (an "M" roof), twin chimneys with two chimney pots apiece, a dozen windows, and a brass name plate on the front door inscribed: "Miss Queenie Watson." The letter and pictures had been sent by Mr. and Mrs. E. H. Short of Dunedin, who had purchased it locally a few years before, completely furnished. The

154

furnishings, which the Shorts augmented from a personal collection of miniature objects, included a silver Queen Anne tea service, hand-carved furniture, and bell pulls with tassels.

An inquiring letter to Mr. and Mrs. Short ten years later disclosed the fact that the dolls' house is now in the Canterbury Museum in Christchurch, the gift of Mrs. J. Ferrier who had bought it from the Shorts. Mr. Short also mentioned in his 1965 letter that after writing to the author in 1955, he and Mrs. Short began searching for the original owners. "After many months, and by sheer accident, we found a Miss Watson, who was one of the two daughters sharing the ownership (of the dolls' house) . . . She mentioned . . . that her parents only allowed them to view it only so often, and (they) were never allowed to play with it or ever to touch it." An interesting bit of documentation of a fact that is often suspected of dolls' houses when they are found in surprisingly good condition, but one that is seldom proved.

A group of Eskimo toys in the Alaska College Museum collected from the Aleutians, the Alaskan Peninsula, Bristol Bay, King Island, St. Lawrence Island and several other arctic regions was described in the *Journal of Home Economics* in 1931. Among the toys discussed was "doll furniture . . . such as little hand-carved plates and bowls of wood or soft sandstone. Miniature seal oil lamps of clay are made by the young girls while the mothers are making the real ones, On Nunivak and Nelson Islands and on the Alaskan Peninsula the girls have little baskets and also small grass mats similar to those the people use for sleeping mats. These last are not seen on St. Lawrence Island because there the people sleep on reindeer and walrus skins."

An assortment of Eskimo toys at the National Museum in Washington among "one of the largest collections of toys in the world" (but, of which, fifty years later, the Museum emphatically denied having any knowledge) was reported by *St. Nicholas* in 1901. The article mentioned particularly the toys the Eskimos carved from walrus tusks. "Often entire villages are made, the huts, canoes and dog sledges being in perfect miniature." The magazine printed a picture of a dog sledge from Labrador, with dogs whittled from white wood, and if the huts were similarly detailed in doll size, Eskimo dolls must have been accurately housed.

In 1919, *Playthings* tucked in among its trade advice the notation that "Eskimo doll houses are sometimes snow huts in miniature," and though we have this intelligence from no more northern authority, such dolls' house building seems almost inevitable in so icy a land.

Shortly before this edition went to press, the writer learned of a remarkable and little-known group of early German and Dutch dolls' houses and shops which has been languishing obscurely in the Denver Art Museum for years.

Collected by Dr. Fritz Rosenberg, a physician who was born in Frank-

"Ambulant Fair Tent," with dry goods, eighteenth century, from the collection of Dr. Fritz Rosenberg at the Denver Art Museum

furt but who has lived and practiced in Colorado since 1938, there are a seventeenth century German dolls' house, 18th and 19th century Dutch houses, and three rare eighteenth and nineteenth century German shops, certainly the most imposing dolls' house aggregation of such early vintage to be seen in the United States.

Inasmuch as the pieces are German and Dutch, but are now to be seen in the United States, they belong really to none of these countries, nor to the chapters (in this book) about them, but are truly international in character. They are included, therefore, in "An International Procession," a chapter which it seems fitting to conclude with this extraordinary collection—a true *grand finale*.

A nineteenth century Dutch "convent piece," from the Rosenberg collection, Denver Art Museum

Dr. Rosenberg and his late wife did their collecting between 1919 and 1938, when it was still possible to find pieces of this antiquity, in travels all over Europe. Two of the houses and all three of the shops were found virtually complete, although some pieces have been added. The seventeenth century German house was assembled. This, which Dr. Rosenberg refers to as "the baroque house," is of more interest for its rare furnishings than for its cabinet which did not originate as a dolls' house. However, the latter is carefully in period, being the upper section of a 17th century cabinet whose lower section with drawers was in such poor condition that it was not usable. Dr. Rosenberg had a carpenter install a rare curving model staircase in his possession, along with inlaid floors and walls made from panels of unusable antique furniture. The house is divided into five rooms, three up and two down, patterned after "the well-known European dolls' houses," such as the Gontard in Frankfurt, and others in Nuremberg, Augsburg, Leyden, and Munich.

Among the beautiful furnishings, perhaps the rarest is a brass two-tiered chandelier that can be dismantled. Exactly like those of a full-sized seventeenth century brass chandelier from the Netherlands that hangs in the author's study, the arms are numbered, with corresponding numbers on the center section as a guide to reassembling. Other rare pieces in this house include a stove model found in an antique shop in Budapest, and a wardrobe that Dr. Rosenberg thinks was very likely an apprentice piece (which an apprentice before becoming a master in his Guild had to show before he could be elected to membership). Some of the early dolls that inhabit these early rooms may have originated, their owner thinks, in Nativity groups.

The eighteenth century "Dutch baroque house" is contained in a glass-fronted cabinet with a most astonishing and delightful addition—a roof garden on top. This, with a charming latticed fence, and swinging gates, is the only dolls' house roof garden (of any country) we know. There are three rooms, one above the other, kitchen, sitting-room, and bedroom, inhabited by dolls of the period. The Rosenbergs acquired the house complete in 1921 from an antiques dealer who had bought it for his daughter (who, upon growing up, had lost interest in it!), adding only a few pieces to what is a thoroughly furnished house.

"Baroque" house in a seventeenth century cabinet. Rosenberg collection, Denver Art Museum

157

The kitchen, which, even more than most miniature kitchens of the period, is overflowing with an astonishing array of utensils of every variety, has many unusual items. One is a box with a special knife which was used to cut the sugar from the heavy (20 pound) conical "sugarhoods." The box, Dr. Rosenberg tells us, "guaranteed no crumbs lost during the splitting process."

Dr. Rosenberg believes the nineteenth century Dutch house to be a convent piece, "probably made within the walls of a convent since the dolls are dressed as nuns. This is a most unusual and handsome trio of three rooms placed horizontally within an arched Gothic framework which also contributes to an ecclesiastical atmosphere. The inlaid floors, Biedermeier furnishings (some of them of the gilt-stenciled, rosewood genre), are not, however, of the spare simplicity one associates with convents. This unusual "house," which also came complete, is a curiosity in another respect. According to Dr. Rosenberg, there is a "lid" to the house, approximately four inches in depth, under one side of which is a drawer sectioned for sewing utensils. Dr. Rosenberg writes, and we concur, that he's never heard of another dolls' house that also serves as a sewing table.

The three shops in this collection are altogether irresistible, two of them, which Dr. Rosenberg refers to as "Ambulant Fair Tents," of eighteenth century origin. These have identical green and white striped awnings stretched across a wooden framework with curious hooks across the awning top for hanging merchandise, shelves for the other stock, and, in each, a counter with a lace-edged cloth. The Ambulant Fair, says the doctor, came twice a year to Frankfurt/Main where, in the early days, it "was likely the cheapest way of replenishing needed household goods."

The dry goods tent, with its hanging baskets and rolls of fabric, is shown, presided over by its 18th century German proprietress. The second tent, containing a china and glassware shop, has a porcelain-headed proprietress (possibly to match her wares?) who appears to be of later date.

Both tents came complete from a collection which two sisters in Wiesbaden had begun. Some merchandise was added by their new owners.

Found in Garmisch, Bavaria, the German milliner's shop, ca. 1840, represents "a miniature collection of native costumes and bonnets as worn by the country girls of the time, but from various areas." This is a delightful piece, its glass-doored cabinet shelves stocked with appealing merchandise, placed at each side of an unusual glass-doored closet through which elegant garments may be seen hanging from a rack. The counter has a charming basket of flowers painted on its front, and several early nineteenth century dolls lend further interest to the premises. The Rosenbergs were able to acquire this lovely shop for the curious reason that it was rejected by the local museum (in Garmisch) as "not rural enough."

It is unfortunate that the Denver Art Museum lacks rooms to keep this rare collection on permanent display, and is limited to brief showings, a recent one at Christmas, 1964.

158

10

TOY
KITCHENS

The TOY KITCHEN, LIKE THE DOLLS' ROOM, ALWAYS HAS LED AN existence quite independent of the dolls' house. Perhaps its originators were hungry fathers with daughters they hoped to see grow up into excellent cooks. They were nothing if not thorough. If early dolls' houses were furnished in sufficient detail to instruct their young owners in housekeeping, early toy kitchens were positively cluttered in their purpose of teaching the highly utensilized art of cookery.

Copper pots, pewter plates, crockery mugs, and assorted utensils of varying sizes, shapes, and purposes lined the shelves and hung, approximately, from the rafters in toy kitchens of the seventeenth and eighteenth centuries. Even to memorize the names of the implements, much less their uses, would seem to have been a considerable achievement for a small girl.

But achieve she did. These were educational toys. We know that the Nuremberg kitchens, if no others, were intended to instruct, and that the so-called modern educational toy has been preceded.

Practically all countries which have had dolls' houses have had kitchens. Although examples from various countries are remarkably similar, there are striking differences in others. The Nuremberg is the classic kitchen, perhaps because the toy center that produced it was seemingly the originator.

Mrs. Jackson tells us that these toys are exact models of the kitchens of South Germany in the seventeenth and eighteenth centuries.

She adds: "We have in our possession a specimen which might be a copy to scale of that in Albrecht Dürer's house in Nuremberg, or of the kitchen belonging to Goethe's mother in Frankfurt where the poet received the inspiration for the great kitchen scene in Faust—the same wide chimney reaching almost down to the big open grate; even the chicken-coops are there, in which the thrifty housewife always kept the next couple of fowls to be killed, that they might be fattened by all the kitchen scraps. These victims, when killed for the table, were at once replaced by another couple."

These poultry coops appear in any number of old toy kitchens of no matter what country. D'Allemagne, in *Les Accessoires de Costume et du Mobilier,* pictures a magnificent specimen from his collection, which is, however, another Nuremberg example, and this one also contains two of these coops. He submits further poultry lore: "In old cook books, there was indicated at what instant one ought to sacrifice an old fowl to improve such and such a very complicated dish of which our ancestors were so fond."

The niceties of the culinary precision that then prevailed are further illustrated by the presence in the same kitchen of the series of twelve frying pans, of varying sizes and thicknesses. Mastering the proper use of each must have amounted to a science. It is notable that d'Allemagne attests to the arrangement of the utensils in this kitchen as "strictly exact," having found in a Nuremberg toymaker's catalogue of the eighteenth century "the picture of a kitchen of this same kind."

To keep the individual members of such a toy in their proper places must have been in itself a challenge to a child, and more attractive than any mere puzzle. Mrs. Jackson's specimen contained 148 pieces of wood, porcelain, brass, copper and pewter (in a space twenty-six inches wide), steak-beaters and toasting-forks, whisk brooms and lanterns. Nor was hers the most comprehensive to be found.

The Illustrated London News, a few years ago, showed an example with 241 utensils, some of them dating from the reign of James II, and with a working oven. This kitchen was large in scale, being almost five feet long. Since it had its own traveling case, possibly its young owner took it back and forth between country and town houses. Such an elaborate toy would have belonged only to a little girl who was herself elaborately housed.

Two kitchens in the author's collection would, between them, provide material for quite a learned thesis on Nuremberg cookery. "Eighteenth century," a time span we originally applied to the specimen pictured, was unquestionably broad. But kitchens, even more than dolls' houses, possibly because metal objects were more likely to have been prized and, therefore, preserved, tend to become accumulations of objects handed down, mixed with later additions. Dating them becomes hazardous, but one ventures to say ca. 1800 of this one after studying a picture of a kitchen so dated at Augsburg. Several important utensils are common to both kitchens.

All Nuremberg kitchens have the big open grate with a wide chimney to carry off the smoky fumes. Charcoal used for cooking on the brick hearth was stored, with wood, in the opening below it—concealed in our photograph by the handsome copper firescreen. The latter was set on the hearth to protect the operator revolving the spit from the heat of the fire. This screen is identical to the one pictured in the Augsburg kitchen* and so is the large copper vessel (with hinged lid) suspended between two metal brackets above the open fire on the hearth. (The position of this imposing utensil assured a continuous supply of hot water, all day long.) Beneath the scales may be seen the lidded copper jug used to carry the water; this, too, is identical to one in the Augsburg kitchen, and there are numerous other similarities.

Matching copper pots in graduated sizes, hanging by their own small brass rings, are lined with tin. Such cooking pans were popular for generations, but "in spite of the highly attractive appearance of a polished and gleaming *batterie-de-cuisine* of this metal," say *The Connoisseur Period Guides,* "the 1850's saw the introduction and acceptance of the more hygienic and more easily managed enamelled iron." Resembling tankards, the glazed dark-blue-handled containers with hinged lids of pierced tin (above the hearth) are sausage pots. The sausages were brought, still in boiling water, to the table.

Of particular interest, on the hearth, is a tin lamp which burned fat in the cup beneath its lid, a wick emerging from its spout, with a saucer base to catch the drippings. An identical lamp may be seen in the kitchen at the Metropolitan Museum of Art.

The second Nuremberg kitchen in the author's collection contains many rare utensils from the eighteenth century, but we shall show only one item which accompanied it—a small German dolls' cook book from the middle of the nineteenth.

Even if only the cover of this small cook book, with its revealing illustration, had survived, it might still have been considered a treasure, but it is intact, faded and a bit wrinkled, like an elderly cook; weathered by the heat of the oven and, possibly, a little gravy.

Printed in Nuremberg in 1858, the title page informs us in German that this is a "Little Cook Book for the Doll's Kitchen," or "First Instruction

* This kitchen, at the Maximilians Museum in Augsburg, may be seen in *Children's Toys of Bygone Days,* by Geoffrey Holme, The Studio, Ltd. London, 1932.

for Cooking for Girls 8–14 Years of Age." So worded, this inscription is an explicit corroboration—if more is needed—that such toys were true educational toys, specifically intended for instruction as well as for play.

Among the late Madame Rubinstein's miniature rooms is an eighteenth century Austrian dolls' kitchen which she bought from a Hapsburg, and which is similar to the Nuremberg species. It, too, has a poultry coop, but instead of Mrs. Jackson's couple, it contains an eighteenth century china turkey, hen, and duck. There is considerable realism; the rough plaster walls are smoke-stained around the hooded stove, leading one to suspect that some little Hapsburg once decided to be realistic in her cooking. If so, it is a mercy that the toy has so perfectly survived, although it is reasonably fireproof with its square-tiled floor and the aforementioned plaster. The sloping sink, though, and the cupboards and shelves are of wood.

Many of these kitchens are occupied, although an occasional discrepancy of costume suggests that the small cooks may have appeared on their miniature horizons at a later date. In the Hapsburg kitchen we have been describing, the cook has been known to hold a gold-mesh fish which, courtesy four links, is capable of squirming. When we saw the kitchen, it appeared to be missing.

The same Hapsburg who had this interesting dolls' kitchen had another, with the utensils in gold, which its owner was at first reluctant to sell, but eventually it, too, came into Madame Rubinstein's possession. It has remained abroad, however, along with many of its owner's treasures.

A toy kitchen in gold doesn't appear quite so startling after one hears of the precious specimen of another sort that belonged to little Louis XVI. This is made of bronze and Dresden china rather than of gold, but it was designed by the celebrated sculptor Caffieri, and is certainly one of the most curious toys that ever has been. Claretie has a delightful description: ". . . it is in the style of the period, with its realism carefully veiled or embellished. The saucepans are decorated with floral wreaths and the little chicken on the spit is an exquisite bit of Dresden china. As for the cook and his assistant they seem to be totally oblivious of the viands they are expected to prepare, but dressed elegantly in satins they simper and pose with an air that is more suited to the dancing of a minuet than to the concocting of sauces. It is a characteristic conception of the period when Marie Antoinette played at farming with snow white sheep at the Petit Trianon."

The "toy kitchen" of bronze and Dresden china that belonged to little, Louis XVI

There is a clock near the top and a cherub above that. Indeed, it seems more a clock than a toy, withal a playful and amusing one. It was shown at the exposition of 1900, and used to be in the collection of Mme. Lelong.

Since early American dolls' houses appear to be a distinct minority, it is interesting that at least three very fine early kitchens are in existence. All are of the Nuremberg type, but two, more similar than the third, have a surprising lot in common. The other member of the trio is unusually comprehensive as similar toys go, containing such traditional American furnishings as a drop-leaf table and slat-back chairs, and is perhaps of earlier vintage. It has more furniture generally than the utensil-filled Nuremberg style. In addition to a hooded stone fireplace with crane, there are stool, chest, towel rack, spinning wheel, churn, baskets, buckets, and "an extraordinary assortment of toleware and treenware . . ."

(There is a curious story attached to our inability to describe personally this kitchen, one that reveals the strange by-ways to which even such innocent work may lead. We wrote to the doll dealer known to possess this interesting toy, and receiving no reply attempted to see her at her shop on a subsequent trip to New York. At this deserted place, a reluctant personage, who plainly eyed us with suspicion, after several minutes came out with it. "It was in all the papers," she kept saying, as if to justify revealing such confidential information. "It was something to do with the dollies." The doll dealer, it seemed, was in prison, the authoress of a quite notorious piece of enemy espionage ([in which her dolls prominently figured]) during World War II. It was impossible to learn what became of the kitchen.)

Another example, which Mrs. J. Insley Blair, of Tuxedo Park, New York, gave to Washington's Headquarters at Newburgh, New York, where it is now on display, came from around Albany, and is believed to have originated in the Hudson River Valley. There are two occupants, lady and servant, in eighteenth century dress, who may or may not be contemporary with the frame, and an antiquarian publication has pointed out that not all of the plenishings are "necessarily of the same date."

The Metropolitan Museum of Art has, unfortunately in storage, a late eighteenth century kitchen very similar to the Nuremberg models, which came to the museum identified as an American toy kitchen from New York State. There are, of course, several possibilities to explain the kitchen's Nuremberg form. The first, needless to say, is that it did not originate in America at all, but was brought over for some affluent colonist's child, with local accessories added, during its early history, to the imported ones. The second possibility is that a transplanted German citizen made the kitchen in New York State in the style which he had employed at home. This, however, would not account for a number of accessories to be seen in the kitchen which are similar to ones found in German kitchens and which, of course, would have been made by assorted artisans. More importantly, it would not account for the fact that the hood of the fireplace, a major feature of the frame, which is to be found in many variations even in Nuremberg versions, is *identical* to one to be seen on a colored lithograph by Johann Michael Voltz, a South German painter and draftsman (1784–1858). The curious similarity was called to our notice by Dr. Elisabeth Wolffhardt of Munich who sent a postcard reproduction of children playing with a Nuremberg kitchen, one of a charming series of Voltz lithographs of Biedermeier home life. Usually the tops of such chimneys are flat or curved; the hollow gable that may be seen on the hood of the Metropolitan's kitchen and on

Cover of "Little Cook Book for the Doll's Kitchen," printed in Nuremberg in 1858

the one in the Voltz lithograph are identically made, and the only ones of this style that we know.

For these reasons we incline to the theory that the kitchen was imported, though very possibly in the eighteenth century. Inasmuch as most citizens whose ancestors may have come to the United States even later than this kitchen consider themselves very American indeed, possibly, with a similar interpretation, the kitchen at the Metropolitan also may be considered American.

In any case, in the Metropolitan's files, an itemized description of the kitchen and its contents may be found, a most ambitious inventory, and such a revealing document with respect to period cookery processes, as well as to the erudition of the noble institution that recorded it, that we list it in part (a companion piece to our illustration):

"Furnishings: at left, built-in dresser with upper cupboard of two drawers and lower of one; next this a built-in shelf with grating below, forming pen for chickens (made of wood); fire-place with hood and trammel at right; back, built-in trough, with strainer at side; at end, built-in table; also table with turned legs and central drawer, flat stretcher connecting legs; stained walnut."

164

Among the utensils, pottery, tin, copper, pewter and woodenware are well represented. Pie dishes, jugs and bowls are among the pottery, and collectors of the ware in full-size would cast covetous eyes upon pieces "aubergine flecked," as is one set of bowls, or at a white pie plate with blue-and-green cross. In tin, such miscellaneous objects as dishpan, spice box, collander, measure, frying pans, cookie tins, and funnels appear. One of the funnels, by the way, with two spouts, is for a whale-oil lamp. And there's a jagging wheel with zigzag edge for cutting cakes or pastry into ornamental figures. Also in tin is a standard with rimmed foot, holding an oil can. Copper pots and pans are present in plenty. A copper tin-lined mold in the form of a cornucopia vies in interest with a cake dish, fluted, with a hole in the middle. In pewter, there are plates, jugs, basins, beakers, domed pudding dishes, a covered baking dish, a tankard. There's a fine wire sieve with flat wooden pestle; and also in woodenware, breadboard and knife (*both* of wood) as well as the inevitable potato masher appear. And there is the customary complement of long-handled wooden spoons. Ladles abound, both pierced and plain, in varying materials, including steel, brass and lead.

Miscellaneous articles include a chopping table with cleaver and meat-chopper; gridiron; lantern with guard on chimney; flatiron (handle covered with leather, and an opening at back for insertion of coals); trivets; a basket of lead knives, forks and spoons; dustpan and brush; long-handled hearth broom; brass mortars and pestles; coffee mill; bellows; brass candle snuffers (a pair); waffle-iron with long wooden handles; kneading board; salt box of lead; and a long-handled shovel.

Among objects in glass are a pair of plain blown decanters with ringed necks—and more interesting—a pear-shaped decanter, blown in mold, with diamond pattern. If this failed to dazzle a glass collector, two hexagonal decanters, blown in mold, with herring-bone pattern, might succeed.

The remarkable picture this total gives not only of a kitchen, but of a person, or persons, working for days and weeks and months to make such a toy for children is certainly extraordinary. It is difficult to imagine how many artisans were involved, and how much time.

The toy kitchen in its most curious form appeared in the middle of the nineteenth century, and in the person literally of a doll. The kitchen doll is better seen (note illustration) than described, but, briefly, she embodies (also literally) a toy kitchen within her full wooden skirt. One example which was left by Lady Grantley to the R.S.P.C.A. and may be seen at their Cheddar branch in the Cotswolds,* was a lady of 1840 with a brick and tile interior, and shelves. Pitchers and utensils hang from hooks on the (in)sides of her skirt. Her kitchen anatomy is not nearly so complex as the Nuremberg models, but she has comparable culinary charms.

---

* According to Miss Faith Eaton, noted English doll-maker, who happened to come across it there, the exhibit, which includes other dolls, is probably on view only during the tourist season.

Mid-nineteenth century kitchen doll, left by Lady Grantley to the R.S.P.C.A. and now on view at their Cheddar branch in the Cotswolds

Even types of toy kitchens more standard than the one this lady conceals beneath her gown vary in quite extraordinary ways. Gröber shows two nineteenth century dolls' kitchens, one Danish and one Swiss, which are entirely different in style from any others we have seen.

Most toy kitchens seem to be wide rather than tall, and have three walls with no roof. The Danish specimen is almost twice as tall as it is wide and has a shallow-gabled roof. Its utensils are relatively few, and most of them are nearly as large as the brick hearth.

The Swiss kitchen is more architectural still; it is, indeed, a complete little building (see illustration), with seven banistered steps leading into it, an exceedingly Tyrolese roof with a tiny gabled window in the midst of its assortment of planes, and a chimney. It has about it a wide-open country air; a closed aperture to what looks as though it might be a hayloft is below the gabled window. A hoist under the latter supports a chained hanger from which are suspended sides of beef. These attest perhaps to the recent activities of a gentleman busy at the chopping block below. He, one might hastily add, and his unattractive goings-on, are out on the little stoop adjoining the steps, and away from the well-furnished interior. Three other personages are bustling about in there, amongst a quite handsome table, several chairs of an Alpine aspect, a tall glassed-in cupboard, and the inevitable hooded stove.

*Kitchen from the Tyrol, early
nineteenth century   Height: 23¼″*

It seems appropriate to conclude this chapter with the tin kitchen, a traditional American toy of the Victorian era, one turned out in a variety of sizes, and degrees of completeness—but of a remarkable similarity in form—by American manufacturers of tin toys during much of the nineteenth century and also by foreign makers.

Often stenciled or embossed, with a hooded stove in the center and a workable pump to one side, a number of these kitchens survive—a tribute possibly to the vast numbers made as well as to their durability.

Since they are often found with their original utensils replaced, and in varying stages of peeling paint, bent tin, and general disarray, the example pictured (from the author's collection) which came out of an old store and is believed to be intact, with its pots, molds, and scoops still in place, is something of a treasure.

*Victorian tin kitchen,
author's collection
Height: 17½″*

167

11

MINIATURE SHOPS

A SOMEWHAT PRECIPITATE WRITER ONCE SUGGESTED THAT IF A dolls' house was the province of little girls, a counterpart for their brothers was the toy soldier. It seemed to us at the time that the model railroad or the toy theater would be a better parallel, and now, while we are about it, how about the toy store?

We of today fancy that we are ever so modern with our educational toys. One would suppose that before the twentieth century no plaything had any intention but to amuse. As we have seen, the interest of quite a number of dolls' houses of the past has been to teach, in a very pretty way, the rudiments of housekeeping to girls. The miniature shop, complete with merchandise, counter and cash, may very similarly have introduced their young brothers to the business world.

In some of the older specimens of these toy shops there is behind the counter a doll salesperson, whom the somewhat larger human proprietor would be obliged, in order to preside, to dispossess. The scale of these toys is frequently greater than usual dolls' house scale, perhaps to better accommodate this vaster custodian.

Although we are not able to trace miniature shops back as far as dolls' houses, they have been known for more than two centuries. It is easy to

Apothecary "cabinet," walnut, ca. 1730; actually an apprentice piece made to show the skill of the apprentice when he took his examination. (Probably from the apothecaries' guild at Delft)

surmise why earlier specimens might have been lost in the shuffle. They would hardly have been as elaborate and expensive as dolls' houses, and therefore neither as carefully cared for, to be handed down to posterity, nor as likely to have been immortalized in any recorded way. Still, as early as 1696, in the Inventory of the Crown, among other toys of the Dauphin's, there is set down, "Nine shops of the marketplace, filled with little figures of enamel." These, however, were more likely to have been enameled tin figures of the type made some sixty years later by Hilpert in Nuremberg.

Most of the early dolls' shops are in museums.

Although an impressive apothecary "cabinet," ca. 1730, in the Rijksmuseum, Amsterdam, is not actually a toy, it is related to dolls' shops in the same way that the Dutch poppenhuizen are related to toy houses, and its irresistible picture is shown above.

Stalls as well as stores are found beginning in the eighteenth century, and the two "Ambient Fair Tents" given by Dr. Fritz Rosenberg to the Denver Art Museum (and described in Chapter 9) are charming examples.

A German lottery stall, also of the eighteenth century, which belongs to the Germanisches Museum in Nuremberg, is pictured by Karl Gröber.* This curious piece, nearly two feet tall, is stocked with exceedingly miscellaneous goods—fans, ladles, and mysterious garments—all of which is presided over by a proprietor as elaborately garbed as a Royal Grenadier. When it is raised, the stall-front not only gives access to the interior, but serves as a rack for some of the merchandise. The front of the counter,

* *Children's Toys of Bygone Days.*

Toy stall, ca. 1800, from Zurich, with toys of wood and gum tragacanth. Author's collection Height: 11"

The small cupboard arrived broken, but a motto was folded neatly inside

The little boy on his hobby horse. A figure of gum tragacanth in the toy stall pictured Height: 1¾"

handsomely painted in a spiral pattern, is flanked on both sides with a panelled, painted gate. A checkerboard floor extends the front.

A toy and sweet stall, ca. 1800, in the author's collection, is similar in style, but considerably smaller, being a mere eleven inches high. Its wares are early and rare. It had been found in Zurich for its new owner who felt very much the Serendip when, upon its arrival, one of its seventy or so small wares unexpectedly disclosed the stall's beguiling secret.

Although the "stock" had been described, by the dealer who found this treasure, as toys of "wood and plaster," and some were indeed of wood, the other figures felt too fragile to the touch to be of such coarse stuff as plaster. It was fortuitous that one tiny cupboard arrived broken, for a bit of paper neatly folded inside it reminded a momentarily distressed collector that this damaged treasure *had* to be of gum tragacanth, the substance which early nineteenth century pastry-cooks combined with meal and sugar, molded into charming novelties with mottoes* inside, and then painted. Gröber, who tells us that the little figures were "for the most part edible," shows in his book examples of a style and size identical to these, oddly enough from a private collection in Zurich, and dated "ca. 1800."

Among the meticulously fashioned articles in the stall are bowls of fruit, a little boy on his hobby horse, a mask for a masquerade, and the cuirass from a suit of armor. The wooden toys include checkerboards,

* Printed in old German, the motto placed a century and a half ago inside the tidbit described above is as fatuous as most "fortune cookie" messages, but a treasure for all that! This shop is featured in *The Toy Shop Mystery* by Flora Gill Jacobs, Coward-McCann, Inc., 1960.

bayonets, hobby horses, tenpins, whips, and tiny musical instruments—horns, drums, and lutes. The booth itself, which has a door in one side, is painted a rusty sienna without, and a pleasant, faded blue within, and is tended by a nicely carved wooden proprietress whose face, alas, is missing.

A general store, found in Zurich with the toy and sweet stall, may be late eighteenth century, and is, at latest, early nineteenth.

The labels on its sixty small drawers are lettered in German: figs, almonds, lentils, marjoram, caraway, candles, sago, and anise—to translate at random—give a key to the type of merchandise they represent. There is a slot in the counter, leading to a money drawer below, and glass doors to display-shelves are behind the counter.

Beneath the bead necklaces hanging in such profusion, a net bag of attractive ceramic fish rests on the counter, near one of two handsome baskets which bear their original price tags. Bundles of candles, a basket of coiled wax tapers, and jars of candy "pills" with parchment lids fastened with thread are on the shelves. Fabrics were obviously a specialty of the shop; bolts of fabric (actually cards of ribbon) are stacked high, and although a museum authority on textiles has told us that they are from the 1870s, considerably later than the shop itself, many, embroidered in lovely old colors and patterns, are late but delightful additions to the stock.

The Biedermeier period is plainly the heyday of the dolls' shop—or at least it appears to be from the number of this vintage to be found. Of these, milliners' shops seem to occur in the greatest numbers.

Possibly because it is shown in color, one of the loveliest appears to be an example from the Germanisches Museum in Nuremberg which is illustrated by Gröber. Here the bonnets of coal-scuttle shape are displayed upon the papier-mâché heads which attractively preceded the cold metal

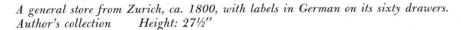

A general store from Zurich, ca. 1800, with labels in German on its sixty drawers. Author's collection   Height: 27½"

A charming Biedermeier milliner's shop from the museum in Nuremberg

display racks of later times.* False curls, both blonde and brunette, may be seen tumbling from boxes on the counter. Only a part of the shop is shown, and one wonders if it is the same described a generation earlier by Mrs. Jackson. The bonnets are also of coal-scuttle shape: "Some are of the finest Dunstable straw plait, some of Leghorn, others of crinoline or buckram, and there are several in skeleton condition, of silk-covered wire. Dainty rolls of coloured ribbons, a few centimetres wide, are kept in some of the cardboard boxes which form the shop fittings; in others, lengths of tulle, net, and hand-made thread laces, for though net was by then made by machinery, lace by the same process was not yet common. Tiny feathers are displayed in some of the glass-covered cases, and a few trimmed hats and bonnets are placed upon stands. A shop-woman stands behind the counter, and a file of bills and quire of wrapping paper testify to her tidy and businesslike methods."

(A charming Bavarian milliner's shop, ca. 1840, in the Denver Art Museum, is described on page 158.)

Two other milliner's shops of the Biedermeier period also are pictured by Gröber, and it is interesting to see what different forms these shops could take. One is Danish from the Dansk Folke Museum and far simpler than the other. The stock is exceedingly random, and the goods displayed rather like a rummage sale. Hats for dolls of various sizes (one is large enough to immerse the proprietor) are casually flung on two shelves. It is evidently Spring, for all the merchandise is straw. Two clotheslines are hung against the door, and umbrellas are among the goods displayed there. The frame and the wooden counter, behind which the proprietor stands talking to a little customer, is of the plainest manufacture.

A more imposing emporium, from the Landesgewerbe Museum at Stuttgart, is nearly nine inches taller, and though it has a comparable entry plan, the doors fold to accommodate its greater width; and its depth, though shallow, is sufficient to contain neat counters with trim drawers. What's more, its doors are of paned glass and when closed correspond to a trio of glass fanlights above. The tidy shelves of the interior are bisected by a mirror, in front of which a chandelier hangs. The bonnets are displayed in an orderly fashion on slender stands. Miscellaneous goods, principally purses, hang from lines on the doors in a style similar to the ones in the Danish shop, but in these more precise surroundings, look quite dignified.

Geoffrey Holme† has a picture of what is literally a doll's shop in the Stadt Historisches Museum, Frankfurt/Main. This one is also of the Biedermeier period, being dated 1830, and has not merely bonnets, but presumably anything a doll could possibly use, including a head. This rather

---

* It must be noted that the gilded, weighted hat stands in a late Victorian milliner's shop in the author's collection have their own charm, however. This shop, all blue and gilt with glazed wall cabinets and much be-feathered and be-flowered merchandise, has the F. A. O. Schwarz West 23rd Street label on the bottom—the New York toy firm's address from approximately 1890 to 1910.

† *Children's Toys of Yesterday.*

unusual mercantile arrangement, a sort of dolls' department store, appears to have, in addition to the aforementioned bonnets and heads, frocks, purses, baskets (suspended from hooks in the ceilings), and all sorts of invisible merchandise, contained, no doubt, in the twenty drawers, divers boxes on shelves, and glass cases on the counter.

Though the majority of dolls' shops seem to have been grocers' or milliners', there has been a variety. Gröber shows a curious one with glass toys. This, from the Bavarian Forest and the first half of the nineteenth century, is of wood, and has a very realistic proprietress and customer compounded of various ingredients. But everything else is of glass. There are pitchers and goblets and potted glass flowers—traditionally glass things; then there are items less realistic, a bird in a glass cage, a small doll, a parrot on a stand, a variety of small birds and animals, for that matter. The *pièce de résistance* appears to be a stag's head, a mounted trophy (with luxurious antlers) of the glass blower's art.

An entirely different sort of plaything, but one which necessarily falls into our miniature business category, is pictured by Geoffrey Holme, and represents a Tyrolese village smithy. This Austrian toy, made at the beginning of the nineteenth century, is from the village of Schwaz and is practically a dolls' house in its architectural detail. Indeed, since the blacksmith's residence appears to adjoin his shop, this toy is part dolls' house and part dolls' shop and is, therefore, for the purposes of this book, a little gem.

The residential section has two stories, two windows and a double door with fanlight on the ground floor, and three windows with shutters above. The smithy, an open alcove with a pitched roof and a tall chimney, clings closely to this superstructure, and a sort of little shed banks that. There are five figures, perfect reflections of both artisan and noble styles of dress. The smith stands near his forge, wielding his mallet. His knee breeches meet neat stockings, whereas his two patrons, one of them seated on a bench in front of his house, have fine boots. The apprentice boy wears trousers; another assistant, a long apron.

The British, for some reason, seem to have made the most attractive butchers' shops. The "attractive" may be taken in any number of ways. A specimen presented to the Victoria and Albert Museum by Queen Mary is of mid-nineteenth century origin and is a beauty, as our illustration shows. One writer, unwilling to overlook its faults, referred to it as "a fascinating if slightly gruesome representation of a typical butcher shop of its day."

It is true that the cuts of meat are considerably gory, and highly anatomical, but they are neatly arranged on hooks and include every cut known. There are even whole haunches. Four little curtained windows are high above. But the vegetarian touch, the sheerly British thought, are the four dear little potted plants on the shelf under the four little windows, scenery for the two short butchers with cleavers and the butcher boy with mallet. This is a tender scene, though, compared to one noticed by a writer in

British butcher's shop, mid-nineteenth century, at Victoria & Albert Museum
Height: 1' 8½"

Two mid-19th century butcher's shops; the upper says "Bull Butcher" but has been seen in a German toy catalogue, ca. 1848 Heights: 13" and 16½"

174

Everyman's in 1906. The writer detected "the butcher in a bloody apron lounging at the door."

Cooper Union in New York City has a butcher's shop almost identical to the Victoria and Albert's, but with an even vaster stock of meats, and such minor additions as a top hat for the butcher. The Museum of Childhood in Edinburgh has a specimen that puts both of these in the shade: there are twice as many cuts of meat, twice as many potted plants, and a bowler hat for the chief butcher who holds in his hand what can only be described as a halberd.

Of several butchers' shops in the author's collection, all considerably more modest than these, a small one labeled "Bull Butcher" offered a surprise when it was discovered in a mid-nineteenth century toy catalogue. Because the sign on it was printed in English, it had been assumed that the shop was made in England. But the catalogue was German, and some of the merchandise pictured in it was labeled in German and some, like this shop, was labeled in English—the latter obviously for export. As a result, another means of identifying the country of origin, one which had previously been relied upon, went out of the window!

Sometimes the exporter is cagey. In a late Victorian grocer's shop in the author's collection, small tins bear charming paper labels picturing the various fruits that are presumably within, but no printed words. Although this might also have been directed towards young children who hadn't learned to read, it is more likely that in avoiding the language problem, it enabled the exporter to send these small tins out into the world regardless of destination.

Mrs. James B. Childs of Washington, D. C. has a delightful grocer's shop that solves the problem in a far more complex way. The rows of packages, drawers, and wooden canisters that line the three walls of her shop are neatly labeled in four languages: French, German, English, and Dutch. Tobacco, cough drops, even green sealing wax, are among the items thus variously identified for the world's children.

There are in this grocery, by the way, the sugar loaves wrapped in blue paper that are found in nearly every toy grocery—the ones of later vintage being more simply represented by wooden pieces of the proper shape painted blue. Sugar hats, Mrs. Childs calls them, and she remembers, upon a childhood visit to an aunt in Germany, helping to chop similar five and ten pound solids with a hammer.

Gröber pictures a German vegetable stall from the Germanisches Museum at Nuremberg, ca. 1850, which is captivating with its rows of baskets filled with bright produce, and set upon small benches. This is very open-air, since the produce is housed in no stall at all, and the proprietress, like her wares, is at the mercy of a sudden turn in the weather.

Mrs. Jackson offers quite a eulogy of the little baskets to be found in such representations. She tells us that the greatest variety of miniature baskets is to be seen in the Nativity and market groups of Naples: "Here each kind of vegetable and fruit on the greengrocers' stalls in the market has its special basket; wee hampers of vegetables stand by the side. The old pointed pottle used for strawberries is there, miniature punnets of chip and crates of osier wands. Miniature figures of women selling butter, eggs, and poultry have their baskets in proportion." (In British museums, the name of Mrs. Mary Greg is to be found near all sorts of miniature shops. In Manchester's Queen's Park Art Gallery is a collection presented by Mrs. Greg— a milliner's, a fishmonger's and a greengrocer's, with fish and fruit in the latter two modeled in wax by the same lady.)

Baskets have not been neglected as saleable items in themselves. The Index of American Design, the unique affiliate of the National Gallery of Art in Washington, which, as part of WPA's Federal Art Project, did 20,000 water color renderings of early American decorative objects, has a charming sketch of a toy basketmaker's shop. The shop, vintage 1870, is of wood, with eighteen baskets of all sizes and guises standing about or hanging from rafters. The proprietor, a painted figure in black coat and brown trousers, strikes a Napoleonic attitude (arm tucked in coat) but looks like a poet.

Since we have mentioned the kitchen doll in our kitchen chapter, it seems only right that we should introduce the pedlar doll into this one. The pedlar doll was after all an itinerant shop and managed to display enough merchandise on her person and thereabouts to stock a well-furnished miniature store. Holme shows such a doll, in wood, of the early nineteenth century, and tells us that in her basket are "flowers, combs, a pin-cushion, and even some novels, 'Lady Elizabeth' and 'Resolution.'" The Metropolitan has an American specimen of the same period.

Queen Victoria, quite the one for making her own toys, made a little bazaar stall which is still to be seen among her playthings. Shoes and beaded bags are among the items on sale.

Rendering of toy basketmaker's shop, ca. 1870, from the Index of American Design

A pedlar doll—a sort of itinerant shop. Museum of the City of New York Height: 12"

175

One of the most astonishing dolls' shops of all must have been a production which *Once a Week,* a London publication, saw at the German Fair in 1859. This was a refreshment stall. "Here we have rolls and sausages and ducks and bottles of champagne and a hundred other dainties; but the children are too cunning; they are only sham-paper. The Berliners who make them call them 'surprises,' for it is rather a surprise to find bonbons for the stuffing of fowls, and sugar-plums tumbling out of simulated pieces of embroidery. Now and then we find a greater surprise still, for there goes a rich plum pudding floating up to the ceiling—an edible balloon."

Mrs. Sumner Parker, of Baltimore, in her attractive collection of old toys, has a contribution to the domain of dolls' shops which is practically an epitome of such toys. This is a whole street of shops, a representation which could be found full-scale in 1850 at the old market square in Baltimore, at "Pratt and Market." The derivation of our neighborhood shopping units of today is plain, with only the parking omitted. There is one structure in which several shops are located, their fronts of glittering glass, small doors leading to interesting upper regions sandwiched between. Here may be found, neatly lettered, "Irmadie Hall," once the meeting house for politicians, and "McCoy's Roof Garden," where presumably "the boys" could retreat for a beer and some entertainment when political warfare got too rough next door. The whole business is topped by a tower with a clock and would make the most leather-hearted old ward-heeler nostalgic.

The New York Times in 1871 seemed quite taken by a grocery store which sounds approximately as realistic as Mrs. Parker's city block and which was manufactured wholesale. This "had real oats and canary seed on sale, and showing its foreign origin, there you saw exposed on the market, pulse and vetches and aniseed. Alongside of this brilliant establishment, and as part of the toy, was the office of this fortunate grocer, with its desk and stool—drawer, with real-looking money, pointing evidently to the reward of assiduous toil, full weight, and unadulterated articles, and in order that amusement and instruction should go hand in hand, there on the wall hung a map of the whole world, showing how necessary it was that all little boys, in order to be good grocers, should have their geography at their fingers' ends."

The foreign origin of some of these toys must have had its perplexing aspects for children who never had seen "pulse, vetches and aniseed," much less been able to pronounce them. The majority of dolls' stores, however, probably were imported right up to World War I.

A toy drygoods store, circa 1880 (illustrated), may be seen at the Museum of the City of New York. The name of this establishment is "Moden-Haus," an identification which must have baffled young American shoppers. It is perpetually bargain day amid these neatly ticketed bolts of cloth on their serried shelves: "Heute Reste-Tag!" a sign above the mirror proclaims, although the proprietor, possibly unaware that it's "Bargain Day Today!", may (eternally) have been getting full price.

A needlework shop pictured in an Italian fashion magazine of 1895

German draper's shop, ca. 1880, Museum of the City of New York Height: 19″

This is quite a large toy, scaled considerably fuller than an inch to the foot, and it would be interesting to know how costly it was when new. Such playthings were to be had, like dolls' houses, at all prices. Wanamaker's in 1899 advertised a butcher's shop for one dollar, complete with butcher.

A grocery store very similar to one in the author's collection is shown in F. A. O. Schwarz's 1910 Christmas brochure. The one pictured has seventeen drawers with metal labels, shelves at each side with canned goods and sugar loaves, and a proprietor in a business suit. In the 1913 Schwarz catalogue, where this was repeated, nine different styles were available in various sizes and styles ranging from a simple affair 20″ wide at $1.75 to a 28″ wide emporium "very complete" at $16.50.* The latter, however, is little more than a booth alongside the whopping 47-inch wide establishment in the collection of Miss Elsa Mannheimer (which is pictured on page 239).

The Bella C. Landauer commercial collection at the New-York Historical Society contains a number of old toy catalogues, of which one 1882 number recalls a somewhat different department in the toy-merchant realm. This was The American Toy Warehouse ("patented") and "just out." This was indeed an educational toy, for it would "convey a very correct idea of the methods employed in the handling and shipment of goods. The interior represents a building four stories high. The elevator extends from bottom to top, and is operated by pulling the endless band at the right. When it is desired to hoist goods or lower them outside the warehouse the adjustable beam over the arched door is pulled out. Then unhook the elevator cord from the elevator carriage and place the cord through the wire ring in the beam."

* It is of interest to note that this same store (with two counters instead of one) was still to be seen in the 1920 Schwarz catalogue—a comment on the number of years almost identical toys often were made; and the difficulties of dating them precisely.

177

The Brooklyn Eagle before Christmas in 1900 told of "an interesting new toy" which though mechanical seems to fall within dolls' shop scope, and offers a vivid portrait of the lavish toys that were available at the turn of the century. This was a summer resort, a town in miniature, which "would occupy the whole of a small room. . . . The whole thing is mechanical and works by electricity, a special battery coming with it. It consists of large grounds brilliantly lighted by little electric lamps, and has a hotel, a theater, chute-the-chute, duck pond, beer garden, etc. These are reached by electric cars which run on real tracks to and from it and all around it." This plaything cost $200, and if you come across it today, don't let it get away.

But it is necessary to return to the earth of the average child. *Playthings* in 1909 announced that for fifty cents or one dollar American-made "toys teaching merchandising" were available. Included were butcher's shop, grocery store, oyster house, and delicatessen, each having a counter with scales at the front and a perspective showing in colors the articles for sale.

At approximately the same time, a Britisher, also interested in disturbing Germany's monopoly in these playthings, came up with a far more realistic way of handling the problem, and apparently made a vast dent in the German trade. His idea, known as "Pets' Stores," consisted of supplying real foods in miniature packages. Whether the maker, a Mr. Ralph Dunn, had commercial tie-ups with the actual food factories whose products were thus wonderfully advertised in miniature, it is not possible to know, but this magnificent idea of facsimile packaging (withal empty insides), persists at much fancier prices today, and no doubt considerably smaller volume.

"You can buy one for a penny, or you can pay thirty shillings for a most perfect set, with everything, even to a wooden counter with drawers behind. Book of shop rules, ball of string, real rubber dating stamp, cashbox full of cash, case of eggs with display labels for all grades, from 'new laid' to 'election eggs,' Quaker Oats, Sunlight Soap, and dozens of other little packages. . . . Remarkable in its completeness is even the penny set (retail), a cardboard box with a shop front and a counter, some real biscuits and sweets, a pair of scales, some printed bags, weights, printed bill-heads, a tiny scoop and some money to trade with."

Sweet, dead days beyond recall. No wonder the list of "Pets' Stores" was increased from the original grocer's shop to a variety. "Five thousand gross of miniature sweet bottles filled with real sweets have gone to make up Pets' Candy Stores. [Did the proprietors promptly eat all the stock?] And the manufacturer has also opened a millinery establishment, post office, fruiterer's, draper's, café, and a newspaper shop stocked with miniature papers, all printed with interesting reading and advertisements." No wonder, also, that in six years "the children . . . opened up nine million Pets' Stores."

A grocery store advertised by F. A. O. Schwarz in 1910

The London *Times* reported an exhibit at the Crystal Palace in 1920, in which an organization of feminine toy-makers that had been making dolls' shops and comparable things since 1916 displayed considerable variety. "A baker's stall with dozens of little rolls and loaves, a greengrocer's, with the pinkest rhubarb and the greenest greens, a fruiterer's, with oranges and apples, and a cake stall, with toothsome-looking tiny cakes." We are not surprised to read that Queen Mary bought the first baker's stall. Her Majesty, as we have implied elsewhere, simply couldn't keep her stately hands off these things!

In modern days, the dolls' shop, like the dolls' house, has not fared as elaborately as in calmer eras. Indeed, fewer shops than dolls' houses have survived since the modern collector engaged in furnishing a costly dolls' mansion is not likely also to be stocking a dolls' shop, which is more exclusively a toy. But dolls' shops still appear from time to time, though very few are as detailed as some of the substantial emporiums of earlier days.

A "Sunshine Valley Store" with forty-one items including metal scales, a counter top of "real varnished wood," and a metal paper cutter "which uses a regular adding machine roll" was sold in 1931 for a dollar.

Craftsmen came on the scene in 1932 in what was at least a temporary renaissance, and fashioned a business block with a restaurant and delicatessen, and a Park Avenue specialty shop with an apartment upstairs. This was included in an elegant dolls' house line conceived by a firm of architects, Messrs. Delano & Aldrich, who organized the project to give work to unemployed draftsmen. (See also page 199.)

In England, a nation of shopkeepers after all, dolls' stores seem to have persisted more earnestly than in America. The British trade magazine, *Games and Toys,* in 1933 reported upon a number of drapery shops and similar wonders, at least one of which is instructive in local custom. This was a miniature of "the newsagent and confectionery shop to be found in nearly every street. It contains a goodly assortment of games, balloons, stationery, confectionery and newspapers, while the confectionery is of the best quality and supplied by one of the well-known confectionery manufacturers." This was made in two sizes, one at five shillings, and one for seven shillings sixpence.

Playing store, like playing doctor or house or nurse, is a game that has among most children always persisted whether appropriate equipment was provided, or not. Using the living-room table for a counter and the family bric-a-brac for merchandise may be inspiring to the imagination, but being provided with such thorough-going appurtenances as some we have described here also has its advantages.

We hear a good deal of talk about small business today. We have no doubt that if only the businesses were as small as those we have been discussing in this chapter, the number of mercantile headaches would drop considerably.

12

THE FACTORY
AND THE
MERCHANT

WE ARE CONCERNED HERE MOSTLY WITH THE PAST CENTURY, AND largely with its second half at that. The commercial dolls' house—the house made wholesale and sold retail—has a long and intricate history. The commercial background of the furnishings of these houses is even more complex.

It is almost impossible to sort the dolls' houses and furnishings of the nineteenth century in terms of the countries in which they are found. Traditionally, the toy industry in the United States, for example, was not truly rooted till World War I, when German sources were terminated. Statistically, less than twenty-five per cent of the toys sold in the United States before the war were made here; after the war, the percentage had risen to ninety. Despite these traditions and statistics, the number of manufacturers of toys in the United States during the nineteenth century is astonishingly large, and research is continually discovering others.

However, there is no question about the accuracy of the statistics; the number of dolls' houses and their furnishings imported to this country up to 1918, particularly from Germany, was overwhelming.

Similarly, England has had a sizable toy industry, considerably earlier and more extensive, needless to say, than that of the United States. Yet England's nineteenth century dolls' houses are nearly as full of furnishings

from Germany as are those of the United States, and when the English dolls'
house historian Vivien Greene asserts that only the English dolls' house is
within her province, she can be talking only of the house itself, and not of
what is placed inside it.

It is Mrs. Greene, incidentally, who shows in her handsome book one
of the earliest of trade cards to advertise such toys in English. This card,
from 1762, offers a lengthy list of sundry items for adults (such as writing
stands and silk purses) all crowded together, with only commas and semi-
colons to set them apart. But it provides a paragraph of its own for the
following sentence: "Fine Babies and Baby-Houses, with all Sorts of Furniture at the lowest Price. Wholesale and Retail."

This advertiser, one Bellamy of Holborn, is, of course, a seller rather
than a maker, who at the outset of his advertisement, mentions "the greatest
variety of English and Dutch toys," again making it impossible to sort out
what was imported and what domestic.

Something more than a generation later, with the opening of the nineteenth century, the trade card was succeeded, in Germany, at least, by the
handsomely illustrated, hand-colored trade catalogue, of which the celebrated Bestelmeier examples have previously been noted. (See pp. 37–38.)

Back to the United States, Inez and Marshall McClintock,* who have
done some thorough research with respect to early toy manufacturing, have
provided some valuable information about the Tower Toy Guild of
Hingham, Massachusetts, which, they inform us, "started rather informally,
probably in the late 1830's." It was begun by William S. Tower, a carpenter
and maker of wooden toys, who has been referred to by the trade magazine,
Toys and Novelties, as "the founder of the toy industry in America."

What William Tower founded was a rare association of craftsmen in
different fields who pooled their efforts and products. Among those who
joined the Guild, there were such well-known toy furniture names as
Loring Cushing and Samuel Hersey. In the author's collection, a card table
of unpainted wood bears beneath a top that still revolves smoothly, this
label: "Manufactured by Samuel Hersey, Hersey Street, Hingham, Mass."
The piece did not have to travel far from Hingham to Somerville, Massachusetts, where it was found in a mid-nineteenth century dolls' house now
also in the author's collection.

Even at mid-century, it is simpler to find information about dolls' house
furnishings than about the houses themselves. In the United States, especially, as surviving early Victorian specimens suggest, the impressive dolls'
houses continued to be handmade by the family carpenter, or a member of
the family.

The Freemans, in *Cavalcade of Toys,** write of dolls' houses dating from
the 'fifties which were manufactured in the United States. "Several American

* *Toys in America.* Public Affairs Press, 1961.
* Century House, 1942.

181

firms who were making other types of woodwork appear to have been the first to turn out these cheap doll houses. Much smaller than any previous they measured not more than twelve by eighteen and were largely unfurnished."

In *The Cricket on the Hearth,* Dickens gives a choice picture of dolls' house making in England at the same time (which we have quoted in Chapter 5). It is of interest as an illustration of a curiously personal sort of manufacturing. Caleb turned out dolls' houses by hand, and in his own living-room. He made enough to supply the middleman, who in turn gave him a fractional profit sufficient to exist on, provided he put in long enough hours to multiply the fractions. Caleb's sure touch still spared the dolls' house from the standardizing machine, though we gather from Caleb's complaint about no staircase and insufficient doors that he was bound by the parsimonious conceptions of his employer.

Hogg's Instructor, in 1852, ran a fascinating series of interviews with English toy-makers of a more independent type who made mostly dolls' house furnishings. Even on their own, though, to judge by their prices, they couldn't have made much more profit than Caleb.

Said one: "I am a white wood toy maker in a small way, that is, I make a variety of cheap articles—nothing beyond a penny in sawed and planed pinewood. I manufacture . . . penny and halfpenny toy bellows, penny and halfpenny doll tables, penny wash hand stands, chiefly for baby-houses, penny dressers, with drawers, for the same purpose, penny bedsteads."

In a day when a dresser with mock drawers brings twenty-five times the amount, it is strange and sad to note this honest workman selling a dresser with honest drawers for a penny. The same gentleman had an interesting footnote on the toy bellows which he said "now have no run. Six or seven years ago there was a great rage for them. Then I made about 12,000 in one year, but you see they were dangerous and induced the children to play with fire, so they soon went out of fashion."

English toys of that period were, like her people, of two classes, upper and lower. A manufacturer for the rich spoke thus:

"I make chiefly copper tea-kettles, coffee-pots, coal-scuttles, warming pans and brass scales; these are the most run on, but I make, besides, brass and copper hammers, sand-pans, fish-kettles, stew-pans and other things. . . . There are sixteen pieces in one copper tea-kettle; first the handle, which has three pieces, seven in the top and cover, one for the side, two in the spout, one for the bottom and two rivets to fix the handle." This artisan could make six dozen tea-kettles out of a copper sheet eight feet square. "They're all fit to boil water in, or cook anything you like, any one of them. You can make broth in them." He turned out an average of 4,992 tea-kettles a year, and these little gems retailed at sixpence each.

Exactly twenty-five years later, *Chambers' Journal* printed what is an interesting 1877 supplement to this aspect of the dolls' furnishing industry:

"Pewter toys are made in London in very large quantities. At one establishment a ton of metal is consumed each month in the production of Lilliputian tea, coffee and dinner sets. English taste may be gathered from the fact that the number of tea-sets made is nearly thirty times larger than either of the other two. Twenty-three separate articles make up a set, and of these two-and-one-half million are made yearly by one house alone. Metal is provided from miscellaneous goods, such as old candlesticks, tea-pots, pots and pans, bought from 'marine' store dealers by the hundred-weight; and when melted, is formed into the regular shapes by different processes of casting in moulds. One girl can make 2,500 small tea-cups in a day. Putting together the four separate pieces of gun metal, she fills it with the molten metal, dips its mouth into cold water, takes it to pieces, and turns out a cup that only wants trimming."

Meanwhile, in America, comparable metal toys were being made by more modern manufacturing methods than these. (This is not to say that these "modern methods" failed to exist abroad.) An article in *Antiques* maintained (in 1934) that "the Quaker City firm of Francis, Field & Francis conducted the first tin toy manufactory during the years 1852–1855, as shown by ads reproduced from a Philadelphia business directory of 1853." The firm reproduced "chairs, tables, clocks and other household pieces for the gentle girl to establish in her doll house." The McClintocks take this factory back a few years earlier, telling of a full-page ad by the same firm in A. M'Elroy's *Philadelphia Directory* for 1848 showing "tin clocks, chairs, bureaus and other furniture for doll houses."

Five years later, another *Antiques* author stated that "a perusal of hundreds of almanacs, city directories, manufacturers' catalogues, circulars, and retail-store catalogues of the 1860's reveals but two firms listed as 'toy manufacturers.' These, recorded in a guide to New York City, published by T. Elwood Zell (1868) are: The American Toy Company, 48 John Street, manufacturers of tin, iron and mechanical toys; and Hull & Stafford, Clinton, Conn. Tin Toys." The Philadelphia firm is presumably not listed since it is believed to have gone both in and out of business in the 'fifties. Louis H. Hertz, in the more recent *Handbook of Old American Toys*, asserts that "While the period immediately following the Civil War saw the great rise of the American toy manufacturing business, there were a number of fairly large firms flourishing before 1865, and certainly the first factory dates back many years previous."

The McClintocks found a number of toy factories operating in the 1850's and 1860's. Two important ones from the dolls' house point of view were George W. Brown & Co. of Forestville, Connecticut, and the J. & S. Stevens Company of Cromwell, Connecticut. The latter's 1868 catalogue of iron toys included many furnishings, "all in the current adult styles and all in doll house size." Among them were "bureaus, wash stands, fruit baskets, cook stoves, laundry stoves, Franklin stoves, coal hods with shovels,

laundry tubs and washboards, sleds, sleighs, water pails, kitchen chairs, rocking chairs, sofas, parlor chairs, cradles, bedsteads, tables for every room in the house, ottomans, mirrors, chopping bowls, skillets, dust-pans, pumps for the kitchen sink . . ."

Brown was another maker of tin toys who, according to the McClintocks, in an early catalogue, printed a long list of items the firm was starting to make, for a particular reason: "To Meet a want long felt we have added to our list a number of Tin Toys expressly for girls." Among the most interesting items mentioned were "tin houses" (see *Harper's Bazar's* description of 1869 tin houses on p. 186), and sets of furniture for parlor or bedroom—the first "imitation rosewood with velvet upholstery," and the second "oak grained." Imitation rosewood upholstery would, of course, describe much of the wooden dolls' house furniture attempted during the nineteenth century, but "imitation rosewood" in tin is reasonably astonishing.

Here, of course, we are considering manufacturers whose sole business was toys. Toys were made as sidelines by miscellaneous makers considerably earlier. According to the Freemans, "Beginning around 1790, the tin makers of Stevens Plains, Maine, and the Patterson brothers of Berlin, Connecticut, were making toy tin ware for children, including toy kitchens."

184

In a Francis, Field & Francis catalogue page reproduced by the Freemans, a tin table is pictured which appears to be almost identical to one in the possession of the author. Our table has a lift top (beneath which a full complement of linens was concealed when it was found) and is elaborately embossed and japanned in black and gold, the top painted to resemble marble. (See illustration.) A canopied bed, very like one pictured in the catalogue of Hull & Stafford, and a dresser with adjustable mirror and workable drawers, are matching pieces. (In his book, Louis Hertz alludes to the rarity of this type of dolls' furniture. "Tin furniture, such as tables, in the old japanned and stenciled tin is scarce," he points out.)

We reproduce two pages from a catalogue of the next generation, an 1874 brochure of tin and mechanical toys got up by Althof, Bergmann & Co., who were extensively set up at 30, 32, 34, 36 Park Place at the corner of Church Street in New York City. This company styled itself "importers of toys and fancy goods, china and Bohemian glassware" and referred proudly to "toys of our own manufacture." "In manufacturing our tin toys," the catalogue points out, "we pay particular attention to avoid all sharp edges and corners. We paint in bright, brilliant colors." A price list which accompanies the catalogue indicates wholesale figures only, but the retail prices probably can be judged. The twelve-piece parlor set pictured, of

ABOVE: *Bedroom furniture and* BELOW: *Parlor furniture in Althof, Bergmann & Co. 1874 brochure*

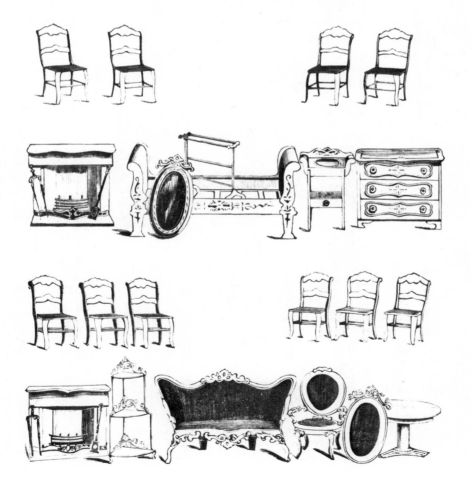

sofa, table, armchair, six side chairs, mantelpiece, étagère and looking glass, was offered retailers at $24 per dozen. The bedroom set, of "bedstead," bureau, washstand, towel stand, four chairs, looking glass and mantelpiece, was more modestly listed at $15 per dozen. Furnished kitchens with pumps that really worked were to be had in varying styles and prices up to $36 per dozen. Individual items were also sold to dealers, by the gross; coal scuttles, for example, at $9; coffee mills at $12.

A few years before, in 1869, *Harper's Bazar* had described dolls' houses of tin, and elaborate ones, too. Reporting on toys for Christmas, they noted "tiny houses of wood" at $3 and then went on to describe "large ones, of tin, painted to imitate brownstone, with real doors and glass windows, and furnished throughout," for $40.

But not all dolls' houses and furniture were of tin, and not all were made in the United States—the last few paragraphs notwithstanding.

Through the courtesy of Mrs. Marg. Weber-Beck of Franz Carl Weber, the celebrated Zurich toy store, we show a page of wooden dolls' house furniture from a ca. 1860 catalogue in the firm's museum collection. The furniture, as its picture shows, is of the simplicity associated with the earlier Biedermeier style. The finish is obviously not meant to represent rosewood or ebony, in the manner of most of the Biedermeier dolls' house furniture. Of course, these forms are not the same as the ones most commonly found, although the bureau (desk) with its drop front is certainly similar to the ones usually seen in "ebony" and "rosewood." It is interesting to note that this maker made his beds (and—with rockers added—cradles) in six sizes.

Another old toy catalogue (Stirn & Lyon, 20 Park Place, New York City, unfortunately undated) is most revealing. Many grades of dolls' house

Wooden dolls' house furniture from a ca. 1860 catalogue. In the possession of Mrs. Marg. Weber-Beck of Zurich

furniture are advertised, at graduated prices. In "oval boxes," there is furniture "common red varnished" and, better, "red polished." Furniture in "square boxes" came in even greater variety: "red polished, fine polished, extra fine polished, and extra fine with marble top tables, bureaus, and washstands and with chairs and sofas covered in silk."

An 1880 "Premium List" for *The Youth's Companion* offers "for one new name" a "Doll's Toy Parlor Set" comprising "eight pieces, including a real marble-top table, sofa, easy-chair and mirror-stand. It is imitation ebony and gold, upholstered in terry." An 1886 *Companion* offered a nine piece set upholstered in "figured cretonne" which, it said," is much handsomer than the cut shows."

The fanciest dolls' houses continued to be imported from Germany. The *New York Daily Tribune,* discussing dolls' houses in 1894, pointed out that "most of them come from Germany in the style of the modern suburban villa, with real windows and having carpets on the floor. Sometimes the whole front elevation can be removed at will . . ."

Great Britain had decided to combat this monopoly in 1889. "The English Toy Company has only just been formed," said *Tinsley's Magazine,* "to put England to a trade similar to that now almost exclusively enjoyed by Germany. The toy that the company particularly prides itself upon bears the attractive name of Miss Dollie Daisie Dimple. This young lady is provided with an elegant detached villa, tastefully furnished, and . . . with all kinds of necessaries and luxuries. She has also a traveling trunk, which contains no less than fifty-four articles, including several fashionable frocks and hats, a birthday book, and many pretty odds and ends calculated to gladden her heart."

There is a sketch showing a family of three ladies and two small boys working at a round table, houses stacked up near by. For the luxurious items meant to gladden Dollie Daisie Dimple's heart "are distributed to the home-workers. These are mostly children, though among them are a considerable number of adults, some of the most competent of whom are able to earn as much as seventeen shillings a week. The youngsters in their cottage homes, find very congenial employment in . . . building up dolls' houses, and the English Toy Company certainly does them a good service in enabling them to earn a few shillings weekly, and at the same time, keeping them out of mischief."

Girl's Realm, eleven years later, revealed a British dolls'-house-making picture that was a bit less grim to behold: "The London dolls' house maker is a very industrious man, and has to work very hard to make both ends meet. The winter is his busiest and most profitable time; during the other months of the year he just contrives to rub along. If he is a married man his wife and family are all engaged in the business. . . . He is chiefly to be found in the East End, and manufactures dolls' houses of the approved English pattern for the large wholesale toy makers, who supply the retail toy shops

with the wares that he turns out. He is the architect as well as the builder and decorator, paper-hanger and fitter of the miniature cottages, villas, and mansions that he makes. And he has the credit of turning out stronger work than the foreigner, whose tasteful and more fanciful work is brought to him to mend, for it soon goes to pieces. I know such a maker. With evident pride he will point to a dilapidated Swiss chalet, German villa, or French chateau that has been sent to him for repair. 'Pretty work,' he says, 'but there's no strength in it. This is one I've done up,' and he points to a foreign mansion that he has put to right, and repainted and decorated. 'And I don't think there is much to complain of in the way I've done it.' "

In America, more elementary doll quarters were being fashioned. In 1896, McLoughlin Bros. listed in their catalogue a folding dolls' house of which the retail price was six cents; a larger one, fifteen. Almost any piggy bank, no matter what its contents, could be suited, and its owner's doll have some sort of a roof over her head. Wanamaker's catalogue in 1899 showed two somewhat more expensive ones, at $1 and at $2.50.

Montgomery Ward's catalogue in 1900 showed what a small sum could buy. This "unique set" consisted of a folding parlor room about twelve inches square with "especially designed and printed walls and carpet; outside walls in perfect imitation of brick in dark red; the corners are doubly hinged with book cloth and warranted to stay bound. The furniture is made of our new lustrous and unbreakable metal, neatly decorated in gold. The three pictures are of different subjects, nicely framed and ready to hang on the wall. One neatly designed mantel fireplace with real glass mirror. Parlor set of four pieces, one settee, two chairs and centre table, one easel and framed picture." This plainly was neat although gaudy, and commemorates a picturesque and defunct furnishing, the painting on the easel. Absolutely all of this for twenty-five cents.

House Beautiful, also in 1900, gave a lavishly illustrated spread to a less commercial and far more expensive dolls' housing scheme. A Chicago woman became interested in doll building, and before she knew it had Longfellow's house, Whittier's and George Washington's all for sale. Craigie House was offered in its remodeled state, complete with piazza and Mrs. Longfellow seated in the parlor. The Whittier house was painted Quaker gray and was of "the severe colonial type of which Craigie is in the fine flower." Mount Vernon, of course, was done stately. The houses came furnished and were made so beautifully and precisely that they were history lessons as well as toys, and an auspicious way for the dolls' house to start the twentieth century. (Thirty years later a commercial firm did popular priced houses in a similar vein, with somewhat different poets. Longfellow was represented again, this time with the Wayside Inn he immortalized, and Emerson and Hawthorne were added. The White House joined Mount Vernon in the presidential department.)

In the same year *Harper's Weekly* printed some informative side-lights on the pewter toy industry which it stated had been introduced into America fifty years before by an Italian who learned the trade in Switzerland. The article discussed the making of "pewter parlor suites, wonderful creations upholstered in plush, and stamped with the most elaborate designs." The writer added that these sets were sold at prices so low that it seemed hard to believe there could be any profit to anyone. The process, however, was mechanical:

"The metal pieces are still cast by hand in brass and steel moulds. The pieces come out of these moulds in the flat, and are then passed into stamping machines that produce at one stroke a perfectly shaped rocking-chair or sofa, upholstered in the most gorgeous fashion. The foreigners still stuff their upholstered toys with sawdust. The American has invented a machine that shapes a piece of straw-board into a swelling cushion. The same action covers it with plush."

Obviously, more than one manufacturer made this type of furniture. It appears, however, to describe most specifically a set of "pewter doll furniture" shown in the McClintocks' book which, according to them, was made by Peter F. Pia of New York, whose business was founded in 1848 and which "was still being actively carried on more than a hundred years later." Oddly enough, however, the author has a set of this furniture in almost the identical horseshoe pattern (with a pink ribbon run through the horseshoe—a thing that would be impossible on the more densely-patterned horseshoe in the Pia set). "The 'Fairy' Furniture," says the printed card under the faded pink plush seat. "INDESTRUCTIBLE"—an astonishing claim, since this is the most infuriatingly fragile furniture to be found. The card further informs the purchaser that the metal is "an alloy of aluminum and white metal," that it has been "Manufactured by Adrian Cooke Metal Works, Chicago, Ill."—and that the patent has been applied for.

Whoever got the patent, the author has a similar set in a different pattern, the well-known set made for the 1893 Columbian Exposition which shows, in great metallic detail, the landing of Columbus, and is "Pat. Aug. 13, '95." Since the exposition was in Chicago, this very likely was also made by the Adrian Cooke Metal Works.

The printed record is necessarily piecemeal till we arrive at the twentieth century. This is due not to a failure on the part of dolls'-house makers to record, but a failure to save what they did record. It is surprising how many of the old-line toy factories neglected to file away so much as one catalogue year by year. Most of those available today are scattered among collectors and libraries.

But after the turn of the century, the toy trade magazine appeared. In America, the most formidable was *Playthings,* in whose back files it has been possible to find a virtual diary of the commercial dolls' house. Before the appearance of this month-by-month toy record, which in its early years, unfettered by buy-America slogans, gives reasonable coverage of foreign as well as American toy markets, the gleanings are sparser.

In 1905 Macy's began to take an interest in playthings and announced, in the *Tribune,* a big "Toy Opening!" Among the items listed were:

A close-up of one of the Bliss Street houses, ca. 1895

Doll houses $1.19 to $29.98	Toy stables 59¢ to $29.96
Doll house furniture 24¢ to $3.19	Kitchens 49¢ to $9.96
Stores and Shops 49¢ to $12.49	

Playthings, in 1907, had an advertiser who took a full-page ad to tell about dolls' houses, which, since it also harks back to 1895, and before, throws manufacturing light on a number of dolls' housing years: "Not many years ago every doll house sold in this country was imported. These goods were unsatisfactory in every way, but nothing else was to be had. About twelve years ago the R. Bliss Mfg. Co. brought out a line of doll houses which was an emphatic success from the very start. A large line was intro-

"Bliss Street." A group of houses in the author's collection made by Rhode Island manufacturer, R. Bliss, at the turn of the century   Height of tallest house: 27"

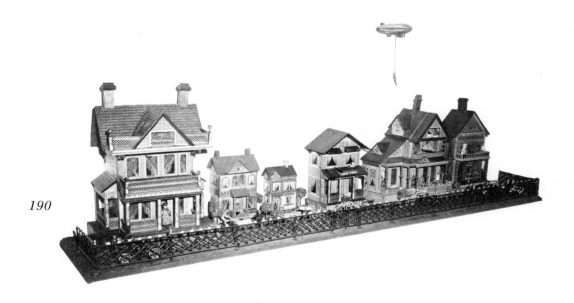

*Lithographed folding dolls' house
shown in a 1908 issue of* Playthings

duced, including Stables, Stores, Cabins, and so forth, as well as houses. All were made in American designs to suit the tastes of American children. [They] are made of well seasoned lumber, and not being subject to climatic changes have eliminated the greatest objection to these goods. Before the introduction of this line many dealers were discontinuing the goods, on account of the fact that if any were carried over from one season to another, there was a serious loss, owing to the warping and cracking of the wood. . . ."

The Rhode Island firm also went on to admire its lithographic work, "true to nature in all respects," and its variety of architecture, and proudly stated that its prices ranged "as high as twenty-five dollars." In the author's possession is a whole street of these Bliss houses, collected house by house, and mostly of the 'nineties. (It is pictured.) The manufacturer thoughtfully put his name on each of his houses, on the door, or elsewhere. In 1960, at a showing of some of Mrs. Homer Strong's dolls' houses at the Rochester Museum of Arts and Sciences, a charming house pictured on a booklet printed in conjunction with the exhibit was (in several high places) mis-called a Bliss house, evidently because, like the Bliss houses, it was of lithographed paper over wood. Innumerable firms both here and abroad made such houses, and it seems of importance to point out this fact.

During the next year *Playthings* announced a line that must have grati-fied the young owners of the above houses. These articles, which were to sell at five cents each, included such "up-to-date" kitchen items as sugar scoop, milk can, nutmeg grater, boiling pot, pail, coal scoop and shovel, alarm clock, candleholder and flat-iron. At the same time, dolls' house furniture generally was consisting of "mission sets, dining room sets in oak, cherry or mahogany, bedroom sets in bird's eye maple, iron beds . . ."

In 1909 an advertiser informed the public that one of the latest wrinkles in the manufacture of wooden dolls' houses was "to have the colors litho-graphed directly on the wood instead of on paper which is pasted over the wood," and announced a series of five houses with especially attractive balconies, roofs, and porches. Another told of a new series of folding dolls' houses which included hotels as well as bungalows and "handsome residences."

The latter could not have been as handsome, however, as a paragon boomed by a competitor. This purported to be "so beautiful and elaborately fitted out that it deserves the name Doll's Palace. Stucco above and imitation red brick below, the entire structure is about three feet broad and three feet high, with a depth of something over a foot. . . . The front porch is a large one containing two blue flowered trees, while just above it juts out a romantic little balcony with a rail piled high with imitation flowers. The entire front of the house swings open and discloses to view five rooms, two on each of the lower floors and one in the garret, and an elevator, run by a clever mechanism, lighted by electricity running up through the cellar of the house and carrying dolls and doll necessities to the various chambers. Each room is fitted out with beautiful doll furniture. . . ." But even this splendor must bow to a piece of perfection reported by *Windsor Magazine* in 1910. By a British manufacturer, "reality was being carried to such a degree that fires can be lighted and smoke go up the chimneys. . . ."

An American firm with a more modest product was specific about the architecture provided. This was a "new line of wooden bungalows, each one of which is made with the second story extending over the porch as is done with so many of these buildings along the seashore and in the mountains."

A contemporary was producing sets of furniture packed in fancy display boxes in one of which he managed to achieve an amusing blend of 1780 and 1911. This was a bedroom set, a "Martha Washington out-fit" in mission which included an easel showing a portrait of Martha.

A very strange dolls' house was described in by *Playthings* in 1913 but, regrettably, was not pictured. This was made of blue and silver wicker, and contained a doll and "doll out-fit." "This is a distinct novelty," said the copy man, in a pretty piece of understatement.

More classical dolls' housing was available at the same time. *American Homes* in 1912 ran a feature about colonial pieces being reproduced in doll furniture in Hingham, Massachusetts. These were undoubtedly made by Ralph T. Jones, one of the last well-known toymakers of the Hingham group, according to the McClintocks. These included cradles and chests of drawers, lowboys and churns, said to be meticulously detailed.

"England manufactures some very high grade wooden toys and she understands the art of charging a high price . . . ," said a trade writer rather cuttingly in 1913. "For a modern mansion doll house with three floors, bath to which water can be laid, walls papered in excellent style, the whole being four feet, six inches high, $42 is demanded."

There followed a description of some mechanical wonders which were comparative newcomers to the dolls' house. Bathrooms, which still were relatively rare in dolls' houses, contained several: "It seems that a good business is to be done in these doll houses with bathrooms. One can get several different models. To play with water is the aim of many a little girl with good clothes to spoil . . ."

"These doll houses with bath generally have a fair-sized tank in the roof which, when filled, contains sufficient water to allow a whole doll family to be bathed. Some of the newer model doll houses have electric lights throughout, an installation costing up to $35. For $40, if the construction of your house will allow, you can have an electric elevator installed. This is electrically driven and the cost includes accumulator and motor. If you have a bath tank and bath you can also have a sink fitted with water laid on."

Playthings in 1912 reported that dolls' houses and their furnishing "offer a profitable field both for individual and manufacturer," and told of a young man "living in a small western city" whose first effort, for his niece, was so widely appreciated that he decided to enter the business. That was "a short time ago," and "today he employs two of his brothers and three other male helpers."

The New York Times in 1917 acknowledged that expensive imported dolls' houses were missing from the current year's toys, but went on to describe a $98 specimen, with a bear-skin rug in the living room, "granite" cooking utensils (a sign of the times) in the kitchen, and a billiard table.

A late Victorian house made by Converse of Winchendon, Mass. Author's collection Height: 23″

Two celebrated firms whose names loom large in the toy trade magazines through the years are Converse, of Winchendon, Massachusetts, and Schoenhut, of Philadelphia.

A maker of wooden boxes who accidentally discovered the toy business when he made his small daughter a tea table from a collar box,* Morton E. Converse turned Winchendon into "the Nuremberg of America." His firm, no longer in existence, was at one time "the largest toy-manufacturing firm in the world."

Among many other toys, he made dolls' house furniture and houses. The small house illustrated (author's collection) has, lithographed directly on wood, the windows, shingles, and bricks that Bliss and other makers lithographed on paper. Although the result is somewhat cruder, there are no delicate bits of paper falling off these houses to dismay collectors a few generations later. On the example shown, the Converse name may be found imprinted on the ground floor within, along with windows, window-shades, and wallpaper. On the outside, red shingles and bricks are lithographed, along with a cat in the attic window, and—peering out of side windows—a pair of rather glum identical matrons.

The Schoenhut bungalow pictured is unmistakably one of those to be seen in a Schoenhut catalogue for 1917,† which describes "a whole new line of doll houses" the firm had just added.

* *Toys in America.*
† Examined through the courtesy of Mrs. Sylvia Brockmon of Philadelphia.

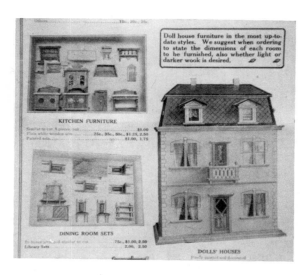

A house and sets of furniture advertised in Schwarz' 1913 catalogue. (The house is obviously a later [and smaller] version of Mrs. Longworth's house, p. 116)

Long famous for toy pianos, dolls, and, somewhat later, circuses, the Philadelphia firm had been founded in 1872 by Albert Schoenhut who had come from Germany after the Civil War. The 1917 catalogue promised that these dolls' houses would be "less expensive than the fine imported doll houses, but at the same time much stronger, more durable and beautiful."

Judging by the excellent condition of the example in the author's collection, this promise of durability was kept. The small bungalow also has considerable charm. The stairs have nicely turned balusters and a proper landing; net curtains on the glass-fronted door and the windows are lace-trimmed; the lithographed wallpapers are exuberant—very striped, very floral, and thoroughly bordered. Perhaps the most amusing feature is one specifically mentioned by the catalogue: lithographed doorways on the walls "showing a perspective view of another room . . . producing the illusion of a house full of fine rooms." There is a glimpse of a bath with footed tub, and a butler's pantry with brightly patterned oiled paper on the

A bungalow advertised in Schoenhut's 1917 catalogue and a Schoenhut bungalow from the author's collection   Height: 20½"

glass doors. There is also a lithographed fire in a lithographed fireplace, and lithographed portières.

As we have mentioned, toy catalogues (even ones as recent as the Schoenhut example), are elusive. Toy sellers as well as toy makers rarely filed away a catalogue, it seems, and therefore we were particularly grateful for the scattered examples that Mrs. Henry Erath of F. A. O. Schwarz permitted us to study. Most of these are late—the firm has only one from before 1910—but these pre-World War I catalogues proved to be astonishingly revealing in rather an inverse way.

From a collector's point of view, the examination has also been somewhat depressing. The celebrated Massachusetts toy collector and dealer, the late Frank L. Ball, once agreed with the writer that catalogues tend to reveal the youth of toys one had believed older. It is true, of course, that a successful line of dolls' house furniture was often continued, with few alterations, for a number of years. Some of the items in Schwarz' 1913 catalogue, which are pictured, were also shown in a 1910 circular, and one was longing to see earlier Schwarz catalogues to know in how many the same item might have appeared, when an 1894 Schwarz catalogue was found which provided a dramatic example:

A kitchen shown in the 1913 catalogue, and to be seen in succeeding ones to 1918, was identically pictured in 1894, establishing *at least* a twenty-four year span for this particular toy.

Architects are incessantly invading the dolls' house picture, and in 1919 we find "one of America's leading country house architects" designing them for a manufacturer. "The grass plot and fence is an original and exclusive feature." These, a pergola (pretty thought!) and chimney, came packed inside the houses.

A kitchen advertised by F. A. O. Schwarz for more than two decades

Assorted dolls' house fixtures advertised by F. A. O. Schwarz in their 1913 catalogue. Many were items which had been similarly made for years

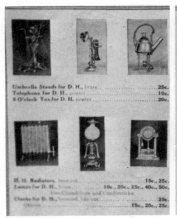

In December of the same year, *Illustrated World* ran a piece revealing that "Four years ago less than twenty-five per cent of the toys sold over American counters were American made; today ninety per cent in the United States are made in this country." The reason is evident—the World War shut out the German supply and left us to forage for ourselves.

Playthings and the toy industry were very pleased in that optimistic year. Cecil B. DeMille in a movie called "We Can't Have Everything" included a scene with a little girl and a large dolls' house. The trade magazine proudly printed a still.

West Coast dolls' house architecture was acknowledged in 1920. One manufacturer reported a California Bungalow type ($3 to $10. Beauty cannot be equalled) with the additional patented feature of a "Magic Floor which enables the dolls to move about the house."

The New England states were always coming forth with colonial dolls' houses and furniture, of which one sponsor already has been noted, and at this time, one of the most successful handicrafters appeared, in Providence, Rhode Island, promoted by two ladies. Both dolls' houses and furniture were exact reproductions of colonial originals, and *Harper's Bazaar* pictured some of the unusual types represented. One was a manor house of eleven rooms with a kitchen wing and a formal garden. Another, a low Nantucket cottage with "its captain's lookout perched high on the sloping roof." Many of the furnishings were exact copies of choice full-size pieces in a famous cabinetmaker's across the street from the Toy Furniture Shop. This was the well-known Tynietoy line, popular for quite a few years. A small undated catalogue of *Tynietoy Doll Houses and Doll House Furniture* is in the possession of Mr. and Mrs. Preston Weatherred, Jr. of Houston, Texas. Among the items listed is a "colonial mansion, unfurnished, with garden $170, without garden, $145." Furnished, this house, with garden, was $267.

Early in 1921 *Playthings* ran a full-page ad illustrating thirteen sets of furniture of a much less beautiful sort, much of it in brown mission, scourge of the era. Most of the sets consisted of ten wooden pieces sewn securely in a box in a manner to simulate the appearance of a room completely if hideously furnished. One curious cubicle included a Victrola and had a picture over the door.

Firemen entered the dolls' house realm a few months later, but not to fight dolls' house fires. Members of the New York Fire Department, weary perhaps of rounds of poker between jobs, decided to take up a more lucrative pastime. Accordingly they built dolls' houses and garages which for some time were enthusiastically marketed by a Fifth Avenue toy shop. They made dolls' house furniture, too, sold by Wanamaker, Best, McCreery and Bloomingdale.

In 1922 there was unveiled a line of dolls' house furniture that monopolized the mass market for a decade and a half. This furniture, its metallic

DOLL'S FURNITURE.

Made of pewter, fancifully painted.
ANY OF THESE ARTICLES BY MAIL, 3c.
EXTRA.

1. WORK-STANDS, 4 inches high, including implements and material. Price......... 23
2. WASH-STAND, 4 inches high, with bowl, pitcher, and sponge. Price.............. 23
3. SEWING MACHINE, 3 inches high. Price. 20
4. KNIFE-TRAY, with forks, spoons, and knives. Price.......................... 25
5. FIRE-STAND, 3¼ inches high, with poker, duster, and pan. Price 22
6. BABY CHAIR, 3 inches high, with dressed china baby doll. Price 20

From The Youth's
Companion, *1878*

charms firmly engraved upon the memories of all of us who wore middy blouses and skirts in the 'twenties, and even thereafter, is the forerunner of the plastic dolls' house furniture that has been the rage of the recent mass market. As today's plastic reproduces actual colonial pieces, the metal furniture was copied from a line of real furniture—but in a style that dates it firmly today. In metal and in plastic, kitchen and bath turned out more realistic than the furniture of other rooms, owing to the queer suitability of the materials. It was known by the quite terrifying name of Tootsietoy. (The kitchen would be green, the bath pink, the dining-room brown, the bedroom blue, the living-room orange. By 1936 it was being promoted as the only line complete with accessories, and for $1 one could get a living-room outfit containing eighteen pieces including clock, flower vase, ship model, parrot on stand, violin, and banjo.)

Such furniture was for small girls of average means. By 1925 the boom was on, and *The Saturday Evening Post* reported the elaborate goings-on in a Fifth Avenue top shop. "Where," said the *Post*, "a poor little rich girl can and often does buy a doll house for $300." The Fifth Avenue shop, which was not named, would not seem to have been F. A. O. Schwarz whose 1926

Furniture advertised by Sears Roebuck in 1909

Dolls' house furniture, vintage 1923, in Playthings

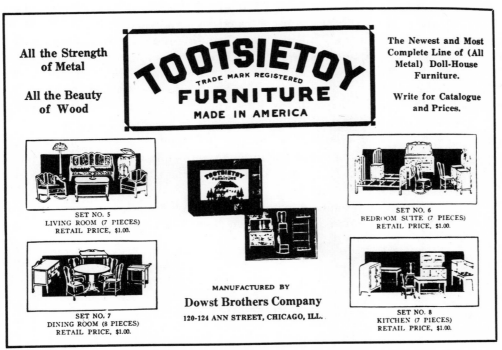

catalogue reported furnished dolls' houses "up to $165." This most expensive style was pictured, a very large affair (38″ wide, 41″ high, 20″ deep) with verandas and stairways and infinite detail. Lesser houses are illustrated, too, and all of them are grand residences.

Schoenhut, in 1927, took a handsome four-page color spread in a toy trade magazine to announce an entire new line of dolls' houses "with or without Garden, Trees, Shrubbery and Garage."

Several months later, a full-page ad heralded a new dolls' house with special brackets for mounting on wall, "thus keeping child off dusty and draughty floors," a notion which many mothers may have joyously welcomed.

A London firm, not bound down to such practical considerations, was featuring "English country homes." " 'Doll houses are always popular with little girls,' " said a toy salesman at Selfridge's, at the same time showing "an imposing model of a Tudor mansion, satisfactorily oak timbered and gabled."

Meanwhile, a knowing manufacturer called Arcade had been putting out extremely handsome bathroom, kitchen, and laundry sets in cast iron. These were marvelously realistic, containing exact models of full-size appliances. They sold mostly for $7.50 per set, and in addition were an excellent ad for the firms whose wares they reproduced. For example the laundry set contained a Thor washer (gyrator type), Thor ironer, Hotpoint electric plate with boiler, and Sanitary laundry tub. Cardboard backgrounds were provided, and the laundry room scene included such local color as a gas meter, which somehow the firm had neglected to reproduce in metal. Two years later they followed a logical custom and got up a lavish dolls' house to contain their product. This had living-room, dining-room, breakfast nook, kitchen, hall with stairs, three bedrooms, and two baths. There were also wings for laundry room and garage, the latter complete with cast-iron autos.

Scientific American in 1928 reported upon a dolls' swimming pool which an opulent dolls' house situated on an adequate piece of real estate might have installed. This included a dressing-room for the doll swimmers, diving platform, and a shower. "The shower has a miniature pump, operated by a lever, which lifts the water from the main basin up to the shower head."

At the time, Marshall Field was running pleasant ads describing their equally pleasant line of dolls' furnishings, which they confessed in one ebullient bit of copy was their "pride and joy." There was almost nothing they didn't make in miniature, including chintz-upholstered chaise longues, marble-top tables, Terry clocks, and fire screens. They also were pleased with their dolls' houses.

The most prominent note the depression sounded in dolls' housing was relatively glorious. A well-known New York architectural firm, Delano

& Aldrich, put unemployed draftsmen and designers to work building very handsome dolls' houses. This worthy project, launched in 1932, was applauded by such diversified publications as the *New York Times, Popular Mechanics,* and the *Art News.* The latter proclaimed "A Georgian example of some ten rooms, with two arcades at either side connecting the wings of the house . . . very much of a triumph" and declared that Delano and Aldrich were "to be congratulated on the originality of their scheme and the artistic success of the venture." The houses were furnished, ranging in price from $15 to $250, and though most were fitted with period reproductions, modern trends were also reflected, some of which twenty years later seem faintly historical. Said the *Times,* admiring the décor, "White-leather covered chairs in a living-room and white-painted furniture in a dining-room follow one of today's smartest vogues."

Actually the depression years seem to have been some sort of heyday for the dolls' house. Perhaps anxious parents, with their family homes mortgaged, were attempting to make their children feel secure, with lavish dolls' homes which were *not* mortgaged. Saks Fifth Avenue was offering in 1932 dolls' houses "of all descriptions" from $7.50 to $250. F. A. O. Schwarz devoted a whole page of its 1934 catalogue to an exquisitely complete line, and listed an immense number of accessories including Persian rugs, radiators, and French phones. They also had dolls' house families for sale, and one could buy two parents, one nurse and one cook for $3.50.

At the same time, but probably not at Schwarz, a doll who *had* lost his shirt could live in an inexpensive house. One type was Disney-inspired, with "authentic reproductions" of Mickey and Minnie Mouse at the front windows. (This failed to take into account that the average doll might not care to share her house with mice.)

To return to F. A. O., the celebrated Fifth Avenue toy emporium has for generations now been a dependable source of the dolls' *mansion.* In December, 1940, both *Life* and *Fortune* considered this establishment, offering a final view of the luxury dolls' house before World War II largely shuttered it. *Fortune* pointed out that Schwarz's own manufactures "account for about five percent of the volume," these chiefly play-houses, dolls' houses and toy garages. The magazine pictured a handsome colonial dolls' residence and reported the presence of running water "for dolly" and what must certainly be noted in this post-war memorandum though it hasn't reappeared since 1940—an automatic stairway.

Life took a retail view of the toy situation at Schwarz, quoting prices, and picturing a dolls' house of ultra-modern design. Of this they said, "The modern child's house is very severely designed. It has glass brick walls, sun terrace, big expanse of horizontal windows. Unfurnished, $25." This price tag, very little higher than the one on today's largest cardboard building, specifically shows what has happened to dolls' housing since the war.

The Southern Colonial house, which *Fortune* pictured, *Life* commented upon. This house, furnished, was to be had for $98. "It is open in back so furniture can be moved. It has a great deal of charm, lights that light, but lacks running water." There appears to be a discrepancy between the running water that *Fortune* located in the Southern Colonial and the running water in the same homestead of which *Life* felt the lack. Perhaps one paid extra for running water. Certainly one could not purchase the house furnished, *with* running water, for $98. *Life,* usually on its toes in such newsworthy incidentals, didn't mention the automatic stairway at all, although it noted that "the doll house hostess now has cherries pasted into her cocktail glasses for Manhattans."

In 1946, a New York State firm doing a mail-order business in dolls' house period furniture reproductions held forth in its bulletin at some length on a new line of dolls' houses it was about to offer. "During the war years," said the advertiser, "we tried many times to find houses, sturdily constructed and of good design but prices were prohibitive. However, we are now ready to accept orders for three and six room houses at $40 and $75 respectively." Since a prospective dolls' house buyer might hesitate before paying $40 for a three-room dolls' house, it seems only fair to mention that considerable detail was promised (in both the $40 and the $75)—cream-colored clapboard, green shingles, glass windows, window boxes, trellises, blinds, bird house, hinged roof and walls, stairway with banister, fireplace, built-in bookcases, closets, a Dutch dresser in the kitchen, and "perfectly finished walls, trim and floors throughout."

It is reassuring to discover that the independent craftsman has been recently at work—in any field. It isn't possible to know how many one-man dolls' house workshops are still to be found throughout the country. We were fortunate to know the late Mr. James W. Butcher of Washington, D. C., who devoted more than twenty years to building dolls' houses.

Mr. Butcher, who took to doll architecture after he retired from the government, "put up" hundreds of dolls' buildings in his basement workshop before his death in 1950. Since Mr. Butcher also did scale models for architects, he almost automatically applied the same sort of careful detail to his dolls' houses. Most of them were tremendous residences (scaled an inch to the foot), usually colonial in design, and generally with wings. Mr. Butcher seemed especially to pride himself on his electrical arrangements, often providing a row of switches to light the rooms individually, or to control separate floors or wings.

The houses usually were sold furnished, with curtains, window shades and other needle-worked matters done by Mrs. Butcher. Butcher houses varied in price according to size and features, but often sold for $200. The architect could dispose of as many as he built, and his work was shipped all over the country. Among the Washington notables who bought Mr. Butcher's houses was the late Evalyn Walsh McLean, of the Hope diamond, who ordered one for her grandchild, Mamie Spears Reynolds.

200

Suitably elegant furnishings for such formidable dolls' houses appear both in the middle and the high price ranges. For a decade or two, a leader in the making of dolls' furnishings was the New England firm to which we have referred, Tynietoy. Their pieces, which were mostly eighteenth century reproductions (with Victorian things later added), were sold by the piece, and were moderately priced, considering that they were good though not extraordinary reproductions and had workable drawers, drop leaves, and other practicable features. They were also charming.

There are, of course, individual craftsmen of miniature furnishings who do custom constructing, and will make to order any item a collector desires. (We refer to several in Chapter 15.) Then the price, to adapt a handy phrase, is between the collector, the constructor, and God. Along with the antique miniature collector, the patronizer of these custom-built fancies is in the stratosphere of his diminutive universe. The collector's whim, not the sky, is the limit. We have seen a handsome little secretary, perfection itself, for which its owner, a concert pianist, paid $350.

But enough of the haut monde! We return to the world of the dolls' cottage and its simpler furnishings. In the 1920's and '30's, as we have noted earlier, metal toy furniture furnished thousands of American dolls' houses from coast to coast. It was neat, strong, and reasonably realistic. It was the rage till World War II swept metal from the face of the civilian earth. During the war, along with most children's toys, dolls' house furniture took a suitably minor and scrawny role. Most low-priced sets were of wood in modernistic motifs, and were dismally ugly.

Then came plastic. In March, 1946, *Collier's,* in a piece entitled "Toys for Tomorrow," mentioned a maker of plastic dolls' house furniture "who expects to sell 150,000,000 pieces this year" and who "has furniture and equipment for every room." "Most original designs," the report continued, "are a model toilet with workable seat and seat cover, a Chippendale dressing table with an intricately carved mirror frame enclosing a real mirror, and a fireplace with andirons and logs."

Anyone who stood near a counter ("near" being as close as an observer often could be) featuring this manufacturer's goods in 1946 will probably be willing to attest that he disposed of his 150,000,000 pieces, and more. In the dime stores, where these plastic furnishings were at first marketed, generally by the piece, his wares sold very rapidly indeed.

This line of plastic furniture duplicated period styles, was amusing and low-cost, and served much the same purpose in plastic that Tootsietoy did in metal. The bathroom and kitchen pieces, realistic in white plastic, are more satisfactory than the over-stuffed sofas and chairs, since plastic upholstery, be it ever so truthfully fashioned, looks like plastic upholstery.

In 1946, therefore, the interior of the low-cost dolls' house was thriving; but its exterior wasn't doing as well. The market in miniature real estate had been inflated in very much the same way as the market in full-size. Since there was no miniature housing shortage, it is difficult to account for this situation. But virtually the only low-cost dolls' houses available were of cardboard, and these were flimsy structures. It was often necessary to pay sixteen dollars, which not long before that would have meant an investment in a sound wooden dolls' house, for a loudly lithographed building in this impermanent material.

It is true that some of these flimsily fabricated dolls' houses had doorbells, and the most expensive featured an electric light or two. The manufacturer of one pasteboard mansion went so far as to include a closet fitted out with small wire hangers. But a generation or so before, one could have, made by Schoenhut, say, a sturdy wooden dolls' residence with a front porch and a carved balustrade, real glass windows, hinged sections, and lace curtains, at a similar cost.

Metal, of course, returned to the dolls' house world a few years after World War II departed—not to the furnishing department, but to the buildings themselves. The modern metal dolls' house, lavishly lithographed inside and out in a riot of color and detail from wallpaper to shrubbery, was to be found, in 1952, in practically every dime, department and drug store in the land. These were chiefly colonial with sun-decks and built-in garages. In more recent years swimming pools and barbecues have been added.

Swimming pools and barbecues are all very well, but Welch's grape juice and Webster's dictionaries also help to make a dolls' house a dolls' home. Early in World War II, an Ohio father named John Stover, who unsuccessfully tried to buy accessories for the dolls' houses he'd built his small daughters, began making his own. As in World War I, such small items, long imported, had vanished from the market.

Mr. Stover found that he liked making dolls' house accessories, and it wasn't long before he was making infinitesimal fish bowls and Federal mirrors for other people's small daughters as well as his own. Under the now illustrious name of Grandmother Stover, he presently makes 75 million miniature items a year.

There was a time, with the coming of television in 1950, according to Mr. Stover, when "doll house play ended and for the next decade little girls spent every hour watching westerns . . . usually with a gun on each hip." Mr. Stover turned to making his miniatures for adults—as party favors. But we are happy to report that in 1962—again a fascinating statistic from Mr. Stover—"a new generation" of small girls showed interest in dolls' houses, and Grandmother Stover Doll House Accessories were (and are) again available.

In any case, collectors of the future will come across many a Stover accessory. Not all are still available, but such celebrated items as the *New York Times,* of which Mr. Stover has "published" close to half a million, and packs of playing cards, of which he has printed close to a million, continue to flourish.

A letter received from Mr. Stover shortly before this book went to press

Grandmother Stover has published close to half a million New York Times and printed nearly a million packs of playing cards

explains why some Stover items have already become history; and furnishes more than a footnote to certain dolls' house items of the past: "So much of the metal silverware and other accessories in our original line had come from the Dowst Company in Chicago," Mr. Stover wrote, "These were produced on the original eighty-year-old Cracker Jack molds. One by one, these molds broke down completely and the Dowst Company no longer exists."

However, it is still possible to obtain, among many other items, *Drano* and *Duz* and *Amy Vanderbilt's New Complete Book of Etiquette* from Grandmother Stover; and multifarious other miniatures from other makers of miniature items (a few of whom are mentioned in Chapter 15.)

Therefore, we are happy to report, the dolls' house in the second half of the twentieth century—at least in the variety of its accessories—continues to flourish.

Investigators of our architecture, like those of our furnishings, will be provided with everything but blueprints by certain representatives of the contemporary dolls' house. As long ago as 1936, the dolls' residence was reflecting the principles of Frank Lloyd Wright. *The New York Times* announced that year that toyland had gone "ultra-modern," and pointed to "a pseudo-concrete, glass and steel mansion with roof garden, terrace and cocktail bar, and with bathrooms which have built-in tubs in all the preferred pastel colors."

We have already referred to a Schwarz contribution to *moderne* in 1940; and might add that the firm in 1952 was selling, in addition to the inevitable but always welcome colonial, a one-story ranch-type house with picture windows, built-in garage, and a living-room and kitchen divided by a counter. (Plus bedroom and bath.)

But the final word on the subject of contemporary miniature architecture must go to *Interiors and Industrial Design* which in October, 1950, reported the marketing of an *avant garde* dolls' house based on San Francisco's Bay Region style. This was the work of Lissa Finney, an architect and the wife of an architect. A redwood exterior was matched by korina paneling within and such features as breakfast bar, barbecue and huge expanse of window. "A boldly cantilevered stair leads to the bedroom balcony over-looking the two-storied living-room," the architectural magazine advised. It also noted, at one side of the house, a covered terrace "which can be closed to the outside with a split bamboo screen" and an "abundance of storage space." This dolls' house, marketed at I. Magnin in San Francisco, undoubtedly found its way into many a korina-paneled nursery.

By the 'fifties and the 'sixties, imported dolls' houses and furnishings, from Germany, England, and other countries again were competing strongly with the native product. It seems of significance that one popular imported line has consisted of a set of rococco rooms. The same nostalgia for the past that has brought about the widespread collecting of full-sized antiques, or of reproductions thereof, is, like almost everything else in the world at large, thus reflected, as usual, in miniature.

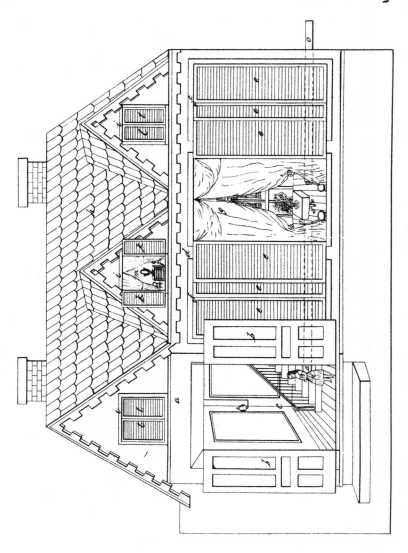

E. S. Russell,

Toy House,

Nº 79,782,

Patented July 7, 1868.

First "toy house" patent, registered by Emily S. Russell of Plymouth, Massachusetts in 1868

13

U. S.
PAT. OFF.

$\mathcal{J}$T IS SURPRISING TO DISCOVER HOW MANY INVENTORS HAVE GIVEN thought to dolls' houses. Few of these inventors, though, want credit for inventing. Scores of mechanical and design patents relating to dolls' houses are on file in the Washington patent office,* but most of them assert in wordy patent-attorney prose that their intent is (but) to "improve." Since patent office files are often found to be a center of unconscious high comedy as well as conscious (and intense) cerebration, these dolls' house improvements take on shapes varied, informative, and amusing.

The first American dolls' house patent goes back to 1868. Since then, the procession of such patents has been sufficient to link together one of those nostalgic architectural sequences which a dolls' house line-up from mingled generations seems always to form. Whether served by a design patent, with mere pictorial invention, or a mechanical patent, requiring varying degrees of manual creation, this procession automatically appears.

It begins quaintly, as a glance at the 1868 dolls' house sketch will show. It is curious, in terms of the times, but natural, in view of the subject matter, that this first patent, and a mechanical one at that, should have been taken out by a woman. Women frequently have mingled their talents with dolls' house devising since.

* For here we shall concern ourselves with American patents only.

The 1868 lady, one Emily S. Russell, of Plymouth, Massachusetts, concerned herself with a "toy house" for paper dolls. Said she: "I claim a toy-house, made of two thin sheets of material secured together, the outer sheet having swinging doors and blinds, concealing or disclosing representations of apartments on the inner sheet, and the space between the sheets being adapted to movements of a doll, . . ."

She mentions that, "It will be obvious that a toy thus made will conduce to the quiet amusement of children old enough to play with dolls, and especially to the diversion of little girls playing together, having great attractions for many children over any toy-houses and furniture requiring building or setting up. There is nothing about the toy liable to break or to get under foot, and it shows, or may be made to show, a great variety of furniture and inside decorations."

Whether or not this last bit of salesmanship helped to market the quaint result was not known when this book first appeared in 1953, though Marian B. Howard, in her excellent brochure on paper dolls' houses also printed that year, described the house manufactured by G. W. Cottrell, 36 Corn Hill, Boston, which, because of the patent date, she suspected was the same one patented by E. S. Russell.

Through the courtesy of Mrs. Frank C. Doble, a well-known Belmont, Massachusetts, collector, we are able to offer the subsequent history of the patent, and to illustrate it, in a manner not often available to researchers.

Through a combination of unusual circumstances, Mrs. Doble has in her possession not only a copy of the Cottrell manufactured version, but a miniature of the dolls' house handmade by Mrs. Russell, who made one for her small daughter and one for her daughter's friend, Maude Spooner. Little Miss Spooner grew up to be Mrs. A. W. Elson from whom Mrs. Doble's husband purchased buildings now occupied by his firm. Mrs. Elson gave the houses to Mrs. Doble who, by a happy coincidence, just happened to have a collection where they would be treated with the care and respect they warranted—a fate, unfortunately, which does not always befall such ephemeral relics of the past.

Mrs. Frank Doble's dolls' house made from the Russell 1868 patent, showing both exterior with shutters open and exterior with shutters closed

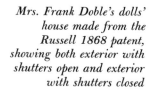

The Cottrell house, as the picture shows, has a name plate on the door—"Muffet." This is explained by twenty-one stanzas printed on the back of the house, "The Story of the Cottage," a whimsical embellishing of the verse about Miss Muffet of tuffet fame.

$2.00 MISCELLANEOUS GOODS.

*McLoughlin Bros. catalogue
showing folding dolls'
house, 1896*

No. 544—FOLDING DOLL HOUSE.

Size of box, 13 x 13 x 1 inch.

The house folds down to the above size. It makes four rooms, Parlor, Dining-room, Bed-room and Kitchen, each 13 inches square, without roof, parted off by partitions 13 inches high. It is designed to be played with on a table. A number of little girls may thus get round it to the very best advantage. It is made of stout binder's board covered with colored designs representing the carpets, walls, windows, mantels, etc., as seen in houses. It is designed to be furnished with paper or other small furniture, and to be occupied by paper or other small dolls.

Single rooms are also put up, instead of four rooms together.

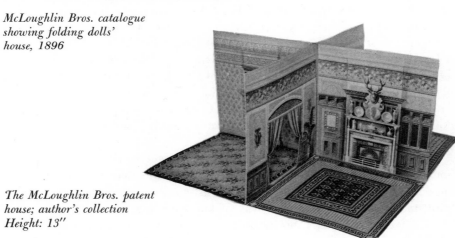

*The McLoughlin Bros. patent
house; author's collection
Height: 13″*

About twenty-five years later, in 1894, another female inventor, from Baltimore, was also successful in marketing her patent. Her dolls' house, actually "a series of partitions radiating from a common hinging point," is obviously the one sketched in McLoughlin Brothers' catalogue of linen and toy books for 1896 (illustrated). Some of its charms are visible in the very Victorian catalogue sketch, and the 1896 copywriter has revealed a few others, but neither does it justice. The writer, who has one of these delightful toys (also illustrated), can report that lithographed stained glass, Brussels carpet, and flowered wallpapers capture an era, in color as lush as the scenery in an African jungle.

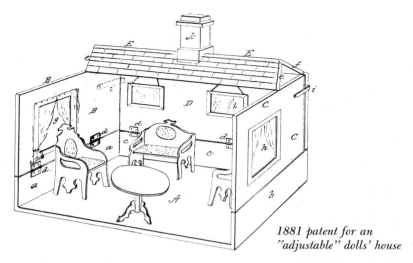

*1881 patent for an
"adjustable" dolls' house*

Innumerable inventors wisely have kept their eyes on the main chance —the chance of marketing their patents. This factor has appeared often to consist of devising collapsible houses, affairs which possess all the household advantages including verandah and bath, but can be knocked down and shipped by a manufacturer with a minimum of bulk, eternal bugaboo of the commercial dolls' house. The result of this wide obsession is a whole category in the patent office devoted to knock-down toy buildings, anticipating their full-sized prefabricated brethren by a number of years.

Two men, one from New Jersey and one from Pennsylvania, patented one example of this telescopic notion in 1881 which is chiefly interesting for being its own box and containing its own furniture, when not in use as a house. This number seems to be more of a dolls' room than a dolls' house, but presumably two such houses could be placed adjacent to form at least a suite (Queen Victoria had no more!). The sketch is reproduced herewith in deference to the furniture, so very expressive both of dolls' house furniture in general and the Victorian era in particular.

Not every inventor has been engrossed in such utilitarian devices as knock-down houses. As early as 1899, a thoughtful man who plainly was concerned with elegance patented a dolls' house with an elevator in it. Unfortunately there is seldom a way of knowing how any of these people, the frankly commercial or this more dreamy type, fared with marketing their ideas. The patent office probably has seen enough of its fledglings after nursing them along for a year or two through the terrible, trying time of "patent pending," and rarely learns whether their subsequent careers are brief, glittering, or non-existent. It may be that several of the roses reproduced here have blushed unseen in dim patent office files these many years.

Number 1,064,124 is shown as an example of probably the fanciest dolls' house patent that ever has been applied for. It was applied for, by the way, in May of 1909 and not granted till June of 1913, a longer interval than appears customary for the time, and it seems possible that the poor patent employees were obliged to take all that time figuring it out. This patent is, of course, for "CARDBOARD STRUCTURE," and it is hard to know whether the means (ninety-eight steps) justify the end, a dwelling not nearly as elaborate as the plan for making it. However, do note that even this building conjures up its own (1909) atmosphere.

The structure is meant to be "readily cut, scored, flexed or folded and glued together," according to its author, who further relates that "The improvement is also intended to furnish intellectual enjoyment as well as instruction for children and adults . . ." The use of the word "intellectual" seems to be no understatement. Even a hearty game of blindfold chess can hardly have given more exercise either to youthful or elderly brains.

There are numerous patents for toy stores. The drugstore is illustrated here because it is rare among the ubiquitous grocers' and butchers' shops, and because, with its grim façade, it may never have existed beyond the patent papers. It is true that small boys like to play "doctors," and miniature stethoscopes and things have been manufactured with their games in mind. But this drugstore featured the word "pill" and bore terrible connotations, perhaps, of castor oil and other fearsome spoonfuls administered to the 1916 children toward whom this design was launched. On the other hand, there must have been any number of ingredients in those dose-sized bottles that an ailing doll might have tolerated with profit.

Also in the design field were several whimsical dolls' house specimens offered by one W. Donahey in 1921. Two of these were shoe houses, and one a derby hat cottage. All have the splendid charm of the truly ugly. Two of the sketches are offered here, the button-shoe house having been chosen

1913 patent page of a cardboard house to be "readily" assembled

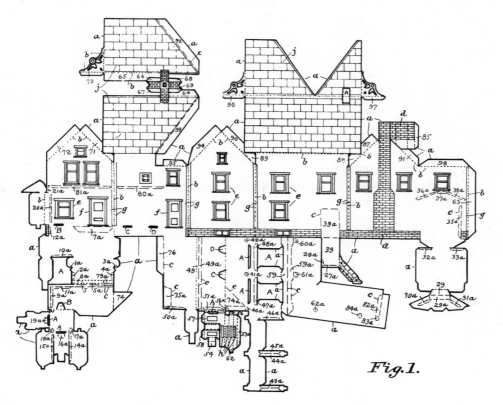

Fig.1.

209

1921 patents for a shoe house and a derby hat cottage, and a 1916 patent for a druggist's shop

over a shoe-laced project because of the realistic quaintness of its missing top button.

Another design sketch—71,072—was called "TOY HOUSE BLANK." What is curious about it appears to be the little girl in a dotted dress who appears eleven times. Just why the 1925 artist, a Mr. McChesney, chose to duplicate the same little girl all around the house seems quite a mystery, and thus worthy of speculation in a work devoted to every sort of doll building, enigmatic as well as informative.

There have been other mysterious dolls' house patents. One, in 1910, had to do with a combined table and dolls' house. With a few simple adjustments one could eat on it or play in it, a versatile object if nothing more.

If quantities of recent dolls' house engineers have devoted themselves to solving the knock-down problem, a different snarl that has troubled all the generations and also has engaged The Thinkers, is the one having to do with the open-front, open-back aspect or How to Look Like a Real House and Be Accessible, Too. Hinged fronts and hinged backs haven't delighted all dolls' house builders. One K. Suyehiro, who described himself as "a loyal subject of the Emperor of Japan," provided a unique solution in 1920. His idea conceals the open side of the dolls' house with a curtain, gathered neatly along a rod. It looks somehow a very Japanese solution.

The success of a relatively recent dolls' house patent, of 1933, is known, for the house was widely advertised for several years. This house featured "views," lighted scenes at the windows which readily could be changed. There have, of course, been houses with views printed on the "windows" but this elaborate variation proved so popular that the manufacturer expanded his house into a series.

This series of houses had more than scenic tricks, one employing "substantial curtain rods" which were "attached to enable the child to hang or take down the curtains but at the same time the rods cannot be lost." This is probably the only dolls' house patent referring to curtain rods there has ever been, or possibly ever will be.

14

THE
MAGAZINES
TELL HOW

*A*LWAYS THERE ARE PEOPLE, TALENTED WIELDERS OF SCISSORS, needle, brush or saw, who prefer to have the pleasure of making items which lesser craftsmen buy in stores. Magazines have been helpful about printing instructions for such handicrafters, and particularly the ladies' magazines have been bountiful with articles about making dolls' houses and doll furniture. Plans are included for bungalows, mansions and apartments, and a good many dwellings in between, and these structures may be built of almost anything, including paper and macaroni! Furniture is fashioned with similar degrees of simplicity and elegance, and materials used are even more varied and surprising.

Most of these articles have been in November and December issues of the magazines in which they appear, with the idea, evidently, that most builders of dolls' houses intend them for Christmas. The December editors seem to have been oddly optimistic in estimating spare time. But a few wiser publications have printed their instructions in October, and it may be that theirs were the houses which turned out best.

In any case, these dolls'-housing schemes, a random selection beginning with 1883 and concluding with World War II, form a parade of architecture, furniture, and people of their own, one to compare and blend with the wider historical pattern of dolls' houses in general.

FIG. 3.—FRONT ELEVATION OF DOLL'S HOUSE.   FIG. 4.—SIDE ELEVATION.

The façade of a most elaborate house for which building instructions were given in 1883 by Amateur Work, *an English publication*

And, should some of the samples culled from these articles inspire other people with talented hands and clever heads, a sort of bibliography of the articles mentioned in this chapter is given as it progresses, guiding these ambitious builders to the nearest library.

An English publication, *Amateur Work,* in 1883,* described in three complex installments the dolls' house that leads off this procession, and anyone who gives the instructions even the most casual perusal knows that building this house is no work for amateurs.

"The Carcase and How to Make It" is the arresting title of the first installment, and one makes haste to say that no summary of the instructions will be found here. After complaining for some paragraphs about houses that open routinely from the front, "The Editor," who thought up an alternative, describes a plan so complex that only a competent patent engineer, one suspects, would be capable of comprehending it. We dimly perceive that two boxes hinged together, with one forming a deep lid to the other, is the crux of the matter, and it is true that the author shows the "carcase" in "isometrical perspective."

* This marvelous article is described through the courtesy of Mrs. Philip Ross-Ross of Ontario, Canada, who located it, and Miss Carolyn Watson of Des Moines, Iowa, who mimeographed and distributed it. We are also grateful to Miss Watson for calling to our notice the fact that a dolls' house pictured in *World of Miniature,* the program of a delightful exhibition of dolls' houses at the Worcester Craft Center in 1961, was obviously made from these plans. The house, which belongs to Mrs. William Mason Smith of New York City, appears to be, except for an excessive supply of panes in the attic dormers, the *Amateur Work* house precisely. Mrs. Ross-Ross' own Domville House, built by her father, was also presumably inspired by the article.

Perhaps a sample sentence will illustrate the problem sufficiently: "As the boxes are drawn apart, and turn on the hinges, the point A travels along the dotted circle, in the direction of the arrow, to A′, F to F′, C to C′, and D to D′, the points B and E describing semicircles, which it is unnecessary, on account of the space that would be taken up, to show in the diagram." Parents who complain today about the complexities of assembling knock-down toys, especially from instructions printed in Japan, would, if they could see these, desist.

Pages composed of small type, filled with sentences loaded with similar geometrical advice, continue, paragraph after paragraph, till the enterprising builder comes to the details that will turn "a bare and unmeaning looking pair of lid-less boxes set on end and linked together by hinges into the semblance of a neat little cottage or so-called villa, sometimes to be met with in the suburbs of London and the larger country towns." He then offers "hints" on constructing windows, chimneys, roof, parapet, and quoins.

But our favorite "hint" is not reached till installment three when the author turns to embellishment of "the triangular ornament shown between the windows in Fig. 3."

"This," he informs us, "may be in fretwork, but incised or carved work is, I think, preferable, and it may be taken advantage of to display the armorial bearings of the family to which the little owner of the house belongs, if that family be really entitled to bear them. Too little respect is paid to heraldry in the present day. I should like to see all who assume armorial bearings, without being able to prove their right to bear them, charged at least a treble rate of duty for the assumption; and as trade-marks partake very much of the nature of heraldic insignia, it is only fair and right that everyone who assumes a trade-mark for the better distinction of his goods should pay a tax for the use of it, as every *armiger* or gentleman is compelled to do who openly bears his arms. I have been led into a slight digression, which I beg respectfully to offer to Mr. Childers as an idea for the Budget of 1884—if he is then still in office."

The editor may be permitted his fit of pique because as the illustration shows, he has constructed a handsome house, truly of its period. We wish there were space to reproduce his equally impressive elevations of the attic dormer window set into the mansard roof, the chimney piece (complete with looking glass, grate, plants, and clock,) and the formidable cross-section of the parapet.

We shall have, instead, to be content with one more quotation: "The imitation of smoke issuant from the chimney—to use a heraldic phrase—as I have seen recommended in other instructions for building a very ordinary doll's house, had better not be attempted."

His earlier "digression" prepared us nicely for the heraldic phrase, and we leave this colorful amateur architect with reluctance.

In an 1893 issue of another English periodical, *The Girl's Own Paper,*

Mrs. Philip Ross-Ross believes that "Domville House," built by her father, was inspired by the Amateur Work *article*

unearthed by doll historian Clara Hallard Fawcett,* there was an almost similarly comprehensive (if less geometric) account of how to construct and furnish a dolls' drawing-room, and we shall attempt to offer no more than its flavor. The room, which was pictured, was modest and homespun, with such fancies as "a writing-cabinet from three match boxes" and—considerably more extraordinary—"an American wicker chair . . . made from a coarse blue and white sailor hat."

With no lambrequin or antimacassar omitted if there was a surface for it to adhere to, this is a period piece if ever there was one. The very materials used are evocative of era. The chimney piece, for instance, is composed in part of "a certain lime and glycerine box." A tall mirror above the mantelpiece was originally to have had a gilded frame, but the author decided "to drape it with chiffon, like the windows, instead, and she added, "I think it looks more artistic."

A few pieces of furniture were bought for the room. "The little grate [was] purchased in London for a shilling," including a miniature set of fireirons. Another piece was a one-octave grand piano (for this was a room larger than usual in scale—thirty-six inches wide and eighteen inches high.) The piano is of interest for the music that its conscientious purchaser provided—"a waltz, specially composed for the one-octave piano, and written as finely as was possible on little sheets of foreign paper with a coloured cover."

In December, 1901, *The Ladies' Home Journal* printed an article by one Gertrude Okie Gaskill, called "How I Made a Dolls' House for $3," and it is probable, the way building costs have gone up, that the house would cost her a good deal more now.

Her ingenuity is evident from the description of her handiwork, and her ideas will be set down in a little more detail here than those of some of her ingenious fellows, since she is one of the pioneers. Her dolls' house, of wood, consists of one room, and the emphasis is on the furniture. It is forty-five inches by twenty-seven and has one side "quite open" which "allows the child to get inside to sweep and dust." There has been a natural preoccupation always with dolls' house architects to leave one or more sides of a dolls' house open so that the contents are easily available to the owner. But this stressing of cleanliness is a variation on the theme, and one that seems quite proper to a ladylike magazine of 1901.

A feature of the house which doesn't seem to have appeared on houses since,† home or factory-made, consists of "ten cent iron handles" at each end of the outside so that it can "readily be carried." But it is the fittings, most of them made from odd items the author found around her house, that show the most ingenuity. One of the innovations which occurs in a number of homemade houses thereafter consists of old photo negatives, washed and

* And reproduced in its entirety in *Hobbies,* August, 1963.
† But is often found on eighteenth century examples.

214

cut for windows. It is a sign of the times that the builder did not omit to have a window seat under at least one of these.

Despite the limitations of a single room, the decorator managed to provide a singular variety of furnishings. For her grandfather's clock, she included the face of a child's ten-cent toy watch. A little writing desk was made from an old cologne-bottle box with an inlaid lid, plus four clothes-pins. The fireplace, of medium rough sandpaper, had a hearth fashioned from an old school slate sawed in two and glued to the carpet.

The bookcase was filled with books, the easy chair covered with velours, and we are told that "the low chair was originally an iron inkstand," and given details of its conversion. The round center table, native to the parlor, was made of a revised walnut shaving stand fifty years old—a bit of destruction which should make any antiquarian quiver.

No detail escaped this lady. She remembered even brass ball feet for sofa, writing desk, side table and bookcase, made from the ends of sockets of extension brass curtain rods.

The only suggestion this architect makes which we hope no one will follow has to do with the fur rug which she says is the skin of a chipmunk which her nephew shot to feed a sparrow-hawk. She describes how she cured it and then says, "Unfortunately the squirrel head [squirrels and chip-munks apparently were one to this lady] had been cut off, else the rug would have been in every particular like a large one."

Delineator in December, 1905, told how to make a "Christmas doll house." This cardboard house, it was promised, would have "window shutters to open and close, doors that will open and shut, and the doors will have little door knobs like real ones. Each room will have a different-colored frieze around the walls, and the floor of the living-room will be covered with a handsome rug."

This handsome rug, by the way, is made of sage-green tissue paper, and there are red tissue paper curtains. This would appear to make the house a Christmasy one for its occupants as well as its recipient, perhaps for all the year. Those doorknobs are of large-sized beads connected by broom-straws. There are three rooms, living-room, bedroom and kitchen, made of three hat boxes. The furniture seems to have been the first of all spool and pasteboard dolls' house furniture, and the number of sewing baskets which must have been plundered in 1905 to make it is too terrible to contemplate.

In 1910, *Harper's Bazar* (the *Bazaar* didn't spell it with a double "a" in those days) ran an article modestly called "A Doll's House," but the title was a misnomer, for it told how to make six. They ran this comprehensive piece, nearly a definitive work, as though to wash their hands of the business, and indeed to this day we've noticed no other dolls' house diagram in their columns. They seemed not to realize that the surface of the subject barely had been scratched.

Their six edifices included a book-house for paper dolls, a cigar-box house for a "tiny china doll," a four shoe-box, four-room apartment for "a little French bisque doll," a log cabin, of corks, for a rag doll, a soap-box house for larger dolls, and a house of heavy wrapping paper for "any doll."

The *Bazar* improved upon a 1904 article of its own in the house for paper dolls. It's surprising that the *Bazar's* only two dolls' house articles should include the paper house, for no other magazine seems to have noticed this pleasant and simple variety whose main ingredient is, after all, the magazine. This appealing 1910 paper house is considered along with its 1904 predecessor in Chapter 16.

Of the other houses in the half dozen, the cigar-box house is most interesting. Whether the *Bazar's* article started the fad or reported a going concern, we do not know, but little girls of the era seem to have waited breathlessly for Papa to smoke the last stogie; and thus the cigar box, vacated by tobacco and renovated for the small doll, became a distinct (doll) architectural style. This *Harper's Bazar* one has wallpaper and pictures of furniture pasted to the walls, or mounted on cardboard and glued to small blocks of wood. The rug and portières may be made of "bright flannel or velvet."

The shoe-box house employs a box per room, kitchen and dining-room downstairs, parlor and bedroom up, mostly filled with match-box furniture upholstered in chintz.

It seems that the log cabin can be made of spools or clothespins as well as corks. A fireplace of clay is advised and "indeed, clay to make these bricks may be found in the toy-shops now."

The soap-box house is a carpentry job. The author asks, "Who said that a little girl couldn't do carpentry?" and hopes that no one will answer.

A plan for a really impressive dolls' house appeared in *Ladies' Home Journal* the same year. Called "The House that Daddy Built," the article told how to make for two or three dollars "a gift that purchased at the stores would cost the buyer thirty-five." Although this mansion had only four rooms, it included a little elevator (pulley). And "Daddy" pointed out that for one dollar a small storage battery, "with four tiny incandescent lights," might be purchased, thereby becoming certainly one of the earliest dolls' house builders to consider electricity.

The front door of this house was "up-to-date oak with a little diamond window," and the house included "a cozy veranda," an item which hadn't yet turned into a mere porch. A little round table with four claw feet, a davenport, "elegant with its padded leatherette cushions and fringed pillow," and a Morris chair further proclaim 1910.

It was *Woman's Home Companion* in October, 1912, hiding behind an innocent-sounding title, "The McKironies' Home," that told how to make a dolls' house and furniture of macaroni—and mucilage and pasteboard. The result has the appearance of a log cabin, with the "logs" dovetailing in the fashion of the pioneers'.

It is suggested that "a shallow tray filled with sand, sawdust or cereal makes a good setting," though to carry out the food motif, cereal would seem most suitable. Barns, sheds, a little fence and a clothesline also are projected. The cabin has a chimney and very little else. The furniture, too, is simple, befitting its pioneer occupants. A chair, table and bench were illustrated.

"The first thing to learn in handling the building material," says the account matter-of-factly, "is how to cut it into the desired lengths. Hacking and sawing will split it. Measure, carefully mark with pencil, lay stick upon table, make slight incision with sharp pen knife, then lift and break."

The apartment house was relatively rare fifty years ago, difficult as that is to realize in this apartment era, and when *Woman's Home Companion* featured in October, 1913, "A Dolls' Apartment House that an Up-to-Date Boy Can Build for His Sister," it was bowing to a new trend. This building was to be made of grocery boxes, and it was claimed that any boy would be able to build it no matter how little experience he had had in handling tools.

The apartment, which is only for one family, and thus perhaps not properly an apartment, is three stories high, but the three units were to be placed side by side during playtime to form a six-room apartment. This allowed for vestibule, reception hall, living-room, dining-room, kitchen, pantry, two bedrooms and a bath, a line-up of rooms which would be unlikely even in a house these space-saving days. The vestibule and reception hall probably are gone forever, and few new-built houses are including pantries. But a pantry in a homemade dolls' house was quite a thought in 1913, and note that here is the first homemade bath to appear. The house has bay windows and a front door of cigar-box wood. The door has a glass panel, and both of these items, bay windows and glass-panelled door, affirm the date. The dining-room, too, is traditional 1913, and "should have a plate rail on which to stand plates (pictures of plates cut from ads and pasted upon cardboard) and the walls below this rail should be panelled."

"A Dolls' Four-Room Bungalow" was described by *Woman's Home Companion* in November, 1914. The four rooms consisted of a living-room, dining-room, bedroom and kitchen. The house was a carpentry job with open sides, and diagrams were shown, but for complete directions, one was obliged to send ten cents. It is interesting to note the list of fifteen pieces of furniture the author considered essential:

These were library table, Morris chair, writing desk, grandfather clock, dining table, dining chairs, buffet, reading lamp, bedstead, wardrobe, washstand, ice-box, kitchen table, stove, and cabinet. The old-fashioned wardrobe, a vast thing with double doors and a lower drawer, was no doubt intended to pinch-hit for the rare closet.

This matter of the closet also turns up in a well-carpentered dolls' house described in *Craftsman* of April, 1916. The finest modern dolls' houses rarely bother with closets, so this one is notable indeed. However, even a built-in receptacle for milk bottles has been thought of in this dolls' house, and it is the first magazine-made residence to mention a stairway. A Mr. Patton, of Erie, Wisconsin, who made it, listed $1.60 as his total cost.

There is at this point a seven-year lull in our cavalcade of magazine diagrams. From 1916 to 1923, there seem to have been no dolls' house how-to articles printed. Possibly people were too busy with the World War and its aftermath. But *Ladies' Home Journal* set to work again in November, 1923, on "A Doll House for Small Folks that any Grown-Up Can Make." And the passage of those seven years shows a vast change in the dolls' house as well as a number of other things. The house still is not impressive architecturally, but it does have a gabled attic, the first to appear in this parade, and inside the house there is much architectural realism. The stairway has a landing (complete with grandfather clock). The kitchen is a wing that lifts off to ease moving day. Not all of the furnishings are homemade; toy plumbing modernizes the bathroom. The upper hall is thirteen inches across and "has a real closet with hooks for the doll dresses, and bonnet shelf."

In the partitions between living-room and hall and hall and dining-room, "arches are cut instead of the conventional doorways, as they give a more spacious air to the house."

Despite these modern touches, there are items that date the house. In the living-room is an upright piano (a block of wood with white paper, heavily ruled, for the keyboard). The dining-room furniture is the inevitable dark, heavy "mission." Pictures are hung with the wire showing. Furniture is often placed cater-cornered instead of parallel to the walls.

A list of materials for furnishing includes "small favors, such as a bird cage, telephone [long-necked], sewing machine and talking machine, many of which may be purchased in confectioner's shops and five and ten cent stores." The great item required in the making of this house, by the way, is fifty feet of bass or poplar lumber, a quarter of an inch thick.

Architecture came truly to the magazine-diagrammed dolls' house in November, 1926, when the *Ladies' Home Journal* told how to build "A Colonial House for the Children's Christmas." This is literally a dolls' house piece; although furniture is shown, there are no directions for making it. Furniture is left to the "ingenuity of" the dolls' house builder, who will need a great deal to duplicate the handsome project author Edward Thatcher has set him.

Attractive color pictures show the house to have four columns, complete with capitals, with a semi-circular fanlight in each of two pediments. The front and back of the house are shown both closed and open, and the latter displays an interesting arrangement of rooms. The living-room and halls, both downstairs and up, run the width of the house and may be viewed both front and back. The colonial stairway ends in a little gallery on the second floor. The front view, in addition, shows dining-room with door leading to kitchen, upstairs nursery and a bedroom. All in all, this was a handsome house.

On a considerably less opulent scale in December of the same year, *Woman's Home Companion* ran a feature called "Santa Claus Designs a House." This seemed to assume that Santa Claus wanted to take some architectural footsteps in which it wouldn't be too difficult for his young friends to follow, for arrangements are simple.

The house itself is two orange crates stood on end and covered with oilcloth, of the type that imitates tiling, to simulate four rooms. The furniture mostly is light wood with slip covers of cloth or crepe paper glued to it. An original idea consists of rag rugs "made of bits of ribbon such as comes around notepaper and candy boxes, braided together and then sewn 'round and 'round." The pictures in the living-room were cut from illustrations of the tops of snuff-boxes, and presumably are not to be run across every day.

"The clock and the little steam radiator were bought in a store where party favors were sold." At last someone remembered to keep the dolls warm.

Edward Thatcher, the same man who told how to make the beautiful colonial house in *Ladies' Home Journal* of 1926, came up with a somewhat untidier model in the same publication for November, 1927.

"A Doll House Made of Odds and Ends," it was called, and the odds and ends included a packing box (the house), pasteboard (the furniture), gummed paper tape (a modern material to which many dolls' house architects are indebted), match boxes, mailing tubes, inexpensive beads, match sticks, pins and glue.

Of the furniture, which for the most part is unimpressive, the only notable item, because of its recent antiquity, is a radio with loud-speaker. This is made of a block of wood ($\frac{3}{4}''$ by $\frac{3}{4}''$ by $3''$) with large and small button molds for dials and loud-speaker.

Ladies' Home Journal for December, 1930, printed an article called "Building Little Sister's Doll House," profusely illustrating a New England colonial and its furnishings. It was plainly a home, sturdy and comfortable, with a baby grand piano in the living-room and an umbrella stand in the hall. But one had to send one dollar for a pattern in order to build it. Possibly the depression had depressed even *Ladies' Home Journal*.

It took a man's magazine like *Popular Mechanics* (for February, 1931) to get around to a dolls' house with running water. This water runs from a built-in tub and the kitchen sink. The supply tank is made of a converted oil can, and quarter-inch copper tubing (the type used for auto gas lines) is used for both feed and drain pipes. The bath tap is a toy steam-engine whistle valve. The painstaking man who invented this system even carved his own bathtub, of white pine, covering it with several coats of white brushing lacquer to give it the appearance of porcelain.

This realistic house is also notable for its possession of a distinctive architectural style. Its author comments that it follows "the California Monterey type, a clean-cut and inviting design which is now very popular on the coast, and had its origin in the homes of the first prosperous American settlers." There are five rooms, upper and lower hall, staircase, fireplace and upstairs balcony. The entire front wall, including the double-decker verandah, lifts off, displaying all the rooms.

There is a six-year lull in our magazine dolls' house parade before, in *Popular Science* for October, 1937, there may be found a piece of miniature architecture elegantly named, "Quality Street Doll House." The builder's objective was a dolls' house that would be an attractive piece of furniture as well as a toy. A table with a drawer went with it. It was a scale model of an actual residence, with electricity, and the total building cost was $9.85.

There are twenty-three windows (of celluloid). And the woodwork has been handled to prevent warping, a problem some dolls' houses have faced. This two-bedroom house in addition to the rooms we have come to expect in modern dolls' housing has a breakfast room as well as a dining-room, with such up-to-date additions as a cloak room near the entrance and a first-floor lavatory. This builder also did his own landscaping, most of it wood painted green, with sidewalks of light gray enamel.

American Home, in December, 1939, told how to build a Dutch Colonial, and, again, a Monterey, the popularity of which, apparently, an eight-year interval had not altered.

These two houses are of most interest because of their modern accessories. The author points out that the barbecue fireplace is "inevitable," and he suggests that it be made of glued-up blocks and painted to resemble bricks. He also provides artificial trees of green sponge rubber, potted box trees, a white picket fence, a sundial, a birdbath and a pergola. Of the Monterey house he remarks, "red doors are having their vogue and are applicable here."

In December, 1940, *House Beautiful* had attractive sketches of three houses "designed and painted by Norman Reeves." The article allowed for the possibility that the young owners might tire of their house, and recommended cardboard rooms which would pull out and push in. Said the story: "These can be interchangeable rooms or sets of them so that one rainy day the house can be Victorian and the next modern."

This ingenious series of houses also had provision for complete façades, to retain all architectural illusion, but included arrangements to unhinge or lift off two sides, for playtime.

The last two houses on our list have a great thing in common. In May, 1943, *American Home* printed an article entitled "House that Scraps Built" and in December, 1944, *Parents' Magazine* did one called "A Doll House Built from Scraps." For everyone knows that during the war builders had to retrench in every way, and this trend was bound to appear even in dolls' housing.

American Home's suggestions were of interest mostly in the matter of furnishings. The use here of inexpensive handkerchiefs for draperies and spreads no one appears to have mentioned earlier, and they dressed the four cartons of this particular house no end. There was also some unusual dining-room furniture of corrugated cardboard. Full instructions for the *Parents' Magazine* piece had to be sent for.

The magazines seemed not to venture into dolls' house planning in 1945 or 1946. The cavalcade continued after building restrictions were eased, but we'll leave those blueprints of an unusually lively art in the lending libraries.*

* Since this is a history, building instructions in this chapter are chosen for their revelations about houses of their times rather than as aids to prospective craftsmen. However, it seems pertinent to mention here that shortly before this volume went to press, *The Dollhouse Book* by Estelle Ansley Worrell, published by Van Nostrand, "Told How" so beguilingly that it became what can only be described as a best seller.

15

THE
CONTEMPORARY
COLLECTOR

*W*HEN THE FIRST EDITION OF THIS BOOK WAS BEGUN IN 1945, AND even at the time it was published in 1953, collectors of dolls' houses and related miniaturia were relatively few, and one seized upon, and attempted to record, the significant details pertaining to every example of merit that came to light.

Today, the chronicler of dolls' houses is faced with an embarrassment of riches. To do the Contemporary Collector justice in the United States alone, one requires a book rather than a chapter. Where, in 1951, one was pleased to learn of a collector of furnishings for one dolls' house, one, in 1965, is confronted with so many important collections that it will be impossible to do more than offer a few highlights from some of these, in the hope of suggesting their scope and variety.

It seems relevant to mention, at least, the collector of miniatures, of which there are several varieties. Most astonishing, to the dolls' house purist, are the ones who must have the *smallest* of all things. Their treasures can generally be accommodated inside a grain of rice (although usually only a position on the head of a pin will do), and they seem to care for very little that can be seen with the naked eye. Their only substantial possessions are magnifying glasses and microscopes, and they are beset with such occupational hazards as dropping on the floor the egg beater that will pass through the eye of the needle, and being obliged to hunt for it for three weeks, often without success. Such oddments are frequently referred to in hobby magazines as "tinies," certainly one of the most alarming words that ever has attempted to crash the English language. (Sir Nevile Wilkinson's "tinycraft" is prissy but more attractive.)

Such collectors are outside the province of this book, but occasionally they have treasures that many a dolls' house would give its front steps for, and then they may be entitled to a paragraph in a dolls' house history.

The celebrated collection of the late Jack Norworth, consisting of 10,000 items, was recently acquired by John M. Blauer of San Francisco, who has incorporated many of them into a 40 room castle he calls "Maynard Manor." There are more than 2,000 pieces in the Manor, including such wonders as a meat grinder, egg beater, and barber clippers that work, and a set of 24 carat gold knives, forks, and spoons in a fitted box. Although Mr. Blauer, who is also a dealer, has such miniaturia as pinhead paintings, he claims to be an inch-to-the-foot man, and he has been true to this scale in his elegant and sizable "Manor."

Jules Charbneau, who is now retired, used to take on tour 28,000 items which considerately could be contained in a trunk, trinkets which would put the mistress of your average dolls' house into a tizzy. There was an electric stove with an inch-size oven that baked bread, and an electric refrigerator, similarly scaled, that manufactured ice cubes. There was a sewing machine that successfully sewed lock stitch, and a camera that took pictures one quarter inch by five-eighths. A model of a Stradivarius that could be played "with a sweet delicate tone" is one and five eighths inches from tip to bridge, and since rabbit whiskers were too thick to string its bow, its maker used hairs from his mother's head.

Another well-known name in this field is that of Joseph H. Gray of Chicago, whose role as a collector is perhaps less familiar than his reputation as a dealer in miniatures of the most extraordinary variety. Mr. Gray, who can provide collectors who do not require antiques with such miniature marvels as "Texas Motor Oil" and "Bass Drum and Traps," specializes in made-to-order items, although the variety to be found on his lists defies one to think up things which are not already in stock.

It is not surprising to learn that Mr. Gray's own collection is even more overwhelming. His miniatures are grouped in categories—tools, fans, games, musical instruments, and such—and his pipes alone number more than a thousand, each different and each smokable! Mr. Gray says these pipes, of which the average size is one inch, are made of materials used in full-sized pipes. "Many are original designs as we ran out of conventional shapes long ago."

As this suggests, Mr. Gray is more interested in pieces made today (he works with other artists to make much of his stock) than in antique items. Mr. Gray says that he has "never gone in for doll houses" himself, but he's had a lot to do with other people's.

Collectors of Mr. Gray's wares, and Mr. Blauer's, are fitting candidates for this chapter because so many of them, in the end, build dolls' houses to contain their miniature pieces.

They then become dolls' house collectors, of which there are several varieties. The most usual type is engaged in the furnishing of a dolls' house, or dolls' rooms, with a blend of pieces current, recent, and sometimes antique, and often with supplements of the collector's own devising.

The latter ingredient depends, of course, upon talent. There is a type of collector who starts out not as a collector but as a builder. It is in these ranks that architects and builders, whose work is more frequently discovered in full scale, are often to be found. Occasionally the dolls' house maker is not professional, but talented nevertheless, and there have been many of these amateur carpenters of remarkably diversified backgrounds. It is after the house is completed, and when this architect begins to furnish the completed house, that architecture ends and collecting begins. This sort of collector may become as dedicated as any.

With pocket knives, and eighteen-inch saws, they turn orange crates and packing cases into small mansions, often with workable sash windows and proper baseboards. There are electric lights and hardwood floors, studio living-rooms and roof gardens. But most of them belong in future dolls' house histories, where they will mirror the times in which they were made to the same degree that houses of the antiquarian collectors of today mirror the past.

It is the latter with whom we are most concerned in this chapter, collectors occupied with bringing or keeping together in an antique dolls' house, or houses, or in a series of rooms, the dolls' house furnishings of an earlier era. Such collectors must also be divided into two categories—those who will admit some reproductions and those—the purists—who will use none. However, those of us who are fanatical in our pursuit and use of period pieces only, appreciate the "amalgamated" dolls' house when it is accomplished with taste, style, and talent, and with fidelity to period.

Both here and abroad, many collections have multiplied to a degree where, ultimately, they have been metamorphosed into private museums. In Bodman, Germany, on the shores of Lake Constance, there is the well-known collection of Frau Maria Junghanns, romantically housed in a castle. The elderly proprietress, who has been collecting for nearly half a century, reportedly conceived the idea of a museum when, after an air raid on her home town of Freiburg, she noticed a pair of old dolls' houses "perched forlornly on the caved-in wall of a gutted house."

She has approximately 90 different dolls' rooms, and the appeal of such a collection is readily attested to by several sentences in a letter we received from a friend who visited the castle in 1964: "Very difficult it was to get there. We had to climb a mountain—I thought I was going to die of a heart attack. . . There was one house and lots of. . .rooms standing in absolute darkness. We got a candle each to try to see, but I could not see very much." Despite these rather picturesque difficulties, the writer's friend reported that Frau Junghanns had had 12,000 visitors to the Museum during the year.

Numerous pictures of the collection we've studied, pending a visit, reveal many treasures, including the most photographed room (not surprisingly, since it is wonderfully photogenic). This is a panelled oak parlor of the end of the nineteenth century with a most dramatic triple stained glass window combined with a pillared arch that somehow epitomizes the solid German middle-class comfort of its period.

It has been reported that the late Queen Mary once offered to buy the collection for a sizable sum, but that "the royal offer was turned down" by Frau Junghanns who has specified that when the collection changes hands, it must *never* be sold abroad.

In another part of Germany, in Würzburg, there is another private museum, this one belonging to a young collector, Fraulein Lydia Bayer, who has recently written her graduate dissertation on the subject of dolls' houses.* Dr. Bayer's collection was begun by her mother, and there are many delightful shops and rooms, as well as houses, including a two-room Biedermeier "Doll Salon and Bedroom" ca. 1830, and a single room furnished entirely with metal filigree furniture, ca. 1860-70, of unusual charm.

It is of interest to note that this furniture stamped out of tin has been made in Germany for generations. One factory in Bavaria, that of Babette Schweizer, which has been in business since the late 18th century, is still making many filigree miniature pieces, some from the original molds. The variety to be found in the earliest pieces is extraordinary. One mid-nineteenth century commode in the writer's collection has its own oil lamp attached to the top, complete with bristol shade.

Although the room in which Miss Bayer's furniture is shown was not with it originally, all the furniture placed in it came to her together.

* *The European Dolls' House from 1550 to 1800.* As this chapter was written this dissertation was at the printer's.

A room furnished entirely with metal filigree furniture, ca. 1860–70, from the museum collection, in Würzburg, Germany, of Dr. Lydia Bayer.

The library of Saltram House, ca. 1865, in Mrs. Vivien Greene's superb museum at The Rotunda, Oxford. The house was made for the family that owned Saltram House, near Plympton in Devon, now National Trust property.   Height: 12"

Before turning to private museums in the United States, one must allude, at least, to the superb collection of Mrs. Vivien Greene in England, perhaps the finest private collection in existence. These, of course, are exclusively English houses, many of them early ones of unusual interest, but they have been described so comprehensively and attractively in the definitive work on the subject of English dolls' houses written by their owner,* that it would be redundant to do more than allude to them here.

There are now thirty-three houses, dating from ca. 1700 to 1886, to be seen in Mrs. Greene's Museum, "The Rotunda," which was recently built on the grounds of their owner's home, "Grove House," Oxford, expressly to display them.

One of the finest collections of dolls' houses (and dolls) public or private, may be seen at Douglassville, Pennsylvania. *Mary Merritt's Doll Museum,* which has been open only a few years, has, for the quality and extent of its collections, as well as for the effectiveness and charm of its display, few equals. Its houses, rooms, and shops are marvelously diversified, and many have their original furnishings, but where the latter have been assembled, great care has been taken to maintain proper period and scale.

Of more than fifty houses, the earliest, of three rooms, is furnished with period pieces set into a Queen Anne cabinet. The Chippendale period

* op. cit.

is also represented by a cabinet house (four rooms), furnished mostly with early things found in the Douglassville area. There is also a Georgian house, and many Victorian ones, early and late, both English and American. A group of larger-scaled rooms (three by four feet) with mostly one-of-a-kind pieces, includes a Pennsylvania Dutch kitchen that features both rush-bottom and balloon-back chairs, a pine, glass-doored cupboard, and framed fracturs on the walls. Of the same genre, a Pennsylvania Dutch barn with hex signs, barnyard, and animals relates to Mrs. Merritt's Amish neighborhood, while her numerous English and Continental pieces reflect the many years she and her family have travelled abroad to import antiques for their sizable antiques business.

On a recent trip to Scotland, Mrs. Merritt acquired an early Victorian house that can only be described as glorious. Above the handsomely panelled door, which is flanked with marbleized columns, "Hope Villa" is inscribed in ornate letters, amid embellishments of a star and two anchors. The brick front shows much rustication, accenting the four bays as well as the coign-ings. Each room opens separately in front and—a most unusual feature— each of the four interior doors to the rooms have locks. Over the front door a window with a lattice-pillared canopy and a pierced railing is another bit of gilt on the elegant gingerbread.

Another recent museum assembled with knowledge and discrimination is housed in an old church in Sandwich, Massachusetts, on a piece of land which, till the new owners bought it from the First Parish Meeting House Committee, had been in the same hands for 325 years. The new owners were Lt. Col. and Mrs. Ronald Thomas who, in their various tours of duty, had collected many of the treasures which are now displayed in their *Yesteryears Museum.*

While Colonel Thomas was stationed in Stuttgart, in particular, Mrs. Thomas found a number of kitchens, shops and other rooms. Of special interest are the Thomas' Nuremberg kitchens which range from 1730 to 1900. Their dolls' houses are mostly English and German, but a recent

"Hope Villa," a thoroughly furnished mid-nineteenth century dolls' house found in Scotland by Mrs. Mary Merritt to add to the many fine houses in her Doll Museum at Douglassville, Penna.   Height: 36"

addition to which they are partial is an ornate Victorian house carved entirely with a penknife by a New York policeman nearly sixty years ago.

Most of the museum collections that have been described thus far emphasize old dolls' houses and rooms found with their original contents. *Steele's Tiny Old New England,* located on the Berkshire Trail in West Cummington, Massachusetts, is a most marvelous museum of Americana that was re-created, but re-created mostly with antique pieces, and with a remarkable degree of what it may be grammatical to call accurate nostalgia.

Alice C. Steele began collecting antique miniatures more than forty years ago, and equipped with these, a memory for precise detail, and a sense of history, she later began to furnish what has now become 54 rooms and a sizable assortment of shops and scenes that reflect, with great veracity, nineteenth century New England. With her husband, Frank Steele, a retired cabinetmaker who fashioned most of the backgrounds, Mrs. Steele has represented, among many, such standbys of the American scene as a Masonic Hall, a church food sale, a country auction, a country store, a quilting party, and, most unusual, "an old-time funeral in a home parlor." In the latter, which has a curious appeal (suggesting that even the awesomeness of death can be diminished in miniature), both casket and occupant are antique.

Mrs. Steele, who says that most of her rooms are replicas of actual ones members of her family once occupied in Hampshire, Franklin, and Berkshire counties, adds, "Everything is old if it is humanly possible to have it so, and the dolls in the rooms represent the people who inhabited the rooms. I have used between 400 and 500 dolls (all old except two), and they are mostly in the five and six inch size. A few are larger."

Visitors from all over the United States, and from England, France, and Germany have found their way to Kokomo, Indiana, to visit Ruth's Doll Museum since its recent opening. Mrs. Ruth S. Hockett is another collector turned entrepreneur who doesn't care for new houses, dolls, and miniatures, and improvises "only when I have to." Two of her large dolls' houses are contemporary copies of two of the oldest houses in Kokomo. A 45-year-old castle, made by Bernard MacMahon, celebrated St. Louis architect, contains 22 rooms. A general store has "for sale" 1,500 items, all old. Mrs. Hockett's museum includes many rare dolls, automata, and other toys. She says that visitors have been so numerous since the opening that she has been too busy to do anything else.

Undoubtedly the most fantastic private museum in the world is that of Mrs. Homer Strong of Rochester, New York. Mrs. Strong's collection, at this writing, numbers approximately 600 doll houses and rooms, and 11,000 dolls, and contains many treasures, including a large eighteenth century Dutch house, and a mid-nineteenth century butcher's shop similar to the one given to the Victoria and Albert Museum by Queen Mary. (See p. 173.)

Mrs. Strong once wrote about how her extraordinary collection began. When she was a child, she related, her mother bought her in Boston, "a charming doll house" that was a replica of James Russell Lowell's house in Cambridge, completely furnished, and, one suspects, unique, inasmuch as it was sold for the benefit of the Red Cross. It was her favorite toy.

When she was eight years old, she began to travel extensively with her parents. The young Margaret Woodbury would be taken out of school, and she says, "away we would go to foreign countries." She remembers being allowed to carry a small bag to put her dolls and toys in, and to add anything she acquired along the way. "Consequently, my fondness for small objects grew." Every year before Christmas, she was required to give away her "most cherished toy" to make room for the presents to come. "I kept the doll house, however," she writes, "because I never admitted it was my treasure until I was twelve years old, when I gave it to my cousins."

When her own daughter was six years old, Mrs. Strong reclaimed the house which was being used as a storage cupboard. "No furniture was returned with it—only one pair of blinds and a door knocker."

Many years later Mrs. Strong was seriously injured in a fall. While she was convalescing, she started to collect dolls' houses. Because she couldn't bend, she had tables built to hold the houses so that she could easily furnish them standing up.

That was the beginning. There are now so many treasures that some disappear into her vast collection almost without leaving a trace. Some years ago, the writer saw for sale a huge four-room dolls' house, made in 1866, for the granddaughter of an early Governor of Rhode Island, which had actually been piped for gas! Suspecting that this extraordinary toy had gone into the Rochester collection, she recently investigated, checking with both the dealer who had sold it, and with Mrs. Strong.

As it happened, the house was indeed in Rochester, and the dealer verified its Newport history, as well as the fact that it had been piped for gas, aspects with which its present owner was unacquainted. Mrs. Strong was pleased to learn of both, but when she then examined the house, she discovered that her assistants who had restored it, and installed electricity, had also removed the pipes, along with a gas ceiling fixture. They are, alas, gone forever, but it is of interest, at least, to know that such a dolls' house was made.

To antiquarians the most appealing parts of this incredible collection are the kitchens and shops, most of which, unlike many of the houses, have been left intact.

Herbert H. Hosmer of South Lancaster, Massachusetts, for years known for his puppet theater and related museum of toy theaters and puppetry, has recently established "The Guild for the Miniature Arts of Decoration" in association with the dolls' house section of his toy museum. The Guild "invites membership of all those interested in the preservation,

study, collecting, restoring, or making of dolls' houses, model rooms, miniature shops, or stables, and the furnishings and accessories." Mr. Hosmer plans to send members several illustrated bulletins annually.

In the Racketty-Packetty House Museum, which is named in honor of a commercially-made, early nineteenth century English house in his collection, there are stables, shops, and kitchens, as well as houses. Of unusually early date is a Dutch Wine Shop, ca. 1840.

In Egg Harbor City, New Jersey, the Antique Doll Museum of Mrs. C. Raymond Kears includes among its imposing collection of dolls and toys two dolls' houses. One is a 27-room "Georgian Colonial" mansion of thirty-five or forty years ago, which is complete from schoolroom to wine cellar. The other is a Victorian house, ca. 1870, with its original furnishings. This house, found in northern New Jersey, was accompanied by its own sizable firehouse, and by a large, three-story barn with handsomely detailed stalls, stairs, and hoist, with old straw showing at the attic windows.

Mrs. Kears says that the barn was empty so she moved her Schoenhut Circus, which was lacking a tent, into it, and tells her guests that "the circus is in its winter quarters." The name "Gerald" is on the back of the barn.

There are many other private museums, and it is trying indeed to be limited by the very fact of their growing numbers to a mere mention of some of them. Like the ones that have been (too) briefly described, they are far-flung. There is Stuart's Castle, an elaborate miniature edifice which was begun more than thirty years ago by Stuart A. Parvin of Woonsocket, South Dakota. (The Reverend Mr. Parvin writes a *Miniaturia* column regularly for *Hobbies Magazine.*)

There are the "Mott Miniatures" at Knott's Berry Farm in Buena Park, California. In a pleasantly but curiously worded reply to a recent inquiry, Allegra Mott wrote, "Antique doll houses have a certain charm because they have been lived with and loved. We have had many pass through our hands during the fifty-four years of our collecting . . . ours are not doll houses, but authentically furnished replicas of real homes. Ours is not the History of Doll Houses, rather it is the history of American living."

It is unfortunate that sometimes those who should most appreciate the role of the dolls' house in domestic history, most misconstrue it.

There are a number of private museums featuring one huge dolls' house, usually in two-fifths scale rather than the customary inch-to-the-foot. In some of these, as in *Susiebelle's House,* a marvelously authenticated "Study in Victorian Living: 1868," by Laura H. Brew, "practically all of the furniture and accessories are either apprentice models, salesman's samples or models for patent application."

Here the pieces have obviously been documented, but this may be as

230

suitable a place as any to admonish inexperienced collectors about the "salesman's sample," a term many antique dealers mistakenly use when a piece is realistically made. One often hears a dealer attach this label even to inch-to-the-foot pieces, though as Mrs. Brew points out in her excellent brochure, all apprentice models and salesmen's samples are made at the scale of two-fifths of the adult size. Even in this larger scale, however, many pieces fashioned with similar care and realism may be found that were made exclusively as toys.

At this point, one arrives at the collectors without museums, or with museums so private that we who have the trappings—the materials and even the facilities, but lack the time to show our treasures on any regular basis—prefer not to call museums even to ourselves.

As her own terrible example of how the addiction can take hold, the author obtrudes a numerical comment about her own collection (which has been described in detail in another volume). A mere three antique dolls' houses when the first edition of this book was published in 1953, it now consists of some forty houses, plus a multitudinous assortment of rooms, (single and double), stables, gardens, stores, and kitchens, most of it nineteenth century. In this collection,* which is still growing, no reproductions are used, and an effort is made when an unfurnished dolls' house is found to furnish it not only in pieces of the proper vintage and scale, but in pieces from the country in which the house originated. (If, for example, the house is English, only furnishings sent from England—and presumably from English dolls' houses, even though they were made elsewhere—are used.)

Since excellent collections of dolls' houses may be found in museums of all the Scandinavian countries (Chapter 9), it is not surprising to find some impressive private collections in these countries as well.

One of the foremost collectors is undoubtedly Fru Estrid Faurholt, of Copenhagen. Mrs. Faurholt, who had been primarily a collector of dolls, and who turned to dolls' houses in relatively recent years, has fine examples ranging from ca. 1800 (a small English house) to about 1890. Only antique furnishings are to be found in the houses, some of which came with their original furnishings.

In answer to a question, Mrs. Faurholt writes: "My collection cannot be called Scandinavian as it consists of nine Danish, eight English, three German, and one American houses, and of two German, one Dutch, one French, and the rest Danish rooms. So you see it is rather universal."

The charming street of three houses which is shown effectively illustrates Mrs. Faurholt's point. The Danish flag flying over the left-hand house announces its nationality. Of about 1890, its four rooms, bath, and attic

* Some portions are mentioned in other chapters.

231

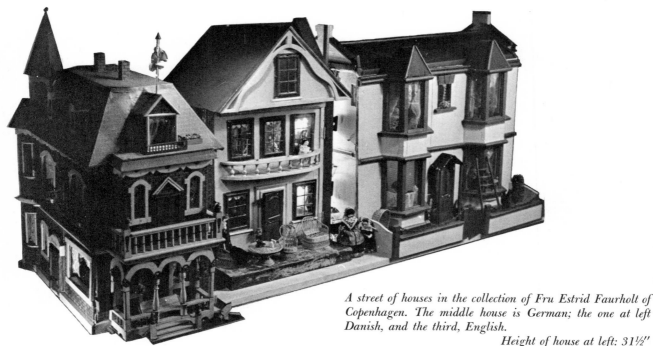

A street of houses in the collection of Fru Estrid Faurholt of Copenhagen. The middle house is German; the one at left Danish, and the third, English.

Height of house at left: 31½″

were fully furnished when Mrs. Faurholt found it. It is 31½″ tall and its façade lifts off.

The middle house, which is German from the middle of the nineteenth century, has a hinged façade which opens to reveal two rooms and, like the English cottage next to it, was found unfurnished. The English house dates from ca. 1870–80, contains four rooms, all of which open to the hall, and a staircase. There are fireplaces in all the rooms, and the front with its small garden lifts off.

Another Danish house, ca. 1840 or earlier, in Mrs. Faurholt's collection, has an intriguing "brick" façade with coigning, casement windows, and a most effective portal. The latter consists of double doors which may be locked with an actual key and a column-supported pediment with the very Scandinavian name painted on it of its long-ago young owner, "Tordis." Above this entrance, another pair of panelled doors leads out to a tiny circular balcony with metal balustrade where a doll may—and does—stand.

Mrs. Faurholt has many rare furnishings in her houses, including miniature hallmarked silver—such gems as a silver candelabrum dated 1716, from Amsterdam, and an English coffee pot dated 1758. The subject of miniature silver alone might fill a book, of course, and it is of interest to remember that such silver toys, as they were called, were so valued in the past that often they were mentioned individually in wills.

It is through the courtesy of Mrs. Faurholt that we have examined pictures of a magnificent house in the collection of Fru Dorothea Baumann, also of Copenhagen. This house is dated 1850, and has its name, "The Three Sisters," on a decorative plaque above the third story. Exquisitely furnished

232

and decorated, with painted ceilings, sumptuous velvet draperies with gilt cornices, and rare furnishings, there is an atmosphere of beauty and elegance that is not often found in houses of the period. The rooms are well populated with dolls, but they give no clue to the identity of "The Three Sisters," whose history is, regrettably, not known.

The same publication that contains pictures of this beautiful house also shows two of the rooms of Fru Signhild Häller of Göteborg, who, according to Mrs. Faurholt, may be said to be "a Swedish Mrs. Thorne." The two shown, of about fifty rooms, studios, and scenes created by Fru Häller, are the interior of a church complete with minister in his pulpit and churchgoers in their pews, and an eighteenth century musicale. Several elegantly dressed ladies and gentlemen in white wigs are listening to a trio—harpsichord, violin, and viola da gamba—play Mozart. The music, unmistakably labeled, is on a tall music stand. Both scenes are done with style and assurance.

Several years ago, at Biot, near the French Riviera, the author was privileged to see what must surely be one of the most unusual dolls' house collections in existence. This is the miniature world, poetic and nostalgic, infused with centuries of family history, of Mme. Madeleine Schlumberger.

"I am not a collector, only the keeper, the poet of the past," Madame Schlumberger once wrote. It is a choice definition, as only this artist and poet could have put it, but she must be described as a collector, too:

"You ask if I use reproductions. O my dear Madame, for me, new things are like a violin without strings. I have only violins *with* strings." Madame Schlumberger's collection began with the dolls' house furniture which she calls "Boule or Duncan Phyfe," ca. 1850, Nuremberg, inherited from a great-aunt. Around this she began: "I create only with old silks and lace, a room, with terrace and lake outside, and I painted a décor . . ."

It is Madame's "décors" which are the key to her art. After she completed the 1850 room, she reconstructed, with 1830 miniatures of yellow wood, "the salon of this grand-aunt as it was, and every window or open door has a décor behind, where I painted the little town, the place, the church, where during 300 years, my ancestors were baptised, married, buried. And so, from the little stories of family, I entered, I don't know how—in the history—and wrote a book. Every window is a chapter."

Madame Schlumberger's rooms numbered fifteen at the time her letters began and they have been augmented since. A small, most unusual house which she found, empty, in Bavaria, is a choice example of her method. The rear façade was crude and so she painted, "What I love for *me,* my own Paradise: birds, dogs, books, grandmothers, and old servants. Both faces were old pale grey with dark grey."

This picture with its *trompe l'oeil* doorway is shown.

A most curious room contains a sofa and four chairs made of "extra-

A house recreated by Mme. Madeleine Schlumberger,
part of her lovely collection at her home
at Biot near the French Riviera

The Watkins baby house. From the collection
of Mrs. William Redd Mahoney of Oak Park,
Illinois   Height: 7' 3"

ordinary blue velvet, gold striped," from the bedroom of King Ludwig II
of Bavaria in 1886, the year of his suicide. Madame Schlumberger has two
letters from the maker, written at Christmas of that year, with the history
and guarantee. It is a most romantic tale, and one longs for the space to
do it justice.

One of the most important private collections in the United States,
one which began in relatively recent years, is that of Mrs. William Redd
Mahoney of Oak Park, Illinois. Mrs. Mahoney's collection is small but
select. She has been fortunate in finding several delightful Victorian houses
complete with their histories as well as with their original furnishings.
Three are outstanding and, of these, the earliest is a small, perfect
English town house, complete with its name and date, "Camden House,
1838," painted at the top of a façade which swings open to reveal three
exquisitely furnished rooms and the original peg wooden dolls. All furnishings were authenticated as of the period by the Victoria and Albert Museum.
The other two are American houses which have been discussed in Chapter 8.
Mrs. Mahoney is exacting about period and scale in houses that do not
come furnished, or so completely furnished, as Camden House.

In the collection of Mrs. Frank C. Doble of Belmont, Massachusetts,
there are many rare and choice pieces (her patent model has been described
in Chapter 13), but perhaps none is more unusual than a lawyer's office,
furnished in tin, ca. 1870.
The notion of a lawyer's office in miniature is unusual to begin with

(as caricatured by such satirists as Daumier and Spy, lawyers usually have their foibles—and their furnishings—magnified rather than diminished), but to find one mid-Victorian and complete is unexpected and curious.

As its picture shows, the furniture itself is unusual. The table, desk, stool, and chairs are of the tin furniture painted to resemble yellow-grained wood which is believed to be from Bavaria, and is not often found even in more conventional parlor shapes. It is supplemented here by an iron safe and a handsome stove—the latter in interesting juxtaposition to a stove-pipe hat. Whether this hat belongs to the lawyer or his client is not known. The former stands by his open safe, the latter by the table on which both a bottle of Scotch and a beer stein are waiting. Perhaps he is hoping to be offered refreshment before he ventures out into what is obviously some weather—as suggested by the presence of a pair of snowshoes under the desk.

Mrs. Doble's collection includes other more conventional pieces, nearly as interesting, including a very complete dolls' house, all original, marked "M. P. H., 1891," which she bought in West Chester, Pennsylvania, and an attractive herb shop, complete with herbs in the drawers, which she found in Portsmouth, New Hampshire.

(One wishes more collectors would, like Mrs. Doble, preserve the sources of their treasures. Perhaps one day someone will come across these words and tell Mrs. Doble more about young M. P. H., who was given such a fine dolls' house in 1891—possibly in or near West Chester.)

Mr. and Mrs. Preston Weatherred, Jr. of Houston, Texas, are toy collectors of long standing, who have, in the past few years, discovered the wiles of the dolls' house world. Although they have not yet found the dolls' house they want to contain their sizable collection of Victorian furnishings, they have, in a relatively short time, gathered a number of smaller houses, shops, and stables; and such related and interesting items as a turn-of-the-century, French swimming pool, and a marvelously complete German toy theater, ca. 1880, with sixteen sets of scenery and four sets of fairy tale per-

Most rare: a lawyer's office, furnished in pieces of painted tin. From the collection of Mrs. Frank Doble of Belmont, Mass.

235

formers, the latter complete with scripts. The toy theater seems as entitled to a place in the doll microcosmos as assuredly as stables and shops, and the Weatherreds', painted in lovely shades of old blue, white, red, and gold, is a superb example.

It is of interest to note that a large part of the Weatherreds' toy collection was exhibited during Christmas, 1964, at the Humble Oil Building in Houston, and received the largest attendance ever recorded there—3,000 in one day— an accolade indeed to the prevailing interest in old toys, as well as to this well-chosen collection.

One of the best-known dolls' houses in the United States is the life-long creation of Miss Faith Bradford of Washington, D. C., who has given her house a theme. Furnished with the honest medley a full-sized home acquires over a period of years, Miss Bradford's house is populated with a family of dolls representing "an American family of the type that is passing, a large family of comfortable means but not great wealth."

For years this family was housed in a large unarchitectural shell, divided into four floors and twenty rooms, which resided quietly on an upper floor of Miss Bradford's home. But when its author retired, some years ago, from her Library of Congress post, she set about realizing an ambition she had long dreamed of for her doll family—residence in the Smithsonian's National Museum. To accomplish this move, more than a snap of the fingers —or even a miniature moving van—was needed. When the museum accepted the gift (and that in itself was an impressive day), the dolls' house had to attain a final perfection.

Since the original house frame was unsubstantial, Miss Bradford decided that larger rooms and other improvements were essential. Accord-

Miss Faith Bradford's house at the Smithsonian's National Museum   Height: 4½'

ingly she had a commercial model-maker construct a shell similar to her original one, but in exact inch-to-the-foot scale. This was in sturdy contrast to the original doll family roof—the lids of two zinc wedding cake boxes!

"Doll houses have a way of having started years ago," someone once wrote. This one had such a beginning in 1887 when little Miss Bradford was given the nucleus of her collection, her sister's four-room dolls' house. Miss Bradford's father was a clergyman and the family moved about a good deal—the dolls' house furnishings traveled in the two wedding cake boxes. This romantic establishment grew to ten rooms, and it grew some more. It was exhibited in historic Gadsby's Tavern in Alexandria, Virginia, a number of years ago where it won a blue ribbon in a benefit doll and toy show. From this Virginia adventure it did not emerge untinged—the butler presently serving the family is one Gadsby. The presence of the latter gentleman may serve to indicate the standard of living of Miss Bradford's miniature family. The placard on the well-lighted glass case that keeps dust (a substance unobtainable in miniature) from invading the petite premises says that this house shows "the way of life of a large and affluent family living in the period 1900 to 1914."

This placard is the key to another task Miss Bradford found when she moved her doll family museumward. Turning from a general theme for her house to a specific era required research. To establish the authenticity of the old-fashioned laundry equipment, for instance (washing-machine with hand-turned wringer and earliest of old-fashioned ironers), she checked—successfully—with a washing-machine firm in Chicago.

Just as a novelist will attempt to make his own characters real to him and later his readers by drawing up a biographical sketch of each one before he sets to work, Miss Bradford knows the name, age and personality of each of the dolls who lives in the house; child, parents, guest and servant. All the rooms are neatly labeled, and most include highly biographical bits about the household. The sewing-room, for instance, realistically provided with a dress form, bolts of cloth, and a garment in process of construction, in addition to a treadle sewing-machine, has this legend: "In a family the size of the Dolls, a great deal of sewing is necessary. Mrs. Doll has a sewing woman in for a fortnight, spring and fall."

The result of this infinite capacity for taking pains has practically displaced the Lindbergh plane as feature attraction at the museum since moving in, in 1951. There's something for almost everybody in the dolls' house. From the furniture in Robin's and Christopher's room, which came from the one-time toy shop near the White House where A. Lincoln bought playthings for little Tad—to the Blue Bird range in the kitchen. From the attic, where herbs hang from the rafters and an old morning-glory phonograph mingles with "discarded" marble tops, to the steamer rug, umbrella, guidebook and copy of *Figaro* with the trunk in the guest room—it is, like many another carefully thought-out dolls' house which presents a bit of the past, all sorts of things to all sorts of people.

The 18-room "Gay Nineties Mansion" with its formal garden. The creation of Miss Gertrude Sappington of Los Angeles, who has furnished it meticulously in antique miniatures (inch-to-the-foot)

One of the most exceptional of dolls' houses is the creation of Miss Gertude Sappington, formerly of Baltimore and now of Los Angeles. "Creation" is a word used advisedly: many years ago, Miss Sappington, with an attractive six-room dolls' house, to which wings were later added, began what is now her 18-room "Gay Nineties Mansion," a name which perhaps does not do full justice to the amount of taste and careful research she has given it, nor to the exquisite antique furnishings she has collected for it (all carefully inch-to-the-foot.)

An example of her care is to be found in the bathroom, for which she studied the craft of marbleizing paper in order to paper the wall in exactly the style and shade she considered appropriate.

An unusually handsome widow's walk crowns the original center section. As its picture also shows, this is a house with a formal garden, its paved walks lighted by French lamp-posts, which illuminate the marble statues, iron garden furniture, and topiary trees. One goes behind the lovely façade to take the twelve foot tour that is the length of the house.

A footnote: this is the only dolls' house known to us which has had its portrait painted room by room. The celebrated house at the Rijksmuseum was painted entire, but we know of no other immortalized in a series of paintings such as the ten lovely canvases commissioned by Miss Sappington and executed by the Baltimore realist painter, Frank Redelius.

238

Recently, Gertrude Sappington bought a remarkable West Coast collection of miniature rooms and Victoriana on which she is now working, and most of which will become "a continuation of the Gay Nineties family."

For nearly half a century, another connoisseur of Victoriana has occupied a spacious St. Paul, Minnesota, apartment that a recent observer described as "half museum, half workshop."

Its occupant, Elsa Mannheimer, like Gertrude Sappington, combines taste, imagination, careful documentation, and the gifts of an expert craftswoman with antique dolls' house furnishings. Where the latter are unavailable, Miss Sappington will resist improvisation, but Miss Mannheimer will get out her tools. Her workshop brims with the materials with which she has furnished and decorated three dolls' houses, two kitchens, fifteen shadow boxes, and assorted shops. Nearly all of these have a Victorian flavor; Miss Mannheimer can draw upon memories of her late Victorian childhood to give it authenticity.

Her stores include an "optical-plus-watch-and-clock shop" (the first we've ever encountered) and an extraordinary toy shop. For the latter, Miss Mannheimer, about twenty years ago, found the empty store, the largest and most elaborate, surely, that ever has been manufactured—even in the extravagant '80s or '90s from which it obviously stems. It is a whopping 47 inches wide and 21 inches high and, as its picture shows, its proprietress has stocked it thoroughly with a beguiling assortment of very small toys of the proper vintage.

One of Miss Mannheimer's dolls' houses, to use her own description, "is done in the gay 'nineties mood—gas jets, gilt radiators, bead portières, brass bed . . . the other house suggests an earlier date."

Many fine antique miniatures may be found in these houses, including such treasures as English brass cornices, ca. 1790, and Baxter prints. Their owner contributes such illusions as edible-looking chicken noodle soup to

A marvelous toy shop re-stocked by Miss Elsa Mannheimer of St. Paul, Minnesota, who restores her houses and shops with great authenticity and craftsmanship   Height: 21"

the silver tureen in the dining-room and a dress form with tape measure in the sewing-room.

Even those of us who resist reproductions have to be impressed when we learn how this craftswoman goes about her work. Needling a bell pull, she got herself a needlework pattern for a full-sized model, and proceeded to reproduce it, stitch for stitch, in a suitable five-inch length!

It's not surprising that Miss Mannheimer has been asked to restore, for the State Historical Society, a dolls' house made for the granddaughter of Minnesota's first territorial governor. (This house has been discussed in Chapter 8.)

Another glowing association of antiques and careful craftsmanship may be found in Aurora, Illinois, where Mrs. Verdelle Flynn's delightful antique houses and shops peacefully co-exist with her reproductions of nostalgic rooms and scenes. A striking and original example of the latter consists of a representation of a painting by Grant Wood: "Dinner for Threshers." The artist's spare style somehow comes through in Mrs. Flynn's effective reproduction. The eight threshers seated at the long table look not like bisque dolls in overalls but like threshers in a painting by Grant Wood.

It is her "old time barber shop," though, that is the measure of Mrs. Flynn as a craftswoman. Shaving mugs even in full-size are a collector's item; in miniature they are an impossibility. An "old time barber shop" without them is unthinkable. Mrs. Flynn studied ceramics, bought a kiln, and made her own!

Mrs. Flynn's dolls' houses range in period, beginning with an English one from the early nineteenth century, but none is as appealing as a four-room, late Victorian cottage reportedly made by, of all people, Mark Twain.

It is to Mrs. Flynn's great regret that years ago, when she bought this house, fully furnished, from an antiques dealer in upstate New York, she was less interested in documentation than she has since become. At the time, she was told that the house was made by Mark Twain for a neighbor's children. Unfortunately, she does not know where. The celebrated novelist's thirty years in Hartford ended in 1900, and the final four years of his life were spent in Redding, Connecticut, where he died in 1910. In 1900, he had settled in New York (for the few years between those dates), so the choice is wide.

In any case, it is known that the beloved humorist was fond of carpentry and children, and though one suspects from the style of the house that he was a better storyteller than architect, his dolls' house, even unauthenticated, is a treasure. Curiously enough, it is not unlike the house he was born in, in Hannibal, Missouri. The upstairs windows of the dolls' house are in pairs, unlike the ones in Hannibal, and two dormers lacking in Hannibal perch on the roof of the dolls' house, but there is the same stoopless front door and a distinct family resemblance for those of us who insist upon seeing one!

The house, Mrs. Flynn says, was in "deplorable condition" when she found it, but it was filled with its original furnishings—commercially made pieces of the type made both before and after the turn of the century.

Several unusually handsome stores, including a delicatessen, ca. 1880, with French labels on the drawers, are to be found in Mrs. Flynn's collection. (The language on the labels is, of course, no proof of the country of origin. A mid-nineteenth century butcher's shop in the author's collection with the label "Bull Butcher" seemed unmistakably British till it turned up in a German toy catalogue featuring labeled stores in both English and German.) Recently, Mrs. Flynn was sent from Paris another lovely old shop, crowned by a sign with "Epicerie" above, and with "Primeurs & Comestibles" on the line below. The "early fruits and/or vegetables" are there, and much other delectable merchandise. This one seems unmistakably Parisian.

A few thousand miles away, and several centuries later in vintage, is a very different sort of dolls' house. This residence, elaborately known as "The Palace of the Princess in the Village of Lilliput" is better known on the West Coast than in the East, but though it doesn't compare in fame to some rival doll realms, it approximates them in a number of other ways. The late Mrs. Elizabeth Larke Blodget of California, more widely known as Mother Larke, conceived this palace which she furnished with one of the largest collections of miniature objects in the world, as well as items fashioned from her own fancy. There were twenty-five thousand of these treasures at one point. They are housed in a palace of thirty-seven rooms built around a central court which is fashioned like a Normandy castle with turrets and towers and battlements. The fountain in the center of the court is a replica of Marie Antoinette's own at the Petit Trianon. There is also a miniature museum which contains "hundreds of overflow pieces of every kind." Like so many dolls' houses, this one has been at the service of underprivileged children, and has been exhibited widely in its own region, including the 1935 Exposition at San Diego.

As serious collectors often do, Mother Larke visited a great many countries in search of her treasures. She spent the better part of a year ransacking fourteen, though this was only a smidgin of more than thirty years of general collecting. As a result of these travels, though, Mother Larke's Lilliput has a decidedly cosmopolitan character. As she once said, "My house covers much territory—French, English, Persian, Spanish, Swedish, a museum whose collections from Russia, the Netherlands, Peru, etc. add to the geographical idea. Egypt is represented by King Tut's golden bed, and many other beautiful miniature objects I bought in Cairo."

But the notable thing about Mother Larke's dolls' palace reflects its West Coast origin—the remarkable series of Oriental rooms. Of these their designer writes, "My Oriental rooms were not copied from anything in existence. They must be very satisfactory, because my most enthusiastic visitors are Oriental people."

A visit to Cliff House, where the palace has been on view* verifies the attractions of several of these Oriental apartments, as well as the sort of ingenuity Mother Larke employed throughout the premises. One, called the Chinese Red Lacquer Room, has murals—taken from an old mah jongg box. A hanging lantern was originally one of the cricket cages in which Chinese children keep crickets as pets. Another room is that of the Chinese Prince (the Princess of Lilliput is not the only royal occupant who lives in this palace) whose most extraordinary furnishing is an exquisitely carved bed which looks more like a small shrine. Some of the carved pieces nearby are of rare red jade. The artist who carved them had died and in 1936, at least, the Chinese Government was "seeking notable examples of his work in order to honor him through the placing of such pieces in a museum collection." The Main Oriental Room is a trove of Eastern lore. Its external features—a beautiful inlaid floor made for Mother Larke by "a gentleman in San Francisco" and Chinese carving on door frames and shrine—are handsome, and so are the furnishings.

Even parts of the palace which are not specifically Oriental seem to have an Eastern cast. One of the most impressive is The Grand Staircase which majestically ascends three stories with grace, branching off into two swirling flights after reaching its first landing. The innumerable ornaments and furnishings on the way emphasize the Oriental atmosphere.

Mother Larke's participation in the dolls' palace went far beyond collecting. Her contributions with her own hands are numerous and surprising. The bed in the Princess' bedroom is made of ivory, but of such miscellaneous offshoots as fan sticks, lemon forks and piano keys. In the same chamber, an outmoded card case, with a few improvements, became a corner cabinet. Mother Larke once wrote, "All my life I've saved bits of broken things, exquisite bits, too, since they were jewelry, carved ivories, wood, odd and unusual beads, trimming, etc. So I had quite a large stock to draw from. And my imagination! It got me spanked at least three times a week when I was a small girl . . ."

In the Spanish Bedroom, Moorish hanging lamps "were obtained from a donkey girl in Spain, who was wearing them as earrings." In the French Drawing Room, the mantel and fireplace set "represent a gathering of ormolu ornaments, part of a lady's hair comb from India, mountings from perfume bottles, and wood from an old walnut bed." The German Bedroom contains a chandelier made from a fish-hook which, according to the booklet, "at one time seemed doomed to destroy the seat of her small boy's trousers." "I made an atomizer for Uncle John (one of the less regal residents of the palace) out of a square bead and nine other objects," said Mother Larke, "after I finished it I had to guarantee it not to squirt!"

For purists who resent the intrusion of such improvisations among more customary works of art, there are sufficient wonders to make them forget a

_____
* A fire interrupted for a time but the palace is again open to the public.

242

difference of opinion. The merits of a number of the collections are of interest considerably outside of dolls' house circles. Mother Larke once said that her Toby jugs, bottles and "Dresden" figures, about half an inch tall "are the envy of all collectors." There is a collection of needle box Baxter prints, measuring an inch by one and three quarters, and a collection of miniature water colors over a hundred years old and painted by Royal Artists, both of which engross connoisseurs.

The Princess of Lilliput has a considerable establishment.

George Washington's office and cabinet room are among the twenty-four miniature rooms of Mr. Edward J. Soller of Chicago, who has been collecting since 1930.

Mr. Soller's rooms, which contain both antiques and finely made reproductions, show interiors of different periods ranging from the seventeenth century to the present. In addition to single rooms, there are a Kentucky Tavern with parlor and dining-room, and an unusual Shaker group which includes assembly and kitchen, and dining, sewing, and bedrooms.

Mr. Soller's collection includes many ivory pieces made by the late Frederick Hosbach whose ivory reproduction of a large printing press about two inches wide, with many surplus parts alongside, may be seen in the Smithsonian.

Joseph H. Gray asserted in *Hobbies* that Mr. Soller's collection is one of the finest—and Mr. Gray should know.

Such nostalgic labels as "After the Ball is Over" and "Return of the Skaters" have been given by Mrs. Richard Fairchild of Bay Village, Ohio, to her 33 miniature rooms. Mrs. Fairchild, who once counted more than a thousand furnishings and—what is awesome—approximately 900 dolls' house and other small dolls in her collection before becoming bored with her indexing project, has many rare antique pieces in her collection. These include a revolving photograph album (which sounds astonishing, to say the least), a filigree-lead washstand with its original bristol fittings, and a set of wooden dishes decorated with Empire-costumed figures and floral sprays. These last came accompanied by the curious and interesting rumor that similar wooden dishes were made, long ago, in the Astabula, Ohio, area, a matter future researchers may wish to check.

Other unusual pieces, including a "rare parian doll with snood and bows," are from a dolls' house bought at the auction of an old mansion on the main street of Norwalk, Ohio, by a generous antique dealer who donated it, and most of its furnishings, to the Milan (Ohio) museum.

Mrs. Fairchild also has an unusual small dolls' house (25″ high, 23″ wide) with mansard roof, much gingerbread trim, fancy lintels over the windows, and a delightful fanlight in a "tree of life" pattern with all the panes of different colors. She was obliged to re-paper the rooms because several layers of paint covered "dozens" of floral and butterfly scrap pictures plus small cards containing proverbs and Biblical quotations, provided by the long-ago young owners. These must have given the house a curious charm, and one would have wished to see it in its heyday. There were traces of stenciling, barely visible on the floor of one room, also covered with layers of paint, when Mrs. Fairchild scraped it to see what lay beneath.

There have been frequent tales of architects turning to miniature building on behalf of miniature daughters, but when an architect finds himself building a dolls' house because he is commissioned to do so, it is apparent that something extraordinary is afoot. When Mrs. Frederick Dent Hammons, of Seattle, Washington, commissioned architect Joseph S. Cote to build a miniature Southern Colonial mansion, he had designed many a full-size Georgian and Colonial, but never had been concerned with miniature blueprints. To judge from an attractive brochure, the result features craftsmanship and attention to detail similar to the perfection of the Thorne Rooms.

Mrs. Hammons writes that this twelfth scale model representing "a house of the Old South restored for present day living . . . began as a dream of Mr. Hammons, the architect and myself." Most of the furniture was copied from antiques, some of these from pieces in the Metropolitan Museum of Art in New York. Numerous craftsmen created the furnishings, including those of an earlier day. Antique miniatures include a European porcelain spill vase which came from a collection belonging to Mrs. Montgomery Blair, wife of the Postmaster-General under President Lincoln.

Several years ago, Claire Bagley Hammons presented this house to Seattle's Museum of History and Industry and then turned to the making of her most ambitious miniature residence, a Beacon Hill house with rooms copied from a number of lovely New England mansions, and containing numerous mementoes of her Massachusetts ancestors.

The extraordinary thing about this tiny house (and the word tiny is used here advisedly) is its scale: the Beacon Hill mansion, which contains three floors, a lovely winding staircase, and fifty workable sash windows, is but 13 inches high, 12 inches across the front, and 9 inches deep. The unusually small scale (one-fourth inch to a foot) has been achieved with a fineness of detail that is evident from the photographs: the realization that a tall-case clock in the banquet hall, a reproduction of an Eli Terry, has a Swiss mechanism and keeps perfect time and yet is only one-and-a-half inches high, is awe-inspiring, to say the least.

Mrs. Hammons, who designed and planned the miniature mansion, also made some of the needlepoint rugs. She gives credit to Joseph H. Gray, the well-known Chicago miniature collector and dealer, for telling her about Frank L. Matter of Seaside, Oregon, an artist and craftsman who built the house and furniture and did the oil paintings.

Interior and Exterior (below) of the almost incredible Beacon Hill house of Mrs. Frederick Dent Hammons of Seattle, Washington   Height: 13" (!)

Architecture may be the most logical profession to invade the dolls' housing field, but related arts often supply representatives. A sculptor, Elizabeth Muntz, worked for four years (1932–36) on an extremely unusual dolls' house, a Cotswold manor of the year 1614. *The Illustrated London News* has pictured this splendid little edifice which boasts such items as wrought-iron banisters, one hundred windows and two secret hiding places! Originally commissioned by an Englishwoman for her daughter, the house has been presented to a Sussex establishment for girls.

An artist who turned to doll architecture, Mrs. Samuel H. Brown, Jr. of Marblehead, Massachusetts, years ago built for her daughter a dolls'

house which occupies much of the second floor hall of the Browns' historic 1728 house. The writer, some years ago, paid a delightful visit to the dolls' house, but Mrs. Brown's own words in a letter that preceded the visit suggest the flavor of the house better than another summary can:

"There are ten rooms—all around twenty-four inches long and deep enough to be in proportion. The furniture (most of it), rugs, etc., we have made ourselves, but the fittings, china, bric-a-brac, etc., have come from all over the world. The dolls are all English and the animals a mixture (mongrels I guess). We have kept the period colonial, the scale one inch to a foot—and have been rather exacting about that—although we 'fudge' a little when something or other that is particularly lovely arrives—as in the case of a silver service, which has the Hall or Guild marks of the maker. Besides the main rooms, there are two bathrooms, halls, closets and dressing-rooms, a barn and a garden—so if it grows much larger, I'm sure we shall just have to buy a lot."

Mrs. Brown, who learned to use tools when she studied jewelry making in art school, built the house and furnished it with replicas of the antique furniture in her home. Also a needlewoman, she made needlepoint copies of her full-sized Oriental rugs.

The number of craftsmen who make *everything*—down to the last doorknob—and collect nothing, would alone fill a volume, as the monthly "Miniaturia" column of *Hobbies* will attest. An example at random is a Hollywood dentist, Dr. Joseph Cooper, who has meticulously reproduced his own living-room—chairs, lamps, figurines—in inch-to-the-foot scale with the tools of his trade. For the furniture, he manufactures his own three-ply wood by gluing together three pieces of mahogany veneer, the center piece set in with the grain running crosswise. The resulting "board," an eighth of an inch thick, he finds suitable for carving, and easier to handle. For such accessories as metal drawer handles and lamp parts, he uses his dental casting machine.

It is obvious that one could go on and on with this procession. Many important collections which have necessarily been dismissed with a few paragraphs were worthy of at least a chapter; and some of them, a volume. Other collections, for one reason or another, have not been covered at all. That of Mrs. Henry P. Kendall of Sharon, Connecticut, for example, is known to be excellent, but it has not been possible to communicate with its owner. For reasons of space and/or time, we, regretfully, can only allude to the houses or collections of Mrs. Claude Callicott of Franklin, Tennessee; Mrs. James Shields of New City, New York; Mrs. H. A. Clopton of Richmond, Virginia; Mrs. John Leininger of Coral Gables, Florida; Mrs. Philip Ross-Ross of Ontario, Canada; Mrs. D. R. Cushing of Westmount, Quebec, Canada; Mr. and Mrs. Paul A. Johnson of North Tarrytown, New York; Mrs. George Grant Mason, Jr. of Arlington, Virginia; Mrs. John Grossman of Trumbull, Connecticut; Mrs. R. H. Ray of St. Paul, Minnesota; and

This miscellany of chairs, from the author's collection, shows a fair cross-section of the variety of furniture styles to be found in Victorian dolls' houses—and collections

Mrs. John Wheeler of West Mystic, Connecticut and Mrs. Marie Berdy of Irving Park, Illinois.*

Obviously there must be many dealers to supply such a host of collectors, and we have earlier alluded to such purveyors of miniature reproductions as John Blauer, Joseph Gray, and Eric H. Pearson. Edith Perry Maxson of Mystic, Connecticut, is another. Elaine Cannon of Batavia, Illinois, makes entire rooms for people who prefer not to assemble their own.

There are a number of dealers who handle both antiques and reproductions, and some of these, such as Carolyn Watson of Des Moines, Iowa, have their own collections.

Various antique dealers who specialize in old dolls or toys, or both, often have this highly particularized merchandise. The famous old New York toy firm, F. A. O. Schwarz, of course, has had, for several years, an antique toy department presided over by Mrs. Henry Erath, a discerning toy collector herself.

Despite these sources, antique dolls' houses and their furnishings are not easily come by, and when they are, they are likely to be expensive. One antique shop out of thirty may have something for this specialized collector. When a shop does have furnishings, though, it often has a number.

The practice of many dealers who buy an old dolls' house at auction, or from a private source, and then "break up" the contents and sell it by the set or item, has been lamented elsewhere in these pages. One can only make a plea on behalf of the rapidly dwindling supply of Victorian dolls' houses which remain intact. With the growing number of collectors of antique toys, it is hoped that a dealer who has been fortunate enough to find such a treasure will attempt to find a collector to buy it who will keep it together and preserve its miniature measure of history—and a flavor of the past that few other relics of the past—particularly in such a modest degree of space— can dispense.

* Other collectors with dolls' houses of unusual national or historic interest are mentioned in other chapters. The decision has had to be arbitrary; much in this chapter might have fitted as well elsewhere.

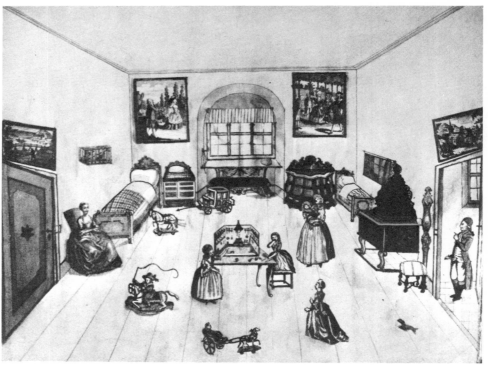

German cut-out books, eighteenth century, from Munich; drawing-room and nursery

248

16

HOUSES
FOR
PAPER DOLLS

$\mathcal{J}$UST AS A NUMBER OF QUITE SUBSTANTIAL DOLLS HAVE BEEN OBLIGED to make do with a trunk-lid over their heads rather than a roof, whole families of paper dolls often have had no residence other than a battered envelope or a volume of *The Decline and Fall of the Roman Empire.* The resulting hibernations that such inadequate housing has made necessary need not have been. Paper dolls' houses have been in existence at least since the eighteenth century, and very handsome ones, too.

Gröber, who has a delightful chapter on paper toys, tells us that German engravers "and especially those of Augsburg," brought out picture series for children to cut out. "Everything conceivable" could be bought, but of most interest here are the dolls' houses which thus came, with the relative cheapness of paper, within the reach of practically all children.

"The little figures," said Gröber, "were neatly cut out and, suitably grouped, stuck on to large sheets of pasteboard, and the background was then painted in." The child did the arranging and the painting. Some of the fruits of this creative toy have been in the Bavarian National Museum at Munich which has had two of these picture-books, dating from the end of the eighteenth century.

"The many sheets show us the complete house from cellar to garret of a well-to-do Nuremberg citizen. Every object portrayed is neatly cut out of

German cut-out books, eighteenth century, from Munich; marketplace and counting-house

250

the sheet of pictures and most carefully stuck together. Nothing is forgotten, and the character of a true plaything is wholly observed. The doors when stuck on their jambs open and shut, so that a glimpse is allowed into all the rooms, however intimate, while the cupboards open and reveal their treasures in clothing and household utensils. In addition there are street scenes, hunting and sledging parties, and children at play in the garden." Gröber shows four pages from the picture-books which substantiate his opinion that they "are among the most delightful things ever produced as playthings." These include such miscellaneous subjects as a market place, nursery, counting house and drawing-room. (See illustrations.)

The nursery is of particular interest because of the toys it contains. In the center of the room two little girls are playing with a toy kitchen which is set upon a table. One of these young cooks is reaching in to place a utensil. A younger cook, who can't attend to her culinary obligations any other way, is standing on a stool, and appears to be tasting some of her cookery. A little brother, evidently unimpressed by these savory goings-on, flourishes a long whip and heads his rocking horse in another direction. Smaller steeds are detached from a miniature carriage in another part of the room. There are beds, chairs, chests, elaborate pictures on the walls, and that inevitable nursery fixture, a bird-cage.

In the drawing room, which has a stove in it dated 1786 and thus precisely identifies the society it warms, a banquet appears to be in progress. It is true that there is nothing but a cloth on the long table, but a goodly company is seated there. One little be-wigged man is reading—perhaps the feast is literary. In the rear of the room a great lady sits grandly on an ornate settee with a little dog in her lap. The young handicrafter seems to have got the pictures on these walls confused with the ones in the nursery: above the great lady is a delicate portrait, amid bulrushes, of a family of ducks, whereas in the nursery the subjects seem to be after Fragonard or Watteau and appear to feature pastoral idylls. The young artist or artists in all four specimens apparently have done their work neatly and suitably. The perspective is occasionally surprising, but this may have been caused by the materials at hand rather than the talents of their users.

Paper furniture, like paper dolls, may have been manufactured at home before it occurred to anyone to print some commercially. The most enterprising interior decorators under ten (or even fifteen), generally like to do their own drawing, as well as their own cutting, coloring, and pasting. As early as 1857, in the United States, there was a handbook for such self-reliant pioneers. The Metropolitan Museum of Art has it, a small, withered book called *Paper Dolls' Furniture. How to Make It,* copyrighted in that year. By one C. B. Allair, it contains furnishings for tracing, coloring, folding, and pasting, and suggests that a sheet of letter paper would be better to use than cardboard. "For you might not succeed in your first attempt, and thus the cardboard, which is rather expensive, would be wasted." The

Warne's Nursery Play Book *shows a mid-19th century dolls' house and the furnishings to "stick" onto the rooms*

manner of tracing suggested is fairly nostalgic. A piece of tracing paper, a little piece of pine wood burned. "Rub back of tracing paper all over with it."

A mere list of part of the furnishings conveys some of the flavor of the era. The kitchen has a queer portion: four plain chairs, one settee table, one common table, one clotheshorse. The dining room consists of one large dining table, one butler's tray, six chairs, one high chair, one plain clock. The parlor, of course, has the fancy allotment: two tête-à-têtes, one lounge, one small pier table, with oval mirror, one picture for the pier, one large rocking chair, one small rocking chair, four mahogany chairs, one patch-work chair, one little work-basket table, two footstools, two figures for mantel shelf, one vase of flowers for pier table. There was also bedroom furniture and servants' furniture.

A New York rare-book dealer a few years ago sold an American paper dolls' house and furniture of this same period, lithographed in colors, which unfortunately it has not been possible to trace, but it is interesting to know that such toys were published as long as a century ago in the United States, since Germany monopolized this as well as other toy fields. It is possible that it was made by a firm mentioned by a writer on paper dolls in *Antiques* who stated that "In the middle of the century, Clarke, Austin and Smith published several series, not only of dolls but also of rooms and furniture. These were styled 'The Girls' Delight,' while a group called 'The Boys' Delight' consisted of animals." By a curious coincidence, one girls' set described by the author was copyrighted in 1857, the same year as the Allair book. It "included sheets of furniture, dolls, and the floor, three walls and ceiling of a room, completely decorated in the most up-to-date style. A page of directions and advertisement went with it. The most expensive item listed was this room at twenty-one cents."

The lush lithography of the turn of the century turned such toys into dazzling miniature spectacles. The same book dealer who sold the mid-Victorian paper house not long ago had for sale a French specimen, circa 1900. This, boxed, was called "l'intérieur de la poupée," and contained a motley, glistening cardboard backdrop which folded into the three sides of a dining-room. The dolls and furnishings required very little cutting. They were linked together on sheets by tabs, and could be practically pulled apart. There were dolls and dishes and purses and furniture, a miscellany temporarily combined in a casually heterogeneous manner. There were peacock feathers in jardinières on the towering sideboard permanently situated on the backdrop. The dinner table sprawled like a centipede till its legs should be folded into position, but its cloth was already laid. The hostess could set the blue plates, though, and the rest of the service.

In this country at the same period both McLoughlin and Bradley were among those publishing similar wonders. In England Raphael Tuck was turning out its luscious creations. The latter in 1910, well-advertised over here, was heralding a "Home Sweet Home for Dainty Dollies." This was "made to form two rooms, with sheet containing twenty-two pieces of

Drawing-room and Bedroom Furniture to cut out. Printed in brilliant colors." The historic Tuck plant was one of the English factories demolished during the war, and many valuable files were lost.

Harper's Bazar in 1904 and 1910 told how to make paper dolls' houses of another sort. These required no help from McLoughlin, Bradley, or Tuck. The only materials needed (according to the 1904 instructions) were "a blank book, some old magazines, a pair of scissors and a pot of mucilage." The home builder was, of course, to cut furniture and accessories from ads. It was suggested that everything be put in place before pasting "to see how it looks, and if it can be improved upon."

The author, of a philosophical turn, it would seem, observed that "The average child is not bound down by any petty consideration concerning art for art's sake. It matters not to her that her table is several sizes too small for her chairs; or that the thermometer with which she decorates her wall is larger than the desk by which it is supposed to hang—undeniably it is a thermometer and whoever demands more is indeed a carping critic." Moreover, impeccable *Harper's B.,* amid profuse illustrations of the quaint house, printed a picture of this weird room, over-size thermometer and all.

There's no limit, the author pointed out; the paper housekeeper can "revel in luxuries" without a thought to expense. Her list of luxuries included a telephone "of course," a phonograph, and "possibly in the papa doll's den, a typewriter." Also for the latter, she provided easy chair, reading lamp, cigars and smoking table, "and any other little masculine comforts which the backs of magazines so thoughtfully suggest." An early model sewing machine, in the bedroom, was up-to-the-minute 1904 furnishing for mama. The paper gardening the author also recommended sounds like a pleasant project, possibly with paper earthworms.

By 1910, the *Bazar* was more fastidious about its paper dolls' houses. Unlike the 1904 piece, this one was particular that the items of furniture be as nearly the same scale as possible. It suggested, for the house, a discarded phone book, with wallpaper covering the pages, and rugs pasted to the floors.

It further advised colored tissue or white lace candy-box paper for curtains, and heavier fancy paper for "portières," a doorway fixture in 1910. This instructor was thorough, and to begin her page-by-page account, revealed that the first two pages would be the hall. "There should be a picture of a winding staircase, a settle, hardwood floors and rugs, and a fireplace. . . ." What has become of that hall—the one that could contain all this furniture *and* a fireplace?

"Following the hall there should be the dolls' parlor, a dining-room, a nursery and a kitchen." Two pages for each room are recommended. "Rooms may be as dainty as any little paper-doll lady can wish, with pictures of brass bedsteads." (!) Remaining pages, the readers were informed, might be used for "a piazza and a garden—the former fitted comfortably with swings, a tea table and piazza furniture."

Neither of these paper houses, please note, neglected the paper garden.

Toy gardens had been occurring as long ago as 1544 (see Chapter 3), but in 1913, a clever woman named Frances Duncan commercialized paper horticulture. *House Beautiful* was enthusiastic about it in its Christmas issue, describing "a charming old-fashioned country house with reasonably spacious grounds, to be laid out as a formal garden. With this comes material for making flagged paths, also pasteboard hedges, trellises, rose arbors, shrubbery and flowers to be cut out and inserted where they will be most effective."

This was not entirely a paper item, it's true. *Playthings,* the toy trade magazine, in a somewhat more detailed report, described "bricks for paths and walls, turf and earth for flower beds, etc., the latter made of blocks of wood covered with paper." However, the plants were in sheets like paper dolls, each with name and time of blooming on its base. Adults might profitably set out hot-stove-league gardens in this fashion.

In April, 1913, a full-page ad in *Playthings* told of "A Book that becomes a Bungalow." With the rather redundant title of "Betty's Bungalow Doll-House," the item evidently became the rage to judge by follow-up ads which declared it the "greatest selling doll house ever made" of which the first run was "exhausted in two weeks." One hundred thousand and more," the maker added, with an eye to the future, "will be ready shortly! . . . When flat it is an attractive book in colors, not over half an inch in thickness, and folded in a box like a beautiful holiday gift book. When opened up it is a two story house with chimney, fireplace, furniture and lawn enclosed with a hedge—all artistically designed and in rich colors, and made in a strong cardboard that will last." Its maker's great inducement, however, was the fact that it could be "opened easily by a child in forty seconds."

Also in 1913 *Ladies' Home Journal* was engaged in a different sort of dolls' housing project. As a matter of fact, this enterprise got under way for Christmas in 1912 and was so successful (or so much of it was left over) that it was repeated for Christmas in 1913.

To any little girl who would send in two new yearly subscriptions, the *Journal* was offering Lettie Lane's dolls' house, complete with Lettie Lane. This they referred to as "the most charming and artistic doll house ever made, and one of the daintiest little dolls ever produced in Germany." Although it is true that Lettie was a little jointed bisque doll, and therefore an unlikely candidate for this chapter, her house was of "heavy coated cardboard" and her furniture of heavy paper "ready to be cut-out, folded, and pasted." Moreover, the original Lettie Lane was a paper doll, as fortunate little girls of that pretty era whose mothers took the *Journal* knew very well. This Lettie could be forgiven for not being appropriately paper, because she wore a braided straw hat.

The house itself, to judge by the pictures (see illustration), was indeed a dream cottage, with trellises of blooming roses and honeysuckle, beds of Shasta daisies and forget-me-nots, and a sentinel bay tree on each side of

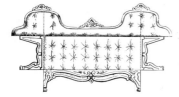

A "Tête-à-Tête," from a ca. 1870 book telling how to make dolls' furniture

254

HAVE you ever seen a more charming doll house than this, or a more charming little doll than the one standing on the terrace? Of course you haven't. Months ago THE JOURNAL's architects and artists were asked to design the most beautiful doll house ever made, and even from the pictures of it here you can see how splendidly they have succeeded.

As for the dainty little girl who lives in this wonderful house, she comes to us from Germany; she is a jointed doll of bisque and practically indestructible. Pretty as she is, her dainty dress and braided straw hat add to her attractiveness. Moreover she just fits the house and harmonizes with every feature of it — its trellises of blooming roses and honeysuckle; its beds of Shasta daisies and forget-me-nots, and the sentinel bay tree on each side of the doorway beneath the lamp. And it is such a *big* house too. To be exact it is two inches wider than this whole page is long, and from front to back three inches deeper. And it is seventeen inches high.

The little mistress is very proud of her home; and she should be, don't you think?

Every Room is Ready for Doll Housekeeping

Its Little Mistress Bids You Welcome

TO TELL the truth another doll bungalow decorated and furnished in such perfect taste does not exist in all Dolltown. The living-room is finished and furnished in dark oak; the dining-room in tan and white and mahogany, while the blue bedroom's woodwork is ivory and its furniture mahogany too, like the charming dining-room. As for the kitchen, the walls, chairs and table appear cleanly painted, while the floor is in imitation of cork.

Moreover the furniture may be placed wherever the little girl who owns the house may choose to place it. For it is printed on heavy paper ready to be cut out, folded and pasted, while the house itself is printed on heavy coated cardboard, all cut out and clearly marked for bending, pasting and putting together. Indeed the setting up of the house and its furniture is one of the most interesting features of it, and yet very easy.

When done the house and furniture become as shown here, only of course much larger, both being in the same proportion to the charming little doll mistress that the actual house in which a real little girl lives, with its furniture, bears to her parents.

How to Obtain the House

ANY little girl may own house, doll and furniture if she will do this: Send to us THREE new yearly subscriptions for THE LADIES' HOME JOURNAL, accompanied by the regular subscription price ($4.50 for the three), requesting Lettie Lane's Doll House, whereupon the house, furniture and doll will be sent, all shipping expenses prepaid.

Remember four things: 1st, these must be 3 yearly subscriptions; 2d, they must all be sent at the same time, and must be accompanied by $4.50 remittance; 3d, they must all be NEW subscriptions (renewals of subscriptions already on the list, or transfers from one member of the family to another, will not count); 4th, the house must be asked for when the order is sent.

Perhaps Mother or Father will

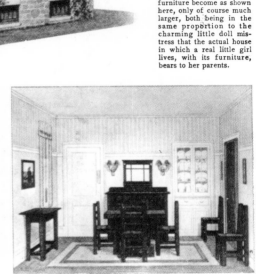

Here is the Model Kitchen With its New Range

Imagine a Doll Dinner Party Being Given Here

Ladies' Home Journal *offers Lettie Lane's dolls' house in 1912*

the doorway beneath the lamp. The copy writer commented that the cottage "is larger than this page," and a *Journal* page was large indeed in those days.

There were living-room, dining-room, bedroom, and kitchen. "Here is the Model Kitchen with its New Range," murmured the copy writer, pointing verbally to a black iron rhinoceros complete with tall stove-pipe. As to other furnishings, there was much mission.

"To tell the truth," the *Journal* concluded, "another doll bungalow decorated and furnished in such perfect taste does not exist in all Dolltown!" Considering the two-subscription cost, such a statement appears perfectly reasonable. It would be interesting to know the statistics, how many new subscribers the *Journal* thus acquired in 1912 and 1913, and how many moppets were made glad with a doll bungalow complete with Shasta daisies.

Magazines were not the only publications concerned with dolls' housing. The newspapers weren't too slow to catch on. According to the Freemans in *Cavalcade of Toys,* "some newspapers of the early twentieth century had interesting supplements of these interesting furnishings. There were parlor sets on bristol board, kitchens of the day with stoves, pots, pans, kettles, dustpans and brooms, colored to give illusion."

In 1943, Katherine R. Hubbard reported in *Hobbies* an exhibit of paper dolls and furnishings in San Francisco. This exhibition, on view at a location with the imposing name of the Junior Museum of the California Palace of the Legion of Honor, displayed among its treasures paper houses and furniture of three generations. The furniture exhibit "showed kitchen, bedroom, parlor, and dining room of 1905; kitchen, dining-living-room, and bed-nursery-room of 1918; and the newest 1941 furniture (found in five and ten's) in its bright yellows and oranges and blues."

Miss Hubbard described most of these. The 1905 furnishings sound most amusing. They seem to have been virtually immersed in mottoes, all cheerful. In the kitchen a wooden chest bore the witticism, "No sauce like appetite," and a wooden water cooler the recommendation that "Water is the best of all things." Stationary "galvanized iron" tubs set in a wooden frame had a different comment on the same subject: "Water washes everything." On the dish closet was a sheet of speckled paper whose message was more terse: "Fly destroyer." In the bedroom, the dresser scarf said "Good Morning" and the alarm clock admonished its listeners to "Improve each hour." Several paper houses were exhibited, "one of the most interesting being the LePageville house, at one time given away with LePage's glue."

The paper doll, it can be seen from this one account alone, has no more lacked variety in her paper residence than in her paper wardrobe. In the 1920's her opportunities were as cheerfully gaudy as those the 'nineties had provided. We remember setting to work with scissors and enthusiasm on a set, circa 1928, which had been presented to a cousin two years our junior and who was, therefore, of little consequence and plainly had no ability for cutting out her own tables and buffets. We recall the outfit with more nostalgia than accuracy, but a very fancy set of cardboard rugs, one per room, remains in mind, and, for some reason, a dark fernery with a green profusion of luxuriant fronds is practically indelible.

To the dolls' house historian, there is something fully satisfying about a sheet of cardboard furniture, absolutely uncut. No out-of-scale hand has ventured to move the be-laced, be-ribboned pincushion from the dresser; every strand of the scalloped fringe on the shade of the oil lamp is in place. The positions of the Britannia butter dish, the crumber-and-tray, and the dresser scarves are exact historical facts, precisely preserved.

When it is possible to add to this lovely minor information a name, date, and place, we feel practically sent back into time, like those characters in historical fantasies who swallow a special potion and are wafted back to 1863 or 1879, or some other distant era. In the case of "Our Dining-Room,"

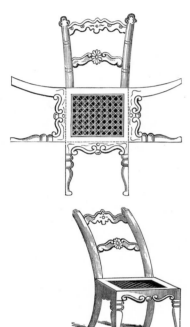

Dining-chairs from "How to make," ca. 1870

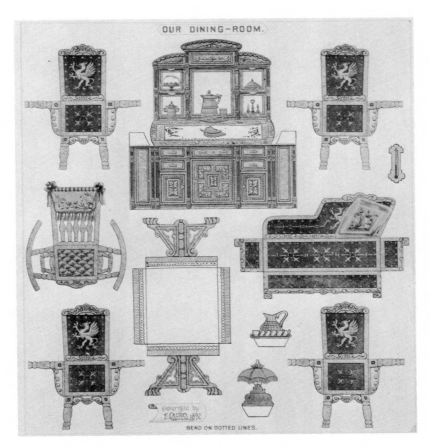

"Our Dining-Room," a sheet of paper furniture to cut out and assemble made by F. Cairo of Brooklyn in 1892

which is pictured (author's collection), we are wafted back to 1892, the year in which this handsomely lithographed room, along with "Our Parlor" and "Our Bedroom," were copyrighted by one F. Cairo of Brooklyn. From the turkey red bedspread to the bright green dining-room settee, it is an informative visit to a paper museum now forever, presumably, intact and inviolate.

In 1953, when most of the preceding chapter was first printed, an attractively illustrated 38-page monograph entitled *Homes for Paper Dolls and Kindred Paper Toys,* was brought out by Marian B. Howard of Miami, Florida. Miss Howard's delightful study contains much valuable information on a subject that necessarily has been little more than touched upon in this chapter, and it is earnestly recommended to anyone who wishes to pursue further this beguiling, and ephemeral, branch of dolls' housing.

A rocking chair, from "How to make," ca. 1870

17

QUEEN MARY'S DOLLS' HOUSE

PEOPLE WHO REFUSE TO TAKE DOLLS' HOUSES SERIOUSLY MAY GO ahead and be brought up short by an item which appeared in a page-one box in the dignified *New York Times* on April 14, 1924. Under a head proclaiming that "Drys Protest Wine Cellars in Queen Mary's Dollhouse," the *Times* reported that these people were "aroused to indignation by the discovery that Queen Mary's million-dollar dollhouse has wine cellars containing miniature cases of champagne, whiskey and other alcoholic beverages which they say no self-respecting doll would drink or even have in the house."

The indignation to which the drys were aroused became somewhat anticlimatic in the final paragraph which tapered off weakly: "Protests have been made, but without results, and Her Majesty's exquisitely furnished replica of an English home, wine cellars and all, will be on view at the Wembley exhibition. . . ."

Since Queen Mary's dolls' house probably is the most famous in the world, it seems not unworthy of a front-page box, and perhaps deserves to be taken more seriously than many dolls' houses, but mark you how seriously it was taken! An informal check has revealed that the beverages in this wine cellar are still untasted, and because of the thirstless nature of its owners, no doubt will continue so for as long as the dolls' house shall survive. Who

The wine cellar in the Queen's Dolls' House disturbed the prohibitionists in 1924
COURTESY COUNTRY LIFE LTD.

knows but what these rare bottles with their few alcoholic droplets sealed in such firm though miniature fashion, shall not hold in future years the most vintaged bottled goods in all the world? One can envision another *Times* front-page box a few centuries hence, telling of a noted connoisseur who couldn't resist, and who in dead of night, stole by jack-knife into the dolls' house wine cellar, and bit, careless of splintered glass, into a bottle of the 1820 Madeira, rapturously spilling the brief contents (unnoticed, the dregs) upon his knowing tongue.

If we seem to loiter here, filling space with supposings, rather than getting down to the business of describing the Queen's dolls' house, it is because this dolls' house has had a sizable book written about it, a delightful piece of literature, in which it has been thoroughly described.

Actually there are two books, and in another sense, three. There is *The Book of the Queen's Dolls' House,* the de luxe limited edition in two volumes, one of them *The Queen's Dolls' House,* and the other, *The Library of the Queen's Dolls' House.* Then there is a one-volume condensation, principally of the first, called *Everybody's Book of the Queen's Dolls' House,* which while curtailed, has much of the text of the original and most of the handsome color plates.

The Queen's Dolls' House, edited by A. C. Benson and Sir Lawrence Weaver, is a collaboration in the same manner that work on the dolls' house itself was a collaboration. "Experts and connoisseurs" wrote the chapters they knew most about and achieved the same sort of delightful results

259

obtained by the innumerable artists and craftsmen (surely every one of note in England) who contributed to the dolls' house itself.

The unique feature of this dolls' house in comparison to other noted ones would seem to be the vast number of objects created expressly for it. Special diminutive china, for example, was manufactured by such great English porcelain makers as Doulton. Where in other famous dolls' buildings like Colleen Moore's Castle or Titania's Palace, precious antique miniatures have been used, practically everything was made new and perfect for the Queen's. Thus, when the house, after four years of extraordinary endeavor, was completed as a "perfect gift" to Her Majesty in 1924, it became a record of English manufacturing arts of the time, as well as a chronicle of the matters most dolls' houses preserve.

The other most striking thing about the Queen's Dolls' House is its library. A good deal of very fine leather, in very small swatches, has gone into covering the miniature books of the world, and collectors today own all sorts of doll-pocket-size volumes of one title or another that can be read with a competent magnifying glass, but there never has been quite such a dolls' house library as the Queen's. It includes not only drawerfuls of prints and original water colors by famous artists, but there are two hundred books written by celebrated authors in their own handwriting specially for this very limited edition library, and these are recorded in full in *The Book of The Queen's Dolls' House Library*.

Some of the contributions were not merely written for a dolls' house; they also were written in a dolls' house vein. The most thorough and interesting of these is *The Haunted Dolls' House* by M. R. James, then Provost of

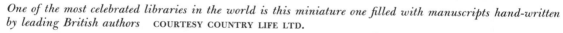

One of the most celebrated libraries in the world is this miniature one filled with manuscripts hand-written by leading British authors COURTESY COUNTRY LIFE LTD.

Eton, to whose minute work we have alluded in Chapter 1. Dolls' houses, for some unearthly reason, have given rise to a number of ghost or horror stories of recent years in slick-paper magazines, and this source has been twice tapped in the Queen's miniature library. V. Sackville-West in *A Note of Explanation* tells about a ghost who visits the Queen's dolls' house. Edmund Gosse also sticks to the subject under the title *A French Dolls' House,* but with little creative effort, merely quoting the brief facts known about the *Chambre du Sublime* given to the little Duc de Maine in 1675 (see Chapter 7). A minor poet (Major Kendall) offers *Songs for a Dolls' House,* some quite charming verses, and Lady Jekyll writes *The Dolls' House Cookery Book.* In the latter, however, the author hasn't troubled to reduce the ingredients to dolls' house proportions, and thus her work actually is beneath our notice here, where only a matchstick of butter and a few crystals of sugar are to scale.

The bulk of contributors to this library, however, did not take their work so literally. A whimsical few compromised with puns based on brevity. Max Beerbohm diminished his stature (physical, not literary) and embroidered this surprising alteration with as large a wit as ever he lavished on a full-size essay. A. E. Housman wrote nothing new, but carefully chose the shortest of his poems. The whimsical Sir James M. Barrie wrote out the briefest of autobiographies.

The innocent merriment described here should not lead anyone to think that the library of the Queen's Dolls' House is limited in scope. The majority of its works are general, and include a well-rounded collection indeed.

Through this very library, the Queen's Dolls' House got into another scrape which caused it notoriety in the *New York Times* comparable to its wine-cellar trouble. It is probably the only dolls' house ever repudiated by the American author, Joseph Pennell. Since these behind-the-scenes tales decidedly may *not* be found in the books about the Queen's Dolls' House, or in the books in the Queen's Dolls' House Library, it might not be amiss here to give at length the searing letter from Mr. Pennell published by the *Times* under the heading, "Mr. Pennell Repudiates Doll's House":

"To the Editor of the New York Times:

"I do not suppose anyone who knows me would credit me with writing the drivel to which my name is signed, printed in your issue today as my contribution to the 'Queen's Dolls' Priceless Library.' I contributed nothing. But, on the other hand, I have received a personal letter of thanks from her Gracious Majesty Queen Mary, in her own royal handwriting, signed Mary R. and addressed to me here from Buckingham Palace, thanking me for doing something—or rather contributing something—I know not what—to a performance I know little about, save that if I had been asked to contribute to this footling display of misdirected nonsense and childishness, I, too, should have been conspicuous by my absence, like Wells, Shaw and Masefield, but even though absent in the flesh—and absent for near three hundred years from my ancestral home—wherever it was—I am remembered and represented in this touching tribute to British royalty and charity. But how, when, where or why, I give up.

"I suppose as the only American represented in this precious library, I ought to be fearfully set up. Though the only American allowed in it, I am still willing to greet my associates and colleagues, but, like the fly in the amber, I wonder how the devil I got there and what I did to get there.

"JOSEPH PENNELL
"New York. August 24, 1924"

The sorely tried Mr. Pennell evidently learned how he "got there" a few days later when the *Times* carried the following item, under the twenty-four-point head, "Pennell Blames Lucas But He Keeps Queen's Letter on Dolls' House Library":

"Joseph Pennell was inclined yesterday to blame E. V. Lucas, Chief Librarian of the Queen's doll house library, for the mix-up which led to naming him as the author of a contribution to the library entitled 'Thoughts,' actually the work of John Pennell connected with the London house which had the contract for the binding of the library.

" 'If the British have come to that sort of thing they are pretty hard up for literature,' Mr. Pennell said of the contribution.

"He said he would take no further action in regard to the error, not even to return the personal letter from Queen Mary thanking him for his supposed contribution."

In justice to Mr. Pennell, we may say that we have perused the trifle assigned by error to Mr. Pennell, and it *is* a sudsy bit of writing. However, Mr. P.'s attitude toward the dolls' house was not shared by such writers as Bennett, Barrie, Chesterton, Housman, and Maugham, who did contribute to the library. It is true that Wells, Shaw, and Masefield, as Mr. Pennell pointed out, are "conspicuous by [their] absence[s]," but they were indeed conspicuous, apart from the formidable two hundred who were present.

No dolls, by the way, live in the Queen's Dolls' House. Mr. Benson, in *The Book of,* elaborately explains why. The gist of it is that "dolls are hopelessly out of place in a Dolls' House. . . . They are impressionist figures and would seriously clash with the exquisite realism of their house. And they would fall down and break things, and small accidents would bring us back with a run from the realms of the imagination to the real world again."

Mr. Benson explains, however, that some representatives of the King and Queen had to be on the premises or stray dolls "would think that it was an unoccupied house and take possession of it." Accordingly, there *are* representatives. The inventory lists them among other "exterior" objects, including:

"Roof Slates
Two Standards
Flagstaff with Crown

Four Sentry Boxes, with
        Guard Instructions inside
Five Sentries:
    One Grenadier
    One Coldstream
    One Irish Guard
    One Welsh Guard
    One Scots Guard
The Pipe-Major"

There is also a tribe of Dollomites, invisible, of course, to ordinary mortals paying their sixpences to walk around the glass case which contains the dolls' house. These creatures, one-twelfth our size, are described in the book in interesting detail, and remarkably hypothetical terms. A sample: "The Dollomites have a lung area 1/144th part of what we have, but, and this is the crux of the matter, their body weight is 1/1,728th part of our body weight—leaving them on balance twelve times as strong." Understand?

According to a 1922 item in the *New York Herald,* a visible population was planned, a notion that evidently miscarried. It is interesting to learn what might have been: "Sir Edwin Lutyens has not failed to introduce a typical humor into his choice of dolls and the order in which they come. They will be six inches in height, dressed in appropriate clothes to scale—the King in his colored robes, the footman in his powdered wig and the journalist with notebook and silk hat.

"In the house there will be a plumber, five sentries, the footmen, two pages, a 'tweeny,' a housemaid, a housekeeper, a chef, a nurse, a prince of the blood, a princess royal, a mistress of the robes, a Queen, a gold stick in waiting and a King. Kept in drawers will be two Prime Ministers, a Lord Chancellor, a General and an Admiral, a Bishop, a doctor, a President of the Allied Republic, a King of Africa, a King of an allied country, a Maharajah Sahib, a journalist and a royal aunt. These will be fetched out only on state occasions."

Since these personages would have contributed so much to the dolls' house's future in terms of their roles in a history of costume, if nothing more, it seems sad indeed that this plan was discarded.

The stately nature of these absent tenants as well as the strictly regal aspect of such apartments as "The Queen's Bedroom," "The King's Bathroom," and "The Strong Room" (where crowns and other valuables are kept), expresses the royal status of this household. You will note, however, that unlike such mythically majestic structures as Titania's Palace and other monarchial miniature buildings described in this book, it is not called "palace," or even "castle." It is called "house."

This is explained by Mr. Benson who says, "The house thus represented is not a palace nor a ceremonious residence, but essentially a home,

The Strong Room, where crowns and other royal treasures are stored

a family mansion belonging to a Monarch who seeks relief from cares of state in a quiet family life and a comfortable rather than luxurious routine." Let it be said, though, that the Queen's Dolls' House is perfectly capable of housing a royal couple in the manner to which it is accustomed.

We have mentioned that the Queen's Dolls' House is contained in a glass case, around which spectators walk. In other words, this, like most English dolls' houses, and unlike the cabinet-like arrangements of the Dutch, and the box-like ones of the Germans, is a realistic building. Instead of a front (or rear) swinging open, the four façades are elevated electrically (the latter detail, to be sure, is *not* realistic) to expose the logically arranged rooms. Sir Lawrence Weaver points this out in contrast to the old jest about "dolls' houses with Queen Anne fronts and Mary Ann backs."

For this panoramic dolls' house, one of England's foremost architects, Sir Edwin Lutyens, was responsible. The exterior is built of wood, "carved and painted to indicate Portland stone." It is similar in style to some of the beautiful Georgian dolls' houses which have survived. A summary from *Everybody's Book* gives a reasonably terse picture of this elaborate shell:

"The House itself is 100 inches long on its main north and south fronts, and 62 inches from east to west. It stands on a base 116 inches by 72 inches and 39 inches high. This base is divided into two parts. The lower 24 inches contains 208 interchangeable drawers, half on the north and half on the south, covered by falling flap doors. Each drawer is 11¼ inches long, and 3½ inches wide and deep, made of cedar and fitted with a drop ring handle of ivory. . . . The upper 15 inches of the base contains the machinery, the electric transformers, the switches, the tank for bath wastes, the wine cellar and store-room for groceries, both ample and suitably victualled. In this part of the base also are two very charming surprises. At the west end a flap falls down, a drawer extends, and, behold, there is a complete garage, with six tiny motor-cars, with an inspection pit in the painted brick paving, and with everything to invite the interest of midget mechanicians! At the east a similar transformation allows a lovely garden to be extended on double runners, so as to display its exquisite imitations."

This summary serves also to suggest some of the unique features of this dolls' house. The garage with its fleet of 1924 limousines, including a Rolls Royce, is already a bit of history as well as an amusing curiosity. It even includes a motorcycle with sidecar. The amount of machinery mentioned hints at the mechanical marvels nearby, with one elevator for the royal inhabitants, and another for the servants. "The tank for bath wastes" indicates the state of realism to which the Queen's Dolls' House extends.

The garden is both beautiful and mechanical, in its special way. Because it is contained in a drawer, the trees have been ingeniously made to lie horizontally, "just clearing the garden flowers," when the drawer is closed. The gate and balustrade are also cleverly tucked in, but when the drawer is open, all of these come into place. The growing things in the garden are intricately fashioned of various metals. Miss Gertrude Jekyll, who (in *The Book of*) describes the garden, relates that "a close search may possibly be rewarded by finding some snails, and even a thrush's nest with eggs."

The baths are as impressive as any stately apartment in the mansion. The Queen's bath is more elegant even than the King's. Her Majesty's has a mother-of-pearl floor, and bath and washstand are of alabaster with silver taps. According to Mr. Percy MacQuoid, who (in *The Book of*) describes this, "It is one of the prettiest sights in the world to see the bath-tub fill with water, the drops swelling slowly from the taps until the whole room is reflected in them, with indescribable, minute beauty; and the reflection of the mother-of-pearl and of the paintings on the ceiling, give added colour to the natural iridescence of these globes of water."

The Queen's Dolls' House, presented by her loyal subjects in 1924 to Queen Mary—and its garden which folds into an ingenious drawer
COURTESY COUNTRY LIFE LTD.

Water systems have been appearing in the more opulent variety of commercial dolls' houses for some years, but it is doubtful whether they ran both hot and cold. Miss Dymphna Ellis (in *The Book of*), mentioning this fact with emotion, in her description of the scullery, reveals other wonders in the kitchen, an apartment fraught with all sorts of machinery, including a knife machine, a weighing machine and a mincing machine. In the midst of these mechanical splendors, as an example of fine upstanding 1924 British conservatism, is the pastry oven operated by "good honest British coal . . . no gas to give the insidious ill flavour, technically called a 'back taste,' and no theatrical display of electricity, the culinary rogue's refuge." The latter a sentiment that, only a generation later, the electric kitchen made antique.

Even the nursery has its small wonders, and if they are less spectacular than some which have been described, they are more charming. Two striking items are an electric-lighted toy theater and "a tiny gramophone, with its first and last gasp whispering, 'God Save the King.' "

Which would bring us, in an indirect sort of way, to music. If its literary library is extraordinary in a dolls' house, the Queen's Dolls' house musical library is equally so. "There are some fifty volumes of music by contemporary British composers, each a little more than an inch square, bound in leather with Her Majesty's monogram. They have been photographed and reduced from ordinary published music, and each volume has been signed by the composer. . . ." There are two pianos on which a toothpick-fingered musician may try these works, one grand and one upright. They are "real" and were numbered and recorded, along with all full-sized instruments, upon the books of the firm that made them. There is also a "gramophone," very 1924, and, like the limousines, already a period piece.

The presence of music by representative British composers underlines the comprehensive record of a period which this dolls' house is destined to become. Almost no field or profession has been neglected. In the book-lined library, along with the authors who have been thus immortalized, there are "two volumes called *The Navy* and *The Army* respectively, bound appropriately to each in blue and red morocco, containing the autographs of the more important officers of both services; a brown volume of the same kind with autographs of *Statesmen,* and another, *The Stage,* with those of our leading actors and actresses. . . ."

We have in our account of this peer of dolls' houses given no space to its luxurious furnishings, made by a multitude of leading British craftsmen, or to its murals and paintings, done by famous British painters, many of whom curbed lush styles to work in the exacting miniature field for the first time. Some of these treasures are comparable to similar magnificences in other great dolls' houses of the present and past. What may well be a unique aspect of the Queen's Dolls' House is the range of individual talents that created these treasures combining them into an extraordinary gift for a well-loved monarch.

18

COLLEEN MOORE'S CASTLE

*I*T IS A TEMPTATION TO COMPARE COLLEEN MOORE'S CASTLE WITH Titania's Palace since both are compounded of fantasy, and were constructed for the purpose of housing fairy royalty. But the resemblance ends there. Miss Moore's themes are largely taken from the realm of Mother Goose and similar species of literature. Sir Nevile Wilkinson decorated Titania's Palace with a more classical mythology in mind. His dolls' house was plainly intended for intellectual fairies. Miss Moore's, on the other hand, is more obviously designed for fairies under ten.

There is one other prominent contrast. Despite its fairyland intentions, Sir Nevile's dolls' house is noticeably realistic—take the magic wand of one of its occupants and cause the castle to become full size, and, with a few alterations here and there, a person of normal size could occupy it pleasurably. Not so Miss Moore's castle: so substantial is its fantasy that even with multiplied dimensions the most adaptable occupant would have singular adjustments to make and might, in the end, restore the lease to Mother Goose.

This, to us, is the peculiar charm of Miss Moore's dolls' house. All sorts of people have announced the availability of theirs for any fairies who might care to fly in. They have even, without offering any really tangible proof, proclaimed their dolls' houses *occupied* by Titania, say, or the Princess of Lilliput. But seldom have any concentrated on making the arrangements suitable or inviting should such possible occupants appear on the premises. They've attended only to the size of things, and let the rest go at that.

It is particularly appropriate that The Castle's décor emphasizes fairy-tale characters dear to children. If dolls' houses are supposed to belong to children (and until a few decades change said dolls' houses into historical documents, they are supposed to), it's surprising that no one before Colleen Moore seems to have thought of designing and furnishing one in a nursery-land spirit. It was a fine notion, and much ingenuity has been employed to follow it through.

Some people have said that the Moore dolls' house is "quite Holly-wood." That is a phrase, of course, which can mean any number of things, but applied to the dolls' house, it means something fairly specific, and it is not untrue. It means that Miss Moore's million-dollar treasure is big (although one inch to the foot, its owner has been photographed sitting inside it), shimmering, and practically beset with precious gems.

Since Hollywood itself is a kind of fairyland, one might say that the shimmer and dazzle and glimmer of this dolls' house are representative of that fairyland, and Mother Goose and Grimm and Walt Disney are representative of another. The blend is impressive. In any case, the dolls' house is a suitable reflection of the celebrated film background of its owner, an autobiographical expression which heightens its historical values. Of all the world's dolls' houses, Colleen Moore's is the one best known in the United States.

One of the most ingenious aspects of the castle is the manner in which it has employed what can well be called connotation. A delightful example of this occurred in such a mundane apartment as the dining-room where inspiration saw instead of a dining-room table King Arthur's Round Table. The dining-room thus became "the great dining hall of King Arthur and his Knights." The walnut chairs have tall shield-backs, each bearing its

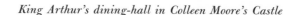

King Arthur's dining-hall in Colleen Moore's Castle

occupant's coat of arms. The table service, seemly for such regal warriors, is of solid gold. A further inspiration may be found on the walls of cast stone—"tapestries" presenting, in the finest of Viennese stitches, a needle-point biography of Sir Galahad.

The kitchen is another worldly room which connotation has cleverly transposed. It is a "magic" kitchen, and the domain of Mother Goose, probably a very good cook. Jack and Jill, Little Jack Horner, Contrary Mary, and Little Bo-Peep are among the notables whose portraits appear on the walls. The copper stove, we are reliably informed, is the one "in which the wicked witch locked Hansel and Gretel."

Similar fancies, represented individually, fill the glistening premises. These range all the way from the bed, in the princess's bedroom, that the Sleeping Beauty slept in, to Hans Brinker's silver skates.

One reassuring matter, in planning this dolls' house, must have been the flexibility of its period. Any one who ever has furnished a dolls' house not entirely of the present, is obliged to fret considerably over anachronism, an 1890 stove in an 1850 parlor, say. The Moore dolls' house, being of magic ingredients, suspends the problem of time. Harold Grieve, its decorator, has said that the period is "Early Faery," but since everyone knows that fairies' lives are timeless, no one had to bother much about errors of era.

In King Arthur's dining hall, for example, there are golden knives and forks, with monograms, if you please, though the latter must be read by magnifying glass. There are also napkins with lace on them. Such table refinements, of couse, weren't even thought of till at least a thousand years later, and with all due respect to a brave set of heroes and their Holy quest, with the sort of table manners they had, no telling what might, some magical night, be the fate of these.

The library, too, is modern rather than medieval, forming a sort of American supplement to the library of the Queen's Dolls' House. The Queen's authors are exclusively British, and the Moore authors are almost entirely American. These, too, are one-volume-only first editions, an assortment of authors about a decade more modern than the Queen's, of which a partial list spans heights and depths of recent literature. The prince and princess can hardly be accused of literary snobbery: Conan Doyle, Edna Ferber, Hendrik Van Loon, Joseph Hergesheimer, Louis Bromfield, Irvin Cobb, Sinclair Lewis, Gene Fowler, Kathleen Norris, Charles Norris, Elinor Glyn, Rupert Hughes, F. Scott Fitzgerald, Fannie Hurst, Booth Tarkington, John Steinbeck, Hervey Allen, Willa Cather, James Hilton, Edgar Rice Burroughs, Carl Van Vechten, Robinson Jeffers, Lloyd Douglas and others. . . . Presumably the psychology behind this selection is that humans like to read about fairies and fairies like to read about humans. It may be that *Main Street* and *The Grapes of Wrath* are fantasy to fairies.

The building has eleven rooms, a "vast" entrance hall and a garden, modest as elderly castles with their hundreds of rooms generally go, but mammoth among dolls' houses. Constructed of aluminum and copper, it is all over battlements and turrets, its tallest pinnacle reaching twelve feet into the fairy atmosphere which necessarily surrounds it. For the rest, it is nine feet square, "rests on the summit of a rugged precipice," and has such practical touches as electric wiring and water piping. The latter has some delightfully impractical uses, most of them splashing fountains. The most appealing outlet, though, is a weeping willow tree that does indeed weep.

This tree is part of Aladdin's enchanted garden, one of the most unusual bits of paradise to be found anywhere in dolls' house circles. The fountains here shimmer only a trifle more than the gold and silver branches of the trees. Indeed this is almost a winter garden in its effect, there is so much silver about. Cinderella's coach is made of this metal, and the four horses who draw it (for the permanent moment, they are drinking from the fountain) are to match. The season, for that matter, is plainly indicated by the presence of Santa Claus who, with his sleigh may, if one looks high up at the castle walls, be seen swooping down to visit an establishment which would not seem to require anything in his pack.

The seasons, though, like the eras, are plainly interchangeable in fairyland. A feathered nightingale really sings in the garden, though in its first public appearance (1935 in New York) its song was hushed owing to a mechanical mishap. And the Rock-a-Bye-Baby swaying in the tree top certainly would not be out there if the weather were unsuitable. Possibly the Wizard of Oz and members of his staff, who are in relief on the castle walls, have something to do with it.

The nightingale's song is not the only sound to be heard by the princess's visitors. Chimes in the steeple sound every fifteen minutes, and in the chapel, one of the loveliest places in the castle, the golden cathedral organ plays by remote control. (A water tank, operated by an electrical pump, if we may so prosaically betray their magic, accounts for most of these mechanical wonders.)

The organ's pipes are six to eleven inches high; there are over a hundred keys, none more than a sixteenth of an inch wide; cherubs in bas relief ornament its cast bronze pillars. The décor here, of course, is based on a more solemn sort of fantasy, which the Colleen Moore booklet best describes (and which our illustration supplements): "The ivory floor is symbolic of events from the Old Testament, telling the story of the Lamb of God, the Dove of Peace, the Ram, the Locusts and the Years of Plenty. In the great center design are the Ten Commandments as hewn in the tablets. The Lights of the World shine forth in hues of purple and gold. The stained glass windows by Brabon depict originals and copies of famous masterpieces of David and Goliath, Moses in the Bulrushes, Daniel in the Lions' Den and the Judgment of Solomon." And there is an embossed ceiling from the Book of Kells, just as there is in the chapel of Titania's Palace.

The wonders of the other rooms are disarmingly miscellaneous. The great hall has a spiral staircase which suggests by its lack of balustrades the sure-wingèd creatures who are meant to use it. The vaulted ceiling is two stories high and its painted domes add Andersen and Grimm to the fairy-tale procession. The library is an interesting combination of sea and sky—nautical below, with fishnets and capstans, sea horses and shells, astronomical above, with constellations in the ceiling. There is also a curious pairing of astrology with the astronomy; the signs of the zodiac inlaid in gold on the floor below. There is a strong-room, reached by a "spidery rope," presided over, in its central mural, by Ali Baba, and refulgent with the jewels and general loot which spill from copper and bronze kegs. The princess's gold hairbrush has silver fox bristles; her washbasin is made of a silver tulip, and has silver tulip faucets to match.

Miss Moore's jewels also have been dealt with in singularly diversified ways. The most celebrated example is the chandelier which hangs from the drawing-room ceiling. This contains some of Miss Moore's choicest diamonds, emeralds, and pearls, the result, assuredly, of the most noble parting of a lady and her jewels known to history. (It is said to have devoured four bracelets, two necklaces, and one six-carat ring.) This chandelier is lit by minute light bulbs which will burn fifteen hours and are almost as celebrated as the gems. (See illustration.) Not all of these sacrifices to personal adornment appear to be as delightfully worthy. Two valuable jeweled clips, for example, which became chair-backs, look more like jeweled clips with legs than anything else.

Most often, though, the castle is beguiling rather than merely glittering, and it has charmed an enormous number of spectators since its gold cornerstone was laid in 1935 by Mrs. James Roosevelt, mother of the late President. Like those of several famous dolls' houses, the proceeds from its exhibitions have gone to charity.

In the chapel of the Moore Castle, the "mighty" organ and the lovely stained glass windows are featured

The celebrated lighted diamond and emerald chandelier in Colleen Moore's Castle

A cook book from the castle kitchen disarmingly, and appropriately, reveals its size

Its owner personifies dolls' house lore. Colleen Moore led up to her castle with seven preceding dolls' houses, the first of which she possessed at the age of two. This was made by her father, Charles Morrison, who was later to supervise her castle's construction. In between she had a three-room bungalow, a two-story house, and ultimately some model rooms.

Since her treasures have been both found and commissioned all over the world, there are innumerable anecdotes about their acquisition, some of them extraordinary. One has to do with Cinderella's glass slippers, which Miss Moore felt belonged in her dolls' house. And she wanted them hollow; however small Cinderella's feet may have been, even she could not have got into slippers which weren't hollow. No glass blower seemed to think the feat possible. Miss Moore went so far as Venice. But even the famed makers of Venetian glass shook their heads. She came home and found a retired glass blower in Jackson, Michigan, willing at least to try. The slippers, somewhat over a quarter of an inch long, with high heels and red glass bows, are now among the museum pieces in the princess's drawing-room.

The castle has now given up its charitable travels, having taken up permanent residence in Chicago's Museum of Science and Industry to which Colleen Moore Hargrave has willed it. There it can be seen, at no admission charge, the year round, an exhibit which "on the road" has drawn as many as 115,000 visitors in a single day.

19

TITANIA'S
PALACE

Sir Nevile Wilkinson, soldier and artist, and creator of one of the three most famous modern dolls' houses, was nearly a victim of one of those tragic coincidences in which two people have the same idea at the same time. Sir Nevile, it is true, didn't find his inspiration for Titania's Palace at the same moment the notion to make the Queen's Dolls' House came into being; he found it about twenty years earlier. But Sir Nevile was one man and had only a few helpers; the numerous participants in the Queen's gift were chosen from the whole British Empire. The results of the two conceptions appeared almost together.

In his autobiography, *To All and Singular,* Sir Nevile does not complain of this coincidence, but he is plainly wistful about it. In the long appendix he devotes to Titania's Palace, he writes with the tact demanded of an Ulster King of Arms whose opponent is personified by his Queen.

"...Titania's Palace was nearing completion," he writes, "when rumours of a great rival reached me: a royal dolls' house which should eclipse all others; designed and constructed by the first architect in the land; to be filled with the work of every craftsman, painter and sculptor of note in the three kingdoms; even the tiny books which filled the library were to contain the actual writing of all the famous writers of the day. In short, all the King's horses were to be saddled, and all the King's men mobilised to make this house not only a gift worthy of Her Majesty's acceptance, but worthy of being handed down to generations to come, as the model of a mansion such as might have been built in the second decade of the twentieth century.

"The position was critical, and the fate of twenty years' work hung in the balance; for I had promised myself at least a year more to complete the hundred and one details whose absence would be noticed when Titania's Palace faced the footlights. But delay meant the danger of being overtaken and overshadowed by the splendid creation of Sir Edwin Lutyens and his thousand helpers."

It may be that Titania herself had a wing in the suitable fairy-tale ending. Sir Nevile already had exhibited one of the most important sections of the palace, the Hall of the Guilds, when the discouraging rumours began, and as a result of its warm reception the completed palace had been invited to accept a formidable spotlight in a prominent exhibition coming up within several months, provided it could be ready in time. It was, of course, and Sir Nevile counted as blessings the 420 pounds earned for charity at this first exhibition, and a bit of charming intervention by Queen Mary.

That gracious monarch who, in her addiction to dolls' houses, is practically the heroine of this book, was hardly likely to ignore even a rival specimen to her own, particularly when charitable motives were included, and Sir Nevile's autobiography includes a photograph of her "opening" Titania's Palace on July 6, 1922. Her Majesty also was first to write in Titania's guest book. Sir Nevile considered it "a happy coincidence" that all this took place on Her Majesty's wedding anniversary, but knowing Her Majesty (by reputation), we suspect that she saved her call on Titania for a special treat on that day.

Although Sir Nevile considers these items "strokes of good fortune," the chances are that Titania's Palace would have got along very well even if it had inauspiciously followed the Queen's Dolls' House. There should indeed be room in the world for two dolls' residences as wonderful as these, and a great many more. Moreover, the Queen's Dolls' House was of course built for Her Majesty, whereas Titania's Palace was built for one whom Sir Nevile chose to call Her Iridescence. By which we mean to imply that the Queen's Dolls' House being meant for little people, and Titania's Palace being intended for little fairies, there is a decided diversity between the two buildings which establishes a need for both of them.

Fraught with all kinds of significance, surely, is the fact that the two most famous dolls' buildings intended for fairy occupancy, this one and Colleen Moore's, are of Celtic origin. The transplanted Erin ancestry of the Moore fairy princess and her train is evident. Sir Nevile, of course, was an Englishman, but he conceived the idea for Titania's Palace under peculiarly Celtic circumstances in Dublin; the construction went on in Dublin, most of it at the hands of Irish craftsmen.

274

It is true that physically the furnishings of the dolls' house are virtually as realistic as those of Queen Mary's. Sir Nevile does make a great to-do about having cupboards for spare wings in the bedrooms, and he omits knives and forks in the dining-room since fairies don't eat, but we feel bound to say that he is not consistent. He includes staircases which obviously no creature with one set of wings, much less spare ones, would use. And he puts toothbrushes in the bathroom. If one does not eat, one is not likely to require so mundane a utensil as a toothbrush.

But these minor discrepancies are, as we have said, physical. The fairy domain which Sir Nevile has chosen to portray is principally spiritual. Many an ethereal idea or appurtenance has, of course, as in Colleen Moore's castle, been given a physical embodiment—such items as the Rose-tree and Tiger-lily which conversed with Alice, and the Clock the Mouse Ran Up. But the larger mythology is something which Sir Nevile concocted himself, and it is a blend of classic legend, the Bible, fairy tale, chivalric ode, English literature, and Sir Nevile himself. The latter includes the elaborate lore he invented for the enrollment of children into the charitable orders Titania's Palace serves.

The key to this compound is best explored in three successful juvenile books which Sir Nevile wrote to go hand-in-hand with the dolls' house. This trio, *Yvette in Italy*, *Grey Fairy*, and *Yvette in Venice*, are travel books which take the Painter (presumably Sir Nevile) and some little girls, principally Yvette, upon some imaginary adventures, sandwiching in occasional room-by-room descriptions of Titania's Palace as well as allusions to the charitable order. (Yvette was an actual miss whose portrait Sir Nevile painted in Dublin at the time of the "troubles," and to whom he told some of the stories which found their way into these books.)

A "FORM to be filled up and forwarded by those who wish to know how they can become COMPANIONS, if Boys, or ROSE-MAIDENS, if Girls, and wear the BADGE given by the Fairy Queen" and "specially perforated so that it can be easily detached" remains the last page in the Library of Congress copy of *Grey Fairy*, eternally unused by Companion or Rose-Maiden. The rather doleful names of the children's charities to which these forms were to be sent were lightened by a notation below: "Chancery of the Most Industrious Order of the Fairy Kiss. Titania's Palace."

The latter is typical of the educated whimsy with which its sponsor has infused his creations. He thought of the dolls' house, and designed it; he collected many of its treasures in years of travel, and created, with wood and paint, innumerable others, but Sir Nevile's personality seems to have been just as much a contribution to Titania's Palace as his material participation.

Which returns us to its Celtic origin. In 1906, according to Sir Nevile, while he was sketching an old sycamore in the wood near his home at Mt. Merrion, his baby daughter got the impression that she saw a fairy disappear amid its roots. It is plain that Sir Nevile's three-year-old was not the only party present on whom the Irish landscape was weaving its sly spell. According to the bewitched autobiographer, "It happened on a still, sunny day, of the kind which is now so rare in Ireland; a day when one could realize to the full the meaning of the words 'vocal woods,' for the chorus of myriads of tiny hoverers roused to a frenzy by the reappearance of the sun . . . grew louder and still more loud, until the listener was almost scared by the volume of sound."

It can readily be seen how a man of Sir Nevile's mystic ilk could proceed from there, as he says he did, to the theory that the Fairy Queen (promptly made regal in his imagination), having gone underground, must have a residence there filled with appropriate treasures which it was a pity people, especially children, couldn't see. He promised his three-year-old to produce this miniature palace, and kept his promise when she was twenty.

In 1923, *Mentor* offered a quite different and somewhat funnier version of how the house came into being. Since this is the same year in which *Mentor* provided an unusual and divergent tale about Peter the Great's dolls' house (see Chapter 6) and the same imaginative reporter may be at work here, we should possibly desist, but briefly: Titania conceived a plan to revive interest in fairies, and putting her plan in action, she alighted on the back of Sir Nevile's armchair and whispered, "I want your help. I want you to build me a palace." When he protested that he wasn't an architect, she said, "It's not the least good your making excuses." He pointed out that she wanted a carpenter and a decorator and a builder . . . "But you haven't a notion, m'am, [it would occur only to Sir Nevile, we suspect, to address a fairy as "m'am," so this at least has an authentic ring] what a lot of different craftsmen it takes to build a palace." "I leave the details to you," she said. "Please wait a moment, give me some idea," said the man. But she flashed off, just touching the tip of his nose with her foot, which woke him up! "My dear," said his wife, "how you have been snoring!"

Frankly we are just a bit suspicious of both of the stories which, under a theory we wish to advance, properly account only for the Titania part of Titania's Palace. This theory is that Sir Nevile had had dolls' houses on his mind for a long time, and had built them, which would have explained Titania's looking him up (in the second version) when she needed a house.

This inclination of Sir Nevile's is further shown in an item about a previous production of his. A toy trade magazine in 1910 undoubtedly picked it up from a London newspaper and printed it with the credit line omitted. The item began with a phrase which mysteriously attaches itself to half the dolls' houses which ever are described, "What is probably the most wonderful dolls' house in the world . . ." This marvel, in any case, "is now on view in the ballroom at Lansdowne House, where a dolls' bazaar organized by Lady Beatrix Wilkinson [Sir Nevile's Lady], is being held in aid of the Children's Union of the Waifs and Strays Society. The miniature mansion was opened by Queen Alexandra two years ago at Wilton House. Her Majesty used a golden key, designed by Captain Nevile Wilkinson, Ulster King of Arms, the architect of the little house. The owner, who is now exhibiting the house is Lady Muriel Herbert, daughter of the Earl of Pembroke."

Here is a pretty example of history repeating itself: Queen Alexandra opening a dolls' house by Sir Nevile in one generation; Queen Mary opening a dolls' house by Sir Nevile in the next. The Earl of Pembroke, by the way, was Sir Nevile's father-in-law, and Wilton House his residence. In the beautiful color series of Titania's Palace postcards brought out by Raphael Tuck some years back, in the nursery view, a dolls' house towers over the other toys. The notation on the back states that "The Dolls' House is an exact copy, reduced to one-twelfth, of the Great Wilton Dolls' House constructed by Sir Nevile Wilkinson in 1904, and opened by H. M. Queen Alexandra." The trade item and postcard notation are the only two references we've encountered of the dolls' house Sir Nevile made for his sister-in-law; he didn't bother to mention it in his autobiography, so presumably its merits were completely overshadowed by those of its successor.

From the written account, however, it had nearly as many rooms. There were fifteen, "one of them a beautiful banqueting hall, with marble pillars, artistic paneling on the walls, exquisite painted ceilings . . ." Moreover, it was seven feet high and about five feet wide, and took five years to build. This house, like its follower, had a visiting book and its autographs were traced in a similarly royal pattern—King Edward and Queen Alexandra—"probably the smallest they ever wrote"—as well as those of Lord Salisbury, Lord Rosebery and "many other celebrated people." The furnishings, we are told, were in many cases as valuable as full-size furniture. The unknown reporter seems to have been most carried away by the grand piano, which "though it could easily be put in one's jacket pocket, yet it [was] so beautifully made that it could be played had one fingers small enough for the keys, and if one's ears were keen enough to catch the tiny sounds, real music might be enjoyed." This was the progenitor, then, of the piano in Titania's boudoir two decades later, for which "fingers small enough" were found: "Sir Hubert Parry played the National Anthem with a sharpened match." And we shall use it for a transition-way into Titania's Palace itself.

Even persons who despair of statistics might find importance in those of the Palace which, next to the dimensions of the Great Wilton project, vividly suggest the scope of Titania's quarters. Her premises, which are built around a hollow "square" called the Fountain Court (laid out as an Italian garden), stand on an area of sixty-three square feet. These dimensions allow for an interesting stroll around the four sides of the house whose façades, similar in fashion to those of the Queen's Dolls' House, must be raised to reveal the rooms. Sir Nevile observes in his autobiography that it would have been relatively simple to design a dolls' house meant to remain

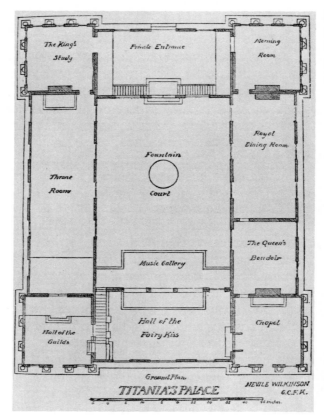

The ground plan
of Titania's Palace

in one room, but that his problem lay in designing a portable mansion, one which could (charitably) tour the world. His solution was to build the house in eight sections, each of which could be lowered into a padded packing case.

The house is only twenty-seven inches high, and its width plus this two-story height gives it a sort of long, low Italian look further augmented by its largely classical architecture. To this sentence, Sir Nevile might have taken exception. Says his autobiography: "There are no styles or periods which must be slavishly copied in fairy architecture. All that is best in design finds a welcome. . . . So on the four corner towers we find pillars of the three great orders of architecture, Doric, Ionic and Corinthian, an echo of Palladio in the broad frieze of triglyphs; while Inigo Jones' uncompleted Palace of Whitehall might have lent the windows. The northern façade, on the other hand, recalls the dignified domestic architecture of Queen Anne; . . . and yet all these styles seem in harmony. . . ."

The exterior is different from most dolls' houses in another respect. Sir Nevile made it of century-old mahogany with oak pillars, and since (according to His Whimsy) imitation is anathema to fairies who insist that "wood must remain wood and not be painted to resemble stone," the outside of Titania's residence grows darker year by year, a finish which gives it a rather special elegance.

If the exterior has its Roman aspects, the interior makes its creator's preference quite plain. Sir Nevile traveled widely, both as soldier and citizen,

The chapel of Titania's Palace contains a reredos (upper rear) which took Sir Nevile Wilkinson four years to complete

and Italy plainly was his favorite country. The manner of the four state apartments is largely Florentine, and even the dozen private rooms, because of the way color is used, and because of the miniature Italian treasures tucked in here and there, give a similar impression.

This undoubtedly is why the *Illustrated London News,* in 1929, referred to Titania's Palace as "A Museum-in-Little of Italian Art." Almost immediately the writer disproved the finality of this title by the following cluster of descriptions: "In the chapel are included a seventeenth century French bronze group . . . and a Holy Family in boxwood, from South Germany on the left. . . . The cross is a copy of the Irish tenth century Cross of Cong." Individually, one should emphasize, the treasures that decorate Titania's Palace are not Italian, but cosmopolitan.

This chapel is one of the four state apartments, of which the others are the Throne Room, the Hall of the Guilds, and the Hall of the Fairy Kiss, and all of which are "two stories" high. All four of these are distinctly related in their lavish warmth of color, and in their opulence of inlay and mosaic, marble and mural, ornament and emblem. Sir Nevile's personal contributions are most evident in this seemingly unlimited garniture. In the chapel is an elaborate reredos that took him four years to complete. (See illustration.) In the Throne Room is a four-inch-wide mosaic frieze. There are five feet of this frieze, and it required a day for him to paint an inch. The Hall of the Guilds is lined with Connemara marble and paved with Carrara. The Arms of the great Guilds of Florence are worked into the tapestries. All of the decoration is the work of Sir Nevile. The miracle seems to be how—even with helpers—Titania's Palace was perfected in twenty years.

In the Hall of the Fairy Kiss, which is equipped with a commodious Minstrel Gallery, and is the formal entrance to the Palace (there is also a family entrance hall, with private staircase and a perambulator), there are several items of more than artistic interest. *Grey Fairy* has quite an elaborate account of how the silver grilles in the upper arches came into being. We shall quote from it at length since it is a suitable example of how Sir Nevile's mythology and his dolls' house are intermingled.

"Titania used often to visit the Man's workshop to see how things were getting on. One day he noticed that she seemed rather upset. 'Is anything the matter, m'am?' he asked politely.

" 'I don't know what's to be done about the two open arches over the staircase,' said the Queen thoughtfully, 'they look very nice and I wouldn't like to fill them up. But the Royal Children are really very naughty about them, they will flash through while visitors are arriving; and it's so undignified! I had a number of most important insects to look over the Palace the other night, and I feel sure that some of them were quite annoyed about it.'

" 'Couldn't we put in some bars, or something like that?' suggested the Man, 'glass would look out of place, I'm afraid.'

" 'Oh, I wouldn't like glass,' said Titania quickly, 'I want plenty of air; but bars wouldn't be any good, because they don't keep out fairies, unless they're made of gold or silver. I really couldn't ask you to go to all that expense!'

" 'I'm afraid gold is out of the question,' he answered, 'but I believe I've got some old silver coins somewhere, and a broken cigarette case.'

" 'Won't it be a pity to melt down the coins if they're old ones?' said the Queen.

" 'They're only the out-of-date five-franc pieces hotel people always gave you in change when you were just leaving France. They don't now because they only use paper. The coins will do splendidly to make into bars for the two openings.' "

Having taught his small readers something about fairy family life, ingenuity in craftsmanship, and French currency, the generous author presumably laid down his pen and lacquered a small cabinet for Her Iridescence.

In the same Hall where the silver bars keep Titania's children in hand, there are two items of more practical interest. One is a portrait of Queen

"The Hall of the Fairy Kiss," is the formal entrance to Titania's Palace

Mary opening the Palace in 1922, and the other is a portrait of Queen Alexandra. The latter also is posed with a dolls' house, and though there is no written information to substantiate our statement, this one is obviously the Great Wilton example we've already discussed. The fact that there are in existence portraits of two English queens with dolls' houses, however miniature, is a stately piece of dolls' house intelligence, and gives a most royal slant to the dolls' house picture.

The Hall of the Guilds (see illustration), which is the anteroom to the Throne Room, contains one of the oldest treasures, a traveler's sample of about 1580. This is a miniature cannon in gilt bronze and iron with non-skid studs, if you please, on iron tires, which bears the initials of Michael Mann, a famous Nuremberg armorer. Sir Nevile, in a magazine article, had "little doubt" that it was made to advertise some improvement in "mobile ordnance" of those days.

Also on the lower floor are several private apartments, the Morning Room, the royal dining-room, Titania's boudoir, and Oberon's study. It is evident from a glimpse of the latter that Oberon has a number of hobbies. There are books and collector's items and chessmen and, most important, his cello. There is also a small piece of the late Princess Mary's wedding cake, in an ivory casket, which might indicate that he is sentimental.

The Hall of the Guilds in Titania's Palace is the anteroom to the Throne Room

Titania's boudoir is more feminine, but not frilly. This contains Titania's piano, to which we can picture Oberon pushing up his cello, and an inlaid Louis XV writing table with a secret drawer. But the most important furnishing, simply because The Painter and his party spend practically the whole of *Grey Fairy* searching for the full-size original, would seem to be the Doria Lantern, a shrine which Andrea Doria, the Genoese admiral and statesman, received as a gift from a Count whose daughter he rescued. (How much of this is truth and how much is Sir Nevile, we do not know. Since Sir N. has an apologia in the front of *Grey Fairy* for moving the Admiral's birthplace for the purposes of his tale, it is well to be suspicious.)

Another major item in the boudoir accounted for in *Grey Fairy* is The Crystal Tear. This delicate bauble is actually an emblem of Wilkinson mythology and charity. "When babies cry because somebody hurts them, or because they are hungry and neglected, the first teardrop always disappears; you can never find it, because it goes straight to Fairyland. It falls on the little golden stand . . . in Titania's boudoir."

A more matter-of-fact apartment is the dining-room. But even this has its ethereal aspects. We have already commented upon the lack of knives and forks. For this limitation, the full responsibility seems to belong to William Blake whose observation that "The Spirits of the air live on the smells of fruit" was accepted by Sir Nevile as truth. Therefore the most substantial fare present is oranges and lemons, though if anyone gets really hungry he can forget his troubles in a bottle of champagne sent by Queen Mary. Why Titania and Oberon need a dining-room under the circumstances, it is hard to say, except to display their rare collection of old Bristol glass. There is plunder in this room from an old Dutch dolls' house. Sir Nevile himself has acknowledged these "Landscapes of marvellous quality . . . painted in 1650 by [Jan Mienze] Molenaer for some rich merchant's baby in Haarlem or The Hague," and one wonders if they escaped from their original walls through some doll house-breaking similar to Utrecht's, or whether they were sold to ease the financial problems of impoverished dolls.

In *House Beautiful,* about thirty years ago, Sir Nevile, writing across the ocean, asserted that the Morning Room contained the "finest collection of miniature lacquer furniture in the world." Sir Nevile, who in his autobiography displayed the curious modesty of describing his handiwork in the third person and admiring it wholeheartedly from behind the privacy of an ambiguous pronoun, did not here mention that this lacquer work was done by himself. In the same way, in describing the reredos, Sir Nevile, instead of admitting he had been honored, circuitously commented that it "earned for its painter, the palace architect, a Vice Presidentship of the Royal Society of Miniature Painters."

On the upper level are the bedrooms and nurseries. Titania's bedchamber has a flower-laden frieze interlaced with the words of the familiar song of the Spring, the first it is believed, ever set to music in English.

Sumer is icumen in,
Lhude song cuccu!
Groweth sed, and bloweth med,
And springeth the wude nu—
Sing cuccu!

Evidently Sir Nevile was proud of the "canopied couch" in this chamber, because in his autobiography he declares that "Nothing that the architect in chief has yet done has pleased Her Iridescence more . . ."

Oberon's dressing room, which in appearance is a full-fledged bedchamber, is probably the most mundane cubicle of any in the palace. There is practically no fairy lore associated with it, and one commentator was driven to mark the presence, on the dressing-table, of "the smallest razor and collar stud ever made." In the dolls' house realm, the smallest this or that is inevitably turning up, like the "most wonderful dolls' house in the world," and there is nothing much to be done about it.

The nurseries, both day and night, are something else again. We have already discussed the dolls' house and the Clock the Mouse Ran Up. There are also delightful little dolls, from a collection dating back to 1820, and other toys, according to Sir Nevile, from India, China, Bavaria and Switzerland. Prince Crystal (whose perambulator is in the family hall) and four big sisters, Daphne, Iris, Ruby and Pearl, rulers of the respective elements, Earth, Air, Fire, and Water, share the nurseries. A floor plan in *Grey Fairy* shows only a Day Nursery and a Night Nursery, whereas the Tuck postcard series pictures the day nursery and two bedrooms, one of the latter for Iris and Ruby, and one for Daphne and Pearl. Sir Nevile was continually making alterations and additions, and most probably this adjustment was owing to the inevitable accumulation of the children's birthdays. (Although they were fairies, we know they had birthdays, because the iris plant on the table in Iris' room was a birthday present.) In any case, it is the princesses' bedchambers which contain the cupboards for spare wings, "for every fairy has a clean pair of wings on Sunday."

There is just one bath for the gossamer inhabitants, "with no vulgar drains or taps" since "early dewdrops suffice to fill their marble bath."

Only one of these fairy secrets has the architect made plain. Heeding the Keats observation that in Fairyland, "The doors all look'd as if they ope'd themselves," he furnished no handles or knobs.

A letter from Ireland from the Countess of Wicklow, widow of Sir Nevile Wilkinson, in April, 1952, informed us that this charming combination of imagination, art and skill had brought more than 80,000 pounds to children's charities all over the world since it was first exhibited "just thirty years ago." Titania's Palace is still on view at the Countess's home Ballynastragh, Gorey, County Wexford, where this earnest work is continued.

20

DUCHESS
DOROTHEA'S
PROJECT

UCHESS AUGUSTA DOROTHEA OF SCHWARZBURG-GOTHA, WHO WAS
born in 1666 and was quite an old lady before her death in 1751, accomplished in her eighty-five years the most documentary dolls' housing project of them all, a microcosm which she prettily called "Mon Plaisir." And since the results have mercifully survived, she performed a considerably cosmic service.

The Duchess,* with the help of her court, undertook to re-create the life about her, noble, bourgeois, and ecclesiastical, in a series of dolls' houses thoroughly populated by dolls. Until a few years ago, the only literature available about this extraordinary collection, apart from articles in German periodicals, appeared to be by Karl Gröber, who had contributed a page of text to a delightful picture booklet on the subject, and had also written of the collection elsewhere. However, in 1959, Dr. Christof Roselt,† in a catalogue of all the collections in the museum at Arnstadt, where "Mon

---

* She became "Princess" when her husband succeeded to the title of Prince, and is referred to by both titles.

† *Kunstsammlungen im Schloss zu Arnstadt*. Eisenach um Kassel O. J. We owe particular gratitude to Dr. Elisabeth Wolffhardt of Munich who not only sent this book, but translated the pertinent section for us.

Plaisir" is now on display, provided an authoritative account of the Duchess' treasure, correcting a number of errors in the information hitherto available.

Dr. Gröber had referred to 26 houses, 84 rooms, and 411 dolls in the booklet, but elsewhere had mentioned "twenty cabinets." Dr. Roselt accounts for this discrepancy: "The original arrangement of "Mon Plaisir" was different from the present one: in the cupboards, which contained and still contain the dolls, the rooms were partly arranged in four stories one above the other and glazed with lead. While the lowest rooms were close to the floor, the highest were too high to be easily viewed." Dr. Roselt adds that these cabinets, which were nearly nine feet tall, may be compared to the baroque cupboards for works of art or "cabinets" on whose numerous shelves precious things were displayed.

The portrait of the Duchess, containing a good deal of ermine, displays her in probable middle age, a decidedly tight-lipped, hard-visaged matron. Matron, that is, by right of the 411 dolls, for like many fellow-creatures similarly deprived who turn to dolldom, she had no children. Neither, when she began upon her project, had she a husband; that nobleman died in 1716, and it was then that the Duchess, according to Gröber, "in the loneliness of her widowhood," set to work.

According to Roselt, the Duchess (Roselt refers to her as Princess) had lived since about 1710 in secluded Augustenburg near Arnstadt, and from the time she was widowed (in 1716) till her death in 1751, she continued to live there "founding the fayence manufactory Dorotheental in the neighborhood of the Augustenburg, collecting pictures and porcelain, and planning the doll town."

She had all sorts of resources and persons at her disposal; Gröber's summary of her background effectively suggests how considerable they were: "Augusta Dorothea was the daughter of Duke Ulrich of Brunswick, and an aunt, therefore, of that Empress Elizabeth who was the consort of the Emperor Charles VI. She herself was married in 1684, to Count—afterwards Prince—Anton Günther of Schwarzburg-Arnstadt. The Princess was childless, but otherwise her married life differed little from that of all the other wives of all the other petty rulers of the rococo period. Prince Anton died in 1716. Augusta Dorothea had been received into the Roman Church the year before, a step that, in those days, did not make for popularity in the sturdily Protestant circles of Thuringia."

Not only was the Duchess provided with all the assistance to which her court position entitled her, and which automatically enlisted the aid of cabinetmakers and chandlers and tinsmiths and all sorts of artisans to duplicate their labors in miniature, and the means to afford them, but from her adopted church she acquired the miscellaneous talents of various individuals whose quiet lives and time to spare ideally fitted them for the exacting and relatively unlimited tasks of such a vast undertaking.

Two spiritual advisers of the princess, Franciscan fathers named Antonius Einhorn and Benedikt Sauer, modeled in wax the heads and hands of the doll population. Their work is delicate and various, a major achievement in a minor art, and it is indeed fortunate that handiwork composed of such a perishable commodity as wax has so perfectly survived.

Traditionally, Roselt tells us, these were likenesses, and the Princess herself, her councilors, other officials, ladies, servants, and other household members are modelled in wax "as like as portraits" (just as the rooms and scenes are believed to be exact likenesses of those of Augustenburg). The pious ladies of the Ursuline order in Erfurt reproduced a convent similar to their own. The large number of ecclesiastical scenes of various types reflect vividly the Duchess' preoccupation with her new religious life.

Das Puppenhaus, * Gröber's picture booklet about "Mon Plaisir," contains more than thirty plates, half of them in color—the exquisite lithography that the Germans seem consistently to produce. All of the pictures but one show a single room, or scene. The exception reveals a unit, or house, with four princely apartments, displayed on two floors, and a windowed structure with balconies above. Upon the projecting balcony, at the center, stand three musicians, all of whom seem to be occupied with wind instruments. They may very well be giving guttural competition to a very different sort of trio in the room below them, a lady singing from a piece of music in her hands, a gentleman playing upon a clavichord and a third patrician performer strumming on a banjo-like instrument. The Duchess must have been fond of music because even in the limited number of views the pictures display, there are sufficient instrumental scenes to provide a considerable and cacophonous concert. One listener stands inside while another listens behind a parapet on the roof.

Although the four rooms below this rather curious musicale were part of one household, the Duchess' creations generally are to be found in more miscellaneous combinations. According to Gröber, "In one of these houses . . . one could see "the princess at her toilet, in the floor below, a curio closet, below that a fair with booths, a puppet-show, clowns, a quack doctor, the town-crier, etc.; beneath this a soap refinery. In another such house there were the princess with a lady at table and three servants in the grey, silver-

* Revised as *Die Puppenstadt.*

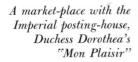

A market-place with the Imperial posting-house, Duchess Dorothea's "Mon Plaisir"

braided livery of the court; in the space below, a town scene, a market-place with the Imperial posting-house, in which the arriving posts, couriers, etc., are forwarded on their way; in the top storey the wife of the post-master is receiving visitors, while in the next room her husband is making up his accounts; below him a country wedding."

To turn the pages of the booklet room by room gives a diversified glimpse into the wonders of "Mon Plaisir." Two rooms placed in a luscious spread of color opposite each other are equally noble in aspect, and seem almost to be counterparts in the similarity of their furnishings. Tables and chandeliers in the two rooms are identical and only a great disparity in wallpapers indicates that two parts of the same chamber are not shown. The wallpapers throughout the princely apartments, incidentally, are remarkably vivid and varied. In one of these two brightly papered rooms, we find court society at cards, and in the other, a formal visit is taking place. The card game is participated in by three ladies and a gentleman. The formal visitor, who is being shown in by a footman, is being received by a hostess whose pug dog (or an ancestor thereof) at her feet must certainly modify the stiffness of even so precise an occasion.

Two other neighboring pictures are of a social nature. In one, described as a reception at court, eleven dolls mill about the long room, the most remarkable an African (evidently a footman) in a white wig that makes a weird frame to his black face. The other party is a men's gathering. There are six gentlemen, in varicolored wigs, who have distributed themselves at two tables. One dandy clings to his walking stick, though he's seated, and another to his long clay pipe. The others look busy, but it's hard to say what they're about. The tables are guiltless of beverages. Various framed maps hang on the walls, maps which must be highly historical geography under a suitable magnifying glass.

The next four plates offered by Gröber are, evidently by design, of a domestic variety. One is of the inevitable lying-in room, a particularly resplendent example in which the canopied bed of the mother is set into a most elaborate alcove whose arch, supported by classical columns with gold capitals, has cherubs sitting on its slopes, clad in such gilded drapery as cherubs wear. Another shows a nursemaid and her charges, one of them a little girl in much lace and a quaintly shaped high chair, and the other an infant in a wicker cradle on wooden rococo rockers. The other two pictures reveal, respectively, milady at her morning toilette (her maid is doing her hair, but she seems more interested in the contents of the cradle by her dressing table), and maids bed-making.

One of the most exquisite of all the rooms is the one Dr. Roselt calls "the miniature cabinet of mirrors," in which, to a visitor with his hat under his arm, the noble host is showing his treasures. They are "original Chinese porcelain vases with blue painting of the K'ang-hsi period,"* placed on gilt

---

* The Emperor K'ang-hsi was a member of the Manchu or Ch'ing dynasty (1662–1722).

288

brackets that cover the walls; "an interesting counterpart," says Roselt, "to the big cabinet of Arnstadt Castle." (Dr. Gröber had incorrectly identified this as porcelain made at Dorotheental when actually the only porcelain for "Mon Plaisir" made there were the fireplaces and tableware.) Strategically placed mirrors multiply the effect of gold and blue produced by the mirrors and porcelain, an effect rather sharply interrupted by two very ordinary looking windows placed against a sudden shade of green.

Mirrors, by the way, are used in all sorts of ways throughout the rooms. Usually in ornate gold or silver frames, they are generally present in pairs. One of the striking differences between these dolls' rooms and Dutch ones is the abundance of small paintings on the Dutch walls which seem to be replaced in "Mon Plaisir" by these mirrors. Whether this reflects an idiosyncrasy of the Duchess, or a deficiency of miniature painters in her court, it is hard to say.

"Princely couple at table" Gröber entitles the next picture. The princely couple who, we are glad to report, have napkins in their laps, are waited upon by two handsomely liveried footmen. They are seated at a surprisingly small table for a meal which, to judge by the lavish but unfortunately unidentifiable course in progress, is dinner. The tablecloth is the strangest item in the picture, being knotted about the table legs in a most curious manner, possibly to forestall tripping.

Two street scenes next appear. In one of these the princess is being helped from her sedan chair (neatly hung with cottage curtains) by a butler and a footman. In the other, a men's quartet is musically engaged. Of their instruments, one is a violin (or possibly viola), one a viol da gamba, and one a recorder. The fourth is one of those spherical horns once startlingly known as a serpent. The two string instruments employ the early bows which, literally bowed, indicate the origin of their name.

The royal kitchen and wine cellar in an ornate two-story combination are next. This kitchen has certainly the tallest ceiling on record, and since it bears on its walls the usual neat clutter of plate and implement and dish on hook and shelf clear to the top, there is the accustomed mystery about how the chef acquires the utensils he needs. Perhaps that is what the large company in the kitchen is conferring about. There is the chef and the pastry cook, both in tall white hats, and three feminine assistants, two with towels over their arms. In the wine cellar there are barrels and tasting glasses.

The following scene is mercantile. The white-wigged lady—perhaps the princess—her back is turned—is at a fashionable mercer's. Bolts of elaborate textiles are on the shelves, and the small proprietress behind the counter is showing one of a red and gold fabric. Rococo bonnet stands hold millinery, though this is in the minority.

An ecclesiastical interior next appears. The governing body of the church, the consistory, are in council. There are three, including one in a wide ruffled collar, standing about a table on which reposes a thick clasped

*The royal kitchen
and wine cellar,
Duchess Dorothea's collection*

volume, presumably the Bible. To judge by the position of their hands, which all are in mid-air, a considerable discussion is in progress.

One of the most amusing scenes follows, the Duke being shaved by the Court Barber. The barber chair is a handsome old wing-back with legs and stretchers in astragal twists, and the Duke is seated erectly. Not for him the coarse cotton apron slung hurriedly around the neck; he is protected by a handsome linen apron edged in two-inch lace! The Court Barber is obviously too dignified to wear a uniform; he is working in his long coat, and his high-heeled shoes. (See illustration.)

Three convent scenes are next. The first shows the needlework hour in the Ursuline boarding school. The young ladies of the Pension, four of them, presided over by two nuns, are engaged with various types of handwork. The second shows the nuns in their refectory where a goodly repast is set upon the table, but where the principal nourishment is spiritual; a clergyman standing on a low balcony is reading to them. The third tableau is simpler—a nun is offering food to a beggar at the convent door.

A segment of the fair, set up against a stately stone building in which two curious personages may be seen at upstairs windows, comes next into view. One of the upstairs spectators is peering between two potted trees on his ledge; the other, who seems to wear a nightcap, stands with a lantern in his window. Below are a chandler's booth (rolls and twists of wax are suspended by cords), a young woman (minus a booth) selling potter's wares, and a cobbler's stall. The pottery is engaging a potential feminine buyer with a basket upon her back, and slippers are being shown two prospective buyers, one of whom is evidently dickering about the price.

One of the most curious and beautiful settings is also the most puzzling. Gröber identifies it as "an Albertineish garden," a term which seems to refer only to the period (Webster defines Albertine as a reference to the younger branch of the house of Frederick of Saxony). Grassy terraces on several levels have potted fruit trees and bushes placed at formal intervals among them. Since cut flowers are not usually seen in gardens, the presence of five enormous blue and white porcelain bowls filled with colorful blooms is most curious. These appear to surround, on two levels, a metal figure or

The Duke is shaved by the royal barber, comfortably

monument of indistinguishable form with an urn at either side. Whether this represented some sort of mausoleum, or had a different kind of religious significance, we do not know. But such common, garden-variety occurrences as a man trundling a wheelbarrow, and a gardener pruning a bush, are also visible, against a handsomely painted backdrop of formal lawns, fountains and pavilions (a kind of "vue d'optique"). A pretty but not unusual green wood summerhouse is in the center.

Italian comedy is being performed in the court theater in the succeeding tableau. The curtain (centered by the Duke's coat of arms) is rolled up and no less than fifteen performers are on stage. The musicians, who are dwarfs, are tucked in a corner at either side of the stage under two tiers of boxes in which members of the audience are established. At least one harlequin, an inevitable presence, is in evidence.

Two domestic offices occupy the next pages. One of these is the headquarters of the steward, and one is the baking room. The steward's office is cluttered with various household utensils and appurtenances, and the steward, seated, appears to be giving instructions to four subordinates, one man and three women. The baking room, which has loaves on its shelves, has two ovens. The pastry cook, a droll-looking fellow, has his hands in dough. One feminine assistant is standing by quite uselessly, but another is balancing by a rod on her shoulders two weights which are invisible in the picture. Here is pastry history, could one identify the mysterious iron implements and other enigmatic utensils in view.

Next, in a great blaze of color and glory, is a slice of the annual fair, two booths and an adjacent dwarf theater. The contents of the two booths seem to be highly miscellaneous. One, engaging the interest of a lady, shows bonnets, gloves, and even a wig. The other is so thoroughly concealed by

An apothecary shop, Duchess Dorothea's collection

three customers that it is difficult to judge what is for sale. An itinerant vendor, who must have been the forerunner of today's pedestrian potato-peeler-and-tie seller, displays his wares upon a folding stand.

An apothecary shop is on the following page. The chemist is weighing powders in a small balance scale he holds, evidently for a customer who is waiting hat in hand. Perhaps it is for the same prescription that an assistant, nearby, is crushing with his pestle some ingredients in a mortar which rests on a very elaborate pedestal standing on the floor. There are bottles and boxes and jars of all sizes on shelves. There is even a little cluster of cone-shaped papers suspended from a hook, apparently to contain the merchandise. One row of china jars is numbered from one to nine in a shorthand which is (we trust) most familiar to the chemist.

The cabinetmaker's workshop which follows is one of the oddest representations in the group. What is shown is almost like an impressionistic stage rather than a room, and the effect given is strangely modern. A huge, scalloped stand, like a palette, is the backdrop; on this saws and other tools of various kinds are suspended. The work benches are, of course, of simple design, and the three chairs in the process of being made are of such a stark aspect, without their upholstery, that even the quaint pair of joiners can't exclude the effect of a scene by Dali.

The Court Tailor, who appears next, has sober premises, by comparison, but even his atelier has its quaint aspects. He and a lady customer and his work tables are standard enough, but on the walls are several amazingly patterned hangings. These, which appear to be tapestry, are five in number. On either side of the door is a pair. In both of these are three major items, a gentleman, a fruit tree growing in an urn, and a dog. The extraordinary thing about the fruit tree growing in the urn is that the urn is nearly as tall as the man, and the tree extends its ample branches over his head. The urn in the first picture is very fancy, having two figures seated upon its indented sides. In the second picture the figures have vanished, the gentleman has moved to the other side of the urn, which has somewhat altered its shape and assumed handles, and the dog which had been romping near the urn is sedately seated, having changed sides with the gentleman. What all this signifies, and one desperately would like to be able to read the motto, illegible in the picture, under the first scene, is utterly incomprehensible. A corresponding pair on the side walls contains (in each) a lady, and a fruit tree in an urn, but the pranks of perspective make the subject matter in these hangings even more enigmatic than in the first pair.

Dr. Gröber sagely concludes his pictorial procession with an amusing group, a bear trainer with two woolly protégés and a bag-piper. One of the bruins is brown and the other white. The brown bear is attached to an iron chain which terminates in a ring through his nose, poor fellow; this would seem to imply that he is not as docile as the unhampered polar who is tamely

Dancing bears, bear trainer, and musician!

begging with his paws in mid-air. However, both of these creatures, marvelously realistic, look as docile as hamsters. (See illustration.)

When we consider that these diversified scenes were considerably less than half of "Mon Plaisir's" total, it is difficult to conceive what has been left unsaid, or rather unshown. Undoubtedly Dr. Gröber has attempted to choose the most interesting glimpses for his booklet, but it must have been almost impossible to decide which those were. One which he has seen fit to omit from the booklet but which was included in an article he did for *The Studio* would seem to be one of the most arresting of all. In this the Duchess was forever immortalized in a different way. The court painter is doing her portrait and she is sitting for it. The painter is sitting for it, too— both painter and subject are comfortably seated in chairs.

Several rooms not to be found in the Gröber booklet are shown by Roselt, among them the "curiosity cabinet" in which paintings of many shapes, sizes, and aspects crowd the walls, and sculptures, along with many other assorted art treasures stand on tables (which are themselves collector's pieces) and on the floor. Mounted on a stand, there is, for instance, a Crucifixion with Christ impaled upon the Cross, that reaches nearly to the ceiling. Roselt comments upon the full-sized rooms of the period that this reflects, in which "pictures, ivory-carvings, cut stones, wax and plaster reliefs, crucifixes and furniture were put together indiscriminately to form an art and curiosity cabinet."

Roselt offers an account of "several fortunate circumstances [which] combined to preserve the collection to the present day without any considerable losses," and is dramatic indeed when considered in terms of what might have been: "When in 1765—fourteen years after the Princess' death—the Augustenburg was pulled down and there was nobody to purchase the collection, the Duke of Brunswick as heir presented it to the newly founded Arnstadt orphanage . . . It was exhibited in the big room of the orphanage in the manner of the old curiosity cabinets together with a collection of minerals, shells, stuffed birds and snakes, and was shown to the public for an entrance-fee two days after Christmas, Easter, and Whitsun."

It seems to have had many visitors, according to Roselt, but when the orphanage was reorganized, he adds, the collection was stored away in an attic where it stood for many years, "unnoticed, uncared for, given to dust and moths."

It was rediscovered in 1882 by Princess Mary of Schwarzburg-Sondershausen, whose name, like that of the Duchess, also should go down in dolls' house history. It was taken to Arnstadt Castle and then, in the 'nineties, rearranged in Gehren Castle. "But it was again forgotten," and although it was in 1919 "awarded" to the Arnstadt museum, it was not set up till 1930. However, since then, interrupted only by World War II and a few years thereafter, it has been on view.

One shudders to think of what might have befallen this "precious document of civilization," as Roselt calls it, in that long and dusty history. Sacheverell Sitwell, who wrote about the collection in 1953 in *Truffle Hunt,* * placed it even more firmly in time. "There is no other such detailed document of one of the Courts of Northern Germany," he wrote, "just as they must have seemed in the eyes of Johann Sebastian Bach, who was Kapellmeister and organist at Arnstadt from 1703 to 1706."

Roselt points out that the interest of visitors is growing year by year. Although their number is limited by the fact that the Arnstadt Palace Museum where "Mon Plaisir" is shown is in Thuringia, behind the "Iron Curtain," we must be grateful that the history which a thoughtful Duchess so attentively created has survived.

* *Truffle Hunt with Sacheverell Sitwell,* Robert Hale Ltd., London, 1953.

21

MRS. THORNE'S ROOMS

*J*T IS FAIRLY IRRESISTIBLE FOR A DOLLS' HOUSE HISTORIAN TO COMPARE the miniature rooms of Mrs. James Ward Thorne, created in the twentieth century, with those of Duchess Augusta Dorothea of Schwarzburg-Gotha, created in the eighteenth.

The Duchess dealt with the present, the life around her, while Mrs. Thorne memorializes mostly the past. But the tomorrow for which the Duchess' dolls' rooms and the majority of Mrs. Thorne's rooms are history is now here. Mrs. Thorne's American, European and Asiatic interiors cover considerably more of the world and many more years than the Duchess's microcosm, but both have served history in a similar way. There is even a numerical similarity. Mrs. Thorne's rooms number ninety-seven, while those of the Duchess are variously estimated at eighty to one hundred.

It is interesting that Mrs. Thorne got started upon her vast project through a great love of dolls' houses. It is ironically interesting in view of the fact that this legend is no longer mentioned in official connection with the Thorne rooms. A representative of Mrs. Thorne's Chicago Art Institute groups some years ago wrote these words, "Except in size they have no relation whatever to dolls' houses as such and are designed for a different purpose and from a completely different point of view. . . . They are serious studies in the history of decorative arts—visual demonstrations—and are in no sense elaborate playthings." In a book devoted to showing that dolls' houses can be utilized for "serious studies in the history of decorative arts," this seems a strange sentence to record. And in terms of the Thorne rooms' debt to dolls' houses for their initial inspiration and for quantities of their furnishings, this attitude seems a bit untoward.

Mrs. Thorne's attraction to dolls' houses grew during a period of years, in which she presented them to innumerable little girls in her family and to several wards of children's hospitals. The houses became more and more elegant till it seemed inappropriate to consign them to the brief life expectancy of toys.

An early account states that Mrs. Thorne had seen the Queen's Dolls' House, and other famous ones in museums abroad, and that it occurred to her "that she might develop an interesting way of constructing rooms in miniature which could be made available for the enjoyment of children." (Adults, the majority of her patrons, must have been a delightful surprise!)

Mrs. Thorne writes that in an antique shop in Rome, she came across "six miniature treasures which were destined to be the nucleus of [the] first room. They had belonged to an Italian noblewoman, in whose family they had been prized possessions for many years. . . . In planning the proper setting for these acquisitions, the idea came to me to build a real room in miniature—a permanent home, into which they would fit." (Mrs. Thorne recorded this information in the interesting catalogue she prepared for the group shown at the Golden Gate Exposition. Later brochures, written by specialists, deal purely in period and contain none of this type of detail.) The six pieces, which may be found in the Renaissance Venetian Room, are curiously in pairs: two delicate bronze chandeliers, set with crystal, lapis lazuli, and amber, two lacy bronze console tables, and two rare polychrome busts which stand on pedestals. (See illustration.)

Mrs. Thorne's Venetian room featuring noble Roman treasures

Elaine W. Rogers, writing thirty years ago* offers an entertaining picture of Mrs. Thorne's initial foray for antique miniatures, as well as an informative glimpse of the numbers and variety then available:

"As she and her husband journeyed leisurely through the cities and hill towns of Italy, they found that somehow word of their coming had always gone before. At every hotel and inn, scarcely would they get to their rooms before they were told a peddler, collector, or dealer waited below with small objects to sell for large sums. Fortunately, the dollar bought more that year than it does now.

"When they were ready to leave Italy for Paris, they had filled their first trunk with tiny trophies—silver wall sconces, inch high wine bottles in braided straw, Venetian glass candlesticks, a credenza and a variety of other objects.

"In Paris, Left Bank shops were ransacked and priceless objects turned up—old silver dinner sets, diminutive toilet articles, vases of silver and porcelain, clocks, everything unbelievably perfect in scale. More and more amazing became the search. She discovered the most beautiful pieces of furniture—a Louis XVI desk with marble top, commodes, consoles, all perfect in workmanship with inlaid wood, antique hardware, locks opened and closed with tiny keys, all true in scale of an inch to the foot."

It's interesting to note how many miniatures Mrs. Thorne found in Italy, a land which never has been emphasized as a likely region for dolls' houses. Although it is only fair to assume that some of the pieces were apprentice pieces, and a few were accessories from elaborate Southern crèche settings, the majority undoubtedly were first made for aristocratic Italian dolls who lived in houses similar to the one shown in Chapter 9.

It is a mild diversion to picture historians of a very future day puzzling over certain of the reproductions created for Mrs. Thorne's rooms, pieces quite apart from these antique miniatures, an unfortunate few which, perhaps, have been lost from their original Thorne nests, and debating in scholarly fashion whether or not they were created for dolls' houses, or for models, and whether indeed they are reproductions from, or survivals of, the centuries they represent.

The Thorne rooms consist of three sets, of which Mrs. Thorne long ago presented two, the American and European groups, to the Art Institute in Chicago. It is the first set that Mrs. Thorne built, consisting of thirty-one miscellaneous American, European, and Asiatic interiors, with which we shall be most concerned here, even though all of the rooms are, both visually and historically, superb. Geographically speaking, however, the first group is the most varied. More importantly, as the *first* group, it absorbed most of Mrs. Thorne's antique miniatures and is therefore of greater interest to dolls' house preservationists.

For these reasons alone, it is gratifying that sixteen of these initial thirty-one rooms, for years the property of International Business Machines

* *Leisure,* April 1936.

298

Corp., are now on permanent display at the Phoenix Art Museum in Arizona. When I. B. M.'s rooms, originally purchased for the company's art collection, were placed in storage in 1961, Niblack Thorne of Phoenix, Mrs. Thorne's son, decided that an addition to the Phoenix Art Museum, then in the process of completion, would be an admirable setting for them. Both I. B. M. and the museum were receptive to such an arrangement, and Mrs. Thorne, after refurbishing the sixteen that were decided upon, presented the group to the museum. Her son, upon the death of his wife, Marie G. Thorne, in 1962, established the exhibit as a permanent memorial in her name.

The rooms, a progression of glassed-in stages set at adult eye level along draped walls, have each their own degree of early morning light, or noonday sun, or starlit night coming through their slight well-polished windows, and these lighting arrangements are not the least of their wiles. Every country and every era seems somehow to be most typically, to the mind's eye, alight with its own peculiar luminosity. Mrs. Thorne has the knack of catching the country at its most typical moment in the day or weather and pinioning the century in a manner to make all minds' eyes imagine they agree. This alone seems to be an unexploited minor art which Mrs. Thorne has cultivated. It adds a dimension which the average dolls' house, its dim daylight reflected from a nursery corner, with a primly modern electric system, cannot have. (This is one of the few advantages the dolls' house will concede to the miniature room in this partisan book.)

Light isn't the only item that comes through Mrs. Thorne's glittering jewelry shop of windows. Always there is a scene. It may be botanical, containing the profusion of an English garden or the pruned sparseness of a Japanese. It might be architectural, a foggy eighteenth century perspective of buildings or a steep twentieth century cluster of skyscrapers. All of these appear—the Japanese garden visible against a whole side of the Japanese room and quite as panoramic in its view and scope as the room itself. For the eighteenth century view from her Georgian library windows, Mrs. Thorne treated an old lithograph, to obtain a proper London drab. For some of the scenes, as the Japanese, she used full-dimensional effects; in others, such as the Georgian, she triumphed with an illusion.

Scenes appear through doors as well as windows, and many of these are of other apartments. Behind a door barely ajar, a very fine grandfather's clock, or a handsome bust on a pedestal may be seen. Outside the English Lodge Kitchen, pins are distinctly in view, for a game of Bowling-on-the-Green. One of the most impressive arrangements of all is the living apartment of a Chinese palace which, while focusing on one "guest" room, actually is a nest of six rooms, one cubicle opening off another.

This Chinese apartment (see illustration) is one of the most captivating of all Mrs. Thorne's creations. The woodwork and furniture are of carved teakwood, and the woodwork, ornamenting innumerable translucent panels, becomes in miniature a lacy and delightful embellishment. The Thorne catalogue is particularly informative about this:

Guests are received, not installed, in the Chinese guest room

"The guest room, so called because here guests are received, exemplifies the Chinese respect for canons of good form. Adjoining it—behind a sliding screen or the wall that backs a prescribed long table and holds a painting or two scrolls with quotations from the classics—is the sacred portion of the house, a room consecrated to a small altar before which deities and the spirit of the family's ancestors are worshipped. In less elaborate homes the sacred shelf serves further as principal element of decoration. Dignified appearance, first requisite of the guest room, has great importance in Chinese thought, as shown by the rule which decrees that only rigid chairs be set here, for otherwise, were they too comfortable, lounging would be encouraged and lead to ungraceful attitudes. Another tradition widely observed is the custom of placing only as many chairs as will be occupied by host, hostess, and the expected number of guests; to have more would be vulgar display. Two stands for flowers, tables for smoking supplies and tea things, and several painted scrolls carefully chosen from the family's collection, complete the setting."

Mrs. Thorne's kitchens are among her most delightful rooms; there are no less than nine of them, five in the first group. Each is a delightful but reproachful reminder of the real living-room that the kitchen used to be. Some of them, it is true, are combination living-rooms, such as an "Early Massachusetts" one from the American collection. This is interesting to compare with the "Early American Kitchen" of Mrs. Thorne's first group, in which date and locale are more general. Other American kitchens include a Pennsylvania Dutch, a Victorian farm, and a replica of the kitchen in the Governor's Palace at Williamsburg. There is an English lodge kitchen, one Breton, one Majorcan, and then the English cottage version of the kitchen-living-room combination. Combine a study of these with a study of the Nuremberg type and other examples in our chapter on dolls' kitchens, and there, practically, is a history of kitchens, including, necessarily, smatterings about the history of cooking.

How can the doughnut become extinct when successive generations will be reminded of it by the dish of toy automobile tires coated with soda which will tempt eternally in Mrs. Thorne's 1885 summer kitchen?

Mrs. Thorne's American group of rooms is of particular interest because it takes, for the most part, a group of historic rooms in specific historic houses which a traveler would have to journey many scattered miles to see and it reduces that mileage to a floor's length.

There are rooms from such shrines as Mount Vernon and Andrew Jackson's Hermitage. Some of the models are composites, combining the most important features of several. There is no complete example from Monticello, but an ingenious "dining room from a 'Jeffersonian' House" displays Jefferson's "passion for ingenious gadgets." The fireplace, which *is* a miniature replica of the one at Monticello, has doors in its side, expediting the arrival of cheer from the wine cellar directly below. There are also trick windows and doors of Jeffersonian contrivance, but the room as a unit borrows from several sources.

A more typical example of Mrs. Thorne's eclecticism may be found in a bedroom of a New Orleans house of 1800–1850. A mantel from a house in the old city, a door and window trim from a plantation on the city's outskirts, and a cornice from a house in the garden district are blended together into a room which outside its slender French windows is graced by a lacy iron balcony that is "typical" rather than specific.

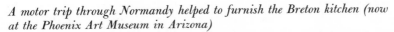

A motor trip through Normandy helped to furnish the Breton kitchen (now at the Phoenix Art Museum in Arizona)

Occasionally Mrs. Thorne has had to make changes based on the necessities of her medium. The stage designer's problem of the missing fourth wall is identical to that of the builder of miniature rooms which more technically are miniature stages. All of Mrs. Thorne's problems are interesting; an entertaining study might be made, alone, of the varied materials she has adapted to her needs. They are invaluable as research material, on the highest plane, for anyone building a dolls' house of any pretensions whatever. The ingenuity exhibited is quite as fascinating, if not as intellectual a study, as the rooms themselves.

Mrs. Thorne's ancestors must have turned the first swords into ploughshares, and have been perfectly capable of transforming sow's ears into silk purses. Metamorphoses seemingly far more extensive have been accomplished. From employing petit point powder box tops for small rugs (she cut up old petit point purses to upholster chairs) and canary feathers for quill pens, Mrs. Thorne has turned to subtler ruses. She captured a chess queen to use as an ivory bust on a credenza, and converted a Spanish comb top for the headboard of a bed.

Rugs appeared like veritable magic carpets. One, found in a Paris antique shop, where it had been used as a lamp mat, proved to be a replica of an Oriental pattern when the kerosene stains were removed, and it stretches now across the stately length of a Stuart salon. Other rugs and carpets were fashioned from pieces of embroidery, but quantities of the floor coverings, which are seen to with the exquisite care of every element of the Thorne rooms, including the great variety of floors they rest upon, were made to order for the rooms. Many Mrs. Thorne did herself; others she supervised. Nearly all of these are miniature replicas of historic rugs. A delightful example of the imaginative detail lavished on these rooms occurs in a small circular rug in a Georgian hallway which "echoes the design of the dome above."

The techniques developed in making the reproductions are a study in themselves, and parallel the experiments made for the Queen's Dolls' House. Similar perplexities had to be solved about textures of cloth, some of which was specially woven, and depth of paint, which if insufficiently diluted might thicken a whole table. Mrs. Thorne participated fully in the creation of reproductions for the early groups, necessarily turning more to gifted craftsmen in the later series. She noted that the two chests at the back of the Italian dining-room were her "first and only effort to become a woodcarver."

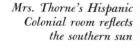

Mrs. Thorne's Hispanic Colonial room reflects the southern sun

302

But she had a gifted finger in almost every other creative process involved, in particular the rug-making mentioned above.

Her assistants are also a story, one of them in particular. Mrs. Thorne has pointed out that in the Federal room, "The table silver and the little ivory-handled knives and forks, one-half inch long, were made by a six-foot Englishman!" The incredibly minute (even in miniature terms) works of this talented London policeman are evident in a number of the interiors.

But the diverting story of extraordinary skills is matched, tale for tale, by that of the remarkable treasure hunt which found for Mrs. Thorne the fruits of skills employed in earlier days. Troves turned up in the most surprising and scattered places. The penthouse dining-hall contains decorated pottery vases, plates, pitcher, and carved stone head that she bought in a small museum near Carthage in North Africa. One of Mrs. Thorne's searches uncovered an especially valuable addition to her Louis XVI dining-room. In a secret drawer, in the back of an old French secrétaire, Mrs. Thorne found an original water-color cartoon of a tapestry, with swatches of vari-colored wools rolled up in it. Intended for a wall of more mammoth dimensions, it has become the impressive backdrop of miniature banquets!

"Good fortune," says Mrs. Thorne, accompanied her on a motor trip through Normandy and Brittany. It led her to the cradle, the spinning wheel, and the tall chest for her Breton kitchen, after she had found the odd bed with doors. (See illustration.) It is irresistible here to add that these must be toys; it is unlikely that travelers' samples would have been made of such modest and purely local furnishings and it is difficult to picture the simple Bretons with curio cabinets.

Mrs. Thorne's early catalogue, by the way, comes right out and says that the furniture in the Victorian parlor is from an English dolls' house of the period. This room confesses its indebtedness to dolls' houses twice—the magazine stand holds "one of the few miniature copies of the London *Times* struck off for the Queen's Dolls' House."

Some materials were found close to home. In the Georgian drawing-room, a corner of Mrs. Thorne's grandmother's paisley shawl has become a rug. Through a picture window in the modern living-room may be seen a red lacquer tea house which Mrs. Thorne had "cherished since childhood." Just above the fireplace in the modern library is a bronze Nubian head which her uncle brought her from Vienna when she was six.

History is made vivid in the Thorne rooms. In a colonial dining-room, a hatchment hangs above the fireplace, a large framed painting of the family coat of arms, which was hung outside on the front door when death came to a household. In a Georgian room, there is a wig stand, reminiscent of the headpiece it once supported for brushing and powdering. In the English cottage is a metal foot warmer, filled once upon a time with hot coals and taken to church of a Sunday. Such items as these, with which the Thorne rooms abound, are informative footnotes to history in general, worthy of full size type for social history in particular.

22

MADAME RUBINSTEIN'S ROOMS

*M*RS. THORNE'S MINIATURE ROOMS ARE INDISPENSABLE. JUST AS they furnished a likely comparison with Duchess Dorothea's, they offer an interesting contrast to the late Mme. Rubinstein's collection.

If one were to line up the small glassed prosceniums of Mrs. Thorne's rooms along one side of a corridor, and the small glassed prosceniums of Mme. Rubinstein's on the other, a cursory glance might detect a strong family resemblance between the two processions. The family resemblance, however, is physical. Where Mrs. Thorne didn't hesitate to supplement her antique pieces with reproductions, Mme. Rubinstein let no miniature objects darken her miniature doors unless they were antique.

There are advantages to both of these policies. Mrs. Thorne's rooms are far more specifically historic and therefore of more documentary value than the cosmetician's. But the latter, though they are disconcertingly labeled in a manner casual as to period or place, are far mellower to behold, and seem to have brooding over them in their subtly lighted cases all their mingled, diversified histories.

Madame collected these treasures over a period of more than thirty years, discovering them in the mapful of countries to which the demands of her international enterprise led her. *Fortune* in 1935 reported that there were "twenty-five little rooms in Madame's Park Avenue triplex apartment—she had to tear down two bedrooms and a bath to make her gallery." The rooms, which were, until her death, housed behind padlocked doors on an upper floor in her Fifth Avenue salon, number only twenty (counting a three-room dolls' house as one), and Madame didn't quite know where the others were.

Her miniature objects are still, to some extent, internationally distributed. "In one of her Paris homes," *Fortune* continued, "she has thirteen more miniature rooms, for which artists like Dufy, Braque, Lurçat and Marcoussis did backgrounds." A writer for a less temperate publication than *Fortune* was carried away and tucked Picasso in among this splendid array. Getting Madame to talk about these wonders was practically impossible. Years ago she was most gracious about showing her rooms to the writer, but was most uncommunicative when asked specific questions. Therefore we resorted to a written list. One of the queries, which referred to the French thirteen, inquired in part: "Does Madame have any idea whether or not these survive? I'd appreciate anything whatsoever she remembers about them, such as what sort of rooms they were, what mood of the artist's is found in them, etc.? Did they have modern furniture?" The answer, in full, noted that "In Paris Madame has thirteen miniature rooms with backgrounds designed by artists such as Dufy and Alice Halicka. These rooms do have modern furniture."

Fortune, which evidently pinned somebody down, further observed, this time in its own inimitable, statistical way, that "There are enough pieces all told for two hundred rooms, and Madame thinks they are worth half a million dollars. She once paid $500 for a single piece of glass." In London, for example, she has a set of Chippendale furniture. This bears, in what must be a microscopic penmanship, the signature of Thomas Chippendale himself.*

Of the rooms in New York, only the illuminated frames are of modern vintage, these rectangular stages composed of wall and floor and door having been built to order by very knowing architects. These, like Mrs. Thorne's, are delightfully supplied with such attractive realities as galleries and alcoves, authentically-patterned wallpapers, and street scenes through windows.

Since the rooms are primarily to entertain, rather than to instruct, and are not, as are most of Mrs. Thorne's, dependent upon fulfilling a sequence of styles or centuries, they are considerably more random in subject matter. Two of Mme. Rubinstein's best-known and delightful interiors are an Old Curiosity Shop and a Montmartre Studio whose haphazard contents are necessarily culled from a number of times and places.

A cliché which relentlessly attests to flaws in the power of observation frequently occurs in dolls' house circles. This, with small variations, goes,

* Shortly before this edition went to press, an attempt to check this proved futile. The Nostell Priory baby house, of course, has exquisite furniture *attributed* to Chippendale.

Dickens' Old Curiosity Shop as reproduced by the late Madame Rubinstein

"Everytime I look I see something I didn't see before." In the case of Madame's Old Curiosity Shop (see illustration) this is less likely to reveal a flaw of the observer than to reflect a tribute to what he is observing. This Old Curiosity Shop has practically everything that Little Nell's had, excepting perhaps the suits of mail. There are for sale in this realistically tarnished establishment no less than five hundred antiquities, representing six countries and three centuries. There are stacks of elderly platters and washstand sets piled on shelves, ancient pitchers and candlesticks loaded on tables, retired lanterns and bird cages hanging from rafters, and other objects, like the "scattered articles" Little Nell's grandfather had "to make his way through," clustered about on the floor. Among these are two items of furniture, a pair of monstrous chairs with incredible backs of a bizarre baroque and feet that are literally the feet of some wayward animal whose head, grotesquely out of place and scale, appears at each knee.

This shop has a wide window, with goods displayed in it, which its original does not appear to have had, but the door seems to have been patterned after its predecessor. "A part of this door was of glass . . ." and in the facsimile the glass is realistically broken. Outside can be seen three steps down (there are three more inside), with a trash barrel alongside, and "The Cheshire Cheese" across the way. There is an odd stove and a desk for the proprietor, and although Little Nell's bit of bedroom is not represented, along with the "distorted figures in china, and wood, and iron, and ivory . . . and strange furniture that might have been designed in dreams," Madame's Old Curiosity Shop looks as though it might have been a very acceptable and interesting place for Little N. to live in, and one which shouldn't have disturbed Master Humphrey at all.

The Montmartre Studio, despite all its casual Bohemian ways, looks inviting. (See illustration.) Perhaps someone thought it looked too inviting, for in an early photograph of the room the neatly turned balusters guarding its gallery bedroom are intact, whereas in the studio, as later seen, two had been removed for a more off-hand, gap-toothed effect.

There is room for all the arts in this sunny attic place. By the light that infuses the premises from a tall window in which several fancily caged birds dwell, and from a slanting attic skylight against the sloping eaves, one notes a grand piano spread with music, plaster nudes, canvases, at various stages, on walls or stacked against them, and shelves arrayed with mingled books and mugs. A table in the middle holds both bottles and a dish of fruit; whether the ingredients of a still life or of the artist's lunch, it is hard to say. A staircase leads to the aforementioned gallery bedroom where bed, chair, and washstand with bowl and pitcher are apparent. A glimpse of this enticing dwelling-place should be enough to send thousands of American students flocking to Paris all over again.

Madame Rubinstein captured the Right Bank in her Montmartre studio

Madame did not hesitate to tuck in here and there, among the more standard inch-to-foot specimens of her collection, a room that is widely discrepant compared with the scale of some of her others. The largest, a mid-Victorian parlor, she referred to as her Victor Hugo room. This, for the numerically inclined, is 22½ inches high, 40½ inches wide and 12 inches deep. The effect given in this parlor is distinctly maroon and gold. The walls are of red damask with gilt mouldings; the furniture is upholstered in red tufted satin bordered in fringe, and a gold lustre tea set is on the center table. A very glittering crystal chandelier suspended from the ceiling and four rococo gilded wood sconces are meant to illumine the handsome gloom cast by this weight of maroon.

There is a gold watch the size of a bead, and a seventeenth century snuff box that literally will hold no more than a pinch of snuff. There is an album of thirty daguerreotypes containing the stately features of members of royalty. A leather-bound volume with somewhat smaller illustrations is antique in a mid-Victorian setting: "Calendrier de la Jeunesse pour L'An 1805." As in most of the rooms, there are dolls, beguiled in this interior by a collection of objets d'art on a what-not, as well as by the daguerreotypes and the reading matter.

The dimensions of the chamber may be compared with the 20 inch width, 14 inch depth and 10 inch height of an "early American sitting room." Where the furnishings in the Victorian parlor are approximately two inches to a foot, the delicate pieces here must be three quarters of an inch to a foot. The legs of the drop-leaf table and chairs are thread-like. Thought has been given to the diversion of the Early American occupants; there is a clavichord in a corner, and at a comfortable distance two chairs pulled up to an ivory chess table complete with its full thirty-two piece complement of castles, knights, bishops, kings, queens and pawns. But spiritual occupations have not gone unheeded; on the built-in bed (set into an alcove) is another of the small leather-bound volumes with which these rooms are well provided, *Le Petit Parisien à L'Enfance,* an old prayer book with steel engravings of saints.

The smallest room in the collection, a Louis XV boudoir, whose exquisite furnishings are doll size compared to those in the Early American sitting room, would practically fit on the table top in the mid-Victorian parlor.

There is diversity in kind, in Mme. Rubinstein's rooms, as well as in subject and size. She sometimes called upon collections which more traditionally occupy cabinets rather than miniature chambers. The most successful example is to be found in a Versailles "Silver Ballroom," where she set silver toys usually to be found on connoisseurs' shelves upon the composition marble floor of a stately hall. The furniture is silver, ornaments are Wedgwood and silver; a piano and harp of silver will accompany the minuet. Gilt plaster decorations decorate the frieze and, to reflect the graces of the ball, the walls are paneled in tall and elegant mirrors.

Another collection assembled under the label of "Rococo China Room" is more properly a case than a room. In this is a delicately motley, predominantly Dresden assortment of china furnishings (trinket boxes in actuality), arranged with no room-like method, but with considerable charm. Here, by dozens, are china fireplaces and dressers, chairs, cradles, pianofortes and chests, some of which camouflage a pin-holding interior and often sprout china forget-me-nots and roses. The dolls' house collector mentally detaches the delicately molded china dishes, which are linked inexorably by kiln to a china surface and to each other on many such pieces.

Also in the collection are rooms which were not "collected" but were dolls' rooms made long ago which now mingle their antique settings with the perfect but contrived walls and doors of Madame's other interiors.

Among the group of twenty, there is an early nineteenth century three-room dolls' house from Poland, the only dolls' house from that country the writer has ever encountered. The rooms, a bedroom and parlor upstairs, and another bedroom down, are set into an unarchitectural framework, and are not furnished in great detail. The wallpapers, which obviously were printed especially for dolls' houses, are an interesting feature. The upstairs bedroom, for example, has a very rococo door printed on the paper along with the design. The bed in this room, by the way, has a canopy crowned with ostrich plumes. Very green wallpaper and antimacassars on chairs and sofa help create the parlor's antediluvian air. The lower bedroom is the least interesting chamber of all, but contains a very odd ivory chandelier with three fat candles. The most interesting aspect of the house is its general effect, which is distinctly Old World.

Madame displayed a "small eighteenth century doll house" (more properly a dolls' room) with her initial group. This has been referred to as an heirloom left to Madame by her great-aunt. Another story says that it "delighted the heart of a little Austrian princess two hundred years ago." Madame, asked point blank about it, would say only that the room was of Austrian origin, though she denied none of the variations on the theme. The caption on the photograph says that "the wall paper is of green, ornamented with gold paper cupids . . . The picture above the mantel is a bouquet of flowers worked out with thousands of tiny colored feathers . . ." and it refers to the "small bronze pieds-de-femme on which the room rests." The last, the matter of a chest or chair being literally "footed," is a connotational inspiration by which, to judge by survivals, a number of baroque craftsmen got carried away.

The French Provincial Bed-Living-Room has more of a story than most, having been "built and assembled around a romantic tale. It is an exact replica of a room in an old French provincial home of the fifteenth century at Martigues Camarague. Originally belonging to an archbishop, and occupied in the eighteenth century by a sea-faring family of captains and fishermen . . . At the table the old retired seaman is reading the minute but legible type of *Exercice du Chrétien*—in Latin with French annotations, while his daughter-in-law stands wistfully looking out to sea, waiting the return of her captain mate in the year 1775."

We are also told that the leather sandals near the Henry II four-poster canopy bed were discovered in Normandy; that on the washstand is an ivory comb with a few teeth missing. More important than this minutiae is the terra cotta floor, the half-timber work over the niches, and the hooded fireplace with built-in benches, all of which are expressions of French provincial styling.

"Room Romantique," Madame called a particularly charming French interior of the early nineteenth century. This has some delightfully Gothic furniture—Venetian petit point tapestry covers chairs and table, but the traceries of the fancy metal framework (as intricate as a cathedral) are more dramatic. An elaborate clock, under a glass bell, is on the equally elegant mantelpiece. A picture of Louis Philippe is on the wall. A bust of Napoleon is on a table. It is evident that this household recognizes the mutations of state impartially.

There are as many treasures in the other rooms. There are both Georgian and Queen Anne dining-rooms. The Georgian dining-room has Hepplewhite furniture, probably made to serve as a model, by a cabinet-maker of the Georgian period. The drop-leaf Queen Anne table is accompanied by six chairs upholstered in green leather. Three less formal rooms are Biedermeier, Dutch and Second Empire. The Biedermeier and the Second Empire are inhabited by little jointed wooden dolls who, in these chambers, seem mostly to be occupied with lovely old sewing cabinets and equally agreeable work-boxes, inevitably containing scissors "that actually cut." A Spanish dining hall and an Italian chamber are companion pieces in a Southern sense. The Italian room has an appropriately religious atmosphere—church figures are set into niches of the brown leather walls, and a curious organ that Madame bought in Poland dominates the furnishings. In recesses at the back of the Spanish dining hall are very tall, black teakwood cabinets with inlaid panels painted in gold leaf. But the most dramatic furnishing is a black oak treasure chest which has a sliding top and a secret drawer in the bottom. The most modern interior is a "Gay Nineties Room" with a French accent, which can only be described as "oo-la-la." If a gentleman doll were present, he undoubtedly would be drinking champagne from a slipper.

23

THE STETTHEIMER DOLLS' HOUSE

*I*N THE LATE 1940's, A NEW YORK ART DEALER ARRANGING FOR A Cubism show discovered that the original of Marcel Duchamp's "Nude Descending a Stair" was on the West Coast with no possibility of bringing it East in time. A resourceful man, he remembered that the artist had specially made a copy of his chef d'oeuvre for, of all art galleries, one in a dolls' house. He borrowed the miniature version right off the small wall of the dolls' residence and hung it on his full-size wall with his full-size paintings. The art critics, presumably busy with mightier matters, failed to mention this delicious occurrence. But it was a considerable coup for dolls' house society.

The by-play behind the very small picture "on loan," however, has for its dramatis personae a selection of characters considerably beyond the range of dolls' house society. The three leading roles belong to an extraordinary trio of sisters who, according to art critic Henry McBride, "ruled, and for almost a generation, one of the acknowledged intellectual salons of the town" (New York). These were the Stettheimers, and the rather footlighted introduction accorded them here is perhaps not unduly metaphorical, for their lives were exceedingly Good Theater.

One of them, Miss Ettie Stettheimer, wrote novels under the pretty pseudonym of Henri Waste. Another, Miss Florine, painted remarkable

pictures. The third sister made a charming dolls' house, and, needless to say, it is the creation of Miss Carrie, the dolls' house Stettheimer, which is the subject here at hand.

But though this is Miss Carrie's story, and though the sisters worked separately, and even privately, at their individual callings, the three inevitably mingle in the saga of Miss Carrie and the dolls' house. Just as the faces and figures of her sisters appear again and again in the wistful but vivid motifs of Miss Florine's paintings, so do the sisters recur in the lore that now belongs to the dolls' house. To the salon that was the one mutual accomplishment of the Stettheimers, the character of the dolls' house and some of its most remarkable features owe a small debt.

Said features considerably diverge from the wonders to be found in what may be called the World's Most Famous Dolls' Houses. The Stettheimer specimen has to offer neither the fantastically detailed opulence of the Queen's Dolls' House (matched by Colleen Moore's and Titania's Palace) nor the combined opulence and antiquity of the remarkable relics which are to be found in dolls' house form in European museums. The appeal of the Stettheimer dolls' house is a subtler matter, and its prompt fame seems to be based upon two ingredients:

*Treasures in the art gallery
of the Stettheimer house include
Marcel Duchamp's miniature
version of his celebrated
"Nude Descending a Stair."
Florine Stettheimer's portrait of
Miss Carrie and her dolls' house,
shown here, is a photograph.*

One of these consists of the artistic qualities imparted by Miss Carrie. The second is composed of some imaginative shenanigans which have come about in behalf of her creation that seem to spring from its colorful Stettheimer heritage. Of the latter, its ability to lend the celebrated Duchamp "Nude" to an exhibition, an elegance already touched upon, is a sample.

Its introduction to the public was comparably novel. This event, in December, 1945, took place in the Museum of the City of New York. It was a Dolls' House Warming, the first such soirée that history records. And it seems fitting and proper that a Stettheimer dolls' house should have been launched in this sociable manner.

Though the dolls' house, like the un-publicity-conscious Stettheimers themselves, was relatively unknown to the public till recently, its creation was in process for a generation, and its progress was known to a very select group of artists who gradually contributed to its Art Gallery. The works in this chamber may be compared, as dolls' house art goes, to the collection of paintings and water colors in the Queen's Dolls' House. Even with Her Majesty's stately (and far larger) assortment in competition, the Stettheimer group manages to be unique. The Queen's canvases, representing the best in British art a generation ago, are conservative indeed next to the small, select group of modern, intellectual works represented in this gallery.

The most celebrated item in the collection is the Duchamp, which art critic McBride has said is "in no way inferior in quality to the famous original." It is the only copy; all other paintings were conceived especially for the dolls' house. These include offerings from two families—Albert and Juliet Gleizes, and Mme. Gela and Alexander Archipenko. Carl Sprinchorn, Marguerite Zorach, Claggett Wilson, Louis Bouché and Paul Thevanaz are other celebrated names from the modern art world represented there. The gallery is dominated by Gaston Lachaise's lovely alabaster "Venus," which is poised in its midst, and seems destined to become a rather celebrated bit of dolls' house statuary.

Miss Carrie's dolls' house has another rare artistic distinction. There is, ironically enough, no contribution of Florine Stettheimer's in the miniature art gallery, since the latter's death interrupted her plans for such a work. But there is, in the dolls' house dining-room, a photograph of her full-size painting of Miss Carrie and the dolls' house. Done in 1923, its enchantments are immediately apparent, though the meanings of some of its motifs are less evident. Miss Ettie interpreted these quite charmingly in a letter written a few years before her death. "The house in the background is an imagined farm, which Carrie often spoke of acquiring, an idea that amused Florine, coming from Carrie. The people at the tea table are the family and a man friend. The waitress was a Margaret whom we had a long time." The dolls' house spirit which the artist captures needs no interpreting. The imposing colonial building supported by flimsy legs somehow typifies the structural insecurities which beset the dolls' houses of the world. The little chair in Miss Carrie's hand seems to epitomize the furnishings thereof.

These external matters, the paintings and the soirées, tend to suggest a setting for the house, and perhaps to indicate the environment that spawned it, but there remains to illustrate the somewhat elusive fact that Miss Carrie has devised her own work of art.

One thing should be noted. Miss Carrie did a remarkable and delightful one-woman job, but it is absurd to compare her creation to the high-powered, multi-craftsmened dolls' mansions (again, the Queen's, Colleen Moore's, Titania's) that look full-size when photographed. The Stettheimer dolls' house looks like a dolls' house when photographed, and that is part of its fascination. On the other hand, perhaps it shouldn't be pictured, except in true color, at all. Like an impressionist painting, which loses far more of its quality in a black-and-white photograph than does a canvas of the realist school, Carrie Stettheimer's dolls' house properly reveals its tenuous charms only in actuality.

Written description of these beguilements is equally elusive, but one ingredient is definable: Miss Stettheimer became an interior designer in "doing" her dolls' house. She probably was born an interior designer, an artist who didn't recognize her gift even when at last it was put to use in her dolls' house. Most of her effects had occurred to no interior designer

314

before, nor are they likely to appear again. Though an enterprising professional might with profit inspect the Stettheimer dolls' house, possibly he might decide that the inspirations which enchant the eye in miniature would fail in full-size, for what one writer has called "the difficulty and beauty of smallness" plays strange pranks.

The Stettheimer dolls' house intends to be realistic. And in one sense it is a perfect household document of the 'twenties, a period that seems too recent to have such a clear line of demarcation in its domestic appearance. Nevertheless, a riffle through the home-making magazines of that era will show, especially in the use of color, a style as decided as Empire or Queen Anne. Miss Carrie has captured this motley style in her dolls' house and has added another dimension directly from her own imagination.

An analogy very close to (the Stettheimer) home may illustrate this dimension more fully. Art critic Henry McBride, describing the increasingly celebrated paintings of Miss Carrie's sister Florine, said: "They commemorate actual events in the family history but always in a playful, satirical fashion—true to the fantastical inner world the artist lived in, and which she charted, possibly unconsciously, in each picture she undertook."

Miss Ettie Stettheimer, the novelist sister, until her death a few years ago the only surviving member of the extraordinary trio, took exception to a point of view that the dolls' house of one sister and the paintings of the other appeared to bear a kinship as related in their employment of color and fancy as the sisters themselves. She pointed out that the two sisters were not in the least alike. Still Mr. McBride's summary of Florine's greater work might be freely paraphrased to do for Carrie's. The "actual events" the painter commemorated on canvas in "playful, satirical fashion—true to the fantastical inner world the artist lived in" might be related to the actual household world the dolls' house maker memorialized in bits of wood and cloth but true to what must have been a comparably interesting dream world of her own. This seems more particularly true since Miss Ettie Stettheimer has commented that none of the rooms in the dolls' house "were at all like any in our own homes."

Where other dolls' houses are more literally miniature households, therefore, the Stettheimer dolls' house is more literally a work of art. When it was placed on public view in 1945, it was promptly misunderstood. One of the miniature furniture makers, newly flourishing in a revived calling and substantial prices, not long after its debut undertook to view the Stettheimer dolls' house and write a critique upon it for its house organ mailed to perspective patrons throughout the country. Secure in its talent for reproducing precisely, the firm observed that the "nicest and kindest thing" it could say for the dolls' house was "amusing." "In the first place," it added, "our memory of the 1920's is pretty clear and we cannot remember any such atrocious color schemes as we saw displayed here."

This distribution of ignorance is upsetting only in terms of the number of impressionable readers it may have reached. However, aside from this minor tugging at its sleeve, so to speak, the Stettheimer dolls' house has not had to bear the usual majority neglect against which art works struggle in garrets. It appears to have had only this one vote cast against it. Otherwise, it has been accorded glowing admiration.

In the Museum of the City of New York the dolls' house is set up with its façades lifted, and the interior exposed to view. The spectator encircles the house—usually more than once! The façades are unimportant. A carpenter built the shell, the only outside help Miss Stettheimer had on her house, and it is the least remarkable feature, a fairly usual colonial exterior.

The only assists to her work which Miss Carrie need acknowledge were of a curiously indirect nature. She employed many arts with paintbrush, glue pot, and needle, for her house, but at no time, except for panels and shelves, did she turn woodworker. She used furniture from widely scattered sources, but even here her creative notions triumphed. If she didn't like the leg on a chair, she'd replace it with a leg from a different chair. The curious, inventive courage such a mutilative course must have required suggest an assured artistic personality.

Probably the most suitable way to describe the house is to begin at the front and present it a side at a time. In the center of this front is one of the most elegant features—the hall with its glass-enclosed elevator. This pretty luxury is given a stately setting, being approached by a comely gangway of green velvet rails gently reminiscent of the old Roxy theater. The same green velvet upholsters the nearby seat of a small, select gilt chair. The hall is papered with an eighteenth century "vue d'optique" cunningly placed to give an air of stately formal gardens disappearing into its depths. The emblem of hospitality painted on the floor is superior in chic to the customary sentiments of mangy welcome mats. It says, "Salve."

To our left in this fashionable dwelling is a more mundane apartment, the kitchen. This is conservatively blue and white and is distinctly the most business-like and least fanciful corner of the house. It has a good 1920 clutter about it, including plate rails.

To the right of the entrance hall is the library, the only limitation of which appears to be a scantiness of books. It does have a comfortable-looking, well-stocked desk, but it seems more properly a game room, principally because it is centered by a table on which mah-jongg tiles are scattered. The decoration of this room has an Oriental flavor, possibly because the principal furniture is painted Chinese red. The walls are silver and the phone is gold, but in miniature, at least, the effect is not unduly glittering. There is an odd box-like ceiling fixture which also manages to look Oriental. The red doors are French, as are most of the doors throughout the house. Miss Carrie plainly was a great one for French doors.

Upstairs, in this section, there is a continuation of the hall with elevator shaft, and décor to match the arrangements below. The hall segment, how-

316

The entrance hall and other rooms behind the front façade of the Stettheimer dolls' house   Height: House, 28″; Façade, 30″

ever, is half the size of its companion piece, to allow for the linen room. One's instinctive reaction to this dainty affair might be to slip it into one's handkerchief case, except that the few furnishings, including a sewing machine, might be more cumbersome than they look. This room is all over white and black lace edging, the latter, among other tricks, framing the doorways, and standing in some mysterious manner at neat right angles to the frames rather than flat against them. Miss Ettie Stettheimer once pointed out that the position of this lace, primly unwilted after many years, was a minor tribute to her sister's handiwork. There is one wall of built-in cabinets, garlanded in a fairly fairy-like manner. The sewing machine has been thoughtfully painted black and white to match the lace.

Dolls' house nurseries are always arresting since toy versions of toys are irresistible. The Stettheimer nursery is a charming example. A favorite fancy of dolls' houses is to have a dolls' house in the nursery, and the Stettheimer nursery is no exception. This one Miss Carrie made herself and the front lifts off. This nursery also has treasures which define the era of the children who grew up in it, a table phonograph with a horn, and a crystal radio set. More traditionally, there is a blackboard.

317

The decoration of the room, though, is what proclaims it Stettheimer and sets it off from other nurseries. The walls have a gay confetti design—Miss Carrie pasted tiny multi-colored slivers thickly upon its white walls. But the crown of this gaiety is a wide Noah's Ark frieze. For this the newly-found artist painted the animals and figures herself, cut them out, and appliquéd them into a procession around the ceiling.

The master bedroom fully reveals its creator's talents as a decorator of furniture. She has gilded the green pieces here in delicate swirls and what again might be described as the Chinese taste, and it is fetching against the pink walls, which are panelled. The baldaquin which was to have hooded the twin beds was among a few matters left incomplete at Miss Carrie's death; unfortunately, for it would have given to the room an exotic contour which is plainly intended.

Going to the left side of the house, one finds the dining-room and a service aspect. That is, a butler's pantry with back stairs, the continuation of this upstairs, and the "couple's" room and bath. It is pleasant to report that the couple's quarters have been accorded as much decorative thought as any in the house. Possibly more. Their bedroom is a distinctly Paisley affair which might have been rather overwhelming to occupants small enough to dwell there, but is quite winsome to full-size spectators glancing in. The Paisley, very red indeed, appears on walls, ceiling, spread, door panel, drawer fronts, chair back and seat, and on the vanity as a cover. It even has been embroidered over as a rug, with figures of the Paisley left glimmering through in an open-work policy here and there. One of Miss Stettheimer's most open decorating secrets is her evident delight in using a motif in all sorts of ways within a room and it is nowhere more apparent than here. The couple's adjoining bath is done in a delicate green, and has a tall scale, the kind you drop a penny in. The back stairs, terminating in the butler's pantry, link together two floors with a gay border of cabbage roses.

The dining-room, which Miss Carrie didn't quite finish, is less interesting than some of the other rooms, but it has its attractions, notably stacks of delicate Limoges plates, much lovelier, one would think, and not much larger, than crown jewels. The table is further set out with amber stemware in buffet party style.

On the other side of the house, upstairs, is the children's bedroom and bath. This bedroom shows Miss Carrie's interior decoration at its most ingenious. Its primary ingredient appears to be chiffon, and its predominant color rose. There are pink and white peppermint striped walls of this material, and the twin beds have a chiffon baldaquin. There is ruching around the ceiling which seems to be "papered" with a chiffon handkerchief to harmonize with the baldaquin, and there is a beautiful gros point wide-striped rose and white rug.

Beneath this pretty room is the parlor. There the effect is pale green and gold, much of it gros point, a medium Miss Carrie employed for upholstery and carpet. The most amusing piece of furniture is a vitrine with minute oddments under glass. It is in this room that one finds two over-door murals by Albert Sterner, delicate things à la Watteau which are copies of a full-size pair the late artist did for a well-known society woman.

The rear of the dolls' house contains its most extraordinary features. Here is the Art Gallery, and over it a sort of roof garden. The latter has espaliered trees, comfortably canopied sitting-room on one side, statues, tools, and grass.

The Art Gallery may be viewed impressively past a grass-and-tile terrace and through three pairs of towering glass doors, thrown open against their arched doorways. The paintings are hung in two rows, one above the other.

It is regrettable that Miss Carrie did not live to see how celebrated her dolls' house was to become. Neither did she quite finish it. The dining-room and a few odds and ends are incomplete, and the doll family Miss Stettheimer planned to make was never begun. Artist Florine was to have painted the doll family's portrait, but even had the dolls been ready for their sittings, her own death preceded her sister's by a few months. Miss Ettie, the surviving sister, had complicated tasks in connection with the works of both her sisters, not the least exacting of which was some finishing touches to the dolls' house. It was she who installed it in the Museum of the City of New York where its glass façades are daily encircled by earnest admirers.

24

FOUR HOUSES
IN SEARCH
OF A CHAPTER

 HEREWITH WE OFFER FOUR DOLLS' RESIDENCES WHICH DON'T
have chapters of their own, but which very easily might have had.

The first is perhaps the rarest and most appealing of all dolls' houses,
with historic and antiquarian values that have been miraculously preserved
after more than two and a half centuries. This house, which was made for an
Archbishop's child, is so literally Queen Anne that it was presented by that
royal personage—to a goddaughter. The giver of the gift is suitably represented in the house; the Queen's portrait, painted on the back of an old
nine of diamonds, hangs above the open fireplace in the drawing-room.

The goddaughter's name was Ann Sharp and *The Connoisseur* saw fit,
in 1917, to devote two installments to an account of her baby house. Since
Ann was born in 1691, and must have received this elaborate toy not long
thereafter, its age may be specifically identified. The date in this case means
more than that of a good many dolls' houses. This one has traditionally
been preserved just as Ann left it, with even the names of the dolls on faded
slips of paper in her writing, pinned either to their dresses, or even more
precisely, to the places where they were meant to stand. An occasional piece
may later have been added by a child or grandchild, but the original order
obviously prevails.

Mrs. Hannah, "ye housekeeper," Sarah Gill, "ye child's maid," a walnut and ivory cradle, etc., from Ann Sharp's house

The dolls are one of the main items of interest in this nine-room town house, and reflect the sort of society to which a daughter of the Archbishop of York would be accustomed. These included "My Lord Rochett," his lady, his son and daughter, "Sarah Gill, ye child's maid," "Fanny Long, the chambermaid," "Roger, ye butler," "Mrs. Hannah, ye house-keeper," an un-named cook and footman, and some guests, "Lady Jemima Johnson," "Mrs. Lemon," an unidentified lady, and "Sir William Johnson," the last-named gentleman lamentably missing. These personages have either enameled wooden heads or elegant wax ones, and the nobles wear magnificent clothes. Lord R., for instance, is elegant in pink satin trimmed with silver lace. His accessories are black buckled shoes, silk stockings, and a bag wig. The ladies are practically as fine. Sarah Gill is as elaborately garbed as they, and has as luxurious a bed as Lady Rochett herself, an indication that her position in the household was by no means menial. There are two other members of the establishment, a parrot in a cage, and another pet often found in fashionable residences of the era—a monkey. This one is wearing a large shovel-shaped hat and, with the parrot, is in Milady's boudoir.

Another idiosyncrasy of the time, as well as of the lady, is reflected in this feminine apartment. On the wall at the back of the room is a framed wax bust of Mother Shipton, the Yorkshire witch, who is said to have been born in 1486. According to Mrs. Willoughby Hodgson, who wrote the 1917 article,* "This phenomenally plain person, who made sensational prophecies concerning Cardinal Wolsey and others, was, in Stuart times, believed in some quarters, which caused considerable alarm in rural districts, and was not allayed till the year was well over." Of course, the presence of this meaningful item in her boudoir needn't imply that Lady Rochett (or Ann Sharp) was a believer—so much as an antique collector!

In Her Ladyship's bedroom, adjoining, there are innumerable things of beauty. One curious imprint of the times appears on so prosaic an item as a blanket. The ones here have at the corner of each an embroidered "clock" in the form of a single flower outlined in green and veined in scarlet, a device which Mrs. Hodgson says "seems to have been used upon all blankets of

* And a further account in *The Quest of the Antique*, Herbert Jenkins Ltd., London, 1924.

the period, and appears again on the nursery blankets in this doll house." The firescreen which stands by the hearth in this bedroom has a notched pole to regulate its height.

Some of the most interesting items in this house are in the kitchen where a plum pudding is boiling in a copper pot over the fire, and a sucking-pig is roasting on the spit. These delicacies sound considerably more appetizing than two from Ann (Sharp) Dering's† book of recipes reproduced in the *Connoisseur* article, one of which was for "Snaill Watter," and one for "Frantiniack Wine." A roast sucking-pig, which according to Mrs. Hodgson "was a favorite second course with 'the quality' in the days of good Queen Anne," is of considerable interest because of the spit upon which it was cooked. The spit and a circular revolving wheel set into the wall high above the fireplace were joined by a pulley. A small, short-legged dog was placed inside the wide rim, and upon his activities, the movement of the turnspit depended. Since he was rotated with another little dog, and since his labours were no more strenuous than running (and staying in the same place!), the custom doesn't seem to have been cruel, but it does set its century in a strange and faraway time. In the dolls' house, the little dogs have disappeared, but the spit remains.

A different era of gastronomy is to some extent reflected in the dining-room, where the oak gate-legged table, according to Mrs. Hodgson, "is laid with a service of old Leeds cream-ware, very finely modelled, moulded, and pierced. This, however, is not the meal to which Lord Rochett and his lady had invited their guests, Leeds cream-ware being unknown in the days when Ann Sharp ruled her doll house." On the side table are two other courses, a fowl and an inevitable leg of mutton. The original service of wooden trenchers, says Mrs. Hodgson, is on the floor, "where the cruet in lignum vitae and ivory, with screw tops, may be seen." This cruet, however, has more than a lignum vitae and ivory personality; it consists of "the Bishop" (the largest bottle), "the Dean," "the Rector," and "the Curates"— a style of castor identity which must have been very much at home in the dolls' house of an Archbishop's daughter.

Although we have referred to this room as the dining-room, it was actually the hall. Says Mrs. Hodgson: "A dining-room would seem to have been considered unnecessary in some high-class residences, and in her letter written many years later, Ann Dering mentions the building of such a room in her home in Yorkshire." The hall, therefore, served as dining-room, the "withdrawing-room" opening out of it, and the fact that "Lord Rochett stands by the door whilst his guests pass out is an indication that the arm-in-arm procession is a fashion of later date—a fashion which, I believe, had its inception in the early nineteenth century."

† Ann married Heneage Dering, Dean of Ripon, in 1712, according to a faded inscription on the back of her portrait (believed to have been painted by Jonathan Richardson, at one time a neighbor of her parents).

Ann Sharp's baby house presented by her godmother, Queen Anne   *Height: 5' 10"*

There are many random things of interest in Ann Sharp's dolls' house. In the drawing room is a red lacquer bracket clock with a metal face and a pewter dial with gilt trim. The words "Beesley, London," microscopically inscribed upon the face, called to (Mrs. Hodgson's) mind the fact that "a clock-maker of this name had a shop in Dean Street in 1725." Among the strangest toys that ever have been made are several bleeding cups at various stations in the dolls' house. These grim tokens of a fortunately departed surgery are to be found here both in pewter and salt-glaze ware, and inevitably turn up in English eighteenth century baby houses, occasionally in silver. The oldest bit of silver, by the way, in Lord Rochett's house is a wonderful little "snuffers and tray" in his lady's bedroom which bears the date-mark 1686. There are a number of treasures in these noble rooms to represent miniature silversmithing, some of them signed, and some merely date-marked; in a roomier book, this delightful art would demand a whole chapter. A dolls' house, which seems to occur to every dolls' home-maker, is made of and furnished with cardboard. "The tiny prints which adorn its walls," writes Mrs. Hodgson, "are believed to represent Bishopthorpe,* with the church in the grounds, and the furniture includes a grandfather clock, flap tables, footstools, a slung looking-glass, dressing tables, kitchen stove and dresser, and many other articles." An adult plaything appears under the table in the butler's pantry where there is a flat basket of plaited straw containing a pack of miniature playing cards. The ace of clubs is inscribed "Cards of the Cries of London, Aesop's Fables, and Emblems of Love," and they were sold at the Grotto Toy Shop, Saint Paul's Churchyard.

It would be of interest to know whether the Queen assembled these furnishings herself, or delegated the project to an underling; and if she attended to the matter personally, just how she went about it. Her Majesty may very well have got the ingredients, even in that early day, in a toy shop. Her contemporary, Jonathan Swift, born in 1667, two years after Queen Anne, says in *A Voyage to Brobdingnag:* "I had an entire set of silver dishes and plates, and other accessories which, in proportion to those of the Queen's, were not much bigger than what I have seen of the same kind in a London toy-shop for the furniture of a baby-house."

This very documentary dolls' house eventually descended to Ann Sharp's great-great-grand-daughter who gave it to Colonel Bulwer, direct descendant of Ann's eldest son, John Dering, and was still in the possession of Mrs. E. A. Bulwer when this edition was printed in 1965. A splendid reflection on the wisdom of Mistress Ann Sharp's descendants would seem to be the fact that they so early recognized the merits of the document she left them, and kept it historically intact.

The second dolls' house in this miscellany has been dramatized by a curious book published in 1857, printed in Frankfurt, written by a man named Carl Juegel, and entitled *Das Puppenhaus.*

Although *Das Puppenhaus* refers to the Gontard dolls' house, a famous old dolls' residence in the Stadtisches Historisches Museum, Frankfurt/M., Herr Juegel's book is not a dolls' house book, but an autobiography. He does devote a long chapter to the dolls' house, but that, and a few introductory remarks, bear the only relationship to his title. The few introductory

* Residence of the Archbishop of York.

Group of implements, including a roasting spit, from Ann Sharp's house

324

remarks, however, provide the meaning, and they add glory to dolls' houses in general, and the Gontard dolls' house in particular. For there Herr Juegel makes a great point of confessing that without the stimulus of this cherished family heirloom, he might not have got around to writing his memoirs at all.

It is doubtful how much these would have been missed (except by dolls' house historians) if they had not appeared. According to the German-born translator who decoded the dolls' house chapter for this book, Herr Juegel's German is of a flowery consistency which is not pleasing to all tastes. We might mention in passing that Herr Juegel precedes and follows his dolls' house chapter with two lengthy eulogies of the dolls' house in verse (as we have seen, several fond dolls' house owners with literary hopes have been similarly carried away), and these, we have been informed, are of too luxuriant a verbiage even to paraphrase.

However, we wish to bless the author for so amply recognizing the merits of the family dolls' house, and so thoroughly enjoying its attractions. This particular house has been most dreadfully neglected by other writers, considering its historic associations. Gröber includes one picture—of three of the dolls, principally, standing in the front hall. Regrettably, Gröber's caption refers to the Gontard dolls' house as "middle of the XIXth Century," possibly a typographical error.

According to Herr Juegel, the Gontard house came from Holland to Frankfurt approximately in 1748, but Dr. Bernard Müller, a former director of the Frankfurt Historisches Museum, writing in a 1913 German publication,* says that *he* is not sure that the dolls' house is of Dutch origin, though he believes that some of the furniture and the dolls with wax heads were probably Dutch. The kitchen and drawing-room fireplaces were not Dutch, according to Dr. Müller, and the bedroom stove resembles the ones found in the Frankfurt area. He concludes that the house might be a mixture of Dutch and German elements, pointing out that there were many reformed Dutchmen in Frankfurt at the beginning of the eighteenth century.

However, Dr. Müller apparently gives no other reasons for his belief that the house was not of Dutch origin, and it would seem that the existence of the German fireplaces and stove in the house can be accounted for by the fact that every time the house changed hands, the dolls and the furniture were adjusted to reflect its new owner's family and home.

In any case, the house was sent to Miss Susanne Maria Gontard by a close friend of the family—and according to Herr Juegel—from Holland. It was much larger and more minutely equipped than most dolls' houses, and was carefully passed from one girl child of the large family to the next. Up to the time Herr Juegel's book was written, there had been six successive owners. The changes that were made for each of these young owners would seem to have tarnished the historic values of the house, but evidently those

* From *Alt-Frankfurt,* 1913, Vol. 1. Through the courtesy of Dr. Elisabeth Wolffhardt who read the article and excerpted the pertinent information.

were preserved along with the new traditions. According to our translator, who cleared away a good deal of Herr Juegel's verbal underbrush, "In the writer's family, the dolls' house was used as a little stage. His young daughter would explain every doll and whom it represented, every piece of furniture and its origin in the family. The 'opening' (as they called it) of the dolls' house was a solemn event."

Despite this tender care of its history, a restoration was eventually undertaken. After the death of the author's wife (his daughter had died earlier), a cousin of hers, Mrs. Belli-Gontard, took it into custody and, carefully considering ancestral quirks, traits and legends, closely restored the house to its eighteenth century appearance.

Herr Juegel mentions quite often, according to our translator, that the dolls' house reminds him of the Goethehaus in Frankfurt, now a museum. It is obvious that he can pay the dolls' house no higher compliment. His evident interest in the poet, in addition to a probable local bond with Goethe which he shared with most citizens of Frankfurt, and combined with a general German affection, may have been heightened by the fact that his wife's aunt, Lilli Schoenemann, had been the beloved of the poet. If such an apparent Goethephile, who must have known the Goethehaus beam by beam, detects a resemblance to the dolls' house, the Gontard heirloom must have historical merits beyond even its immediate family ones.

There was evidently a strong likeness between the Gontard dolls' house and the Gontard ancestral home, as well as between the dolls' house and the Goethehaus. According to Herr Juegel, the dolls' house may not be an exact copy of the great "merchant house," as it was called, situated "under the Kraeme" but it comes very close to it. Juegel considers it room by room, and since a number of details are similar to those of other German dolls' houses of the period, we shall allude only to the unusual ones.

Juegel logically "enters" the large hall, whose floor is covered with red and cream flagstones. Here he finds it necessary to tell us that "Cool twilight envelopes the furniture and the entire room," a bit of emotion which may be unconsciously dependent on the fact that twilight is the eternal light of most unelectrified doll residences. This hall is of particular interest in terms of Gröber's pictured fragment thereof. It is Juegel who describes it: "In the rear rises the solid staircase. It is made of stained wood and leads straight up to the landing, where it turns to the right and reaches the upper floor. The railing—like the one in the famous Goethehaus—is outstanding because of its fine balusters . . . The dolls liven the scenery. A servant standing on the staircase has just announced the arrival of two visitors—dolls representing the nieces of Mrs. Gontard, first owner of the dolls' house."

Staircase, balusters, nieces, flagstones, are all in view. Also visible is one of the doors "on either side," although owing to the limitations of the photograph it is not possible to see above it (or above its companion-piece), the sur-porte pictures by Junker and Snyder. These "depict savory dishes and delicious fruit, proving that good food was highly prized here."

Detail of the pantry and cellar, Gontard house

It is plain from his loving description of some of the good food that Herr Juegel was as partial to gastronomy as to nostalgia. He observes that from the staircase landing, a door leads directly to a gallery, right under the ceiling of a big store room combining pantry and cellar. "From up here," he says, with evident satisfaction, "one can survey the provisions of the household":

"Sacks of peas, lentils, beans, rice, barley, and millet are placed on sturdy tables, which stand in the center of the room. Huge loaves of bread are piled up for drying. We also see butter barrels, twisted rolls of butter, baskets of eggs, and cheese loaves. All kinds of vegetables such as turnips, carrots and potatoes and many others are kept here. Hanging from the walls are all kinds of meat: hams, sausages and various sorts of smoked meat. For gourmands, we find such delicacies as a basket of domestic fowl, bohemian pheasants, and even a heath cock. Jars of all shapes and sizes, containing preserves and jams, sweet and sour pickles, are filed on the shelves. For dessert we discover baskets of oranges and homegrown fruit of best quality. Boxes and jars of dried fruit, truffles and mushrooms provide spicy ingredients to the meals. Coffee in various containers and a battery of sugar loaves cover the floor. Bottles of fine oils, various sorts of vinegar and mustard, fill the spaces in between."

A housekeeper, by the way, sitting in the center of the cellar, has a

The historic Gontard dolls' house, eighteenth century, from Frankfurt Height: 7' 3"

blackboard on which to render account of the consumption of these victuals. Near her are big wine barrels and a large scale with a set of weights. In the kitchen, there is the usual battery of pots and pans and utensils for preparing the abundance above-mentioned. We are told that the cook, a fat little doll, is stuffing a turkey.

The upstairs hall, where the youngest daughter is awaiting her guests, has several interesting features. The oddest furnishing, artistically fashioned, was described by Juegel as a napkin-wringer and he went to some pains to explain how this object served, in its day, to restore the finish to the table linen after each use. This sounded vaguely unsanitary, but seemed a curiosity worth reporting. However, Dr. Müller, in his article,* calls it not a napkin-press but a fruit press. Another furnishing that is entirely contemporary stands in a corner, "a wash basin with a little water tank above it, for the use of servants." Here Juegel may be somewhat in error, for such pieces were generally for the use of the elegant but fairly unwashed family members. This particular house had better-washed occupants than most of the period; in the bedroom of the mistress is a wash basin of embossed silver on a matching tripod.

Several paintings, which are too large for the other rooms, are upon the walls in the hall. Among the Biblical scenes they portray is a lavish representation of Daniel in the Lion's Den.

The third dolls' house in this quartet is by far the most modest, but has such a curious and special history, that it seems to require singling out among more antique or elaborate specimens. This was the dolls' house of Frances Hodgson Burnett who later wrote that classic of children's literature, *Racketty Packetty House*.

It was a dolls' house acquired late in life. Its mistress described the house and its English origin lovingly in an article devoted to the subject in *Ladies' Home Journal* in April, 1915. There is no point in attempting to paraphrase Frances Hodgson Burnett, who knew how to wrap any reader with an ounce of sentiment around her little pen. We shall quote as much of her account as conceivably the traffic will bear.

"I invariably stop and look into toy-shop windows wheresoever I come across them—whether in Paris, where they are too deliciously beautiful for words; in London; in little English, German, or Italian country towns or villages, anywhere and everywhere I plant myself unashamedly before them, and disregard all else. The day before the Jacobean cabinet revealed its true character to me I was walking through a village and saw a small shop whose window presented objects before which I paused transfixed. There were a small Japanese tea-table, and six small chairs made of bamboo. On the table was a tiny Japanese tea-set of green ware, the tea-pot with a wicker handle. And around the tea sat a small Japanese family, composed of a mamma, a

* Previously noted.

papa and three unextinguishably beautiful Japanese babies, all in dazzling kimonos and with shaved heads except the mamma, who wore fans in her hair. It was impossible to resist and pass them by.

" 'I will go in and buy them' I said in that sneakingly specious manner in which we always make plausible excuses for our weakness. 'I can give them to some child.'

"The unadorned truth was I did not want to give them to 'some child.' I wanted them for myself because they were so human and so delicious and tiny and quaint . . . I entered the shop, and finding an enchanting old human there—like a sort of fairy godmother—I went . . . into her back room and bought a dozen things: the Japanese family, a tiny and perfectly attired nursery-maid wheeling a tiny white and blue perambulator, with a baby just the right size in it; a bath fitted up most satisfactorily with another baby; a piece of pink soap, a sponge, and a towel on a rack . . . When I returned home I carried into the Red Room a collection of little boxes. I looked around the room uncertainly.

" 'Where shall I put them? If one buys half a toy-shop, one must put it somewhere.'

"Perhaps the Jacobean cabinet had been slightly bored that afternoon and truly wanted something to do. It looked at me as I glanced toward it. 'Give them to me. I'll take care of them,' it said.

"It was the very place for them. The lower part of it, when its doors were opened, revealed two substantial shelves. I opened the doors and kneeled down. I took out one delightful thing after another and set them in order, arranging a little scene, and while I did so the most satisfactory and logical reasoning argued my case for me.

Mrs. Burnett's dolls' house as shown in a 1915 issue of Ladies' Home Journal

" 'When children are brought to see one,' I murmured as I set the table for the Japanese family, 'They are expected to sit perfectly still and behave beautifully while their elders and betters amuse themselves with gossiping in their ridiculous, grown-up away . . . The poor little things have nothing to do and are bored to death. The unfairness and lack of consideration in grown-up people are really revolting. How should we behave if we were invited to a place and shut entirely out of the conversation? Personally I should behave disgracefully. Why not have things in one's house for the poor little lambs to play with? From this time forward I shall always keep a Toy Cupboard—and this shall be it' . . .

"When it was brought, four years ago, to Long Island, everything it contained was distributed to enraptured recipients in Kent. Then came the inspiration of dividing the two shelves into four, papering their walls and furnishing them luxuriously as rooms. The lower half became a Dolls' House. It contains a drawing-room hung with pale green brocade, a combined nursery and bedroom with chintz on the walls, a dining-room of massive leather-upholstered furniture and a kitchen replete with luxury and modern convenience. In the drawing-room the ladies are always either playing on the piano, or writing invitations at the desk with the telephone on it, or pouring out tea for visitors. In the dining-room various members of the family are always dining, the footman is always serving them from the sideboard, a parlor maid, in a white cap and apron, is perpetually handing things to someone who won't take them, the collie dog stands waiting to be fed by the grandpa who never feeds him, and the table is spread with the richest viands and rarest hot-house fruits (done in plaster of Paris), . . . the oranges and grapes relatively the size of cannon-balls. No one ever eats anything, so the housekeeping bills are small.

"In the nursery children of different sizes are continually ready for a walk, or a perambulator, or bed, and a nurse never ceases giving a totally undressed baby a bath (you can turn on a real shower if you pour water into a thing at the top, but it sometimes wets the nursery maid and the carpet and always wets your clean frock, if you are six). A rather severe cook with a bunch of keys at her waist prepares banquets in the kitchen and inspects varieties of vegetables piled on a table in neat bowls and baskets. The cat sits at her feet and the kittens are in a basket. She pays no attention to the vacuum cleaner, the carpet-sweeper, the broom, and the wringer, which are rather ostentatiously grouped about the kitchen. This must be through mere pride of possession, as no one uses them and the Dolls' House is never cleaned unless I fall to myself or have a visitor who is a good house-keeper, in which case she usually drops on her knees before the Toy Cupboard, sticks her little head inside and has a housecleaning, from which she emerges glowing and triumphant."

Vivian Burnett, in a biography of his mother, *The Romantic Lady*, gives a picture, from a different vantage point, of the dolls' house proprietress and her young guests: "Nothing delighted her so much as kneeling down upon cushions with her little visitors before this cupboard so that she herself could explain all the marvels, and see the wonder and delight grow in their faces. Only her sense of duty to the guests in her house would prevent her playing this way for hours. She would laughingly admit the accusation, when she was told that she had the doll house quite as much for herself as for the youngsters."

There has been no more glowing tribute to the dolls' house, any dolls' house, than a paragraph Mrs. Burnett included in her Journal eulogy: "I have built houses and furnished them; I have made gardens in various countries and revelled in them; I have written quite a number of things; but I do not think that anything I have done has been more amusing and satisfactory to me . . ."

Our final dolls' house is not really in search of a chapter, or even an author—it is present because it found an author, and a very special one. It is a literary dolls' house and we yield to a substantial description of it, from Katherine Mansfield's haunting short story, *The Doll's House*.

330

"There stood the doll's house, a dark, oily spinach green, picked out with bright yellow. Its two solid little chimneys, glued onto the roof, were painted red and white, and the door, gleaming with yellow varnish, was like a little slab of toffee. Four windows, real windows, were divided into panes by a broad streak of green. There was actually a tiny porch, too, painted yellow, with big lumps of congealed paint hanging along the edge . . . The hook at the side was stuck fast. Pat pried it open with his penknife, and the whole house swung back, and there you were, gazing at one and the same moment into the drawing-room and dining-room, the kitchen and two bedrooms. That is the way for a house to open! Why don't all houses open like that? How much more exciting than peering through the slit of a door into a mean little hall with a hatstand and two umbrellas! That is—isn't it?—what you long to know about a house when you put your hand on the knocker. Perhaps it is the way God opens houses at the dead of night when He is taking a quiet turn with an angel . . . All the rooms were papered. There were pictures on the walls, painted on the paper, with gold frames complete. Red carpet covered all the floors except the kitchen; red plush chairs in the drawing-room, green in the dining-room; tables, beds with real bed clothes, a cradle, a stove, a dresser with tiny plates and one big jug. But what Kezia liked more than anything, what she liked frightfully was the lamp. It stood in the middle of the dining-room table, an exquisite little amber lamp with a white globe. It was even filled all ready for lighting, though, of course, you couldn't light it. But there was something inside that looked like oil and moved when you shook it. The father and mother dolls, who sprawled very stiff as though they had fainted in the drawing-room, and their two little children asleep upstairs, were really too big for the doll house. They didn't look as though they belonged. But the lamp was perfect. It seemed to smile at Kezia, to say, 'I live here.' The lamp was real."

"I seen the little lamp," says our Else, the poor, wistful little figure who has been permitted briefly to see the splendid toy in which the little lamp is housed.

"I seen the little lamp," says she to whom it will never belong at the end of the story, in what is assuredly one of the most haunting lines in literature. And one wonders if the dolls' house Katherine Mansfield has so exquisitely fashioned to make her social point was the one of her own childhood which she tenderly recalled in her *Journal.* This "was a beautiful one with a verandah and a balcony and a door that opened and shut and two chimneys . . . I had gone all through it myself, from the kitchen to the dining-room, up into the bedrooms with the doll's lamp on the table, heaps and heaps of times." Surely this lamp was The Little Lamp which our Else "seen."

Whatever the genesis of the dolls' house of the story, it somehow epitomizes all dolls' houses and thus appears to warrant the last words in this history.

Museums in which dolls' houses, shops, kitchens and related toys may be found:

Austria
    VIENNA: Historisches Museum der Stadt Wien
               Osterreichisches Museum für Volkskunde
               Kunstgewerbe Museum

Canada
    BRUCE MINES, ONT.: Bruce Mines Public Museum

Denmark
    COPENHAGEN: Dansk Folkemuseum

Finland
    HELSINKI: Finland's National Museum

France
    PARIS: Musée des Arts Décoratifs (The Louvre)
           Musée de Cluny
           Musée Carnavalet
           Musée d'Histoire de l'Éducation

Germany
    ALTONA: Altonaer Museum
    ARNSTADT: Schlossmuseum
    AUGSBURG: Maximilians Museum
    BODMAN: Puppen-Museum
    FRANKFURT/M: Stadtisches Historisches Museum
    HANOVER: Vaterlandisches Museum
    MUNICH: National Museum
    NUREMBERG: Germanisches Museum
    PASSAU: Museum
    STUTTGART: Landesgewerbe Museum
    WÜRZBURG: Museum Lydia Bayer

Great Britain
    England   BERKSHIRE: Windsor Castle, Windsor (The Queen's Dolls' House)
                    CAMBRIDGESHIRE: Cambridge and County Folk Museum,
                              Cambridge
                    DEVONSHIRE: Natural History Society Museum, Torquay
                    DURHAM: Bowes Museum, Barnard Castle
                    GLOUCESTERSHIRE: Blaise Castle Folk Museum, Bristol
                              *Snowshill Manor (nr. Chipping Campden)
                    KENT: Maidstone Museum, Maidstone
                        Royal Tunbridge Wells Museum and Art Gallery,
                              Tunbridge Wells
                    LANCASHIRE: Queen's Park Art Gallery, Manchester
                        City Art Gallery, Salford

LONDON: Bethnal Green Museum
Guildhall Museum
Gunnersbury Park Museum
London Museum, Kensington Palace
Victoria and Albert Museum
MIDDLESEX: * Uppark, Belmont
NORFOLK: Castle Museum, Norwich
OXFORDSHIRE: The Rotunda, Grove House, Iffley Turn, Oxford
STAFFORDSHIRE: Museum of Childhood and Costume, Blithfield
Hall, (nr. Rugeley)
SUSSEX: West Pier, Brighton (Batty Dolls' House)
Toy Museum, Rottingdean, Brighton
Hove Museum of Art, Hove
Worthing Museum and Art Gallery, Worthing
YORKSHIRE: Bolling Hall, Bradford
Cliffe Castle Museum, Keighley
Abbey House Museum, Kirkstall Abbey, Leeds
* Nostell Priory, Wakefield
Castle Museum, York
WARWICKSHIRE: Doll Museum, Oken's House, Warwick

Scotland EDINBURGH: Museum of Childhood
Wales CARDIFF: Welsh Folk Museum, St. Fagan's Castle
* The National Trust

Hungary
BUDAPEST: National Museum
Ireland
GOREY, CO. WEXFORD: Ballynastragh (Titania's Palace)
Italy
BOLOGNA: Museum of Industrial Art
Netherlands
AMSTERDAM: Rijksmuseum
ARNHEM: Openluchtmuseum
HAARLEM: Frans Hals Museum
THE HAGUE: Gemeente Museum
UTRECHT: Central Museum
New Zealand
CHRISTCHURCH: Canterbury Museum
Norway
BERGEN: Veslandske Kunstindustri Museum
OSLO: Gamle Folkemuseum, Bygdøy
Sweden
STOCKHOLM: Nordiska Museet
UPSALA: University of Upsala
Switzerland
BASEL: Historisches Museum
Schweizerisches Museum für Volkskunde
ZURICH: Schweiz Landesmuseum
Franz Carl Weber

United States

ARIZONA	Phoenix: Art Museum
CALIFORNIA	San Francisco: Cliff House
	John M. Blauer's "Maynard Manor"
	Buena Park: Knott's Berry Farm
COLORADO	Denver: Art Museum
DELAWARE	Wilmington: Delaware Historical Society
DISTRICT OF COLUMBIA	Washington: National Museum, Smithsonian Institution
ILLINOIS	Chicago: Art Institute
	Museum of Science and Industry
	Chicago Historical Society
INDIANA	Kokomo: Ruth's Doll Museum
MASSACHUSETTS	Boston: Harrison Gray Otis House
	Children's Museum
	New Bedford: Old Dartmouth Historical Society
	Plymouth: Plymouth Antiquarian Society
	Salem: Essex Institute
	Sandwich: Yesteryear's Museum
	South Lancaster: Racketty-Packetty House Museum
	Wenham: Wenham Historical Association
	West Cummington: Steele's Tiny Old New England
MICHIGAN	Dearborn: Ford Museum
MINNESOTA	St. Paul: Minnesota Historical Society
NEW JERSEY	Egg Harbor City: Antique Doll Museum
	Newark: Newark Museum
NEW YORK	Brooklyn: Brooklyn Museum
	New York: Cooper Union Museum
	Metropolitan Museum of Art
	Museum of the City of New York
	New-York Historical Society
	Van Cortlandt Museum
	Rochester: Mrs. Homer Strong's private museum
OHIO	Cleveland: Cleveland Museum of Art
	Western Reserve Historical Society
	Fremont: Rutherford B. Hayes Library
	Lebanon: Warren County Museum
	Milan: Museum
PENNSYLVANIA	Douglassville: Mary Merritt's Doll Museum
	West Chester: Chester County Historical Society
RHODE ISLAND	Newport: Newport Historical Society
VERMONT	Brattleboro: Museum of Old Dolls and Toys
	Shelburne: Shelburne Museum
VIRGINIA	Woodlawn Plantation, Mount Vernon
WASHINGTON	Seattle: Museum of History and Industry
WISCONSIN	Milwaukee: Museum
	Milwaukee County Historical Museum

d'Allemagne, Henri-René, *Histoires des Jouets,* Paris, 1903.

————, *Les Accessoires de Costume et du Mobilier,* Paris, 1928.

————, *Les Jouets à la World's Fair en 1904 à St. Louis,* Paris, 1908.

The Art Institute of Chicago, *Handbook to the European Rooms in Miniature,* 1943.

————, *Miniature by Mrs. James Ward Thorne,* 1943.

————, *American Rooms in Miniature,* 1941.

————, *Period Rooms in Miniature,* International Business Machines Corp., 1946.

Becq de Fouquières, L., *Les Jeux des Anciens,* Paris, 1869.

Benson, A. C. with Sir Lawrence Weaver, *The Book of the Queen's Dolls' House,* London: Methuen & Co., Ltd., 1924.

————, *The Book of the Queen's Dolls' House Library,* London: Methuen & Co., Ltd., 1924.

————, *Everybody's Book of the Queen's Dolls' House,* London: Methuen & Co., Ltd. and The Daily Telegraph, 1924.

von Boehn, Max, *Dolls and Puppets,* translated by Josephine Nicoll, London: G. C. Harrap & Co., 1932.

Boesch, Hans, *Kinderleben in der Deutschen Vergangenheit,* Leipzig, 1900.

Boger, Louise Ade and H. Batterson, *The Dictionary of Antiques and the Decorative Arts,* New York: Charles Scribner's Sons, 1957.

Caiger, G., *Dolls on Display,* Tokyo: The Hokuseido Press, 1933.

Calmettes, Pierre, *Les Joujoux,* Paris, 1924.

Casal, U. A., *The Doll Festival,* (paper read at Kobe Women's Club, March 1, 1938.)

Claretie, Leo, *La Jeune Fille au XVIII Siècle,* Tours, 1901.

————, *Les Jouets de France,* Paris, 1920.

————, *Les Jouets, histoire, fabrication,* Paris, 1898.

Coleman, Evelyn, Elizabeth and Dorothy, *The Age of Dolls,* Washington, D. C., 1965.

Colleen Moore's Doll House, (Brochure), Garden City Publishing Co., 1930.

Colleen Moore's Fairy Castle, Chicago: The Museum of Science and Industry, 1964.

Crump, Lucy Hill, *Nursery Life 300 Years Ago,* New York: E. P. Dutton & Co., 1929.

Daiken, Leslie, *Children's Toys throughout the Ages,* New York: Frederick A. Praeger, Inc., 1953.

————, *World of Toys,* London: Lambarde Press, 1963.

Deutschen Spielzeugmuseum Sonneberg, *Spielzeug,* Leipzig: Im Prisma, Verlag, 1963.

Finlands Nationalmuseum, *Dockor och tennsoldater,* Helsingfors, 1961.

Foley, Dan, *Toys through the Ages,* New York: Chilton Books, 1962.

Fournier, Édouard, *Histoire des Jouets et de Jeux d'enfants,* Paris, 1889.

Franklin, Alfred, *La Vie Privée d'Autrefois,* Paris, 1896.

Freeman, Ruth and Larry, *Cavalcade of Toys,* Watkins Glen, New York: Century House, 1942.

Gordon, Lesley, *Peepshow into Paradise,* London: George G. Harrap & Co., Ltd., 1953.

Greene, Vivien, *English Dolls' Houses of the Eighteenth and Nineteenth Centuries,* London: B. T. Batsford, Ltd., 1955.

Greg Collection of Dolls and Doll Houses, Catalogue of, Manchester Art Gallery, Manchester, England.

Gröber, Karl, *Children's Toys of Bygone Days,* translated by Philip Hereford, London: B. T. Batsford, Ltd., 1928.

————, *Das Puppenhaus,* (a pamphlet), Leipzig, no date; reprinted *Die Puppenstadt,* Konigstein im Taunus: Verlag Karl Robert Langewiesche, no date.

Hertz, Louis H., *Handbook of Old American Toys,* Wethersfield, Conn.: M. Haber, 1947.

Holme, Geoffrey, *Children's Toys of Yesterday,* London: The London Studio, Ltd., 1932.

Howard, Marian B., *Homes for Paper Dolls and Kindred Paper Toys,* Miami, Florida, 1953.

Jackson, Mrs. F. Nevill, *Toys of Other Days,* London: Country Life, Ltd.; New York: Charles Scribner's Sons, 1908.

335

Juegel, Carl, *Das Puppenhaus*, Frankfurt, 1857.

Kaut, Hubert, *Alt Wiener Spielzeugschachtel*, Vienna: Hans Deutsch Verlag A. G., 1961.

Lane, Margaret, *The Tale of Beatrix Potter*, London: Frederick Warne & Co. Ltd., 1946.

Lessing, Julius and Bruning, Adolf, *Der Pommersche Kunstschrank*, Berlin, 1905.

Lockwood, Luke Vincent, *Colonial Furniture in America*, New York: Charles Scribner's Sons, 1913.

London Museum, *Toys and Games*, London: Her Majesty's Stationery Office, 1959.

Low, Frances H., *Queen Victoria's Dolls*, London: George Newnes Ltd., 1894.

McClintock, Marshall and Inez, *Toys in America*, Washington, D. C.: Public Affairs Press, 1961.

Muller, S. and Vogelsang, W., *Holländische Patrizierhäuser*, Utrecht, 1907.

Museum für Völkerkunde und Schweizerische Museum für Volkskunde, Guidebook for a toy exhibition, Basel, December, 1964–April, 1965.

Museum of Childhood, Edinburgh, *Descriptive Handbook*, Libraries and Museums Committee, Edinburgh, 1961.

Museum of Science and Industry, *Colleen Moore's Fairy Castle*, Chicago, 1964.

Nishizawa, Tekiho, *Dolls of Japan*, Tokyo: Society for International Cultural Relations, 1934.

Notes on the Collection of Dolls and Figurines at the Wenham Museum, Wenham, (Mass.): Historical Association, 1951.

Period Dolls' Houses from Many Lands, (Catalogue of an Exhibition), London, 9th December, 1955 to 7th January, 1956.

Rabecq-Maillard, M. M., *Histoire du Jouets*, Paris: Hachettex, 1962.

Rijksmuseum, Amsterdam, *Poppenhuizen*, 1955.

Roh, Julian and Hansmann, Claus, *Altes Spielzeug*, Munich: Verlag F. Bruckmann, 1958.

Roselt, Christof, *Kunstsammlungen im Schloss zu Arnstadt*, Eisenach and Kassel: Im Erich Roth Verlag, no date.

Schwindrazheim, Hildamarie, *Altes Spielzeug aus Schleswig-Holstein*, Heide in Holstein: Westholsteinische Verlagsanstalt Boyens & Co., no date.

Sézan, Claude, *Les Poupées Anciennes*, Paris, 1930.

Singleton, Esther, *Dolls*, New York: Payson & Clarke, Ltd., 1927.

————, *Dutch and Flemish Furniture*, London: Hodder & Stoughton Ltd., 1907.

————, *Dutch New York*, New York: Dodd, Mead & Co., 1909.

Stockbauer, Dr. J., *Die Kunstbestrebungen am Bayerischen Hofe unter Herzog Albert V. und Seinem Nochfolger Wilhelm V.*, Vienna, 1874.

Victoria & Albert Museum, *A Picture Book of Dolls and Doll Houses*, London, 1960.

Von Wilckens, Leonie, *Tageslauf im Puppenhaus*, Munich: Prestel Verlag, 1956.

Wilkinson, Sir Neville, *Grey Fairy and Titania's Palace*, London: Oxford University Press, 1922.

————, *To All and Singular*, London: Nisbet & Co., Ltd., 1925.

————, *Yvette in Italy and Titania's Palace*, London: Oxford University Press, 1922.

————, *Titania's Palace. An Illustrated Handbook*, 1926.

Worcester Craft Center, *World of Miniature*, (Program of an exhibition) Worcester, Mass., Oct. 22, 1961.

Note: This bibliography is partial, the bulk of research material for the uncharted course that has been doll house history having come from magazines, newspapers, museums and private persons. We might cite separately the complete files of *Playthings*, American toy trade magazine, New York: McCready, 1904 ff. Virtually all periodical and newspaper references are cited in the text.

INDEX

Adam dolls' house, 58
Albrecht V, Duke of Bavaria, ix, 23–6
Allair, C. B., 251
d'Allemagne, Henri-René, 19, 36–7, 82, 91–2, 95–6, 160
Alsatian dolls' house, 85–7
Altadena's dolls' house, 121–2
Althof, Bergmann & Co., 185
Althouse, Eunice, 59
Amateur Work, 212
Amen, Mrs. Marion Cleveland, 116
American Home, 220–1
American Homes, 192
American Toy Company, 183
American Toy Warehouse, 177
Amsterdam dolls' house, 72–4, 77
Antiques, 18, 53, 183, 251
Antwerp, 80
apprentice pieces, 10, 230–1
Arcade, 198
architects, 5, 43, 47, 62, 108, 179, 193, 198–200, 203, 224, 228, 244, 264
Architectural Forum, 67
Architectural Review, 54
art, miniature, 70, 72, 80–1, 112, 121, 158–9, 239–40, 244, 260, 266, 281, 283, 294, 305, 313–4, 319
art cabinets, 15, 20–3
Art News, 199
Art Nouveau dolls' house, 57
Asia, 141
Augsburg, 20, 23–4, 161, 247
Augusta Dorothea, Duchess of Schwarzburg-Gotha, 28, 41, 285–95, 296
Austria, dolls' houses of, 145, 173
automobiles, miniature, 265

Badger, Leonidas Vergil, 114
Baeumler house, 16
Ball, Frank L., 195
Ballycastle toy industry, 151–2
Baltimore town houses, 110–1
basketmaker's shop, 175
Batty, Tom, 65–6
Baumann, Dorothea, 232
Bayer, Lydia, 226
Becq de Fouquières, 15
Beerbohm, Max, 201
Benson, A. C., 3, 259, 262–3
Bestelmeier's catalogue, 37, 97
Biedermeier, 61, 103, 129, 131, 147, 171–2, 186, 225, 310
Bingham dolls' house, 120–1
Blaauw dolls' house, 69, 75–6
Blackett Baby House, 50

blacksmith's residence, 173
Blair, Mrs. J. Insley, 163
Blauer, John M., 223, 247
Bliss, R., Mfg. Co., 190–1
Blodget, Elizabeth Larke. *See* Mother Larke
Blossom, Mrs. Dudley S., 120
Boehn, Max von, 20–1
Boesch, Hans, 17, 22, 24–5, 28
Bolshevik toys, 144
Bolton, Frances P., 120
books, miniature, 56, 102–3, 161–2, 260–2, 269, 308
Bradford, Faith, 236–7
Bradley toy company, 252
Brandt, Mrs. Milton K., 104
Breton kitchen, 303
Brett family, 101–3
Breughel, Peter, 68, 80–1
Brew, Laura H., 230–1
Brockmon, Sylvia, 193
Brönte, Charlotte, 62
Brooklyn Eagle, 178
Brown, George W., & Co., 183–4
Brown, Mrs. Samuel H., Jr., 245–6
brownstone dolls' houses, 108–9
Bulwer, Mrs. E. A., 324
Burnett, Frances Hodgson, 328–30
Burnett, Vivian, 330
Butcher, James W., 200
butcher's shops, 173–4, 177, 228

cabinet dolls' houses, 68–80, 103–4, 106, 111, 129, 134, 145, 157, 286
Caffieri, 112
Caiger, C., 139
Cairo, F., 257
Caleb the toymaker, 62, 182
Calmettes, Pierre, 90
Cambridge Cottage dolls' house, 125
Cane End House, Reading, 41
Cannon, Elaine, 247
cardboard dolls' houses, 134, 201–2, 209, 215
Carter, Mrs. E. J., 8, 176
Casal, U. A., 139
catalogues, 37, 177, 183–6, 188, 195–6
chairs, 4, 36, 51, 135, 171–3
Chamberlain, Benjamin, H., 118–9
Chambers' Journal, 182
Chambre du Sublime, 92–4, 261
chandeliers, 37, 129, 131, 157, 271–2
Charbneau, Jules, 223
Charles III of Bourbon, 7, 19
Chelmsford dolls' house, 47
Cheney, Elizabeth, 53
Chester County house, 104

ciety, 127; Zagorsk Museum (Russia), 143
musical instruments, miniature, 9, 19, 25, 59, 63, 66, 72, 126, 266, 277, 287, 289

Netherlands, dolls' houses of, 68–80, 155–8, 228, 310, 325
New York Daily Tribune, 187, 190
New York Fire Department, 196
New York Herald, 263
New York Times, 20, 144, 176, 193, 199, 202, 203, 258, 261–2
New Zealand, dolls' houses of, 154–5
Nichols, Mr. and Mrs. Walter, 142–3
Nishizawa, Tekiho, 138
Noah's Ark, 7
Noble, John, 102
Norra Lindved Castle, Scania, 134–5
Norway, dolls' houses of, 135–7
Norworth, Jack, 223
Nostell Priory baby house, 46–7, 305
Notes & Queries, 40
Nuremberg, 27–35, 37, 57, 169; kitchens, 159–62

Once a Week, 176

Palace of the Young Pioneers, 143
paper dolls' houses, 126–7, 206, 216, 249–57
Parents' Magazine, 221
Paris Exhibit of 1900, 89
Parke-Bernet Galleries, 51, 101
Parker, Mrs. Sumner, 110–1, 176
patents, dolls' houses, 189–90, 205–10
Patterson brothers, 184
Pearson, Eric H., 117, 247
pedlar doll, 175
Pennell, Joseph, 261–2
penny toys, 9, 132, 182
Penthièvre, Duke de, 98
Peter the Great, 63, 68, 72–4
"petit ménage," 83–5
pewter toys, 183, 189
pharmacy, miniature, 75–6, 169, 293
Philbrick, Mrs. Lawrence S., 122–3
Philip II, Duke of Pomerania, 20
Pia, Peter F., 189
plastic toys, 201
Playthings, 126, 144, 152, 155, 178–9, 190–3, 196, 254
Poland, dolls' house from, 309
Popular Mechanics, 199, 220
Popular Science, 220
Potter, Beatrix, 10, 123
Praz, Mario, 4
prehistoric miniatures, 16
Price, Edith S., 125
private museums, 111, 224–31
Pylkkanen, Riitta, 137

Queen Alexandra, 277
Queen Anne, 47, 320

Queen Anne dolls' houses, 43, 47–51, 58–9, 136
Queen Mary, 56–7, 173, 179, 258–62, 274
Queen Mary's dolls' house, 56, 258–66, 269, 273–5, 312–3; library of, 10, 259–62, 266
Queen Victoria, 55, 175

Racketty Packetty House, 328–30
Ramsey-Fairfax, John, 152–4
Ricardo, Emmée, 58
Richelieu, Cardinal, 91, 92
Riisöen, Mrs. Thale, 135–6
Roberts, Sonia, 5
Rogers, Elaine W., 114, 298
Roh, Juliane, 37
Rome, toys of, 14–6
Roosevelt (Theodore) family, 116–7
Roscoe, Jervis, 66–7
Roselt, Dr. Christof, 285–8, 294–5
Rosenberg, Dr. Fritz, 155–8
Ross-Ross, Mrs. Philip, 212, 246
Royal Magazine, 56, 64
Rubinstein, Mme Helena, 162, 304–10
Rückert, Dr. Rainer, ix
Russell, Emily S., 206
Russia, toys of, 143–5

St. Nicholas, 55, 155
Saks Fifth Avenue, 199
Saltram house, 226
Sappington, Gertrude, 238–9
Saturday Evening Post, 197
Saxony, Prince of, 22
scale, 15, 122, 130, 136, 168, 177, 230–1, 244
Schlumberger, Mme Madeleine, 233–4
Schoenhut, 193–5, 198
schoolroom, miniature, 39
Schwarz, F. A. O., 9, 106, 117, 177, 195–6, 199, 203, 247
Schweizer, Babette, 225
Schwegler, Johann, 20, 22
Scientific American, 198
Scotland, dolls' houses of, 152–4
Sears Roebuck furniture, 197
Selfridge's, 198
Sévigné, Mme de, 94
Sézan, Claude, 85
Sharp, Ann, 47–8, 320
Sheraton dolls' house, 51
shields of arms, 40–1, 44, 213, 303
Shinto palaces, 140
shoe-box dolls' house, 216
shops, miniature, 148, 168–79, 209, 240–1, 292–3, 305–7
Short, Mr. and Mrs. E. H., 154–5
silver toys, 12, 48, 50, 70–2, 83–4, 102–3, 118–9, 232, 323–4, 308, 323
Singleton, Esther, 80–1, 83–4, 97, 139–40
Sitwell, Sacheverell, 10, 295
Soller, Edward J., 243
Sotheby's, 58